CANOE TRAILS
DIRECTORY

CANOE TRAILS DIRECTORY

James C. Makens

A DOLPHIN BOOK
DOUBLEDAY & COMPANY, INC.
GARDEN CITY, NEW YORK
1979

Formerly published as *Makens' Guide to U.S. Canoe Trails.* Copyright
© 1971 by James C. Makens

Library of Congress Cataloging in Publication Data
Makens, James C
Canoe trails directory.
(A Dolphin book)
Published in 1971 under title: Makens' guide to
U.S. canoe trails.
Bibliography: p. 340.
1. Canoes and canoeing—United States—Guide-books.
2. United States—Description and travel—Guide-books.
I. Title.
GV776.A2M34   1979   917.3
Library of Congress Catalog Card Number 76–42426
ISBN: 0-385-12428-7

*This book is dedicated to
my good friends and fellow canoeists,
Neal Robinson, Bernie Asner,
John Dunagan, and George Demski.*

FOREWORD

Welcome to the world of canoeing. Leave behind the rush of freeway traffic, the sound and fury of exploding growth, and the disarray of man in confusion. Enter with us a new world, a world to match the moods of any man.

Challenge the fury of white water or dream and for a moment forget as you glide on silent ribbons of beauty.

Use this book as simply one key to the world you seek. Select your trail, consult maps, other guide books, and spoken words of those who know the river. Discover each river's major secrets before you enter her waters. The value of each book far exceeds the cost.

Like those she carries in her crest, a river can be moody and deceptive. A temper of violence spits and foams as a river gorges the charge of a sudden thunderstorm. Sandbars grow and disappear. Snags and whirlpools appear, then hide. Pollution fouls and destroys where before there existed beauty. Man builds fences, dams, and bridges. He dredges, he dumps, he blocks, and he gnaws into the heart of his river. He forces peaceful rivers to grow surly and then turns to damn the spirit of those he calls wild and useless.

The world of canoeing can accommodate many. Miles of streams and rivers are seldom broken by paddle. They remain waiting to be found and experienced.

A legacy of pleasure and adventure can be left to others by each canoeist. Descriptions of new canoe trails and additions or corrections to those now recorded will be warmly received for inclusion in a later printing. New runs will bear the names of canoeists who first record and send descriptions to me, care of the publisher.

The thrill of discovery around each new river bend, the sound of solitude, the challenge of boulders and rapids—each is food for man's soul. Each in its own way punctures and scrapes the hardened crust of man the machine to expose man the mortal.

Enter the world of canoeing. Take with you your fears, your bitterness, and your sorrow. Leave them, but leave them only. Return with the trash of a throw-away mentality. The careless clutter of but one reader who uses this book destroys the purpose of all who caused this book to be.

It is man the mortal who must now save our rivers, for he knows and feels that indescribable something that only the river provides.

CONTENTS

Further Sources Suggested

CANOE TRAILS
DIRECTORY

WARNING

We are not responsible for accidents that may occur on any canoe trail due to any errors or omissions in this book. This material is subject to change as rivers change. Canoeists should not use these data alone, but also gather up-to-date maps and other information concerning the rivers or streams they intend to float.

It is also each canoeist's responsibility to use common sense, all necessary and required safety equipment, and to keep craft and gear in excellent condition.

RECORDING YOUR CANOE TRIP

Here is an opportunity to help provide enjoyment to adventure lovers for years to come. Record your canoe trip and send the information to James C. Makens, c/o Doubleday & Company, Inc., 245 Park Avenue, New York, New York 10017.

We will also appreciate corrections, changes, or additions to trails already described.

Please be as accurate as possible. Remember, your information can actually save lives.

Stream
State
County
Water level
Put-in location
Take-out location
Distance between points in river miles:_____ in hours:_____.
Date of trip

Special Information:

Danger points
Difficulty rating
Obstacles
Portages or lining
Dams
Type of bottom
Pollution

Campsites
Seasonal fluctuation in water level
Access points
Scenic interest
Special historical points
Special precautions necessary
Fish and fishing

EXPLANATION OF DIFFICULTY RATING

Difficulty Rating in Roman Numerals

I. Easy
II. Medium
III. Difficult
IV. Very difficult
V. Exceedingly difficult—seldom attempted even by the most experienced canoeists
VI. Limit of navigability—cannot be attempted without risk of life

Difficulty Rating System for Streams of West Virginia taken from A Canoeist's Guide to the Whitewater Rivers of West Virginia *by Bob Burrell and Paul Davidson*

A. Standing or slow flowing water, not more than 2.5 m.p.h.
B. Current between 2.5 and 4.5 m.p.h., but backpaddling can effectively neutralize the speed.
C. Current more than 4.5 m.p.h. and backpaddling cannot neutralize the speed of the current. Simple obstacles may occur that require a certain amount of boat control.

1. Easy
2. Medium difficulty
3. Difficult
4. Very difficult
5. Exceedingly difficult—skilled only
6. Utmost difficulty—risk of life in running

List of Abbreviations

bdry.	boundary
ctry.	country
cfs.	cubic feet per second
dif.	difficult or difficulty
is.	island
lndg.	landing
par.	parish
ptg.	portage
sec.	section
st.	state

TRAILS INDEX

Trail	State	Trail	State
Brazos River	Tex.	Cascade River	Minn.
Brice Creek	N.C.	Cascade River	Wash.
Brimstone Creek	Tenn.	Cass River	Mich.
Broad River	Ga.	Cassadaga Creek	N.Y.
Broad Run River	Va.	Catatonk Creek	N.Y.
Brokenstraw Creek	Pa.	Catoctin Creek	Md.
Brule River	Mich.	Catoctin Creek	Va.
Brule River	Wis.	Cattaraugus Creek	N.Y.
Bruneau River	Nev.	Catwissa Creek	Pa.
Bruneau River, W. Fork	Nev.	Cays River	Mich.
		Cayuta Creek	N.Y.
Brushy Creek	Ala.	Cedar Creek	Mo.
Bryant Creek	Mo.	Cedar Creek	Va.
Buchannon River	W.Va.	Cedar River	Wash.
Buffalo Creek	N.Y.	Center Creek	Mo.
Buffalo Creek	Pa.	Chadakoin River	N.Y.
Buffalo River	Ark.	Chain of Ponds	Me.
Buffalo River	Ind.	Chama River	N.M.
Buffalo River	Tenn.	Champlain Canal	N.Y.
Buffalo River	Wyo.	Chappepeela River	La.
Bull Creek	Mo.	Charles River	Mass.
Bull Pasture River	Va.	Charlotte Creek	N.Y.
Bulow Creek	Fla.	Chartiers Creek	Pa.
Butternut Creek	N.Y.	Chassahowitzka River	Fla.
Cabbossee Stream and Lakes	Me.	Chatanika River	Alas.
		Chattahoochee River	Ga.
Cacapon River	W.Va.	Chattooga River	Ga.
Cacapon— N. River Tributary	W.Va.	Chattooga River	S.C.
		Chauga River	S.C.
		Cheat River	W.Va.
Cache Creek	Cal.	Cheat River, Black Fork	W.Va.
Cache River	Ill.	Cheat River, Dry Fork	W.Va.
Cahaba River	Ala.	Cheat River, Glady Fork	W.Va.
Calamus River	Neb.	Cheat River, Shavers Fork	W.Va.
Calcasieu River	La.		
Canal Feeders	N.J.	Chehalis River	Wash.
Canandaiqua Outlet	N.Y.	Chemung River	N.Y.
Canaseraga Creek	N.Y.	Chena River	Alas.
Caney Fork River	Tenn.	Chenango River	N.Y.
Caney River	Kan.	Cherry Brook	Conn.
Canisteo River	N.Y.	Cherry River	W.Va.
Cannon River	Minn.	Cherry Valley Creek	N.Y.
Canoe River	Mass.	Cherwack River	Wash.
Cape Cod Canal	Mass.	Chest Creek	Pa.
Carabassett River	Me.	Chestatee River	Ga.
Carp River	Mich.	Chester Creek	Pa.
Carson River	Cal.	Chicopee River	Mass.
Cartecay River	Ga.	China Lake and Stream	Me.

Trail	State	Trail	State
Dearborn River	Mich.	Ellicott Creek	N.Y.
Dearborn River	Mont.	Ellis River	N.H.
Decker's Creek	W.Va.	Embarras River	Ill.
Deerfield River	Mass.	Embarras River	Wis.
Deerfield River	Vt.	Emory River	Tenn.
Deer Trail Creek	Wis.	Entiat River	Wash.
Delta River	Alas.	Escanaba River	Mich.
Delaware River	N.J.	Esopus Creek	N.Y.
Delaware River	N.Y.	Estero River	Fla.
Delaware River	Pa.	Etowah River	Ga.
Delaware River and	N.J.	Everglades	Fla.
Raritan Canal		National Park	
Denny's River	Me.	Exeter River	N.H.
Denton Creek	Tex.		
Depot Stream	Me.		
Des Moines River	Ia.	Fall Creek	N.Y.
Des Moines River	Minn.	Fall River	Kan.
Des Plaines River	Ill.	Fall Stream	N.Y.
Deschutes River	Ore.	Falls River	Mass.
Deschutes River	Wash.	Farmington River	Conn.
Devil's River	Tex.	Farmington River,	Conn.
Dismal River	Neb.	E. Branch	
Dismal Swamp	N.C.	Farnum Creek	Va.
Traverse		Fawn Brook	Conn.
Dismal Swamp	Va.	Fawn River	Ind.
Traverse		Feather River,	Cal.
Dog River	Vt.	E. Branch,	
Duck River	Tenn.	Feather River,	Cal.
Dugdemona River	La.	Mid. Fork.	
Dungeness River	Wash.	Feather River,	Cal.
Duwanisn River	Wash.	N. Fork	
		Fence River	Mich.
		Finley Creek	Mo.
E. Creek	Vt.	First Fork Creek	Pa.
E. Machias River	Me.	Fish Creek	Alas.
Eau Claire River	Wis.	Fish Creek	La.
Econfina River	Fla.	Fish Creek	N.Y.
Econlockhatchee	Fla.	Fish River	Me.
River		Fish River,	Me.
Eel River	Cal.	E. Branch	
Eel River	Ind.	Fish River Lakes	Me.
Eel River,	Cal.	Fish Stream	Me.
S. Fork		Fishing Creek	Pa.
Eighteen Mile Creek	Ky.	Fishkill Creek	N.Y.
Eighteen Mile Creek	N.Y.	Five Mile Creek	N.Y.
Eleven Point River	Ark.	Flambeau Flowage	Wis.
Eleven Point River	Mo.	Flambeau River	Wis.
Elk River	Pa.	Flambeau River,	Wis.
Elkhorn River	Neb.	S. Fork	

Trail	State	Trail	State
Huron River	Mich.	Kankakee River	Ind.
Huzzah Creek	Mo.	Kansas River	Kan.
		Kaskaskia River	Ill.
Ichetucknee River	Fla.	Kayaderosseras Creek	N.Y.
Illinois River	Ill.		
Illinois River	Okla.	Keechi Creek	Tex.
Illinois River, Michigan Canal	Ill.	Kenai River	Alas.
		Kennebago River	Me.
Illinois River, Mississippi Canal	Ill.	Kennebec River	Me.
		Kentucky River, Mid. Fork	Ky.
Illinois River, Mississippi Feeder Canal	Ill.	Kentucky River, S. Fork	Ky.
Indian Creek	Mo.	Kern River	Cal.
Indian River	Mich.	Kettle Creek	Pa.
Indian River	N.Y.	Kettle River	Minn.
Indian Head Creek	Pa.	Kezar Lake	Me.
Inguadona Canoe Tour	Minn.	Kiamichi River	Okla.
Inland Lakes Route	Mich.	Kickapoo River	Wis.
Intermediate Chain of Lakes	Mich.	Kinderhook Creek	N.Y.
		Kings River	Cal.
Iowa River	Ia.	Kisatchie Bayou	La.
Iroquois River	Ill.	Kishacoquillas Creek	Pa.
Ischua Creek	N.Y.		
Israel River	N.H.	Kiskiminetas River	Pa.
		Klamath River	Cal.
Jack's Fork River	Mo.	Konkapot River	Mass.
Jackson River	Va.	Kootenai River	Mont.
James River	Mo.	Kunjamuck Creek	N.Y.
James River	S.D.		
James River	Va.	Lackawaxen River	Pa.
Jarbridge River	Nev.	Lake Bistineau	La.
Jefferson River	Mont.	Lake Cumberland	Ky.
Jellico Creek	Ky.	Lake D'Arbonne, Mid. Fork	La.
John Day River	Ore.		
Johnson Creek	N.Y.	Lake Tahoe	Nev.
Jordan River	Mich.	Lamoille River	Vt.
Jump River, N. Fork	Wis.	Lampasas River	Tex.
		Lamprey River	N.H.
Jump River, S. Fork	Wis.	Laurel Creek	N.C.
		Laurel Creek	Tenn.
Juniata River	Pa.	Laurel Hill Creek	Pa.
Juniata River, Raystown Branch	Pa.	La Vaca and Navidad rivers	Tex.
		Lawrence Brook	N.J.
		Lehigh River	Pa.
Kachees River	N.Y.	Lemonweir River	Wis.
Kalamazoo River	Mich.	Leon River	Tex.
Kankakee River	Ill.	Lewis River	Wash.

Trail	State	Trail	State
Marais des Cygnes River	Kan.	Molunkus Stream	Me.
		Monocacy River	Md.
Marias River	Mont.	Monongahela River	Pa.
Marengo River	Wis.	Montreal River	Wis.
Maries River	Mo.	Moodna Creek	N.Y.
Marsh Creek	Ky.	Moorefield River	W.Va.
Martins Brook	Mass.	Moorman's River	Va.
Mattaponi River	Va.	Moose Pond	Me.
Mattawamkeag River	Me.	Moose River	Me.
		Moose River	Minn.
Mattawamkeag River, W. Branch	Me.	Moose River	N.Y.
		Moose River	Vt.
Mattole River	Cal.	Moose River, Mid. Branch	N.Y.
Maumee River	O.		
Maurice River	N.J.	Moose River, N. Branch	N.Y.
Maury River	Va.		
McKenzie River	Ore.	Moosehead Lake	Me.
Meadow River	W.Va.	Mooseleuk Stream and Lake	Me.
Medicine Creek	Neb.		
Medina River	Tex.	Moreau River	Mo.
Meeker Run	Pa.	Moshannon Creek	Pa.
Menominee River	Mich.	Mosquito Creek	Pa.
Menominee River	Wis.	Mt. Landing Creek	Va.
Meramec River	Mo.	Mountain Fork River	Okla.
Merced River	Cal.	Mousam River	Me.
Merrimack River	Mass.	Mud Creek	N.Y.
Merrimack River	N.H.	Muddy Creek	Pa.
Methow River	Wash.	Mulberry River	Ark.
Michigamme River	Mich.	Mullica River	N.J.
Mid. Fork of Lake D'Arbonne	La.	Munsungan Stream	Me.
		Muscatatuck River	Ind.
Mid. Loup River	Neb.	Musconetcong River	N.J.
Mill River	Kan.	Muskegon River	Mich.
Millers River	Mass.	Muskegon River, W. Branch	Mich.
Millinocket River	Me.		
Millstone River	N.J.	Muskingum River	O.
Mineral Fork of Big River	Mont.	Musquacook Stream	Me.
Minnesota River	Minn.	Namasket River	Mass.
Missisinewa River	Ind.	Namekagon Lake	Wis.
Missisquoi River	Vt.	Namekagon River	Wis.
Mississippi River	Minn.	Nantahala River	N.C.
Missouri River	Mont.	Nanticoke Creek	N.Y.
Missouri River	Neb.	Narraguagus River	Me.
Missouri River	N.D.	Nashua River	Mass.
Moccasin Creek	Va.	Nashua River	N.H.
Mohawk River	N.Y.	Naugatuck River	Conn.
Mohican River	O.	Navarro River	Cal.
Mokelumne River	Cal.	Navesink River	N.J.

Trail	State	Trail	State
Paul Stream	Vt.	Popple River	Wis.
Paulins Kill	N.J.	Portage Lakes	O.
Pautuxet River	R.I.	System	
Paw Paw River	Mich.	Potholes Lakes	Wash.
Pawcatuck	R.I.	Potomac River	Md.
and Wood River		Potomac River	Va.
Peabody River	N.H.	Potomac River,	Md.
Peace River	Fla.	N. Branch	
Pearl River	La.	Potomac River,	Wis.
Pecatonica River	Ill.	N. Branch	
Pecatonica River	Wis.	Potomac River,	W.Va.
Pecos River	Tex.	N. Fork of	
Pedernales River	Tex.	S. Branch	
Pelican River	Wis.	Potomac River,	W.Va.
Pemigewasset River	N.H.	S. Branch	
Penns Creek	Pa.	Potomac River,	W.Va.
Pennsylvania Canal	Pa.	S. Fork of	
Penobscot River	Me.	S. Branch	
Penobscot River,	Me.	Powell River	Tenn.
E. Branch		Powwow River	Mass.
Penobscot River,	Me.	Presque Isle River	Mich.
W. Branch		Provo River	Ut.
Pequest River	N.J.	Pushepatapa Creek	La.
Père Marquette River	Mich.	Puyallup River	Wash.
Peshtigo River	Wis.		
Pigeon River	Ill.	Quaboag River	Mass.
Pigeon River	Ind.	Queets River	Wash.
Pigeon River	N.C.	Quinapoxet River	Mass.
Pike River	Wis.	Quinault River	Wash.
Pilchuck Creek	Wash.	Quinault River,	Wash.
Pilchuck River	Wash.	N. Fork	
Pine Creek	Pa.	Quinebaug River	Conn.
Pine Island Bayou	Tex.	Quinnipiac River	Conn.
Pine River	Mich.	Raccoon Creek	Ia.
Pine River	Wis.	Raccoon River	Pa.
Piscataqua River	Me.	Rahway River	N.J.
Piscataqua River	N.H.	Rainbow River	Fla.
Piscataquis River	Me.	Raisin River	Mich.
Piscataquog River	N.H.	Ramapo River	N.J.
Piscataquog River,	N.H.	Ramapo River	N.Y.
S. Branch		Rancocas River	N.J.
Pit River	Cal.	Rangeley Lakes	Me.
Platte River	Mich.	Rapid River	Me.
Platte River	Neb.	Rapidan River	Va.
Platte River	Wyo.	Rapidan River, Upper	Va.
Pleasant River	Me.	Rappahannock River	Va.
Plum Creek	Neb.	Raquette River	N.Y.
Pomme de Terre	Mo.	Raritan Canal	N.J.
River		Raritan River	N.J.

Trail	State	Trail	State
Saranac River	N.Y.	Shrewsbury River	N.J.
Satilla River	Ga.	Silver Brook	N.H.
Satsop River,	Wash.	Sinking Creek	Ky.
Mid. Fork		Sinnemahoning	Pa.
Satsop River,	Wash.	Creek	
W. Fork		Sipsey River	Ala.
Saugatuck River	Conn.	Six Mile Creek	La.
Saugus River	Mass.	Skagit River	Wash.
Sauk River	Wash.	Skokomish River	Wash.
Savage River	Md.	Skookumchuck River	Wash.
Saxtons River	Vt.	Skykomish River	Wash.
Schenevus Creek	N.Y.	Skykomish River,	Wash.
Schoharie River	N.Y.	S. Fork	
Schroon River	N.Y.	Slippery Rock	Pa.
Schuylkill River	Pa.	Creek	
Seboeis River	Me.	Smith River	Cal.
Seely Creek	N.Y.	Smith River	Mont.
Seneca Creek	W. Va.	Smith River	N.H.
Sequatchie River	Tenn.	Snake Creek	N.D.
Seven Mile Stream	Me.	Snake River	Id.
Shade Creek	Pa.	Snake River	Minn.
Shawangunk Kill	N.Y.	Snake River	Neb.
Shawsheen River	Mass.	Snake River	Ore.
Sheepscot River	Me.	Snake River	Wyo.
Shell Rock River	Ia.	Snohomish River	Wash.
Shenandoah River,	Va.	Snohomish River,	Wash.
N. Fork		N. Fork	
Shenandoah River,	Va.	Snohomish River,	Wash.
S. Branch		S. Fork	
Shenandoah River,	Va.	Soleduck River	Wash.
S. Fork,		Soucook River	N.H.
Shenandoah River,	Va.	Souhegan River	N.H.
S. Fork		South River	Mass.
and Back Creek		S. Loup River	Neb.
Shenandoah River,	Va.	S. Moreau Creek	Mo.
S. Fork,		S. Prairie River	Wash.
N. River		S. Santiam River	Ore.
Shenandoah River,	Va.	S. Vermillion River,	Ill.
S. Fork		Mid. Fork	
S. River		S. Vermillion	Ill.
Shenango River	Pa.	River, N. Fork	
Shepaug River	Conn.	S. Vermillion River,	Ill.
Shetucket River	Conn.	Salt Fork	
Shiawassee River	Mich.	Spencer Stream	Me.
Shoal Creek	Ill.	Spoon River	Ill.
Shoal Creek	Mo.	Spring Creek	Kan.
Shoal Creek	Kan.	Spring Creek	La.
Shoal River	Fla.	Spring Creek	Tenn.
Shoshone River	Wyo.	Spring River	Kan.

Spring River	Mo.	Temperance River	Minn.
Spring River	Mont.	Temple Stream	Me.
Spring River	Okla.	Ten Mile Creek	La.
Spruce Creek	Fla.	Ten Mile River	N.Y.
Squam River	N.H.	Teton River	Id.
Squamscott River	N.H.	The Branch	N.H.
Squannacook River	Mass.	The Cut	Mich.
Stanislaus River	Cal.	Thornapple River	Mich.
Station Camp Creek	Ky.	Thornapple River	Wis.
Still River	Conn.	Thornton River	Va.
Stillaquamish River	Wash.	Three Lakes—	Wis.
Stony Brook	Mass.	Eagle River Trail	
Stony Brook	N.H.	Thunder Bay River	Mich.
Stony Brook	N.J.	Thunder Bay River	Wis.
Stony Creek	Pa.	Thunder Bay River,	Mich.
Stony Creek	Va.	S. Branch	
Sturgeon Creek	Ky.	Tickflaw River	La.
Sturgeon River	Mich.	Tieton River	Wash.
Sucker River	Mich.	Tilton River	Wash.
Sugar Creek	Ind.	Tioga River	N.Y.
Suiattle River	Wash.	Tionesta Creek	Pa.
Sulphur River	Tex.	Tioughnioga River	N.Y.
Sun River	Mont.	Tippecanoe River	Ind.
Suncook River	N.H.	Tittabawassee	Mich.
Sunday River	Me.	River	
Susquehanna River	N.Y.	Tobyhanna Creek	Pa.
Susquehanna River	Pa.	Toccoa River	Ga.
Susquehanna River,		Tolt River	Wash.
W. Branch		Tomahawk River	Wis.
Suwannee River	Fla.	Toms River	N.J.
Swan Creek	Mo.	Tonawanda Creek	N.Y.
Swan Lake	Alas.	Totogatic River	Wis.
Swan River	Mont.	Toxaway River	N.C.
Swanson River	Alas.	Trail to Ohio	Pa.
Swatara Creek	Pa.	River	
Swift Creek	Va.	Trinity River	Cal.
Swift Diamond	N.H.	Trinity River	Tex.
River		Trinity River,	Tex.
Swift River	Me.	Clear Fork	
Swift River	Mass.	Trinity River, E. Fork	Tex.
		Trinity River, Elm Fork	Tex.
Tahquamenon River	Mich.	Trout Creek	La.
Talking Rock Creek	Ga.	Trout River	Vt.
Tangipahoa River	La.	Trout River	Wis.
Taunton River	Mass.	Truckee River	Cal.
Tavern Creek	Mo.	Truckee River	Nev.
Taylor River	Col.	Tsala Apopka	Fla.
Tchefuncte River	La.	Chain of Lakes	
Tchoutocabouffa	Miss.	Tuckaseigee River	N.C.
River		Tulley River	Mass.
Tellico River	Tenn.	Tulpehacken Creek	Pa.

Trail	State	Trail	State
Tuolumne River	Cal.	Westfield River	Mass.
Turkey River	Ia.	Wet Beaver Creek	Ariz.
Turnback Creek	Mo.	Weweantic River	Mass.
Turtle Creek	Pa.	Wharton Creek	N.Y.
Turtle Creek	Minn.	Whiskey Chitto Creek	La.
Turtle River	Wis.	White Creek	Tenn.
Tuxachanie Creek	Miss.	White Deer Creek	Pa.
Two Hearted River	Mich.	White Oak River	N.C.
Tygart River	W.Va.	White River	Ark.
		White River	Mich.
		White River	Vt.
Umpqua River	Ore.	White River	Wash.
Unadilla River	N.Y.	White River	Wis.
Upper Iowa River	Ia.	White River,	Ind.
Upper Mohawk River	N.Y.	E. Branch	
Upper Tangle Lakes	Alas.	White River,	Ind.
		E. Fork	
Verde River	Ariz.	White River,	Ind.
Verdigre Creek	Neb.	W. Fork	
Verdigris River	Kan.	White Rock Creek	Tex.
Vermillion River	Ill.	Whiteoak Creek	Tenn.
Vermillion River	La.	Whitefish River	Mich.
Volga River	Ia.	Whitewater River	Ind.
Wabash River	Ind.	Wild River	Me.
Wacissa River	Fla.	Willamette River	Ore.
Wading River	N.J.	Williams River	Mass.
Wailua River	Hi.	Willimantic River	Conn.
Waiska River	Mich.	Willomemoc River	N.Y.
Wakopa Game	N.D.	Wills Creek	Md.
Management Area		Wills Creek	Pa.
Walhonding River	O.	Wilson Stream	Me.
Walkill River	N.J.	Winhall River	Vt.
Wallkill River	N.Y.	Winooski River	Vt.
Wallenpaupack	Pa.	Wisconsin River	Wis.
Creek		Withlacoochee	Fla.
Wappinger Creek	N.Y.	River	
Wapsipinicon River	Ia.	Withlacoochee	Ga.
Wards Creek	Va.	River	
Ware River	Mass.	Wolf River	Wis.
Waupaca Chain	Wis.	Wood Creek	N.Y.
of Lakes		Wood River	R.I.
Waupaca River	Wis.	Wynoochee River	Wash.
Weaubleau Creek	Mo.	Wytopitlock Stream	Me.
Weber River	Ut.		
Wekiva River	Fla.	Yahara River	Wis.
Wenatchee River	Wash.	Yakima River	Wash.
W. Canada Creek	N.Y.	Yampa River	Col.
W. Clear Creek	Ariz.	Yellow Breeches	Pa.
W. River	Vt.	Creek	

REGIONAL LISTINGS

REGION I — Maine, Vermont, New Hampshire, Massachusetts, Connecticut, Rhode Island, New York

REGION II — Pennsylvania, Maryland, Delaware, Virginia, West Virginia, North Carolina, South Carolina, New Jersey

REGION III — Mississippi, Alabama, Tennessee, Georgia, Florida

REGION IV — Ohio, Illinois, Michigan, Wisconsin, Kentucky, Indiana

REGION V — Texas, Louisiana, Arkansas, Oklahoma

REGION VI — North Dakota, South Dakota, Nebraska, Missouri, Iowa, Minnesota

REGION VII — Washington, Wyoming, Oregon, California, Idaho, Montana, Colorado, Utah, Nevada, Arizona, New Mexico, Alaska, Hawaii

REGION I
Maine, Vermont, New Hampshire, Massachusetts, Connecticut, Rhode Island, New York

Trail	State	Trail	State
Adirondack Rtes.	N.Y.	Ashuelot River, S. Branch	N.H.
Allagash Wilderness Waterway	Me.	Assabet River	Mass.
		Attean Lake	Me.
Allegheny River	N.Y.	Ausable River	N.Y.
Allegheny River	Pa.	Ausable River, E. Branch	N.Y.
Ammonoosuc River	N.H.	Ausable River, W. Branch	N.Y.
Ashuelot River	N.H.		

Bagaduce River	Me.	Chenango River	N.Y.
Baker River	N.H.	Cherry Brook	Conn.
Bantam River	Conn.	Cherry Valley Creek	N.Y.
Baskahegan River	Me.	Chicopee River	Mass.
Bass River	Mass.	China Lake	Me.
Batten Kill	N.Y.	and Stream	
Bear River	Me.	Chiputnecook Lakes	Me.
Bearcamp River	N.H.	Chittenango Creek	N.Y.
Beards Brook	N.H.	Claverock Creek	N.Y.
Beaver Brook	Mass.	Clyde River	Vt.
Beaver Brook	N.H.	Cocheco River	N.H.
Beaver Kill	N.Y.	Cockermouth River	N.H.
Beaver River	N.Y.	Cohocton River	N.Y.
Belgrade Lakes	Me.	Cold River	N.H.
Circle Trip		Cold River	N.Y.
Bellamy River	N.H.	Concord River	Mass.
Bennett River	N.Y.	Conewango Creek	N.Y.
Big Black River	Me.	Connecticut River	Conn.
Black Creek	N.Y.	Connecticut River	N.H.
Black River	N.Y.	Connecticut River	Vt.
Black River—	Vt.	Contoocook River	N.H.
northern Vermont		Contoocook River,	N.H.
Black River—	Vt.	N. Branch	
southern Vermont		Crooked River	Me.
Blackledge River	Conn.	Cupsuptic River	Me.
Blackwater River	N.H.		
Boreas River	N.Y.	Damariscotta River	Me.
Boston Brook	Mass.	and Lake	
Bouquet River	N.Y.	Dead Diamond River	N.H.
Buffalo Creek	N.Y.	Dead River	Me.
Butternut Creek	N.Y.	Dead River, N. Branch	Me.
		Dead River, S. Branch	Me.
Cabbossee Stream	Me.	Deerfield River	Mass.
and Lakes		Deerfield River	Vt.
Canandaiqua Outlet	N.Y.	Denny's River	Me.
Canaseraga Creek	N.Y.	Depot Stream	Me.
Canisteo River	N.Y.	Dog River	Vt.
Canoe River	Mass.		
Cape Cod Canal	Mass.	E. Creek	Vt.
Carabassett River	Me.	E. Machias River	Me.
Cassadaga Creek	N.Y.	Eighteen Mile Creek	N.Y.
Catatonk Creek	N.Y.	Ellicott Creek	N.Y.
Cattaraugus Creek	N.Y.	Ellis River	N.H.
Cayuta Creek	N.Y.	Esopus Creek	N.Y.
Chadakoin River	N.Y.	Exeter River	N.H.
Chain of Ponds	Me.		
Champlain Canal	N.Y.	Fall Creek	N.Y.
Charles River	Mass.	Fall Stream	N.Y.
Charlotte Creek	N.Y.	Falls River	Mass.
Chemung River	N.Y.	Farmington River	Conn.

Trail	State
Farmington, E. Branch	Conn.
Fawn Brook	Conn.
Fish Creek	N.Y.
Fish River	Me.
Fish River, E. Branch	Me.
Fish River Lakes	Me.
Fish Stream	Me.
Fishkill Creek	N.Y.
Five Mile Creek	N.Y.
Flint Creek	N.Y.
Genegantslet Creek	N.Y.
Genesee River	N.Y.
Grand Lakes Chain	Me.
Grass River	N.Y.
Great Chazey River	N.Y.
Great Ossipee River	Me.
Great Ossipee River	N.H.
Green River	Mass.
Green River	Vt.
Honeoye Creek	N.Y.
Hoosic River	N.Y.
Housatonic River	Conn.
Housatonic River	Mass.
Hubbard Brook	Mass.
Hudson Brook	Conn.
Hudson River	N.Y.
Indian River	N.Y.
Ischua Creek	N.Y.
Israel River	N.H.
Johnson Creek	N.Y.
Kachees River	N.Y.
Kayaderosseras Creek	N.Y.
Kennebago River	Me.
Kennebec River	Me.
Kezar Lake	Me.
Kinderhook Creek	N.Y.
Konkapot River	Mass.
Kunjamuck Creek	N.Y.
Lamoille River	Vt.
Lamprey River	N.H.

Trail	State
Limestone Creek	N.Y.
Little Androscoggin River	Me.
Little Androscoggin River, Nelinscot Branch	Me.
Little Black River	Me.
Little Madawaska River	Me.
Little Ossipee River	Me.
Little River	Me.
Little Salmon River	N.Y.
Little Spencer River	Me.
Livingston Creek	N.Y.
Lovell River	N.H.
Lower Magalloway River	Me.
Machias River	Me.
Macwahoc Stream	Me.
Mad River	Conn.
Mad River	N.H.
Mad River	Vt.
Magalloway River	Me.
Magalloway River	N.H.
Martins Brook	Mass.
Mattawamkeag River	Me.
Mattawamkeag River, W. Branch	Me.
Merrimack River	Mass.
Merrimack River	N.H.
Millers River	Mass.
Millinocket River	Me.
Missisquoi River	Vt.
Mohawk River	N.Y.
Molunkus Stream	Me.
Moodna Creek	N.Y.
Moose Pond	Me.
Moose River	Me.
Moose River	N.Y.
Moose River	Vt.
Moose River, Mid. Branch	N.Y.
Moose River, N. Branch	N.Y.
Moosehead Lake	Me.

Mooseleuk Stream and Lake	Me.
Mousam River	Me.
Mud Creek	N.Y.
Munsungan Stream	Me.
Musquacook Stream	Me.
Namasket River	Mass.
Nanticoke Creek	N.Y.
Narraguagus River	Me.
Nashua River	Mass.
Nashua River	N.H.
Naugatuck River	Conn.
Nefourd River	N.H.
Neversink River	N.Y.
New York City	N.Y.
Newfound River	N.H.
Niagara River	N.Y.
Nicatous Lake and Stream	Me.
Nine Mile Creek	N.Y.
Nissequoque River	N.Y.
Nissitissit River	Mass.
Normanskill	N.Y.
N. River	Mass.
Norwalk River	Conn.
Oatka Creek	N.Y.
Old Stream River	Me.
Olean Creek	N.Y.
Ompompanoosuc River	Vt.
Oneida Creek	N.Y.
Orange River	Me.
Ossipee Lake and River	Me.
Oswegatchie River	N.Y.
Otego Creek	N.Y.
Otselic River	N.Y.
Ottauquechee River	Vt.
Otter Brook	N.H.
Otter Creek	Vt.
Otter River	Mass.
Ouleout Creek	N.Y.
Owego Creek	N.Y.
Owego Creek, W. Branch	N.Y.
Palmer River	Mass.
Paul Stream	Vt.

Pautuxet River	R.I.
Pawcatuck and Wood rivers	R.I.
Peabody River	N.H.
Pemigewasset River	N.H.
Penobscot River	Me.
Penobscot River, E. Branch	Me.
Penobscot River, W. Branch	Me.
Piscataqua River	Me.
Piscataqua River	N.H.
Piscataquis River	Me.
Piscataquog River	N.H.
Piscataquog River, S. Branch	N.H.
Pleasant River	Me.
Powwow River	Mass.
Quaboag River	Mass.
Quinapoxet River	Mass.
Quinebaug River	Conn.
Quinnipiac River	Conn.
Ramapo River	N.Y.
Rangeley Lakes	Me.
Rapid River	Me.
Roundout Creek	N.Y.
Sacandaga River	N.Y.
Sacandaga River, E. Branch	N.Y.
Sacandaga River, W. Branch	N.Y.
Saco River	Me.
Saco River	N.H.
St. Croix River	Me.
St. Francis River	Me.
St. John River	Me.
St. John River, Baker Branch	Me.
St. John River, N.W. Branch	Me.
St. John River, S.W. Branch	Me.
St. Regis River	N.Y.
Salmon Brook	Conn.
Salmon Brook	N.H.
Salmon Creek	N.Y.
Salmon Falls River	Me.

Trail	State	Trail	State
Salmon Falls River	N.H.	Swift Diamond	N.H.
Salmon River	Conn.	River	
Salmon River	N.Y.	Swift River	Me.
Sandy Brook	Conn.	Swift River	Mass.
Sandy Creek	N.Y.		
Sandy River	Me.	Taunton River	Mass.
Sangerfield River	N.Y.	Temple Stream	Me.
Saranac River	N.Y.	Ten Mile River	N.Y.
Saugatuck River	Conn.	The Branch	N.H.
Saugus River	Mass.	Tioga River	N.Y.
Saxtons River	Vt.	Tioughnioga River	N.Y.
Schenevus Creek	N.Y.	Tonawanda Creek	N.Y.
Schoharie River	N.Y.	Trout River	Vt.
Schroon River	N.Y.	Tulley River	Mass.
Seboeis River	Me.		
Seely Creek	N.Y.	Unadilla River	N.Y.
Seven Mile Stream	Me.	Upper Mohawk River	N.Y.
Shawangunk Kill	N.Y.		
Shawsheen River	Mass.	Wallkill River	N.Y.
Sheepscot River	Me.	Wappinger Creek	N.Y.
Shepaug River	Conn.	Ware River	Mass.
Shetucket River	Conn.	West Canada Creek	N.Y.
Silver Brook	N.H.	West River	Vt.
Soucook River	N.H.	Westfield River	Mass.
Souhegan River	Mass.	Weweantic River	Mass.
S. River	Mass.	Wharton Creek	N.Y.
Spencer Stream	Me.	White River	Vt.
Squam River	N.H.	Wild River	Me.
Squamscott River	N.H.	Williams River	Mass.
Squannacook River	Mass.	Willimantic River	Conn.
Still River	Conn.	Willomemoc River	N.Y.
Stony Brook	Mass.	Wilson Stream	Me.
Stony Brook	N.H.	Winhall River	Vt.
Suncook River	N.H.	Winooski River	Vt.
Sunday River	Me.	Wood Creek	N.Y.
Susquehanna River	N.Y.	Wood River	R.I.
		Wytopitlock Stream	Me.

REGION II
Pennsylvania, Maryland, Delaware, Virginia, West Virginia, North Carolina, South Carolina, New Jersey

Trail	State	Trail	State
Alloways Creek	N.J.	Baab Creek	Pa.
Anthony Creek	W.Va.	Back Creek	Va.
Antietam Creek	Md.	Bald Eagle Creek	Pa.
Appomattox River	Va.	Batsto River	N.J.

Beaver River	Pa.
Beech Creek	Pa.
Bennett Creek	Md.
Big Nescopeck Creek	Pa.
Big Pipe Creek	Md.
Big Sandy River	W.Va.
Big Totuskey River	Va.
Big Walker Creek	Va.
Black Moshannon River	Pa.
Blacklick Creek	Pa.
Blackwater River	W.Va.
Brandywine River	Del.
Brandywine River	Pa.
Brice Creek	N.C.
Buchannon River	W.Va.
Buffalo Creek	Pa.
Bull Pasture River	Va.
Cacapon River	W.Va.
Cacapon River, N. River Tributary	W.Va.
Canal Feeders	N.J.
Catoctin Creek	Md.
Catoctin Creek	Va.
Catwissa Creek	Pa.
Cedar Creek	Va.
Chartiers Creek	Pa.
Chattooga River	S.C.
Chauga River	S.C.
Cheat River	W.Va.
Cheat River, Black Fork	W.Va.
Cheat River, Dry Fork	W.Va.
Cheat River, Glady Fork	W.Va.
Cheat River, Shavers Fork	W.Va.
Cherry River	W.Va.
Chest Creek	Pa.
Chester Creek	Pa.
Clarion River	Pa.
Clinch River	Va.
Cohansey Creek	N.J.
Conemaugh River	Pa.
Conestoga Creek	Pa.
Conewango Creek	Pa.

Connoquenessing Creek	Pa.
Conodogniast Creek	Pa.
Cooper River	N.J.
Cowpasture River	Va.
Cranberry River	W.Va.
Crooked Creek	Pa.
Cross State Canoe Route	N.J.
Crosswicks Creek	N.J.
Dark Shade Creek	Pa.
Decker's Creek	W.Va.
Delaware River	N.J.
Delaware River and Raritan Canal	N.J.
Dismal Swamp Traverse	N.C.
Dismal Swamp Traverse	Va.
Elk River	Pa.
Farnum Creek	Va.
First Fork Creek	Pa.
Fishing Creek	Pa.
Flat Brook	N.J.
French Broad River	N.C.
French Creek	Pa.
Gifford Run	Pa.
Goose Creek	Va.
Grays Creek	Va.
Great Egg Harbor River	N.J.
Green River	N.C.
Greenbrier River	W.Va.
Hackensack River	N.J.
Hazel River	Va.
Holston River, Mid. Branch	Va.
Holston River, N. Fork	Va.
Holston River, S. Fork	Va.
Honey Creek	Pa.
Hughes River	Va.

Trail	State	Trail	State
Indian Head Creek	Pa.	Mosquito Creek	Pa.
		Mt. Landing Creek	Va.
Jackson River	Va.	Muddy Creek	Pa.
James River	Va.	Mullica River	N.J.
Juniata River	Pa.	Musconetcong River	N.J.
Juniata River	Pa.		
Raystown Branch		Nantahala River	N.C.
		Navesink River	N.J.
		Nesamining Creek	Pa.
Kettle Creek	Pa.	Neshannock Creek	Pa.
Kishacoquillas	Pa.	New River	W.Va.
Creek		N. Anna River	Va.
Kiskiminetas River	Pa.	N. River	W.Va.
		Nottoway River	Va.
Lackawaxen River	Pa.		
Laurel Creek	N.C.	Oconaluftee River	N.C.
Laurel Hill Creek	Pa.	Octararo Creek	Pa.
Lawrence Brook	N.J.	Oil Creek	Pa.
Lehigh River	Pa.	Oswego River	N.J.
Licking Creek	Pa.		
Little Juniata	Pa.		
River		Pamunkey River	Va.
Little Pine River	Pa.	Passage Creek	Va.
Little River	Va.	Passaic River	N.J.
Little Tennessee	N.C.	Paulins Kill	N.J.
River		Penns Creek	Pa.
Little Totuskey	Va.	Pennsylvania Canal	Pa.
River		Pequest River	N.J.
Little Walker Creek	Va.	Pigeon River	N.C.
Lost River	W.Va.	Pine Creek	Pa.
Loyalhanna Creek	Pa.	Potomac River	Md.
Loyalsock Creek	Pa.	Potomac River	Va.
Lycoming Creek	Pa.	Potomac River,	Md.
		N. Branch	
Mahoning Creek	Pa.	Potomac River,	W.Va.
Maiden Creek	Pa.	N. Fork of	
Manasquan River	N.J.	S. Branch	
Mattaponi River	Va.	Potomac River,	W.Va.
Maurice River	N.J.	S. Branch	
Maury River	Va.	Potomac River,	W.Va.
Meadow River	W.Va.	S. Fork of	
Meeker Run	Pa.	S. Branch	
Millstone River	N.J.		
Moccasin Creek	Va.	Raccoon Creek	Pa.
Monocacy River	Md.	Rahway River	N.J.
Monongahela River	Pa.	Ramapo River	N.J.
Moorefield River	W.Va.	Rancocas River	N.J.
Moormans River	Va.	Rapidan River	Va.
Moshannon Creek	Pa.	Rapidan River, Upper	Va.

Rappahannock River	Va.	Slippery Rock Creek	Pa.
Raritan Canal	N.J.	Stony Creek	Pa.
Raven Fork River	N.C.	Stony Creek	Va.
Red Bank Creek	Pa.	Stony Brook	N.J.
Reed Creek	Va.	Susquehanna River	Pa.
Ridley Creek	Pa.	Susquehanna River,	Pa.
Roanoke River	Va.	W. Branch	
Rockaway River	N.J.	Swatara Creek	Pa.
Russell River	Va.	Swift Creek	Va.
Saddle River	N.J.		
Savage River	Md.	Thornton River	Va.
Schuylkill River	Pa.	Tionesta Creek	Pa.
Seneca Creek	W.Va.	Tobyhanna River	Pa.
Shade Creek	Pa.	Toms River	N.J.
Shenandoah River,	Va.	Toxaway River	N.C.
N. Fork		Trail to Ohio River	Pa.
Shenandoah River,	Va.	Tuckaseigee River	N.C.
S. Branch		Tulpehacken Creek	Pa.
Shenandoah River,	Va.	Turtle Creek	Pa.
S. Fork		Tygart River	W.Va.
Shenandoah River,	Va.		
S. Fork and		Wading River	N.J.
Back Creek		Walkill River	N.J.
Shenandoah River,	Va.	Wallenpaupack Creek	Pa.
S. Fork of		Wards Creek	Va.
N. River		White Deer Creek	Pa.
Shenandoah River,	Va.	White Oak River	N.C.
S. Fork of		Wills Creek	Md.
S. River			
Shenango River	Pa.		
Shrewsbury River	N.J.	Yellow Breeches	Pa.
Sinnemahoning	Pa.	Creek	
Creek		Youghiogheny River	Pa.

REGION III
Mississippi, Alabama, Tennessee, Georgia, Florida

Alafia River	Fla.	Blackburn Fork	Tenn.
Alapaha River	Ga.	Blackwater River	Fla.
Alcovy River	Ga.	Brimstone Creek	Tenn.
Alexander Springs	Fla.	Broad River	Ga.
Creek		Brushy Creek	Ala.
		Buffalo River	Tenn.
		Bulow Creek	Fla.
Beaver Creek	Tenn.		
Beaverdam Creek	Miss.		
Black Creek	Fla.	Cahaba River	Ala.
Black Creek	Miss.	Caney Fork River	Tenn.

Trail	State	Trail	State
Cartecay River	Ga.	Little Pigeon River	Tenn.
Chassahowitzka River	Fla.	Little Sunflower River	Miss.
Chattahoochee River	Ga.	Little Tennessee River	Tenn.
Chattooga River	Ga.		
Chestatee River	Ga.	Loxahatchee River	Fla.
Chipola River	Fla.		
Clear Creek	Tenn.		
Clear Fork River	Tenn.	New River	Tenn.
Clearfield Creek	Tenn.	Nolichucky River	Tenn.
Clinch River	Tenn.	N. Whiteoak Creek	Tenn.
Collins River	Tenn.		
Conasauga River	Tenn.		
Coosawattee River	Ga.	Obed River	Tenn.
Crystal River	Fla.	Ochlockonee River	Fla.
Cumberland River, S. Fork	Tenn.	Ocmulgee River	Ga.
		Ocoee River	Tenn.
		Oconee River	Ga.
		Ogeechee River	Ga.
Daddy's Creek	Tenn.	Okefenokee Natl. Wildlife Refuge	Ga.
Duck River	Tenn.		
Econfina River	Fla.		
Econlockhatchee River	Fla.	Peace River	Fla.
		Powell River	Tenn.
Emory River	Tenn.		
Estero River	Fla.		
Etowah River	Ga.	Rainbow River	Fla.
Everglades Natl. Park	Fla.	Red River	Tenn.
		Roaring River	Tenn.
Flint River	Ga.	St. Mary's River	Fla.
French Broad River	Tenn.	Salt Springs Run	Fla
		Satilla River	Ga.
		Sequatchie River	Tenn.
Harpeth River	Tenn.	Shoal River	Fla.
Hatchie River	Tenn.	Sipsey River	Ala.
Hermosassa River	Fla.	Spring Creek	Tenn.
Hiwassee River	Tenn.	Spruce Creek	Fla.
Holmes Creek	Fla.	Suwannee River	Fla.
Holston River	Tenn.		
		Talking Rock Creek	Ga.
Ichetucknee River	Fla.	Tchoutocabouffa River	Miss.
		Tellico River	Tenn.
Laurel Creek	Tenn.	Toccoa River	Ga.
Little River	Ala.	Tsala Apopka Chain of Lakes	Fla.
Little River	Tenn.		
Little Emory River	Tenn.		

Wacissa River	Fla.	Withlacoochee River	Fla.
Wekiva River	Fla.	Withlacoochee River	Ga.
White Creek	Tenn.		
Whiteoak Creek	Tenn.	Yellow River	Fla.

REGION IV
Ohio, Illinois, Michigan, Wisconsin, Kentucky, Indiana

Au Sable River	Mich.	Clinton River	Mich.
Au Sable River, S. Branch	Mich.	Clinton River, N. Branch	Mich.
Au Train Waters	Mich.	Courderay River	Wis.
Aux Vases River	Ill.	Crystal River	Wis.
		Cumberland River, N. Fork	Ky.
Bad River	Mich.	Cuyahoga River	O.
Bad River	Wis.		
Baraboo River	Wis.		
Bear Creek	Mich.	Dearborn River	Mich.
Bear River	Wis.	Deer Trail Creek	Wis.
Belle River	Mich.	Des Plaines River	Ill.
Betsie River	Mich.		
Big Elk River	Wis.	Eau Claire River	Wis.
Big Manistee River	Mich.	Eighteen Mile Creek	Ky.
Big Muddy River	Ill.	Embarras River	Ill.
Big Sable River	Mich.	Embarras River	Wis.
Black River	Mich.	Escanaba River	Mich.
Black River	Wis.		
Blue River	Ind.	Fawn River	Ind.
Boardman River	Mich.	Fence River	Mich.
Bois Brule River	Wis.	Flambeau Flowage	Wis.
Brule River	Mich.	Flambeau River	Wis.
Brule River	Wis.	Flambeau River, S. Fork	Wis.
Buffalo River	Ind.	Flat River	Mich.
		Flint River	Mich.
Cache River	Ill.	Ford River	Mich.
Carp River	Mich.	Fox River	Ill.
Cass River	Mich.	Fox River	Mich.
Cays River	Mich.	Fox River	Wis.
Chippewa River	Wis.		
Chippewa River System	Mich.	Goose Creek	Ky.
Chippewa River, W. Fork	Wis.	Greasy Creek	Ky.
		Great Miami River	O.
Cisco Chain	Mich.	Green River	Ill.
Clam River	Mich.	Green River	Ky.

Trail	State	Trail	State
Horsehead—	Wis.	Little Wabash River	Ill.
Lac du Flambeau		Little Wolf River	Wis.
Trail		Looking Glass River	Mich.
Huron River	Mich.	Lower Ox Creek	Wis.
		Lower Platte River	Mich.
Illinois River	Ill.		
Illinois River,	Ill.	Mackinaw River	Ill.
Michigan Canal		Main Creek	Wis.
Illinois River,	Ill.	Manistique River	Mich.
Mississippi Canal		Manistique River,	Mich.
Illinois River,	Ill.	W. Branch	
Mississippi		Manitowish River	Wis.
Feeder Canal		Maple River	Mich.
Indian River	Mich.	Marengo River	Wis.
Inland Lakes Route	Mich.	Marsh Creek	Ky.
Intermediate	Mich.	Maumee River	O.
Chain of Lakes		Menominee River	Mich.
Iroquois River	Ill.	Menominee River	Wis.
		Michigamme River	Mich.
Jellico Creek	Ky.	Missisinewa River	Ind.
Jordon River	Mich.	Mohican River	O.
Jump River,	Wis.	Montreal River	Wis.
N. Fork		Muscatatuck River	Ind.
Jump River,	Wis.	Muskegon River	Mich.
S. Fork		Muskegon River,	Mich.
		W. Branch	
Kalamazoo River	Mich.	Muskingum River	O.
Kankakee River	Ill.		
Kankakee River	Ind.	Namekagon Lake	Wis.
Kaskaskia River	Ill.	Namekagon River	Wis.
Kentucky River,	Ky.	Net River	Mich.
Mid. Fork			
Kentucky River,	Ky.	Ocqueoc River	Mich.
S. Fork		Ontonagon River	Mich.
Kickapoo River	Wis.	Ontonagon River,	Mich.
		E. Branch	
Lake Cumberland	Ky.	Ontonagon,	Mich.
Lemonweir River	Wis.	Mid. Branch	
Licking River	Ky.	from Agate	
Little Fox River	Wis.	Otter River	Mich.
Little	Mich.		
Manistee River		Paint Creek	Wis.
Little Miami River	O.	Paint River	Mich.
Little	Mich.	Paw Paw River	Mich.
Muskegon River		Pecatonica River	Ill.
Little	Ken.	Pecatonica River	Wis.
S. Fork River			

Pelican River	Wis.	Spoon River	Ill.
Père Marquette River	Mich.	Station Camp Creek	Ky.
		Sturgeon Creek	Ky.
Peshtigo River	Wis.	Sturgeon River	Mich.
Pigeon River	Ill.	Sucker River	Mich.
Pigeon River	Ind.	Sugar Creek	Ind.
Pike River	Wis.		
Pine River	Mich.		
Pine River	Wis.	Tahquamenon River	Mich.
Platte River	Mich.	The Cut	Mich.
Popple River	Wis.	Thornapple River	Mich.
Portage Lakes System	O.	Three Lakes— Eagle River Trail	Wis.
Potomac River, N. Branch	Wis.	Thunder Bay River	Mich.
		Thunder Bay River	Wis.
Presque Isle River	Mich.	Tippecanoe River	Ind.
		Tittabawassee River	Mich.
Raisin River	Mich.		
Red Bird River	Ky.	Tomahawk River	Wis.
Red Cedar River	Mich.	Totogatic River	Wis.
Red River	Ky.	Trout River	Wis.
Rifle River	Mich.	Turtle River	Wis.
Rock River	Ill.	Two Hearted River	Mich.
Rock River	Wis.		
Rockcastle River	Ky.	Vermillion River	Ill.
Rockcastle River, Mid. Fork	Ky.		
Rockcastle River, S. Fork	Ky.	Wabash River	Ind.
		Waiska River	Mich.
Roundstone Creek	Ky.	Walhonding River	O.
Russell River	Ky.	Waupaca Chain of Lakes	Wis.
		Waupaca River	Wis.
Saginaw River	Mich.	White River	Mich.
St. Croix River	Wis.	White River	Wis.
St. Joseph River	Ind.	White River, E. Branch	Ind.
St. Joseph River	Mich.		
Saline River	Ill.	White River, E. Fork	Ind.
Salt Creek	Ill.		
Sandusky River	O.	White River, W. Fork	Ind.
Sangamon River	Ill.		
Shiawassee River	Mich.	Whitefish River	Mich.
Sinking Creek	Ky.	Whitewater River	Ind.
S. Vermillion River, Mid. Fork	Ill.	Wisconsin River	Wis.
		Wolf River	Wis.
S. Vermillion River, N. Fork	Ill.		
S. Vermillion River, Salt Fork	Ill.	Yahara River	Wis.
		Yellow River	Wis.

REGION V
Texas, Louisiana, Arkansas, Oklahoma

Trail	State	Trail	State
Amite River	La.	Eleven Point River	Ark.
Angelina River	Tex.		
Atchafalaya Basin	La.	Fish Creek	La.
		Flint Creek	Okla.
Barren Fork	Okla.	Frio River	Tex.
Bayou Bartholomew	La.		
Bayou Chitto	La.	Garcitas Creek	Tex.
Bayou des Canes	La.	Glover River	Okla.
Bayou Dorcheat	La.	Grand Bayou	La.
Bayou La Fourche	La.	Guadalupe River	Tex.
Bayou L'Outre	La.		
Bayou Rigolette	La.	Hickory Branch	La.
Bayou Sara	La.		
Bayou Teche	La.		
Bayou Toro	La.	Illinois River	Okla.
Beckwith Creek	La.		
Big Cypress Bayou	Tex.	Keechi Creek	Tex.
Big Piney Creek	Ark.	Kiamichi River	Okla.
Black Lake Bayou	La.	Kisatchie Bayou	La.
Blanco River	Tex.		
Blind River	La.		
Blue River	Okla.	Lake Bistineau	La.
Bogalusa Creek	La.	Lake d'Arbonne,	La.
Boggy Creek	Tex.	Mid. Fork	
Bogue Chitto River	La.	Lampasas River	Tex.
Brazos River	Tex.	La Vaca and	Tex.
Buffalo River	Ark.	Navidad rivers	
		Leon River	Tex.
		Little Red River	Ark.
Calcasieu River	La.	Little River	La.
Chappepeela River	La.	Little River	Okla.
Cimarron River	Okla.	Little River	Tex.
Cocodrie Bayou	La.	Llano River	Tex.
Colorado—	Tex.	Long King Creek	Tex.
Highland Lakes			
Comite River	La.		
Concho River	Tex.	Medina River	Tex.
Corney Creek	La.	Mid. Fork,	La.
Cossatot River	Ark.	Lake D'Arbonne	
Curry Creek	Tex.	Mountain Fork	Okla.
		River	
		Mulberry River	Ark.
Denton Creek	Tex.		
Devils River	Tex.		
Dugdemona River	La.	Neches River	Tex.

Osyka River	La.	Spring River	Okla.
Ouachita River	Ark.	Sulphur River	Tex.
Paluxy River	Tex.	Tangipahoa River	La.
Pearl River	La.	Tchefuncte River	La.
Pecos River	Tex.	Ten Mile Creek	La.
Pedernales River	Tex.	Tickflaw River	La.
Pine Island Bayou	Tex.	Trinity River	Tex.
Pushepatapa Creek	La.	Trinity River, Clear Fork	Tex.
Richland Creek	Ark.	Trinity River, E. Fork	Tex.
Rio Grande River	Tex.	Trinity River, Elm Fork	Tex.
Sabine River	Tex.	Trout Creek	La.
Saline Bayou	La.		
San Antonio River	Tex.		
San Bernard River	Tex.	Vermillion River	La.
San Gabriel River	Tex.		
San Marcos River	Tex.	Whiskey Chitto	La.
Six Mile Creek	La.	White River	Ark.
Spring Creek	La.	White Rock Creek	Tex.

REGION VI
North Dakota, South Dakota, Nebraska, Missouri, Iowa, Minnesota

Trail	State	Trail	State
Arkansas River	Kan.	Bourbeuse River	Mo.
		Boy River	Minn.
Bear Creek	Mo.	Bryant Creek	Mo.
Beaver Creek	Mo.	Bull Creek	Mo.
Big Blue River	Neb.		
Big Creek	Mo.	Calamus River	Neb.
Big Fork River	Minn.	Caney River	Kan.
Big Piney River	Mo.	Cannon River	Minn.
Big River	Mo.	Cascade River	Minn.
Big River, Mid. Fork	Mo.	Cedar Creek	Mo.
		Center Creek	Mo.
Big Sugar Creek	Mo.	Cloquet River	Minn.
Black River	Mo.	Cottonwood River	Kan.
Black River, E. Fork	Mo.	Courtois Creek	Mo.
		Crane Creek	Mo.
Black River, Mid. Fork	Mo.	Crow River, Mid. Fork	Minn.
Boone River	Ia.	Crow River, N. Fork	Minn.
Boundary Waters Canoe Area	Minn.	Crow Wing River	Minn.
		Current River	Mo.

Trail	State	Trail	State
Des Moines River	Ia.	Marais des Cygnes River	Kan.
Des Moines River	Minn.		
Dismal River	Neb.	Maries River	Mo.
		Medicine Creek	Neb.
Eleven Point River	Mo.	Meramec River	Mo.
Elkhorn River	Neb.	Middle Loup River	Neb.
		Mill River	Kan.
Fall River	Kan.	Minnesota River	Minn.
Finley Creek	Mo.	Mississippi River	Minn.
Flat Creek	Mo.	Missouri River	Neb.
		Missouri River	N.D.
Gasconade River	Mo.	Moose River	Minn.
Gorden Creek	Neb.	Moreau River	Mo.
Grand Auglaize Creek	Mo.		
		Niangua River	Mo.
Gull River	Minn.	Niobrara River	Neb.
		N. Fork River	Mo.
Harlan County River	Neb.	N. Loup River	Neb.
Huzzah Creek	Mo.	N. Platte River	Neb.
		N. Turtle River	Minn.
Indian Creek	Mo.		
Inguadona Canoe Tour	Minn.	Osage Fork of Gasconde River	Mo.
Iowa River	Ia.		
		Platte River	Neb.
Jacks Fork River	Mo.	Plum Creek	Neb.
James River	Mo.	Pomme de Terre River	Mo.
James River	S.D.		
Kansas River	Kan.	Raccoon River	Ia.
Kettle River	Minn.	Red Cedar River	Ia.
		Red Lake River	Minn.
Little Blue River	Neb.	Red River	N.D.
Little Fork River	Minn.	Red Willow Creek	Neb.
Little Missouri Public-use Area	N.D.	Republican River	Kan.
		Republican River	Neb.
Little Niangua River	Mo.	Rice River	Minn.
Little Piney River	Mo.	Roaring River	Mo.
Little Sac River	Mo.	Rock Creek	Mo.
Little St. Francis River	Mo.	Root River	Minn.
		Rum River	Minn.
Little Sioux River	Ia.		
Little Sugar Creek	Mo.		
Little White River	S.D.	Sac River	Mo.
Logan Creek	Neb.	St. Croix River	Minn.
Loup River	Neb.	St. Francis River	Mo.
Lyons Creek	Kan.	St. Louis River	Minn.

Shell Rock River	Ia.	Turnback Creek	Mo.
		Turtle Creek	Minn.
Shoal Creek	Kan.	Tuxachanie Creek	Miss.
Shoal Creek	Mo.		
Snake Creek	N.D.	Upper Iowa River	Ia.
Snake River	Minn.		
Snake River	Neb.		
S. Loup River	Neb.	Verdigre Creek	Neb.
S. Moreau Creek	Mo.	Verdigris River	Kan.
Spring Creek	Kan.	Volga River	Ia.
Spring River	Kan.		
Spring River	Mo.	Wakopa Game Management Area	N.D.
Swan Creek	Mo.		
		Wapsipinicon River	Ia.
Tavern Creek	Mo.	Weaubleau River	Mo.
Temperance River	Minn.		
Turkey River	Ia.	Yellow River	Ia.

REGION VII
Washington, Wyoming, Oregon, California, Idaho, Montana, Colorado, Utah, Nevada, Arizona, New Mexico, Alaska, Hawaii

American River	Cal.	Cache Creek	Cal.
American River, Mid. Fork	Cal.	Cascade River	Wash.
		Cedar River	Wash.
American River, N. Mid. Fork	Cal.	Chama River	N.M.
		Chatanika River	Alas.
American River, N. Fork	Cal.	Chehalis River	Wash.
		Chena River	Alas.
American River, S. Fork	Cal.	Cherwack River	Wash.
		Clackamas River	Ore.
Animas River	Col.	Clark Fork River	Mont.
Arkansas River	Col.	Cle Elum River	Wash.
		Colorado River	Cal.
Bear River	Cal.	Colorado River	Col.
Beaverhead River	Mont.	Columbia River	Wash.
Big Bear River	Ut.	Conejos River	Col.
Big Blackfoot River	Mont.	Cowlitz River	Wash.
		Crab Creek	Wash.
Big Hole River	Mont.		
Birch Creek	Alas.		
Bitterroot River	Mont.	Dearborn River	Mont.
Bogachiel River	Wash.	Delta River	Alas.
Bruneau River	Nev.	Deschutes River	Ore.
Bruneau River, W. Fork	Nev.	Deschutes River	Wash.
		Dungeness River	Wash.
Buffalo River	Wyo.	Duwanisn River	Wash.

Trail	State	Trail	State
Eel River	Cal.	Mad River	Cal.
Eel River,	Cal.	Marias River	Mont.
S. Fork		Mattole River	Cal.
Entiat River	Wash.	McKenzie River	Ore.
		Merced River	Cal.
Fish Creek	Alas.	Methow River	Wash.
Flathead River	Mont.	Mineral Fork	Mont.
Flathead River,	Mont.	of Big River	
S. Fork		Missouri River	Mont.
Forty Mile River	Alas.	Mokelumne River	Cal.
Garcia River	Cal.	Navarro River	Cal.
Gila River	Ariz.	Nisqually River	Wash.
Gila River	N.M.	Nooksack River	Wash.
Grand Coulee	Wash.	Nooksack River,	Wash.
Chain of Lakes		N. Fork	
Grand Ronde River	Ore.	Nooksack River,	Wash.
Green River	Col.	S. Fork	
Green River	Ut.	N. River	Wash.
Green River	Wash.	North Santiam	Ore.
Green River	Wyo.	River	
Greys River	Wyo.	Noyo River	Cal.
Gros Ventre River	Wyo.		
Gualala River	Cal.		
Gulkana River	Alas.	Okanogon River	Wash.
Gunnison River	Col.	Owyhee River	Ore.
Gunnison River	Ut.		
		Passage Creek	Wash.
Henry's Fork	Id.	Pilchuck Creek	Wash.
Hoback River	Wyo.	Pilchuck River	Wash.
Humptulips River	Wash.	Pit River	Cal.
		Platte River	Wyo.
		Potholes Lakes	Wash.
Jarbridge River	Nev.	Provo River	Ut.
Jefferson River	Mont.	Puyallup River	Wash.
John Day River	Ore.		
		Queets River	Wash.
Kenai River	Alas.	Quinault River	Wash.
Kern River	Cal.	Quinault River,	Wash.
Kings River	Cal.	N. Fork	
Klamath River	Cal.		
Kootenai River	Mont.		
		Redwood Creek	Cal.
Lake Tahoe	Nev.	Rio Grande River	N.M.
Lewis River	Wash.	Rio Grande River,	Col.
Little Colorado	Ariz.	S. Fork	
River		Rogue River	Ore.
Lost River	Wash.	Russian River	Cal.

Sacramento River	Cal.	Swan River	Mont.
Salmon River	Id.	Swanson River	Alas.
Salmon River,	Id.		
Mid. Fork		Taylor River	Col.
Salt River	Ariz.	Teton River	Id.
Sammamish River	Wash.	Tieton River	Wash.
San Joaquin River	Cal.	Tilton River	Wash.
Sandy River	Ore.	Tolt River	Wash.
Satsop River,	Wash.	Trinity River	Cal.
Mid. Fork		Truckee River	Cal.
Satsop River, W. Fork	Wash.	Truckee River	Nev.
Sauk River	Wash.	Tuolumne River	Cal.
Shoshone River	Wyo.		
Skagit River	Wash.		
Skokomish River	Wash.	Umpqua River	Ore.
Skookumchuck River	Wash.	Upper Tangle Lakes	Alas.
Skykomish River	Wash.		
Skykomish River,	Wash.	Verde River	Ariz.
S. Fork			
Smith River	Cal.	Wailua River	Hi.
Smith River	Mont.	Weber River	Ut.
Snohomish River	Wash.	Wenatchee River	Wash.
Snohomish River,	Wash.	W. Clear Creek	Ariz.
N. Fork		Wet Beaver Creek	Ariz.
Snohomish River,	Wash.	White River	Wash.
S. Fork		Willamette River	Ore.
Soleduck River	Wash.	Wynoochee River	Wash.
S. Prairie River	Wash.		
S. Santiam	Ore.	Yakima River	Wash.
River		Yampa River	Col.
Spring River	Mont.	Yellowstone River	Mont.
Stanislaus River	Cal.	Yuba River	Cal.
Stillaquamish	Wash.	Yuba River,	Cal.
River		N. Fork	
Suiattle River	Wash.	Yuba River,	Cal.
Sun River	Mont.	S. Fork	
Swan Lake	Alas.	Yukon River	Alas.

DESCRIPTION
OF TRAILS

ALABAMA

Brushy Creek: Winston Co., W. B. Bankhead Natl. For. Below dam at Brushy Lake Rec. Area to U.S. 278 at Lake Lewis Smith, 20 mi., much debris, swift in high water, rocky in dry season, fair to poor fishing, run in high water only.

Cahaba River: Jefferson, Shelby, Bibb, Perry, Dallas cos.; U.S. Hwy. 280 brdg. to Alabama River at Old Cahaba, 162 mi.; primitive, some rapids. N. of Centerville water fast moving, rel. clear, cool; S. of Centerville river slows, widens, and warms. Fish—N. of Centerville, sunfish, spotted bass; S. of Centerville, large-mouth bass, bluegill, shellcrochess, cats, some crappie and striped bass. Trips—U.S. 280 brdg. to U.S. Hwy. 31 brdg., 7 mi., 5–9 hrs.; Hwy. 31 to Co. Rd. 52 brdg., 7 mi., 5–9 hrs.; Co. Rd. 52 brdg. to Boothton Ford, 11 mi., 8–12 hrs.; Boothton to Ardela-Piper brdg., 8 mi., 6–10 hrs.; A-P brdg. to Co. Rd. 27 brdg., 6 mi., 4–8 hrs.; Co. Rd. 27 brdg. to U.S. Hwy. 82 brdg. (Centerville), 8 mi., 6–10 hrs; Hwy. 82 brdg. to Harrisburg brdg., 9 mi., 7–11 hrs.; Harrisburg brdg. to Jericho brdg., 8 mi., 6–10 hrs.; Jericho brdg. to St. Hwy. 14 brdg., 8 mi., 6–10 hrs.; St. Hwy. 14 brdg. to Redford brdg., 7 mi., 6–10 hrs.; Redford brdg. to Suttle brdg., 6–10 hrs.; Suttle brdg. to Dry Creek brdg., 6 mi., 4–8 hrs.; U.S. Hwy. 80 brdg. to St. Hwy. 22 brdg., 10 mi., 8–14 hrs.; St. Hwy. 22 brdg. to Old Cahaba (mouth of Cahaba River), 7 mi., 6–10 hrs.

Little River: Trip is through Little River Canyon put-in—take Hwy. 20 out of Rome, Ga., to Ala. Rte. 35, turn right onto 35, cross Little River at brdg., take first left after brdg., and go approximately 12 mi. to the ski lift, put in ¼ mi., carry down canyon side, 7-mi.-long-trip, Dif. III–V, open boats need flotation, two major drops on this trip—can be ptgd., much action, for experts only. (Credit—Georgia Canoeing Association)

Sipsey River: Winston Co.; W. B. Bankhead Natl. For. Sipsey River Picnic Area on St. Hwy. 26 E. of Haleyville to marina, where U.S. 278 crosses Sipsey Fork of Lake Lewis Smith, 20 mi., much debris, swift in high water, rocky in dry season, fair to poor fishing, run in high water only.

ALASKA

Birch Creek: Dif. overall II, some rapids III or IV. Gradient—overall 14 ft., some upper sections 30 ft. USGS quads.—Circle B-1, B-2, B-3, B-4, C-1. Fish—grayling, northern pike. Start of trail—access at N. Fork Brdg., Milepost 94, or ptg. ¼ mi. from Milepost 95 to N. Fork—Birch Creek Jctn. N. Fork shallow to Birch Creek; Four Dif. IV rapids—lining recommended; end at brdg., Milepost 147. Total, 140 mi.

Chatanika River: Dif. II. DANGER—overhanging trees. Gradient —14 ft. USGS quads.—Circle A-6, B-6, Livengood A-1, A-2. Fish—grayling, sheefish, whitefish. Start of trail—access at Milepost 61 (Cripple Creek), numerous access points of Steese Hwy. downstream to Chatanika. Upper river not navigable in low water. Access at Chatanika brdg., Milepost 39; 26 river mi. from Cripple Creek and 19 mi. to end of canoe trail at brdg. Milepost 11, Elliot Hwy.

Chena River: Dif. I overall; upper river, II. Gradient overall 4 ft.; upper end, 7 ft. USGS quads.—Fairbanks D-1, D-2, Big Delta D-5, D-6. Fish—grayling, northern pike, sheefish. Start of trail—access at end of Chena Hot Springs Rd., access to Chena Slough off Badger Loop at Peedee, Block, and Persinger rds. End of trail at Fairbanks. Total trip, 70 mi.

Delta River: Dif. generally II, for 2 mi. downstream from ptg. III. Gradient—overall river, 16 ft. USGS quads.—Mt. Hayes A-4, B-4. Fish—lake trout, grayling, whitefish, burbot in Tangle Lakes, grayling in river. Start of trail—access at Tangle Lakes Cmpgrnd., paddle N. through lakes. Fall—2 mi. below last lake, ¼ mi. ptg. trail provided from right bank. 200 yds. after re-entering river, traverse to left bank to run dif. rapid. Glacial water enters at Eureka Creek. End of trail—Delta swings to Richardson Hwy. at Milepost 212.5, extremely dangerous, Dif. IV beyond this pt. Total trip, 35 mi.

Fish Creek: Dif. I–III, hanging trees and narrow channel. Gradient—11 ft.; last mi., 30 ft. USGS quads.—Anchorage B-8, C-8. Fish—rainbow trout, Dolly Varden, silver salmon. Access to canoe trail from Big Lake Rd. at Big Lake. First 4 mi. shallow with gravel bars, next 8 mi. are excellent Dif. I water, last mi. Dif. III water. End of trip—Knik Rd. brdg. Total trip, 13 mi.

Forty Mile River: Dif. overall II; some rapids III and IV. Gradient—overall 9 ft., some 25 ft. USGS quads.—Eagle A-1, A-2, A-3, B-1, C-1, D-1, Tanacross D-2, D-3. Canadian maps—Forty Mile 116-C7, Cassiar Creek 116-C8, Sheel Creek 116-C9, Mt. Gladman 116-C-10. Fish—grayling, burbot, sheefish. Start of trail—access at brdg. Milepost 49, 32 river mi. to access at brdg., Milepost 75. There is an access below Chicken Airstrip 40 river mi. from access at brdg. Milepost 75 to next access. Three dangerous rapids between (5 mi. below Milepost 75 access, immediately below N. Fork, and 2 mi. upstream from Milepost 112 access). Access at brdg. Milepost 112. 45 river mi. to Clinton Creek brdg. access, 3 dangerous rapids between (Deadman Riffle, Eldon

Landing, and 5 mi. upstream from Clinton Creek brdg. access, last rapid most dangerous, line from either bank depending on water level, high water use N. bank; this rapid is in 2 secs. separated by ¼ mi. calm water). Access at Clinton Creek brdg., 51 mi. to Eagle. End of trail—last access pt. on Taylor Hwy., 160 Yukon River mi. to Circle.

Gulkana River: Dif. II, III, IV; Gradient—overall, 16 ft. USGS quads.—Gulkana B-3, B-4, C-4, D-4. Fish—rainbow trout, grayling, king salmon, whitefish. Start of trip—access at Paxson Lake, 45 river mi. to access at Sourdough; First 3 river mi. Dif. III, next 15 mi. Dif II; canyon rapids, ptg. or lining from left bank along marked trail next 8 mi. Dif. IV with 50-ft. gradient remainder of river to Sourdough Dif. II. Access at Sourdough, Milepost 147, Richardson Hwy. Gradient to Gulkana—15 ft. to 25 ft. Dif. II to III. End of canoe trail at Gulkana, Milepost 127 Richardson Hwy. Total trip, 80 mi.

Kenai River: Dif. Kenai Lake to Skilak Lake III, IV; Skilak Lake to Kenai, II; Gradient—Kenai Lake to Skilak Lake 14 ft.; Skilak Lake to Kenai 4 ft. USGS quads.—Kenai Lake to Skilak Lake— Seward B18, Kenai B-1; Skilak Lake to Kenai—Kenai B-2, B-3, C-2, C-4; Fish—Dolly Varden, rainbow trout, pink salmon, silver salmon, red salmon. Start of trail—access at Sterling Hwy. brdg., Milepost 49, 17 mi. to Skilak Lake; access at Sterling Hwy. brdg. Milepost 52, Dif. II rapids at Schooner Ben, keep against right bank. Most difficult rapids on Kenai River just downstream from Jean Creek, 2-mi.-long canyon—Dif. IV, Skilak Lake—6 mi. on lake to upper Skilak Lake cmpgrnd., lake dangerous during windy weather—use caution. Access at lower Skilak Lake cmpgrnd., 2 mi. to river, 12 mi. to Sterling Hwy. brdg. at Soldatna, and 51 mi. to Kenai, Dif. III rapids. Numerous access pt. downstream to end of trail at Kenai. High bluffs border near Kenai, access dif. Total trip, 81 mi.

Swan Lake: Dif. Moose River I; Gradient—4 ft. USGS quads.— Kenai C-2. Fish—rainbow trout, Dolly Varden, red salmon, silver salmon. Start of trail—access at Canoe Lake and access at Ptg. Lakes, 1-day canoeing from either to Bavia Lake, total 3 days to Sterling Hwy. brdg. (end of trail). Ptgs. usually short, longest ½ mi., many lake shores soft and wet. Good fishing except Birch, Teal, Mallard, Raven, Otter, Big Mink, and Ptg. lakes. Rough lake water seldom a problem—lakes are small or sheltered by trees. Total trip, 60 mi.

Swanson River: Dif. Swanson River I. Gradient—Swanson River 4 ft. USGS quads.—Kenai C-2, C-3, D-2, D-3. Fish—rainbow trout, Dolly Varden, silver salmon. Start of trail—access at Paddle Lake near end of Swan Lake Rd. One full day of canoeing to Gene Lake, ptgs. generally short—longest ½ mi., many lake shores soft and wet, good fishing except Barry and Redpole lakes. Rough lake water seldom a problem; lakes are small or sheltered by trees. From Gene Lake 19 mi. on Swanson River to Swanson River cmpgrnd., 24 mi. from cmpgrnd. to end of trail at terminus of N. Kenai Rd.

Upper Tangle Lakes: Upper Tangle Lakes to Dickey Lake; Dif. lake canoeing with ptgs. Gradient—none. USGS quads.— Gulkana D-4, D-5, Mt. Hayes A-5. Fish—lake trout, grahoin, whitefish, burbot. Start of trail—access at Tangle River boat launch site, then S. through 4 Tangle Lake Creek connecting lakes No. 2848 and No. 2865 (see USGS maps), navigable only at high water. At low water easier to portage to Upper Tangle Lake then to lake No. 2865. Creek to Tangle No. 4 deep and navigable except for 100 yds., 1 mi. ptg. to Dickey Lake, no marked ptgs.—must rely on maps. Total trip to Dickey Lake, 9 mi. Possible to run Mid. Fork from Dickey Lake. No information on this trip. It is known that the first 6 mi. are exceptionally hazardous, gradient to 100 ft. per mi. with ptgs. necessary.

Yukon River: Dif. I, II. Gradient 3 ft. USGS quads.—Eagle C-1, D-1, Charley River A-1, A-2, B-2, B-3, B-4, B-5, B-6, Circle C-1, D-1. Fish—grayling in most tributaries, Yukon unproductive for hook and line. Last hwy. access 160 river miles from Eagle. In Alas., the Yukon River is broad and fast-moving, no known rapids, waters silt-laden and deep; use caution. Yukon also accessible in Yukon Territory at Whitehorse and Dawson. Rapids exist in Canadian portions.

(Credit all trails in Ak.—*Alaska Canoe Trails* and information from U. S. Fish and Wildlife Ser. concerning canoe trails in Kenai National Moose Range.)

ARIZONA

Gila River: Gila, Graham, Greenlee cos.; Hwy. 666 to Solomon, 25 mi., 11 ft. per mi. drop, pleasant, not outstanding; runnable March and April only; Coolidge Dam to Christmas, 25 mi., 15 ft. per mi. drop, brushy, quite spectacular at times, runnable summer due to irrigations releases; Christmas to Ashurst-Hayden Diversion Dam, 35 mi., 10 ft. per mi. drop, runnable same time as Coolidge Dam to Christmas segment, generally more open desert ctry. (Credit—John McComb)

Little Colorado:
> *Trip 1*—from Cameron to Old Hope trail crossing, 7 mi., put-in—just upstream from hwy. brdg. at Cameron, can run with 300 cfs. in rubber raft, scenic, need pickup truck for access to take-out pt., don't miss take-out—a canyon is next.
> *Trip 2*—Grand Falls to Black Falls, muddy, 12 mi., spectacular waterfall at Grand Falls, wide channel, best above 1,500 cfs., some good rapids, side canyons to explore.
> (Credit—Scott Holzhauser)

Salt River: Gila Co.; Rafts only—no open canoes. Hwy. 60 to Hwy. 288, 52 mi., 4 days, 23 ft. per mi. drop, 4-man rafts at 400–1,000 cfs.; above 1,000 cfs., rough, April–May, at one point river drops 45 ft. per mi., beautiful, much white water, ptg. at head of "jump-off can," drowning has occurred in second falls.

Tel. 602-273-5900 Phoenix for flow information.; above Hwy. 60 river not runnable for at least 5 mi. (Credit—John McComb)

Verde River: (rather than try to combine two different descriptions, both are included) Yavapi, Maricopa cos.; Prescott Natl. For.

> *Description 1:* From U.S. 89A brdg. to Verde Hot Springs (Childs), 45 mi., some small rapids, some logs in water. CAUTION—irrigation canals, junked cars, barbed wire, water volume changes markedly, run March–April, scenery and water can change rapidly in space of few miles; from brdg. at Cottonwood to last brdg. at Camp Verde—broadest part of Valley. CAUTION—last curve before Camp Verde brdg., there are 3 brdgs. near Camp Verde, OK for beginners around Camp Verde, below Camp Verde action begins, 800 cfs. best level below Camp Verde; below Camp Verde is long, flat stretch, then rapid where river enters lava. CAUTION—3-ft. waterfall in these rapids, then shortly beyond is "The Falls"—4 ft. falls; then river less demanding on to Childs, don't run in high water, check gauge above Horseshoe Dam, OK for open canoes above Camp Verde, below Camp Verde for *rafts only* and experienced persons. (Credit—Scott Holzhauser)
>
> *Description 2:* From Camp Verde to Tangle Creek above Horseshoe Dam, 50 mi.; 19 ft. per mi. drop, similar to Salt River but not as spectacular, not as much white water, April best, *no open canoes.* (Credit—John McComb)

W. Clear Creek: Originates above the Mogollon Rim on the Col. Plateau, channel rapidly becomes narrow, steep-walled canyon with only foot access above the Mogollon Rim, except in flood stage this river is a series of pools connected by shallow rocky rapids, popular for hiking and fishing, impossible even in flood stage to run in canoe or on raft. (Credit—Robert B. Gillies, Jr.)

Wet Beaver Creek: Same description as W. Clear Creek. (Credit—Robert B. Gillies, Jr.)

ARKANSAS

Big Piney Creek: 67 mi. Newton, Pope, Johnson cos.; deep canyons, narrow valleys, rapids, long quiet pools, dangerous high water, steep slopes, beautiful. Ptg.—Haw Creek Falls. Trip—3 access pts. above Fort Douglas or Hwy. 123 brdg. Indian Creek to Long Pool, Dif. II, III, white water, some obstacles on Indian Creek, gorge.

Buffalo River: 150 mi. Trips—above Boxley no good; Boxley Hwy. 21 brdg. to Ponca low-water brdg., Hwy. 74, spring exciting; 6 mi., 2½ hrs., skilled canoeists only; Hwy. 74 brdg. to Boy Scout Camp Orr, 10 mi., 5 hrs., exciting, beautiful, fast water, rapids, experienced canoeists only; Dam at Boy Scout camp; Camp Orr to Pruitt, 15 mi. blind corners, obstacles in water; Pruitt to Big Creek, 12 mi., intermediate canoeists, narrow and swift below riffles, deep pools, good fishing; Big Creek to Mt. Hershey, 7 mi., pleasant, good current; Hershey to Wollum, 8½ mi., riffles, scenic, superb canoeing, some hazards, river disappears underground in low water (2 mi.).

Cassatot River: 28.5 mi., Devil's Hollow Falls to Hwy. 70–71 brdg. Trips—Devil's to Ladd Brdg. (Hwy. 380), 18.5 mi. rocky ridges, forested banks, mountain stream, rapids, falls (threatened by Gilham Dam); Ladd Brdg. to Hwy. 70–71 brdg., 10 mi., looks like bottomland stream; small-mouth, large-mouth bass. Gen. Dif. of river I–VI. Hwy. 246 brdg. to Devil's Hollow Falls, 7.3 mi., not canoeable except by experts in kayaks—sometimes, Dif. V–VI; wild ctry. Devil's Hollow Falls to Clinton Ford, 17.3 mi., continuous irregular rapids, long N.–S. stretch, E.–W. stretches have long pools, at low level OK for novice, at medium level OK for novice with experienced canoeist, at medium-high segment above dam becomes Dif. III–IV, not for novice, at high water

III–IV, expert only. Mid. Cassatot, 12 mi., Clinton Ford to Hwy. 70–71 brdg., OK for novice except in high water, Dif. I–II; Lower Cassatot, 33.5 mi., Hwy. 70–71 brdg. to jctn. with Little River, snags and jams, peaceful and beautiful. Access pts.—Ed Banks Rd. low-water brdg., Hwy. 4 brdg., Duckett low-water brdg., end of govt. property at Gilham Dam site, Ladd Brdg., Hwy. 70–71 high-water brdg., Hwy. 24 high-water brdg., New Cent. E. Rd. Hwy. Brdg. CAUTION—in high water, section between Hwy. 4 to Hwy. 380 for experts only Dif. IV–V. (Credit—Jack Welborn, Jr.)

Eleven Point River: Randolph Co.; originates near Willow Springs, Mo., and flows S., cold, clear, swift, unpolluted, quiet deep pools with many shoals and rapids, many access pts.; U.S. Hwy. 62, 63, 67, brdgs. at Thomasville, Greer, Riverton, Narrows (Mo.), Dalton, Hwy. 90 at 11-pt. store, Block's Ferry, and U.S. Hwy. 62. (Credit—Harold D. Bly)

Little Missouri River: 80 mi. Narrows Dam to jctn. with Red River, white water, rushing, below dam with gates open; too low with gates closed; S.W. Power Adm. Trout, 3–4 mi. below dam; no fish rest of way.

Little Red River: Cleburne, White cos.; Greers Ferry Dam to Pangburn brdg., 25 mi., very cold, water release each weekday at midmorn., swift, approx. 9 shoals, no gravel bars, access limited —most posted priv. land, few campsites, trout.

Mulberry River: From Cass to Mulberry, a popular white-water run, not for beginners.

N. Fork River: Baxter Co.; Norfolk Dam to Norfolk on White River, 4½ mi., very cold, boat dock halfway, quick river rises, trout.

Ouachita River: Camden, Ark., to Monroe, La., 169 mi., big wide river, no rapids, 3 locks, beautiful, wild ctry., danger—water moccasins, don't bother fishing lines, may end up shot, large-mouth bass, no pollution, good camping, wildlife, mild current, run locks in high water, not particularly suited for canoeing, few access pts. From old brdg. at Pine Ridge to Lake Ouachita, 40 mi., can float about 1 m.p.h., 9 lndgs. are in operation and 2 more are planned, upper waters are narrow with many fast-flowing rapids interspersed with clear pools, river becomes larger downstream, pools become deeper, meanders along high, massive rock bluffs, wooded banks, camping on For. Ser. land in Ouachita Natl. For., small-mouth and large-mouth bass, bream cats, walleye, white bass near Lake Ouachita. (Credit—Ouachita River Float Trip, U.S. For. Service)

Richland Creek: Falling Water brdg. to Eula; experts only, Dif. IV, V, decked canoes or kayaks, min. 3 craft, 25 ft. fall per mi.; high water only; Access: For. Ser. cmpgrnd., Hwy. 7 via For. Ser. rd.

White River: Baxter, Marion, Stone, Izard, Ind. cos.; Bull Shoals Dam to Lock 8, Dam No. 3, 101 mi., very cold, wading limited but dangerous, quick river rises, sandbars for camping, several access pts., approx. 4 shoals.

CALIFORNIA

Albion River: Mendocino Co. From Boat Harbor upriver 4–5 mi., 1 day, OK for beginner, much wildlife, trashy. (Credit—*Canoeing Waters of California*)

American River: Folsom Dam to jctn. with Sacramento River, few minor rapids, flows about 5 m.p.h., dikes hide signs of civilization. From Sacramento via Hwy. 50 to Hazel Ave. off ramp, then N. on Hazel 1 mi. to Winding Way, then left on Winding Way and left again at Ill. Ave. to Sailor Bar; Sailor Bar to Watt Ave., 4 hrs., few submerged logs, some swift but easy rapids, nice trip. American

River: USGS Folsom, Citrus Heights, Carmichael. Here is a second description that covers part of the already described area.

From Nimbus Ave. to Watt Ave., 12½ mi., 1 day, OK intermediates, San Juan Rapids below Sunrise Ave. good for practice, good current, snags in water. CAUTION—Arden Rapids—*don't run,* rest of river fairly easy.

(Credit—*Canoeing Waters of California*)

American River—Mid. Fork: Placer Co.; note as of writing Mid. Fork threatened by Auburn Dam, description may be history; from Ralston Afterbay to Rte. 49, 27 mi.

Trip 1—Ralston Afterbay to Greenwood Brdg. site, 16 mi., Dif. III–IV–V, experts only, gradient 40 ft. per mi., 3 ptgs. at 600–1,000 cfs., pretty scenery, heavy rapids; put in—generating station; take out—McKeon Rd. off the Auburn-Foresthill Rd.

Trip 2—Greenwood Brdg. site to Rte. 49, 11 mi., Dif. III, 1 unrunnable rapid, beautiful gorge. DANGER—Murderer's Bar (ptg. these rapids); above Rubicon Jctn.—no runs.

(Credit—Charles Martin)

American River—N. Fork: Placer Co.; Colfax to N. Fork Dam, 18 mi.

Trip 1—Colfax (Ia. Hill Rd.) to Weimur (Ponderosa Way), 9 mi., Dif. IV at 500–1,000 cfs. to Shirttail Canyon, Dif. II Shirttail to Ponderosa Way. Put-in—dirt rd. off Colfax Exit I-80, take-out—dirt rd. off Weimar Med. Cent. exit of I-80, 2 possible ptgs.—scout rough areas before running.

Trip 2—Weimar to Lake Clementine (N. Fork Dam), 9 mi., Dif. II until lake, OK for open canoes, no ptg. around dam, cannot run river below dam. Giant Gap Run—*don't run,* unrunnable.

(Credit—Charles Martin)

American River—N. Mid. Fork: Placer Co.; Mosquito Ridge Rd. brdg. to Mid. Fork, 2.1 mi., gradient 100 ft. per mi., Dif. IV–V, experts only, beautiful river, run in spring only, 2 ptgs.

(Credit—Charles Martin)

American River—S. Fork: El Dorado Co.; Kyburz to Salmon Falls Rd., approx. 40 mi.; above Kyburz, too steep to run.

Trip 1—Kyburz to Riverton, 7 mi., Dif. IV–V, experts only. DANGER—diversion dam 1½ mi. below Kyburz, Dif. VI drop below dam, *don't run,* put in below dam.

Trip 2—Riverton to Peavine Ridge Rd. brdg., 3½ mi., Dif. III–IV, OK for intermed. canoeist, 1 ptg. around heavy rapids—visible from Rte. 50.

Trip 3—Peavine Ridge Rd. to El Dorado Powerhouse, 8½ mi., Dif. VII, wilderness gorge, impossible to run, *don't try it.*

Trip 4—El Dorado Powerhouse to Chile Bar, unknown, no data.

Trip 5—Chile Bar to Coloma, 6 mi., Dif. III–IV; put-in— Rte. 193 brdg., ptg. "S" rapids half-mile above Coloma after houses seen on bank; take-out—picnic area beyond State Hist. Park.

Trip 6—Coloma to Lotus, 4 mi., Dif. II–III, OK beginners; put-in—picnic area, exciting rapids but not particularly dangerous; take-out—short rd. off Rte. 49 near river bend.

Trip 7—Lotus to Salmon Falls Rd. (Folsom Lake), 9 mi., Dif. II–IV, OK intermediates, flows through granite gorge. DANGER—"Satan's Cesspool" near start of drops through granite.

(Credit—Charles Martin)

Bear River: USGS Lake Cambie, Colfax, Chicago Park; Placer and Nev. cos.; from Placer Co. Cmpgrnd. to Lake Van Geisen, 8 mi., 1 day, advanced canoeists only, beautiful, canyon haystacks, drops, and sharp turns, rapids Dif. II–III, line or ptg. if necessary. CAUTION—rapid above Dog Bar Brdg.; scout first. (Credit— *Canoeing Waters of California*)

Big River: Mendocino Co.; from Mendocino upriver 8 mi., 1 day, wildlife, birds, redwoods, OK beginners. (Credit—*Canoeing Waters of California*)

Cache Creek: USGS Rumsey, Guinda, Brooks, Esparto: Yolo Co.; from Rumsey to Guinda, 6 mi., 1 day, OK intermediates, riffles, desert ctry., run in spring, trash on banks, barbed wire. (Credit—*Canoeing Waters of California*)

Carson River—E. Fork: USGS Markleeville, Topa 3 Lake, Mt. Siegel; Alpine Co.; from Markleeville to Gardnerville, 20 mi., 2 days, advanced canoeists only, many haystacks, rocky, swift current, submerged logs. CAUTION—bad rapid halfway, good campsites, many rapids. CAUTION—dam in lower river hidden by willows. (Credit—*Canoeing Waters of California*)

Colorado River:

Trip 1—Hoover Dam to Willow Beach, 12 mi., 1 day, run spring or fall, OK beginners, beautiful, wildlife, little current, some rapids, *don't run* in low water.

Trip 2—Willow Beach to El Dorado Canyon, 16 mi., 1–2 days, slow current, OK beginners, wildlife, side canyons, no rapids, good camping.

Trip 3—El Dorado Canyon to Davis Dam, 50 mi., slow going. CAUTION—heavy winds.

Trip 4—Davis Dam to Needles, 30 mi., 2 days, OK beginners to intermediates, wildlife, water rises very high, strong current, no rapids.

Trip 5—Topock to Jop's Lndg., 20 mi., 1 day, OK beginners to intermediates, beautiful, scenic gorge, wildlife, Indian petroglyphs, slow current, can be windy.

Trip 6—Earp to River Bend, 28 mi., 2 days, OK beginners, clean water, wildfowl, good fishing, swimming, 1 small rapid.

Trip 7—Walker's Camp to Imperial Oasis, 40 mi., 2 days, OK beginners, scenic. CAUTION—logs and current forcing canoes into banks, shallow water, sandbars.

(Credit—*Canoeing Waters of California*)

Eel River: USGS Laytonville, Spyrock, Kattanpom, Alderpoint, Blacksburg, Weott; Trinity, Humboldt cos.; from Dos Rios to S. Fork, 82 mi.

Trip 1—Dos Rios to Alderpoint, 50 mi., 6 days, advanced canoeists only, scout rapids first, remote, rapids start above jctn. with Mid. Fork. DANGER— waterfall at Is. Mtn., sharp

turns before and after, after Is. Mtn. several isles with rapids and drops. CAUTION—rattlesnakes, wildlife, few people.
Trip 2—Alderpoint to S. Fork, 32 mi., 3–7 days, OK beginners to intermediates; CAUTION—rattlesnakes, Indian petroglyphs, birdlife, wildflowers, wildlife.
(Credit—*Canoeing Waters of California*)

Eel River—S. Fork: USGS Garberville, Weott; Humboldt Co.; from Richardson Grove State Park to Weott, 40 mi., 3–4 days, cold water, OK beginner to intermediate; ptg. low-level brdg. before Benbow Lake, campsites limited, many people. (Credit—*Canoeing Waters of California*)

Feather River: USGS Gridley, Sutter, Yuba City; Sutter, Butte and Yuba cos.; from Gridley to Yuba City, 18 mi., 2 days, OK beginners to intermediate, good fishing, snags, fallen trees, easy run. (Credit—*Canoeing Waters of California*)

Feather River—E. Branch, N. Fork: Virgilia to Belden, 8 mi., Dif. III–IV; put-in—picnic table 8 mi. above Belden below waterfall, exciting rapids. (Credit—Charles Martin)

Feather River—Mid. Fork: Plumas Co.; Winton to Lake Oroville, 82 mi.
Trip 1—Winton to Sloat, 35 mi., some pollution, little drops in river.
Trip 2—Sloat to Nelson Point, 9 mi., Dif. III, beautiful, easy run, go in late April and May, no difficult rapids.
Trip 3—Nelson Point to Lake Oroville, 38 mi., Dif. VII, *don't run,* impossible.
(Credit—Charles Martin)

Feather River—N. Fork: dammed up, not runnable. (Credit—Charles Martin)

Garcia River: USGS Pt. Arena; Mendocino Co.; from Eureka Hill Rd. to Hwy. 1, 7 mi., 1 day, peaceful, run in spring, OK beginner, not widely used, some riffles. (Credit—*Canoeing Waters of California*)

Gualala River: USGS Gualala, Stewarts Pt., Ornbaun Valley; Mendocino Co.; from Annapolis Rd. brdg. to Hwy. 1 brdg., 9 mi., 1 day, OK beginner, run after rain, some snags, few people. (Credit—*Canoeing Waters of California*)

Kern River: USGS Isabella; Kern Co.; from Kernville to Lake Isabella, 5 mi., ½ day, advanced canoeists only, cold water, rapids, *don't canoe* above brdg. with open canoes, scenic. (Credit —*Canoeing Waters of California*)

Kings River: Fresno Co.
  Trip 1—Zumwalt Meadows to Cedar Grove, 6 mi., Dif. II–III, check to see if run is legal.
  Trip 2—Mid. and S. Fork jctn. to Upper Kings Cmpgrnd., 9 mi., Dif. IV–VI, experts only, many ptgs.; put-in—hike 3 mi. down trail from Rt. 180 to gauging station, tough going, waterfall 3½ mi. after start at Garlic Creek, beautiful cliffs, dangerous and extremely difficult.
  Trip 3—Upper Kings Cmpgrnd. to Kirch Flt. Cmpgrnd., 8½ mi., Dif. III–IV, OK intermediates. DANGER—Banzai Rapids near start.
  (Credit—Charles Martin)

Kings River: USGS Isabella, Pine Flat, Wahtoke, Piedra; Fresno Co.
  Trip 4—From brdg. below Pine Flat Dam to Centerville, 13 mi., 1 day, advanced canoeists only, good current, scenic. DANGER—weirs, ptg. weirs, LIVES HAVE BEEN LOST AT WEIRS, cold water.
  Trip 5—From Centerville to Reedley, 20 mi., 1 day, advanced canoeists only, easier than Trip 4, less scenic, use caution.
  (Credit—*Canoeing Waters of California*)

Kings River—N. Fork: runnable only near mouth. (Credit— Charles Martin)

Klamath River: USGS Techah Creek, Ship Mt., Regun, Fean

Canyon, Seiad Valley, Conney Mt., Hornbrook; Del Norte, Humboldt, Trinity, and Siskiyou cos.; Good canoeing on upstream portions, some dangerous parts, very dangerous in heavy runoff in upper parts, almost dry in July and August; best time—medium flow; from Interstate 5 brdg. to Requa, approx. 125 mi., 12–14 days.

Trip 1—From I.H. 5 brdg. to Tree of Heaven Cmpgrnds., 12 mi., 1 day, advanced canoeists only, several rapids. CAUTION—rapid above brdg.

Trip 2—From Tree of Heaven Cmpgrnds. to Beaver Creek, 12 mi., 1 day, advanced canoeists only; CAUTION—Hamburg Falls, many difficult rapids.

Trip 3—Beaver Creek to Scott River, 18 mi., 2 days, OK intermediates, some rapids, fairly easy.

Trip 4—Scott River to Seiad Valley, 9 mi., 1 day, many rapids, advanced canoeists only.

Trip 5—Sommes Bar to Orleans, 8 mi., 1 day, advanced canoeists only. CAUTION—Big Ike and Little Ike rapids, several challenging rapids; DANGER—Ishi Pishi Falls above put-in.

Trip 6—Orleans to Weitchpec, 17 mi., 2 days, advanced canoeists only; CAUTION—rapids before and after Bluff Creek, beautiful gorge.

Trip 7—Weitchpec to Johnson, 21 mi. 1½ days, OK intermediates, wide, sand beaches, some waterfalls, some rapids, scout rapids first, boulders in river.

Trip 8—Metak Creek to Requa, 30 mi., 2 days, OK beginners, headwinds, good fishing, wide river, slow, riffles, some snags, wildlife. (Credit—*Canoeing Waters of California*)

Mad River: USGS Blue Lake, Buttes; Humboldt Co.; from Maple Creek to Blue Lake, 18 mi., 2 days, advanced canoeists only, mostly wilderness. CAUTION—narrow gorge near Maple Creek, ptg. bad spot in gorge. (Credit—*Canoeing Waters of California*)

Mattole River: USGS, Pt. Delgado, Scotia, Cape Mendocino, Garberville; Humboldt Co.; from Ettersburg to Petrolia, 36 mi., 4 days.

Trip 1—Ettersburg to Honeydew, 18 mi., 2 days, advanced canoeists only, canyon, remote; CAUTION—3 rapids near end.

Trip 2—Honeydew to Petrolia, 18 mi., 2 days, OK beginners, pastureland, clear water, good campsites.

(Credit—*Canoeing Waters of California*)

Merced River: Above Lake McClure, Mariposa Co.; El Portal to Bagby, 35 mi.

Trip 1—El Portal to Briceburg, 20 mi., Dif. I–V, scout from rd. first, start to Indian Flat cmpgrnd., experts only, below Indian Flat cmpgrnd. OK beginners.

Trip 2—Briceburg to Bagby, 15 mi., Dif. III–IV, 1 or 2 ptgs.; put-in—Bear Creek, small river, good ptgs. on right side, first 3 mi. below Briceburg, Dif. III with some Dif. IV, next 2 mi. easy, then hard Dif. IV rapids. Obstacles— 4-ft. dam, tough rapids below weir, ptg. in high water. DANGER—20-ft. waterfall—*don't run,* poison oak in path of ptg. around waterfall, rapids easier below waterfall.

(Credit—Charles Martin)

Merced River: Below Lake McClure.

Trip 3—McConnell St. Park Rec. Area to Hagaman Co. Park, 9 mi., 1 day, OK beginners to intermediates, some sharp bends, several snags, much trash, pastureland. (Credit —*Canoeing Waters of California*)

Mokelumne River: Amador, Calaveras cos.; above Comanche Dam.

Trip 1—Electric powerhouse to Rt. 49, 3 mi., Dif. II, OK beginners, some easy rapids.

Trip 2—Rt. 49 to Middle Bar (Pardee Res.) 2 mi., Dif. II, some good rapids below start, may be illegal to make this run.

(Credit—Charles Martin)

Mokelumne River: Joaquin Co.; below Comanche Dam.

Trip 3—From Comanche Dam to Victor, 11½ mi., 1 day,

OK beginners to intermediates, beautiful, OK all summer, some riffles, some overhanging branches, snags, and downed trees. (Credit—*Canoeing Waters of California*)

Navarro River: USGS Booneville, Navarro; Mendocino Co.; from Hendy Woods St. Park to Navarro-by-the-sea; 26 mi., 2–3 days.
Trip 1—Hendy Woods St. Park to Dimmich St. Park, 16 mi., 1–2 days, OK intermediate, many riffles, a few fast chutes, ptg.—downed tree, little civilization.
Trip 2—Dimmick St. Park to Navarro-by-the-sea, 10 mi., 1 day, snags, OK beginners, moderate–slow current, scenic, a canyon, redwood-for. hills.
(Credit—*Canoeing Waters California*)

Noyo River: Mendocino Co.; from Noyo Mooring Basin upriver, 2 mi., ½ day, some snags, trashy, small river, OK beginner.
(Credit—*Canoeing Waters of California*)

Pit River: Madoc, Lassen cos.;
Trip 1—Fall River Mills brdg. to Rte. 299 brdg., 9.7 mi., Dif. IV–V, experts only. DANGER—Pit Falls; this is a 30-ft. waterfall, ptg. waterfall on right.
Trip 2—Lake Britton to Pit No. 3 powerhouse, very brushy, 5.7 mi., Dif. III.
Trip 3—Pit No. 4 dam to Pit No. 4 powerhouse, 7 mi., Dif. IV, experts only, beautiful scenery, 1 ptg.—around a Dif. V rapid.
Trip 4—Pit No. 5 dam to Pit No. 5 powerhouse, 9 mi., Dif. IV with 1 Dif. V rapid, experts only, Dif. II–III below Big Bend, first 4 mi. exciting; ptg.—rapid 1 mi. from put-in.
(Credit—Charles Martin)

Redwood Creek: USGS Orick, Rodgers Peak, Coyote Peak; Redwood Natl. Park; from Bald Hills Rd. upstream to spot where it's impossible to go farther and back down, beautiful redwoods.
(Credit—*Canoeing Waters of California*)

Russian River: USGS Ukiah, Purdys Gardens, Hopland, Cloverdale, Asti, Geyserville, Jim Town, Healdsburg, Kelseyville, Guerneville, Duncan Mills; Sonoma and Mendocino cos.; from Ukiah to Reins Beach, 80 mi., parts for experienced canoeists only.

Trip 1—From Ukiah to Hopland, 16 mi., 1 day. CAUTION—old car bodies; CAUTION—broken dam in first mi., some snags, little civilization, OK intermediate.

Trip 2—From Squaw Rock to Cloverdale, 7 mi., 1 day, advanced canoeists only, white water, scout rapids first, fast current. CAUTION—rapids below suspension brdg., big rocks in water, attractive.

Trip 3—Cloverdale to Healdsburg, 30 mi., 2–3 days, OK beginners–intermediates, some riffles, some junk cars, popular stretch, some swift sections. CAUTION—dam in Healdsburg.

Trip 4—Healdsburg to Reins Beach, 27 mi., 2–3 days, OK beginners, many homes along river; CAUTION—partial dams, 1 between Hilton and Guerneville and 2 between Guerneville and Monte Rio, sec. between Hilton and Guerneville is junglelike: Can extend trip to Duncan Mills or Jenner.

(Credit—*Canoeing Waters of California*)

Sacramento River: USGS Red Bluff, Corning, Willows, Butte City, Chico, Maxwell, Sutter Buttes; Shasta, Tehama, Colusa, Glenn, Butte cos.; from Redding to Colusa, 122 mi., 8–10 days.

Trip 1—From Redding to Red Bluff, 32 mi., 2–3 days, intermediates, OK all year, large river, strong current, eddies, haystacks, cold water. CAUTION—supports under Anderson Brdg.; some camping. CAUTION—Chinese Rapids in Iron Canyon.

Trip 2—From Red Bluff to Colusa, 90 mi., 6 days, OK novice, OK all year, windfalls, slower current than Trip 1, polluted water, many insects.

(Credit—*Canoeing Waters of California*)

San Joaquin River: near Fresno, nice easy stretch below the Friant Dam, Lake Millerton Res., not exciting, pleasant. (Credit—Max Gardner)

Smith River: USGS Crescent City; Del Norte Co.; from Jedediah Smith St. Park to Public Boat Ramp, 10 mi., 1 day, clear water, excellent fishing, OK beginners, some riffles. (Credit—*Canoeing Waters of California*)

Stanislaus River: Calaveras Co.; threatened by Melones Dam, description may be history: Camp Nine afterbay to Parrots Ferry brdg., 9 mi., 4 hrs., Dif. III–IV, OK advanced intermediate, scout rapids, bad ones not visible from rd., ptg.—bad rapids; Parrots Ferry to long rapids, river then flattens, OK beginners. (Credit—Charles Martin)

Stanislaus River: USGS Knights Ferry, Oakdale, Escalon, Riverbank; from Knights Ferry to Oakdale Brdg., 13½ mi.;
> *Trip 1*—From Knights Ferry to Orange Blossom Rd., 7 mi., 1 day, beautiful small canyon, OK intermediate, small rapids, much underbrush, snags, barbed wire, narrow, some short ptgs.
> *Trip 2*—Orange Blossom Rd. to Oakdale Brdg., 6½ mi., 1 day, ranch ctry., some snags, OK beginners, shallow in spots in summer.
> (Credit—*Canoeing Waters of California*)

Trinity River: USGS Hoopa, Ironside Mt., Hyampom, Willow Creek, Hayfork, Weaverville, Trinity Dam; Trinity, Humboldt cos.; from Lewiston to Weitchpec, approx. 90 mi., 9–10 days.
> *Trip 1*—Lewiston to Douglas City, 16 mi., 1–2 days, OK intermediates.
> *Trip 2*—Douglas City to Junction City, 12 mi., 1 day for intermediate skills, rapids Dif. II.
> *Trip 3*—Junction City to Eagle Creek, 10 mi., 1 day, OK intermediates, rapids in lower part. CAUTION—Pidgeon Point Rapids in low water.
> *Trip 4*—Big Bar to Cedar Flat, 14 mi., 2 days, advanced canoeists only.
> *Trip 5*—Hawkins Bar to S. Fork Jctn., 7 mi., 1 day, rocky gorge, good current, rapids mostly in first part.
> *Trip 6*—S. Fork to Knights Park, 9 mi., 1 day, OK beginner, OK into summer.

Trip 7—Knights Park to Tish Tang Cmpgrnd., 4½ mi., ½ day, advanced canoeists only. CAUTION—several steep drops. CAUTION—drop beyond big bend at Sugar Bowl Ranch.

Trip 8—Tish Tang Cmpgrnd. to Hoopa, 4 mi., ½ day, OK intermediates, fairly easy, OK into summer.

Trip 9—Hoopa to Weitchpec, 12 mi., 1 day, advanced canoeists only, gorge, beautiful; CAUTION—Weitchpec Falls, scout before running, best to ptg.; rapids and drops on this run.

(Credit—*Canoeing Waters of California*)

Truckee River: USGS Tahoe, Tahoe City; from Tahoe City to River Ranch, 3½ mi., ½ day, OK intermediates, good fishing, some riffles, rapids above Rte. 89 brdg., ptg.—first brdg.; CAUTION—bend around River Ranch some snags and broken brdg. at this bend, popular trip. (Credit—*Canoeing Waters of California*)

Tuolumne River: Tuolumne Co.; Don Pedro Res. threatens river up to Wards Ferry.

Trip 1—Tuolumne Meadows to Hetch Hetchy (Tuolumne Grand Canyon), 25 mi., *don't run,* waterfalls, unrunnable.

Trip 2—Cherry Creek to Lumsden Brdg., Dif. IV–VI, experts only, very difficult, many ptgs., much walking; put-in—dirt rd. to Cherry Lake; take-out—Lumsden Falls.

Trip 3—Lumsden Brdg. to Lumsden Cmpgrnd, 2 mi., Dif. IV–V, experts only, has unrunnable rapids, scout rapids first.

Trip 4—Lumsden Cmpgrnd. to Wards Ferry Brdg., 18 mi., Dif. III–IV at 800–2,000 cfs., Dif. IV–V at 2,000–8,000 cfs., Dif. VI over 8,000 cfs., experts only, deep wilderness canyon, continuous heavy rapids. DANGER—Clavey Falls at mouth of Clavey River—ptg. if necessary.

Trip 5—Wards Ferry Brdg. to Jacksonville, 6 mi., Dif. III–IV, first 2 mi. tough (IV); below this, Dif. I, threatened by new dam, description may be history.

(Credit—Charles Martin)

Yuba River: USGS Yuba City, Browns Valley (this description overlaps with part of Yuba River—N. Fork, below; rather than combine them we decided to give you both).

From Parks Bar brdg. to Yuba City, 15 mi., 2 days, OK intermediate skill, good fishing, series of haystacks on river. CAUTION—dam halfway down, ptg. left, slow going after dam, little current, few campsites, many people. (Credit—*Canoeing Waters of California*)

Yuba River—N. Fork: Sierra, Yuba cos.

Trip 1—Sierra City to Downieville, 12 mi., Dif. IV–VI, experts only, 2 ptgs.—difficulty drop below Ladies Canyon and long V–VI rapid farther down.

Trip 2—Downieville to Goodyear's Bar, 4 mi., *don't run,* unrunnable.

Trip 3—Goodyear's Bar to Rte. 49, 9 mi., Dif. III–IV, 1–2 carries; DANGER—near end, 10-ft. drop through rock slit, ptg.

Trip 4—Rte. 49 to New Bullard's Bar Res., 4 mi., Dif. III.

Trip 5—Rte. 20 brdg. to co. dump, 10 mi., Dif. I–II, OK beginners.

(Credit—Charles Martin)

Yuba River—S. Fork: Nev. Co.; The Washington Edward's Crossing, 10-ft. waterfall ½ mi. below Humburg Creek, check water level, ranges between too much and too little. (Credit—Charles Martin)

COLORADO

"Most of the stream portions above 8,000 ft. in elevation are rushing torrents, made up of one dangerous rapid after another with very little still-water area. Stream flow speeds range from 15–25 m.p.h. In the stream portions between 8,000 ft. and

6,500 ft. in elevation, certain stretches of still water are available. However, hazards such as rapids, irrigation diversion, dams and fences, crossing the streams may require many portages. Irrigation diversion in the stream portions below 6,500 ft. in elevation result in intermittent flows or dry streambeds." (Credit—B. G. Bovce, Adm. Asst., Parks and Recreation Planning Dept. of Natl. Res., St. of Col.)

Animas River: San Juan Co.; Silverton to Steel RR brdg., 26 mi.; river parallels narrow-gauge RR, Silverton to Elk Park, Dif. III on scale of VI, no stretches of flat, still water, ptg.—fallen logs. Elk Park to Needleton, Dif. III–IV rapids, cold water may be necessary to ptg. some rapids. Needleton to end, may be necessary to ptg. some rapids, Dif. III–IV; has been run only once according to our information by kayaks; trout. (Credit—Bill Winn)

Arkansas River: Canon City downstream 10 mi. to Florence.

Colorado River: Loma, Colo., downstream 12 mi. to Col.-Utah st. line.

Conejos River: 24 mi.; Roaring Gulch (above jctn. with S. Fork) to Broyles Brdg.; shallow, rocky, meandering, cottonwood- and willow-lined, swift, obstructions, 200-ft. drop in 15 mi., no falls or major rapids, narrow, canoeable till late summer, 4 cmpgrnds., resorts, trout. (Credit—Tom Eberhard)

Green River: Utah-Col. st. line downstream 20 mi. to Dinosaur Natl. Mon. bdry.

CONNECTICUT

A special word of thanks to Stewart Coffin, who generously shared his notes with me. These were collected over many years by a great canoeist.

Bantam River: Litchfield Co.; E. of Litchfield to Shepaug River, 14 mi.; Dif. I–IV; swampland above Bantam Lake. Ptg.—⅛ mi. below Bantam, dif. run to Shepaug River. NOTE: It is strongly recommended that you purchase and consult the *AMC New England Canoeing Guide* for further information.

Blackledge River: USGS Sheets: Moodus and Deep River; see Salmon River description; from Farm Brook to Leesville, 10 mi., start where Blackledge joins Fawn Brook, good current, easy rapids, Dif. I to Rivers Rd., iron brdg. ½ mi. above jctn. with Salmon River; there is ⅓ mi. easy rapids to jctn. with Salmon; whirlpool at jctn., next 2½ mi. to broken dam best part of river, continues as easy rapids Dif. I–II, through Hemlock woods, best to run March 1 to May 15, ptg. right around broken dam, then easy rapids ½ mi. to covered brdg. and Rte. 16 brdg., after Rte. 16 brdg. the next 4–5 mi. fast current, pleasant to backwater of dam above Leesville, ptg. dam, take out below Rte. 151 brdg. on right or go on 2 mi. into Conn. River. (Credit—Stewart Coffin)

Cherry Brook: Runs from N. Canton through Canton Center to the Farmington; not canoeable. (Credit—*The Farmington River and Watershed Guide*)

Connecticut River: Canoeable through entire state; 1 ptg., Windsor Locks; use canal, avoid dam and rapids.

Farmington River: Hill & Dale Inn at Otis to Goodwin or Hogsback Dam, white water, rocky, high water only, experts only, Dif. II–III to Rte. 8 steel brdg., below Rte. 8 Dif. III–IV; Goodwin Dam to Riverton, 30–40 min., Dif. I–III rapids; Riverton to Satan's Kingdom, 11 mi., Dif. I–III, first half wild ctry., some whirlpools; DANGER—chute 4½ mi. below Riverton; Satan's Kingdom to Collinsville, 5 mi., 2 hrs., scenic, challenging, no open canoes in high water, Dif. III–IV in gorge, drop in midgorge—scout ahead, ptg. Collinsville Dam—hard Collinsville to Unionville, 6 mi., rapids, dangerous right turn and washed-out power dam. Unionville to Tariffville, 9 hrs., smooth and swift mixed, some rips. Ptg.—5-ft. dam near brick house with white picket fence. DANGER—rapids below Tariffville Dam—skilled only. Tariffville to Spoonville, white water, to Rte. 187 brdg., experts only; below 187, standing waves, rapids, line if necessary; Spoonville brdg. to Poquonock, flat water, ptg.—Rainbow Dam, shallow below dam; Poquonock to Conn. River, 2 hrs., Dif. II rapids, shallow. (Credit—*The Farmington River and Watershed Guide*)

Farmington River—E. Branch: (Hubbard Brook). Hubbard Brook flows through Granville St. For., not open for canoeing. (Credit—*The Farmington River and Watershed Guide*)

Fawn Brook: USGS Moodus, Deep River. See Salmon River descriptions.

Housatonic River: Fairfield, Litchfield cos., 81 mi. Dif. I–IV. Falls Village to Kent Rapids, beautiful, submerged rocks. DANGER—in high water below W. Cornwall, ptg.—Bulls Brdg. Dam and rapids, heavy pitches from jctn. with Ten Mile River to New Milford, dangerous sometimes, many dams between New Milford and Derby, tidewater below Derby. Best sec.—Falls Village to Kent; Start—river mi. 75.9 below Hartford Elec. Lt. Co. powerhouse, white water to Kent Hwy. brdg. at river mi. 57; below Bulls Brdg. Dam, dif. ptgs., not good short stretch white water.

Norwalk River: Not recommended, too shallow, too many ptgs. (Credit—Stewart Coffin)

Quinebaug River: See description under Massachusetts.

Quinnipiac River: New Haven Co.; Hanover Pond to New Haven, 25 mi.; Dif. I–II; smooth, 5–6 dams marshy, meanders from New Haven to New Heaven.

Salmon Brook: USGS Tariffville; 4 mi. canoeing in high water, put-in at main road S. of Granby or on N. Branch. N. of Granby,

through farm ctry. to Tariffville, clear, sandy stream. (Credit
—Stewart Coffin)

Salmon Brook: Rte. 10, either branch to Farmington River; check
water level. (Credit—*The Farmington River and Watershed
Guide*)

Salmon River: USGS Moodus, deep river; sec. above jctn. with
Blackledge River is steep, sporty white-water run; sec. down
Blackledge River and lower Salmon is attractive, popular with
novice white-water fans; from old Rte. 2 Brdg. to Blackledge
River, 3 mi., run in high water, normally Mar. 1–Apr. 15, narrow
stream, swift current, many rapids. Dif. III–IV, rapids need scouting, overhanging trees in first sec., put in where old Rte. 2 crosses,
1½ mi. to millpond and dam at N. Westchester, take out, ptg.
100 yds., cross at 149 brdg., put in on right, then 1½-mi. run,
strong current, nice scenery, rapids Dif. II, to jctn. with Blackledge River. (Credit—Stewart Coffin)

Sandy Brook: No good till Rte. 8, scout between Robertsville and
Riverton before run. (Credit—*The Farmington River and Watershed Guide*)

Saugatuck River: Fairfield Co.; Lyon to Long Is. Sound, 10 mi.
Dif. I–III. Easy current, dams, tidewater below Westport. (Credit
—*The Farmington River and Watershed Guide*)

Shepaug River: Fairfield, Litchfield cos.; Bantam River outlet to
Housatonic River, 21½ mi. Dif. I–V; beautiful, exciting, dif.
parts, sharp turns, scout. DANGER—Rosburg Falls ptg.—land
well above—approach hidden.

Still River: Fairfield Co.; Beaver Brook to Housatonic River, 10
mi. Dif. I–II, winds through marshes; Rte. 8 where Sandy Brook
crosses to Farmington River, experts only. (Credit—*The Farmington River and Watershed Guide*)

Willimantic and Shetucket rivers: USGS Stafford Springs, South
Coventry, Columbia, Willimantic, Scotland, and Norwich: from

Stafford Springs to Greenville, 25 mi., ptg.—many dams, water fluctuates due to dams, below Willimantic are series of millponds, many areas not canoeable in dry season, some rapids in first part between Stafford Springs and Willimantic. (Credit—Stewart Coffin)

DELAWARE

Brandywine River: Chester, Delaware cos.; W. Branch, 1 long day, some riffles, pleasant interm. canoeists, high water only; Lenape to Rockland, Del., 1 day, novice, some riffles, pleasant; Rockland to Wilmington, 1 day, skilled only, mixed smooth and rapids, 9 dams, can run at med. to high water, 3–4 rapids.

FLORIDA

Alafia River: Near Tampa, Topo Quads, Lithia, Dover, Riverview, and Brandon; Hillsborough Co. From Alderman Ford Park to Bell Shoals Rd., 12½ mi., 1 day, put in Alderman Ford Park on St. Rd. 39, swift-moving water, limestone bed, shoals in low water, can be challenging trip. (Credit—*Florida Canoe Trail Guide*)

Alexander Springs Creek: In Ocala Natl. For., Paisley, Fla. From Alexander Springs Rec. Area to 52-B Lndg., 7 mi., 4 hrs. From put-in to St. Hwy. 445, 1.3 mi., ¾ hr., from put-in to Ellis Lndg., 3 mi., 1½ hrs., pleasant trip. OK for beginners, can rent canoes at boat concession stand in Alexander Springs Rec. Area, nice semitropical scenery. (Credit—U.S. For. Ser. For information contact Boat Concession, Alexander Springs Rec. Area, P.O. Box 77, Paisley, Fla. 32767)

Blackwater River: USGS Crestview, Munson, and Harold. Santa Rosa and Okaloosa cos. From St. Rd. 180 to Blackwater River St. Park, 40 mi., 2–3 days. Put-in is 2 mi. S. of Ala.–Fla. st. line; river flows through Blackwater River St. For., dense canopy of trees, many beautiful white sandbars for camping, good fishing. Watch out for old brdg. pilings in spots, some wading in dry weather, check USGS gauge at St. Rd. 4 brdg.—if it is around 4 there will be logjams. (Credit—*Florida Canoe Trail Guide*)

Bulow Creek: USGS Flagler Beach W., Flagler Beach E., Ormond Beach. Flagler and Volusia cos. From put-in 3½ mi. N. of public boat ramp at Bulow Ruins (locate—Bulow St. Park) to entrance to Intercoastal Waterway on St. Rd. 201, 13 mi. if you start at Bulow Ruins, then go to northern end, then back and to take-out, 6 mi. from put-in to take-out without northern trip, water takes on coastal appearance—brackish near end, good fishing whole trip, nice coastal marsh scenery, 1-day trip. DANGER—large boats on Intercoastal Waterway. (Credit—*Florida Canoe Trail Guide*)

Chassahowitzka River: Source to Gulf of Mexico, spring-fed, crystal clear, undeveloped, natural, flows through Chassahowitzka Natl. Wildlife Refuge.

Chipola River: Jackson, Calhoun, and Gulf cos. USGS, Marianna, Oakdale, Altha West, Clarsville, Frink, Dead Lake, and Wewahitchka. From Florida Caverns St. Park to St. Rd. 71, 50 mi., 3 days, flows 3 river swamps, hardwood for., high limestone bluffs and rapids. DANGER—"Look and Tremble" rapids above St. Rd. 274 Brdg., *don't run*—ptg. instead, some logjams and submerged rocks in northern part of trip, distance between roads, start to 167 is 1½ mi., 167 to U.S. 90 is 2 mi., U.S. 90 to 280A is 7½ mi., 280A to 278 is 9½ mi., 278 to 274 is 8 mi., 274 to 20 is 9½ mi., 20 to 392 is 13 mi. (Credit—*Florida Canoe Trail Guide*)

Econlockhatchee River: USGS Sanford, Sanford S.W., For. City. Orange and Seminole cos. From St. Rd. 50 9 mi. E. of Orlando to St. Johns River, 28 mi., 2 days, shallow at first, narrow and twisty, hardwood forests, high sand hills, many underwater hazards. In dry periods put in at St. 419 due to logjams, many campsites, many sandbars, river subject to extreme and rapid changes in water level, river becomes dangerous after heavy rain, use lifejackets, river widens halfway downstream, deeper and more placid in second half, much wildlife and birds, excellent fishing. (Credit—*Florida Canoe Trail Guide*)

Estero River: Lee Co. USGS Ft. Myers Beach and Estero. From Koreshon St. Park to Carl Johnson Co. Park on St. Rd. 865, easy 1-day trip, trail goes 4 mi. through mangrove swamp to mouth at Estero Bay, then 2½ mi. across Estero Bay head S.W., avoid boat channel N. of shoals, select own route through mangrove isles. DANGER—don't cross bay in bad weather (Credit—*Florida Canoe Trail Guide*)

Everglades Natl. Park: Old Homestead Trail; 15 mi. through Bear Lake to Gator Lake via Bear Lake Canal, to E. Cape, OK novice. W. Lake Trail 8 mi., through W. Lake, between small bays to "the Lungs" into Alligator Creek, on to Flamingo along shore of Florida Bay. Hells Bay Trail—8 mi. to cmpgrnd., rugged, dense brush, from dock near W. Lake through shallow natural waterway, mangrove tunnels, trails well marked, birdlife, alligators. (Credit—Natl. Park Ser. Everglades Natl. Park and *A Guide to the Wilderness Waterway of the Everglades National Park*)

Hermosassa River: Limited canoeing, industrial development on river (Credit—David S. Arthurs)

Holmes Creek: USGS Vernon, Millers Ferry; Washington Co. From St. Rd. 79 at wayside park boat ramp to boat ramp owned by Game and Fresh Water Fish Comm. 1 mi. N. of St. Rd. 284 brdg., 17 mi., 1 day, excellent trip, a variety of scenery, high banks at start to low-lying swampland, logs, sharp twisting bends,

ptgs. necessary in low water, much birdlife, good fishing. (Credit
—*Florida Canoe Trail Guide*)

Ichetucknee River: USGS Hildreth. Suwannee Co. From Ichetucknee Springs St. Park 6 mi. N.W. of Ft. White to U.S. 27, 3½
mi., one of safest streams in Fla., shallow in most places, many
springs, moderate flow, no underwater obstructions, beautiful
stream, good for beginners, popular for tubing, much wildlife,
good fishing (bass, shellcrocker, other panfish), trail entirely
within st. park, leisurely trip, 1–1½ hrs. (Credit—*Florida Canoe
Trail Guide*)

Loxahatchee River: USGS Rood and Jupiter. Martin and Palm
Beach cos. From St. Rd. 706 Brdg. to Jonathan Dickinson St.
Park, 7 mi., 1 day, blend of temperate and subtropical wilderness, very scenic, only wild river left in S.E. Fla., many cypress
trees, much wildlife, and many birds, shallow water in spots,
deadfalls, and logs, don't go in dry weather—can get stranded;
good side trips on tributaries. (Credit—*Florida Canoe Trail
Guide*)

Ochlockonee River: USGS Lake Talquin, Smith Creek, Thousand
Yard Bay, Sanborn, McIntyre, St. Teresa, and Lighthouse Point.
Leon, Wakulla, and Liberty cos. From St. Rd. 20 to Ochlockonee
River St. Park, 67 mi., 2–3 days, river can be swift and treacherous, wear lifejackets, scenery varies from banks of high pine
bluffs to dense cypress and hardwoods, flows through Apalachi-
cola Natl. For., some snags, some ptgs. in dry weather, water fluctuates without notice due to release from Lake Talquin Dam, several public campsites and fishing camps with accommodations,
much wildlife, including bear, good fishing (black bass, bream,
catfish, perch), some posted land along river, always within 15 mi.
of public campsite or fishing camp. (Credit—*Florida Canoe Trail
Guide*)

Peace River: USGS Bartow, Homeland, Bowling Green, Wau-
chula, Zolfo Springs, Gardner, Limestone, and Nocatee. Polk, De

Soto, and Hardee cos. From St. Rd. 60 at Bartow to St. Rd. 70, W. of Arcadia, 83 mi.

Trip 1—Put in to U.S. Hwy. 98 brdg., 16 mi., beautiful, cypress-studded, primitive camping on W. bank just past U.S. 98 brdg., logjams and ptgs. in low water, hyacinth jams make sections impassable at times.

Trip 2—From U.S. Hwy. 98 brdg., E. of Ft. Meade to St. Rd. 70 W. of Arcadia, 67 mi., nice canoe trail, dense for. most of way, few signs of civilization, historic river—used to be bdry. between Indian territory and whites', some stretches of rapids, then shallow pools, nice side trips on tributaries much wildlife and birds, longest distance between access pts. is 40.6 mi. between St. Rd. 64 and St. Rd. 70; others do not exceed 9 mi. (Credit—*Florida Canoe Trail Guide*)

Rainbow River: 7 mi., side trip off Withlacoochee River, Start-Dunnellon, crystal clear, great skin diving. (Credit—David S. Arthurs)

St. Mary's River: Baker and Nassau cos. in Fla. and Charlton Co. in Ga. USGS Macclenny, St. George, Toledo, Folkston, and Boulogne, From Fla.-Ga. st.-line brdg. on St. Rd. 121 to Camp Pickney Park in Ga., 63½ mi., several logjams in dry season, some ptgs., flows through beautiful wilderness, many white sandbars for camping, can also camp under brdg., rights-of-way, and at Camp Pickney Park and Trader Hill Park. Distances between brdgs.—start to Stokes Brdg. 9 mi., Stokes Brdg. to Hwy. 2 Brdg. 17 mi., Hwy. 2 Brdg. to Hwy. 301 and 23 37 mi., then 5 mi. to end. (Credit—*Florida Canoe Trail Guide*)

Salt Springs Run: Marion Co., Ocala Natl. For., flows into L. George, 3 mi., beautiful.

Shoal River: USGS Laurel Hill, Crestview, and Holt. Walton and Okaloosa cos. From St. Rd. 285 to St. Rd. 85, 24 mi., very scenic, many twists and turns, narrow river, high sandy hills, broad sandbars, deep pools, many campsites, very little civilization, excellent fishing, you can continue another 7 mi. after St. Rd. 85 to jctn. with Yellow River. (Credit—*Florida Canoe Trail Guide*)

Spruce Creek: Volusia Co., USGS Somsula and New Smyrna Beach. From Moody Brdg. off Taylor Rd. to Bunk's Landing off St. Rd. 5A in Port Orange, 4½ mi., scenery ranges from hardwood wilderness to coastal saltwater marsh (Credit—*Florida Canoe Trail Guide*)

Suwannee River: USGS Fargo S.W., Benton, White Springs E., White Springs W., Oak E., Hillcoat, Ft. Union, Ellaville, The Pocket, Strange Is., Fargo, Needmore, and Council; Fla. Columbia, Hamilton, and Suwannee cos. in Fla. Ga. cos.— Clinch and Echols. From Lem Griffis Hunting and Fishing Camp in Ga. to Suwannee River St. Park in Fla., 107 mi., put-in is 18 mi. N.E. of Fargo off St. Rd. 177, many access pts. along this trail, can divide trail into 1-day trips or longer, several camp-sites with accommodations. DANGER—white-water shoals above White Springs—ptg. (Credit—*Florida Canoe Trail Guide*)

Tsala Apopka Chain of Lakes: Access to Withlacoochee River via Orange St. Canal off Hernando Outfall Canal, other access pts. near Inverness, Floral City, and Hernando. (Credit—David S. Arthurs)

Wacissa River: USGS Wacissa and Nutall Rise. Jefferson Co. From Wacissa Springs E. of Tallahassee to U.S. Hwy. 98, 6 hrs., beautiful trip, primitive river, water is crystal clear for much of trip, deep pools, narrow river and swift, many overhangs, much wildlife, many tributaries to explore, wilderness camping except for park at Goose Pasture 10 mi. from put-in, river forks below Goose Pasture, take far right channel, near end of trail is canal dug by slaves in 1850, take the canal entrance to end of trail, willows overhang entrance. (Credit—*Florida Canoe Trail Guide*)

Wekiva River: USGS Sanford, Sanford S.W., and Forest City;

Lake and Orange cos. From Wekiva Springs St. Park to Emanuel Lndg. on High Banks Rd. off U.S. 17 and 92, 15 mi., 1 day. Combination pine and hardwoods upland and dense swampland, crystal-clear waters, mixture swift and placid water, many islands, tributaries, and lagoons, isolated campsites, good fishing, bird watching, some overhangs, some submerged snags, many squatters' shacks from beginning to RR tracks. (Credit—*Florida Canoe Trail Guide*)

Withlacoochee River: USGS Clyattville, Pinetta, Octahatchee, Ellaville. From Ga. St. Hwy. 94 crossing 10 mi. N.W. of Valdosta, Ga., to Suwannee River St. Park in Fla., 55 mi., very scenic, flows past sandy beaches, swamplands, limestone buttes, many rapids, sometimes high waves, many bends, overhangs, fallen trees, can be high and swift during rain, rapids appear in dry weather, also some wading in dry weather, some ptgs. in dry periods, wear lifejackets. (Credit—*Florida Canoe Trail Guide*)

Withlacoochee River: USGS Lacoochee, St. Catherine, Nobleton, Wahoo, Rutland, Stokes Ferry, Dunnellon, N.E., Dunnellon, Yankeetown, Yankeetown S.E.; Citrus, Hernando, and Pasco cos. From Coulter Hammock Rec. Area in Withlacoochee St. For. to Florida Power Co. Dam 100 mi.

Trip 1—Start to Silver Lake about 9 mi. S. of Bushnell, 17 mi., 1 day, campsites in Coulter Hammock and Silver Lake Rec. Areas, submerged logs, some ptgs.

Trip 2—From I-75 at Silver Lake about 9 mi. S. of Bushnell to Fla. Power Co. Dam, 82 mi., get a good map before going, river separates into many streams and sloughs, many are dead ends, dense cypress swamps, at first the river flows through sandhills, then hardwood forests, then cypress ponds, some cabins in spots, many access pts. no more than 17 mi. apart, excellent fishing, much wildlife, many birds including wild turkey, alligators, only 1 developed campsite on trail with fee charged. DANGER—Wysong Dam 3½ mi. below St. Rd. 44. Indian shell mounds along banks, short side trips up spring-fed runs.

(Credit—*Florida Canoe Trail Guide*)

Yellow River: USGS Crestview, Holt, and Harold. Okaloosa and Santa Rosa cos. From St. Rd. 2 to St. Rd. 87, 50 mi., 2–3 days, nice canoe trails, hardwood forests and high sandy banks at first, then cypress marginal swamp terrain; fast-flowing river at first, then widens and deepens, much wildlife, fishing excellent in tributary streams, some overhanging brush in spots, camping available in several spots, many access pts. (Credit—*Florida Canoe Trail Guide*)

GEORGIA

Alapaha River: Willocoochee to Statenville 83 mi., remote ctry., clearest Ga. river, high sandbanks, small rapids with wave, minor obstacles, rises and is swift after rain, 4 campsites. Dif. I, easy. Trips—Willocoochee to Ga. U.S. 168 brdg., 20 mi.; on to U.S. 129 brdg., 18 mi.; on to U.S. 84 brdg., 18 mi.; on to Ga. 187 brdg.—Mayday, 12 mi.; on to Statenville, 15 mi. (Credit—*Canoe Guide to the Alapaha River*)

Alcovy River: From Hwy. Brdg. 213 near Covington to take-out pt. 9 mi. below, 5–6 hrs., primarily a flat, gentle river, some easy rapids. Dif. I–II, OK beginners, below take-out pt. is a ¼-mi. stretch of rapids—Dif. III. (Credit—Georgia Canoeing Association)

Broad River: From St. Hwy. 281 to St. Hwy. 172, 6 mi., 3 hrs. Dif. II–III. 5 rapids on this stretch, wide river, 100 yds. wide in places, combination long, flat stretches with rapids at end, canoeist usually has choice of running rapids or not due to width of river; a 5-ft. slide on this stretch can be run in open canoes. (Credit—Georgia Canoeing Association)

Cartecay River: From Ga. 52 5 mi. E. of Ellijay to gauging station on Ga. 52 just outside of Ellijay, 11 mi., not for beginners.

Dif. I–III, small, fast-flowing, 6 major rapids, rapids begin after first noticeable is., 4 rapids Dif. II, 2 rapids Dif. III, scout before running, toughest rapids are twisting drops over ledges with powerful current, last 5 mi. contain Dif. I rapids, beautiful trip, wild ctry., run during rainy season, min. flow 1.80 on gauge 1½ mi. above Ellijay on Ga. 52, optimum conditions around 2.50. (Credit —Georgia Canoeing Association)

Chattahoochee River: Habersham, White, Hall cos.; Upper Chattahoochee—above Lake Lanier; Hidden Valley Campsite off Georgia Rte. 105 to Lake Lanier; Hidden Valley Campsite to Chattahoochee Paradise Park, 3½ to 4 hrs., several Dif. II rapids with Dif. III rapids at Smith Is., Buck Shoals, and the Horseshoe, experienced canoeists only. Ch. Par. Park to Bellton Brdg. Rec. Facility, 10 mi., 4 hrs., 3 or 4 Dif. II rapids and several Dif. I. Below Bellton Brdg., backwaters of lake, OK beginners; last take-out point—Clark's Brdg. Rec. Facility; trout fishing in upper river, white and black bass in lower river; access points—Georgia 75, Georgia 255, Georgia 254/115, Duncan Brdg. Rd. (S. 1759), Bellton Brdg. Rd., and Georgia 52.

Chattooga River: USGS Ga.—S.C., N.C. Walhalla; Rabun Co. in Ga., Ocones Co. in S.C.; borders S.C.; from Nicholas Ford to Tugaloo Lake, 33 mi., Dif. II–IV.

Trip 1—Nicholas Ford to St. Hwy. 28, Dif. II–III, 4 mi., no partic. dangers, small, clear river.

Trip 2—St. Hwy. 28 brdg. to Earl's Ford, 7 mi., Dif. I–III. DANGER—one 5-ft. ledge, scout first, flat and slow river.

Trip 3—from Earl's Ford to U.S. Hwy. 76 brdg. 15 mi., Dif. III–V. DANGER—3 falls and several Dif. V rapids, fast river, very narrow in spots, white-water experts only.

Trip 4—from U.S. Hwy. 76 brdg. to Tugaloo Lake, 7 mi., Dif. III–VII. DANGER—5-ft. falls, narrow canyon, contin. rapids IV–VI, very dangerous, white-water experts only, good all year, good trout fishing.

(Credit—*Canoeing White Water River Guide* and *Canoeing Georgia's White Water Rivers*)

Chestatee River: Lumpkin Co.; Waters Creek off Ga. 19 to 5976, Dif. II through Good Spring Run IV. Below 5976 is a 50-ft. waterfall—this stretch experts only, old interesting gold and copper mines.

Coosawatee River: Gilmer Co.; St. Hwy. 5 to st. line, some good Dif. IV rapids, no other information.

Etowah River: Lumpkin, Dawson cos.; easy Dif. II river, some challenging rapids and shoals, access from U.S. Rte. 19 near Dahlonega, Ga. at 2 pts. and from Ga. Rte. 53 and Ga. Rte. 136. DANGER—10-ft. falls Ga. 136 to Tobacco Pouch Creek River, 3 hrs. good most of year; Hwy. 52 to Lake Altoona, 45 mi., fair fishing, canoeable.

Flint River: From St. Rte. 19 Brdg. near Woodbury to Pobiddy Rd., 25 mi., Dif. I–III.
> *Trip 1*—OK from St. Rte. 18 Brdg. to Sprewell Bluff, 14 mi., beautiful, 6–8 hrs., mostly flat, easy 2-ft. ledge near end.
> *Trip 2*—OK beginners, Sprewell Bluff to St. Rte. 36, 5 mi., 3 Dif. II ledges, 2 hrs.
> *Trip 3*—OK intermediate, from St. Rte. 36 to Pobiddy Rd., 6 mi., 3 hrs., Dif III, maximum level for open canoes 10.0 ft. on gauge under St. Rte. 36 Brdg., should read 7.0 for good run.
> (Credit—Georgia Canoeing Association)

Ocmulgee River: From Rte. 18 brdg. N. of Macon to Spring Street in Macon, 16 mi., 5–6 hrs., OK beginners, a large river, first 9 mi. through and across rock outcroppings, nice scenery, Dif. I rapids, unique rock formations. (Credit—Georgia Canoeing Association)

Oconee River: From Oconee St. Park to Oconee River Brdg., 4 hours, OK beginners. (Credit—Georgia Canoeing Association)

Ogeechee River: Jenkins Bullock, and Chatham cos.; from Rocky Ford to Atlantic Ocean, 40 hrs., no danger pts. Dif. I (A and B, mostly B); obstacles—fallen trees; ptgs.—none; sand bottom, no pollution, wilderness area, good camping, fishing—good in low water for bass and bream, tide affects lower parts; beautiful trip, great for family.

Trip 1—Rocky Ford to U.S. 301, 5 hrs.
Trip 2—U.S. 301 to Ga. 24, 7 hrs.
Trip 3—Ga. 24 to Ga. 119, 12 hrs.
Trip 4—Ga. 119 to U.S. 80, 3 hrs.
Trip 5—U.S. 80 to Ga. 204, 4 hrs.
Trip 6—Ga. 204 to U.S. 17, 4 hrs.
Trip 7—U.S. 17 to Atlantic Ocean, 5 hrs. (Credit—G. R. Mitchell)

Okefenokee Natl. Wildlife Refuge: Charlton, Ware, Clinch cos., in S.E. Ga. near Fla. line, Waycross, Ga. Area extends 38 mi. from N. to S. and 25 mi. at widest pt., 412,000 acres, open all year, spring best time, swampland, filled with wildlife and birds, good fishing—need Ga. license, can't use live bait, bass, bream, catfish pickerel, don't collect plants or animals, camping by permit only and in assigned area, must use assigned trails, can't move from camp after dark, must have Coast Guard-approved lifejacket, must have compass and flashlight, no swimming, must launch before 10 A.M., no motors on canoes, no littering, max. party is 10 canoes, rtes. are marked with colored canoes and white-topped posts, OK to leave vehicles overnight with permit. There are 13 approved rtes.: (1) Kingfisher–Maul Hammock–Big Water–Stephen Foster, 3 days; (2) Kingfisher–Bluff Lake–Floyds Is.–Stephen Foster (via Floyds Prairie), 3 days; (3) Kingfisher–Bluff Lake–Floyds Is.–Stephen Foster (via Suwannee Canal Run), 3 days; (4) Suwannee Canal–Duck Island–Suwannee Canal, 2 days; (5) Suwannee Canal–Suwannee Canal Run–Stephen Foster, 2 days; (6) Suwannee Canal–Cedar Hammock–Floyds Is.–Stephen Foster (via Floyds Prairie), 3 days; (7) Suwannee Canal–Cedar Hammock–Floyds Is.–Stephen Foster (via Suwannee Canal Run), 3 days; (8) Stephen Foster–Cravens Hammock–Stephen Foster, 2 days; (9) Suwannee Canal–Cedar Hammock–Floyds Is.–Suwannee Canal, 3 days; (10) Suwannee Canal–Cedar Hammock–Floyds Is.–Bluff Lake–Kingfisher, 4 days; (11) Kingfisher–Maul Hammock–Big Water–Floyds Is.–Bluff Lake–Kingfisher, 5 days; (12) Kingfisher–Bluff Lake–Kingfisher, 2 days; (13) Kingfisher–Maul Hammock–Big Water–Stephen Foster–Floyds Is.–Bluff Lake–Kingfisher, 6 days. (Credit—*Wilderness Canoeing in Okefenokee,* Slash Pine Area Planning and Development Commission, also Refuge Mgr. of Okefenokee Natl. Wildlife Refuge)

Call for reservations well in advance to Refuge Mgr. of Okefenokee Natl. Wildlife Refuge, P.O. Box 117, Waycross Ga., 31501; phone 912-283-2580. Canoe rentals at Suwannee Canal Rec. Area, Rte. 2, Folkston, Ga. 31537; phone 912-496-7156.

Satilla River: Approx. 260 mi., beautiful river. Trips—area above Waycross 94 mi., low in dry season, raging in rainy season, good canoeing section, many small passages, obstructions in river, 30 access pts.; Waycross to Hoboken (Hwy. 121), 20-mi. seasonal water flow, many obstructions, 3 dangerous sections, high bluffs; Hoboken to Nahunta 29 mi., deeper than upstream clear streambed; Nahunta to Atkinson 23 mi., few obstructions, deep; Atkinson to Burnt Fort 41 mi., motorboat traffic, wide and clear channel; Burnt Fort to Atlantic Ocean 52 mi., very wide and deep, salt marsh border, tide influence, motorboat traffic; best portion above Waycross to Woodbine; bass, crappie, red bellies, bream. (Credit—*Canoe Guide to the Scenic Satilla River* and Raymond S. Cannon for Slash Pine Planning and Development Committee)

Talking Rock Creek: From Hwy. 156 Brdg. to where 156 recrosses the river, 18 mi., 5–6 hrs., uninhabited, OK intermediates, very scenic, 6 mi. of Dif. I, then Dif. II for 12 mi., when Etowah River is low, Talking Rock Creek is impossible. (Credit —Georgia Canoeing Association)

Toccoa River: Fannin Co. Canoeable from Cooper Creek to McCaysville, through Blue Ridge Lake, lightly traveled. Dif.— Gen. II, some III rapids, beautiful, forest, good trout fishing. Deep Hole Res. Area to Blue Ridge Lake, 12 mi.

Withlacoochee River: Ga. 94 brdg. to Suwannee River St. Park, Fla., 56 mi., swampland, sandy beaches, many rapids, high waves, bends, minor obstacles, ptg. Aug.–Sept. over sandbars and rapids, high and swift Mar.–May. Dif. III, fairly easy. Trips—Ga. 94 brdg. to U.S. 84 brdg., 8 mi.; U.S. 84 to Rocky Ford Rd. brdg., 12 mi.; Rocky Ford to Fla. 145 brdg., 4 mi.; 145 to Fla. 6 brdg., 20 mi.; Fla. 6 to finish, 12 mi. (Credit—Coastal Plains Area Tourism Council)

HAWAII

The estuaries of a few rivers on the island of the Kauai offer some canoeing potential. These include the Wailua River (2 miles by 100 yds.), the Hanalei River (3 miles by 100 ft.), and the Huleia River (2 mi. by 250 ft.).

The best of these appears to be the Wailua River. A boat-launching ramp, park, and restaurant complex stands at the river-mouth and a fleet of sight-seeing boats conduct daily upstream runs to a scenic spot called Fein Grotto, a distance of 2 mi.

(Credit—Stanley Shima)

IDAHO

Buffalo River: Fremont Co., Targhee Natl. For. River crossing off dirt rd. E. of Is. Park Vil. to Is. Park Res., approx. 8 mi., canoeable.

Henry's Fork: Madison, Fremont cos., Targhee Natl. For., St. Anthony-Targhee Natl. For. Headquarters to Is. Park Res., approx. 50–60 mi. DANGER—Warm River through Sheep Falls (rafts only), experts only in Box Canyon below Is. Park Res.; Macks Inn to Big Springs, 6 mi., canoeable.

Salmon River: "River of No Return," rubber rafts, kayaks, power-boats, flat-bottom barges, 40 stretches of rapids, most dif. rapids —Pine Creek, white water, stretches of calm water and deep pools, some Dif. V rapids, some fallen trees, boulders, granite walls, Corn Creek Cmpgrnd. (46 mi. W. of N. Fork, Ida.) to Wind River Park Brdg., 81 mi. Chinook, sockeye, steelhead, rainbow, eastern brook, Dolly Varden, cutthroat, small-mouth bass, whitefish.

Salmon River—Mid. Fork: 106 mi., wild river, no open canoes, kayaks and rubber rafts, dangerous, Chinook salmon, steelhead, rainbow trout, Dolly Varden.

Snake River: Bonneville, Jefferson cos. Below Palisades Res. to Neije, approx. 35 mi., canoeable.

Teton River: Madison, Teton cos., Patterson Creek to N. Fork, canoeable, approx. 20 mi.; jctn. with N. Fork to first all-weather rd., rubber rafts only, approx. 15 mi., past first all-weather rd. canoeable for several mi.

ILLINOIS

Big Muddy (Aux Vases): Franklin, Williamson, Jackson, Union cos., 90 mi. Rte. 14 brdg. W. of Benton to Mississippi River. Trips—Rte. 14 brdg. to Rte. 51 brdg. S. of De Soto, 41 mi., poor canoeing, many logjams. Rte. 51 brdg. to Murphrysboro, 8 mi., good canoeing; Murphrysboro to mouth, 41 mi., good; wild area in Jackson and Union cos.; poisonous snakes, take care camping; end—Rte. 3 brdg.

Cache River: Johnson, Pulaski cos., approx. 60 mi. Trips—Hollis Spur to brdg. between Foreman and Belknap, 21 mi., 16 hrs., tough trip. Belknap to Rte. 37, 2 mi.; Rte. 37 to co. rd. E. of Rte. 51 and new Rt. 57, 7 mi. Alt. rte., low water, Karnak to brdg. S. of Perks, 4–5 hrs. Avoid access via Rte. 37 and 51 brdg.; Perks Brdg. to Ohio River, approx. 30 mi.; poisonous snakes.

Des Plaines River: Cook, Du Page cos., 7 mi., ½ day. Willow Springs to Lemont Rd.; heavily polluted, poor canoeing, mud bottom; dangerous pt.—Sante Fe RR crossing; river runs from northern Lake Co. to join Kankakee in Will Co.—no information on other sections.

Embarras River: Douglas, Coles, Cumberland, Jasper, Richland, Crawford, Laurence cos.; 130 mi.; Rte. 130 S. of Villa Grove to Wabash River; logjams, silt, sand, gravel bottom, good wading, river rises fast after rain; Access pts.—hwy. brdgs. and city access pts. Trips—Villa Grove to Rte. 133 brdg., 16 mi.; Rte. 133 to Rte. 16 brdg., 11 mi.; Rte. 16 to Lake Charleston, 3 mi.; Rte. 130 brdg. to Newton Dam. 50 mi.; Newton to St. Marie, ½ day; Laurenceville to Wabash River, 2 days. Dams—low rock dam near spillway Lake Charleston, Newton Dam—be careful. Fishing —good catfish, spotted bass in fast water.

Fox River: McHenry, Lake, Kane, Kendall, La Salle cos., 95 mi. from bottom of Chain of Lake to Ill. River; approx. 120 mi. from Wis. line to Ill. River; entire river good canoeing, slow current, sand and gravel bottom, silt and sewage, sludge bottom—Kane Co., some riffles, fair fishing. Access pts.—Oak Pt. St. Park, 40 private docks on Chain of Lakes (charge), McHenry Dam St. Park, Rte. 14 brdg., Algonquin City Park, E. Dundee, Elgin City Park, Fabian Forest Preserve, Batavia City Park, Rte. 30 brdg., Yorkville Dam, other brdgs.—check first. Dams—Algonquin very dangerous, don't run; Yorkville; Norway; Dayton—long carry— ptg. right; may be others.

Green River: Lee, Whiteside, Bureau, Henry cos., approx. 100 mi.; Rte. 26 brdg. to mouth at Green Rock. Access—Rte. 26

brdg., Rte. 88 S. of Deer Grove, Rte. 92 W. of Normandy, Rte. 78 N. of Annawan, Rte. 82 N. of Genesco, may be others; shallow river, sand bottom, steep banks, small-mouth bass, and catfish.

Illinois-Michigan Canal: 25–30 mi.; Gebhard Woods St. Park to Channon St. Park.; sand and mud bottom, little current, some sewage pollution, cruise any season, good for beginner; above U.S. Rte. 66 canoeing difficult. Illinois-Mississippi Canal: approx. 60 mi.; Henry, Bureau cos.; Rock River to Ill. River; same general characteristics as Ill.-Miss. Feeder Canal; 21 locks between Ill. River and Feeder Canal—ptg. all; walleye and large-mouth bass, pools 22, 23, 24.

Illinois River: 272 mi., Grafton to Dresden Isle Lock and Dam. Trips—Grafton to Morris, 263 mi., Illini St. Park, 247 mi., Ottawa, 240 mi., Lacon, 189 mi., Hwy. 166 in Peoria, 166 mi., Havana, 120 mi., Beardstown, 88 mi., Naples, 65 mi., Pearl, 43 mi., Hardin, 21 mi., Père Marquette St. Park, 5 mi.; many dams on river, highly polluted areas, sudden high winds, lightning, large cruisers and barges, mileage markers on river, many access pts., best fishing from Grafton to Staved Rock, safety equipment required.

Little Wabash River: Shelby, Clay, Wayne, White cos., 4–5 days; Rte. 15 brdg. to New Haven. Trips—Sections N. of Rte. 15 brdg., poor canoeing; Rte. 15 to Carmi, 2–3 days; Carmi to New Haven, 25 mi., 2 days. Dam—Carmi; lower river—few roads and brdgs., scenic, canoeable all year, many birds, watch for rock shoals above New Haven Brdg., good fishing, channel cat, bullhead, carp.

Mackinaw River: McLean, Woodford, Tazewell cos., 100 mi.; Rte. 51 to Ill. River. Trips—above Rte. 51, no canoeing, river full of debris; Rte. 51 to Rte. 150 canoeable except low water, ptgs., 20 mi., 1 day, beautiful trip; Rte. 15 to Rte. 9, 20 mi., junk in water near 174 brdg., fast water, watch bends, low banks, fairly free of obstructions; Rte. 9 to Rte. 121 high banks, some obsta-

cles, pleasant trip; Rte. 121 to Rte. 29, 1 day; Rte. 29 to Ill.
River, 1 day, flat, marsh terrain; best portion—Rte. 9 to Ill.
River, 60 mi.; channel cat, carp, small-mouth bass, flathead cat.

Pecatonica River: Stephenson, Winnebago cos., 76½ mi. in Ill., 4
days, Winslow to Rock River; all-year canoeing, steep banks,
several towns ½ mi. from river. Access—limited, use brdgs. and
street ends; Freeport VFW property E. edge of town, Fairgrounds
at Pecatonica. Trips—Winslow to Freeport, Freeport to Pecatonica to Harrison-Shirland, Harrison-Shirland to Rock River, 1
day each. River dangerous in high water. Ptgs.—low dam at
Freeport, broken dam at Ridott. Take right bank and right fork of
river 1⅓ mi. above Freeport Dam to avoid logjam.

Rock River: Winnebago, Ogle, Whiteside, Henry, Rock Island
cos., 150 mi., st. line at Beloit to Blackhawk St. Park and Miss.
River; excellent canoeing, can stay in hotels at night and eat in
restaurants, some shallow riffles, good current, bottom mostly
bedrock and gravel, some mud. Trips—st. line to Rockford, 1
day; Rockford to Oregon, 1 long day; Oregon to Dixon, 20 mi., 1
day; Dison to Sterling, 1 day; Sterling to mouth, no dams, Ext. 50
mi. Ptgs.—Rockton Dam, in summer paddle head race canal to
paper mill water wheel, ptg. to river; Rockford Dam, stay clear of
head race, dangerous, land on split between dam lip and head race,
steep carry; Oregon Dam, easy ptg.; Dixon Dam, ptg. left. Sterling
—Rock Falls, 2 dams 1 mi. apart, ptg. E. side both; river heavily
polluted, fish below dams, channel cat, bullhead, crappie, walleye,
carp.

Saline River: Gallatin, Hardin cos., 9 hrs.; Equality to Saline
Landing; good canoeing, high clay banks, easy cruise. Trips—
brdg. S. of Equality to mouth Eagle River, 4 hrs.; Eagle River to
Saline Mines, 3 hrs.; Mines to Saline Landing, 2 hrs., fair fishing
below Saline Mines, bluegill, crappie, channel cat.

Salt Creek: McLean, DeWitt, Logan, Menard, Mason cos., E.
bdry. Logan Co. to mouth, 50 mi., good canoeing. Trips—Clinton
(Rtes. 10, 51, 54) to Lincoln, beautiful but very difficult to canoe,

brush piles, fences, fast current, sharp curves, submerged logs; Lincoln to Sangamon River, 1 day; few riffles, excellent canoeing, good for novice; Dam—Lincoln Dam; fair fishing, channel cat, green sunfish, rock bass, flathead cat, carp.

Sangamon River: Macon, Christian, Sangamon, Menard, Cass cos., 93 mi.; Lincoln Trail Homestead St. Park W. of Decatur to mouth at Beardstown; upper portion above co. rd. brdg. S. of Argenta not good, brush pile, fences, wading; below Lincoln Trail, good current, some riffles, sand and gravel bottom, muddy bottom below Springfield, sewage pollution from Decatur to Springfield, poor fishing; ptg. Springfield Dam, Petersburg Dam ptg. right; Springfield to Lincoln's New Salem Park., 1 day; then 14 mi. more to mouth Salt Creek; then 35 mi. to Beardstown.

Shoal Creek: Bond, Clinton cos., 57 mi., Hwy. 40 brdg. to Ill. 161 brdg.; easy canoeing except for brush piles, sand and mud bottom, high and steep banks. Trips—3 hrs. Rte. 40 to 143 to Jamestown, logjams and brush jams, 2 ptgs.; below Jamestown brdg., 3 ptgs.; 4 hrs. to Frogtown Rd.; U.S. 50 to Ill. 161 ruined by trash; catfish, carp fishing.

S. Vermillion River—Mid. Fork: Vermillion Co., no canoeing above Potomac; 10 mi., Power Plant Rd. N. of Kickpoo River St. Park to Danville, good trip except in low water, steep banks.

S. Vermillion River—N. Fork: Vermillion Co., poor canoeing, sharp bends, logjams, some wading, ptg. rapids 50 yds. above Bismark Rd., swift and treacherous current at Bismark Rd. Brdg. logjam, low-hanging vines and trees.

S. Vermillion River—Salt Fork: Champaign, Vermillion cos., 25 mi., Rte. 49 to jctn. with N. fork; shallow, sandy silt and clay bottom, forested banks, good canoeing, access limited to hwy. brdgs., bass fishing in Stoney and Jordon creeks, carp, sucker, panfish in Salt Fork.

Spoon River: Stark, Knox, Fulton cos., 120 mi., Elmore to mouth at Havana; good canoeing, sand, gravel, and some mud bottom, steep banks, water levels vary, some wading, best in spring, big logjam between Rte. 17 and Elmore Brdg., many brdg. access pts. Trips—Elmore to Wolf Brdg., 22½ mi.; Wolf Brdg. to London Mills, 20 mi., 1 day; London Mills to Rte. 9 brdg., 18½ mi.; Rte. 9 brdg. to Bernadotte, 22 mi.; Bernadotte to Havana, 36½ mi. Ptg. Bernadotte Dam, dangerous, start ptg. far from dam; end— Rte. 78 brdg., Havana; good catfish in deep pools.

Vermillion River: La Salle, Livingston cos.; 90 mi.; 5 mi. N. of Chatsworth to mouth; wild river, high bluffs, mostly gravel bottom, many riffles, great scenery, fences. Trips—N. of Chatsworth to Pontiac Dam, 30 mi., 1 day, tough canoeing; Pontiac Dam to Rt. 23, Streator, 28 mi.; Streator to Lowell Brdg., 17 mi.; below Lowell Brdg., high water only, experienced canoeists, 5-ft. waves, rapids, 10 mi. to Rte. 71. DANGER—Wildcat Chute aim just left of haystacks in center, Marquette Cement Co. Dam, run chute at right, turn to left with current to avoid rocks in center of opening; good fishing, carp, bass, bluegill, bullhead. Dam—Pontiac Dam, Marquette Cement Co.

(Credit for Ill. information—*Illinois Canoeing Guide*)

INDIANA

Blue River: Washington, Harrison, Crawford cos., 77 mi.; jctn. of mid. and W. forks to Ohio River at Leavenworth. Trips—jctn. S. of Salem to Fredericksburg, 19.5 mi.; Fredericksburg to St. Rd. 64 at Milltown, 23.8 mi.; Milltown to dam at Sharp's Mill, 12.9 mi.; Sharp's Mill to St. Rd. 62 at White Cloud, 6.3 mi.; White Cloud to Ohio River, 14.4 mi.; avg. fall per mi., 317 ft.; best portion for canoeing from Fredericksburg to Ohio River. Access— below Fredericksburg, above and below Milltown, Sharp's Mill,

White Cloud, Leavenworth. Ptgs.—above and below Milltown, at Sharp's Mill, above White Cloud.

Blue River: Henry, Rush, Shelby, Bartholomew cos., 45 mi.; Freeport Dam to Columbus; 1 ptg.

Eel River: Whitley, Wabash, Miami, Cass, Carroll, Tippecanoe cos., 74 mi. from brdg. on Wash. Rd. S. of Columbia City to Wabash River. Trips—Columbia City to South Whitley, 8.9 mi.; S. Whitley to Collamer Dam, 2.6 mi.; Collamer to Liberty Mills Dam, 6.2 mi.; Liberty Mills to N. Manchester Dam. 6 mi.; N. Manchester Dam to Laketon, 4.3 mi.; Laketon to Roann, 8.5 mi.; Roann to Denver, 14.4 mi.; Denver to Wabash River, 23.1 mi.; avg. fall per mi., 2.7 ft. Best portion for canoeing—S. Whitley to Logansport. Access—S. Whitley, Laketon, Roann, Denver, Logansport. Ptgs.—2 below S. Whitley, 1 below N. Manchester, 1 below Laketon, 2 below Roann, 2 below Denver, 1 at Lake Freeman.

Eel River: Putman, Clay, Owen, Greene cos., 56.5 mi.; from U.S. 40 at Manhattan to Worthington. Trips—U.S. 40 at Manhattan to jctn. with Mill Creek, 5.6 mi.; Mill Creek jctn. to Bowling Green, 13.3 mi.; Bowling Green to Worthington, 37.5 mi.; avg. fall per mi., 1.8 ft. Best portion from Hwy. 40 brdg. at Manhattan to Worthington. Access—Walnut Creek approx. 6 mi. above Mill Creek jctn., approx. halfway pt. between Mill Creek jctn. and Bowling Green, at Bowling Green, approx. 8 mi. below Bowling Green, approx. 6 mi. above Worthington, at Worthington. Ptgs.—Cataract Lake.

Fawn River: Steuben, LaGrange cos.; 20 mi. from Crooked Creek at Snow Lake to Mich. st. line. Ptgs.—3.

Kankakee River: St. Joseph, LaPorte, Starke, Porter, Jasper, Lake, Newton cos., 55 mi.; Kankakee St. Game Preserve to Ill. st. line. No ptgs.

Mississinewa River: Miami, Grant, Delaware, Randolph cos., 110

mi. from Ind.-Ohio line to Wabash River at Peru. Trips—Ind.-
Ohio line to Ridgeville, 12.5 mi.; Ridgeville to Albany, 15.5 mi.;
Albany to Eaton, 12.9 mi.; Eaton to Mattheus, 12.1 mi.;
Mattheus to Jonesboro—Gas City, 11.7 mi.; Jonesboro—Gas
City to Marion, 7.2 mi.; Marion to Redbridge, 25.7 mi.; Red-
bridge to Wabash River at Peru, 12 mi.; avg. fall per mi., 3.3 ft.
Best portion for canoeing from Eaton to Peru. Access—Eaton,
Marion, Peru. Ptgs.—S. of Mattheus, N. of Marion.

Muscatatuck River: Jefferson, Jennings, Scott, Jackson, Washington cos., 39 mi. from N. of Austin to Sparksville. No ptgs.

Pigeon River: La Grange Co., 35 mi. from dam to Mongo to
Mich. st. line. Ptgs.—4.

St. Joseph River: Elkhart, St. Joseph cos., 35 mi. from Bristol
west to Mich. st. line. Ptgs.—4.

Sugar Creek: Clinton, Boone, Montgomery, Parke cos.; 90.3 mi.
from source to Wabash River. Trips—source to U.S. Hwy. 421 at
Kirklin, 8.5 mi.; Kirklin to St. Rd. 39 at Thorntown, 10.6 mi.;
Thorntown to dam at Darlington, 13.1 mi.; Darlington to dam at
Crawfordsville, 10.2 mi.; Crawfordsville to Shades St. Park, 16.1
mi.; Shades St. Park to Turkey Run St. Park, 11.1 mi.; Turkey
Run St. Park to Wabash River, 12.5 mi.; Wabash River to U.S.
Hwy. 36 at Montezuma, 4.7 mi.; avg. fall per mi., 5 ft. Best por-
tion from Crawfordsville to Wabash River. Access—Thorntown,
at dam below Darlington, Yountsville, Montezuma. Ptgs.—dam
below Darlington, dam below Crawfordsville, dam below Turkey
Run St. Park.

Tippecanoe River: Kosciusko, Fulton, Marshall, Pulaski, White,
Tippecanoe cos., 75 mi. Best portion from Rochester to Lafayette;
avg. fall per mi., 2 ft. Access—Rochester, Leiters Ford, Monterey, Tippecanoe River St. Park, Winamac, Monticello. Ptgs.—2
(1 above Monticello, 1 at Lake Freeman).

Wabash River—Sec. A: Well, Huntington, Wabash, Miami, Cass,

Carroll, Tippecanoe cos. Total length of Wabash, 451 mi. from Ind.-Ohio st. line to Lafayette. Trips—Ind.-Ohio st. line to Linngrove brdg., 20.8 mi.; Linngrove brdg. to St. Rd. 1 at Bluffton, 11.9 mi.; Bluffton to St. Rd. 3 at Markle, 13.4 mi.; Markle to St. Rd. 105 at Andrews, 18.6 mi.; Andrews to St. Rd. 15 at Wabash, 14.2 mi.; Wabash to U.S. Hwy. 31 at Peru, 14.6 mi.; Peru to U.S. Hwy. 35 at Logansport, 18 mi.; Logansport to U.S. Hwy. 421 at Delphi, 23.8 mi.; Delphi to Main St. Brdg. at Lafayette, 14.2 mi.; avg. fall 2.2 ft. per mi. Access—all towns on river. Ptgs.—1 at Markle.

Wabash River—Sec. B: Tippecanoe, Warren, Parke, Vermillion, Vigo, Sullivan cos., 139 mi. Lafayette to Hutsonville. Trips—Main St. Brdg. at Lafayette to U.S. 41 brdg. at Attica, 23.9 mi.; Attica to U.S. 136 at Covington, 16.7 mi.; Covington to St. Rd. 32 at Perrysville, 6.8 mi.; Perrysville to U.S. 36 at Montezuma, 24.4 mi.; Montezuma to St. Rd. 63 at Clinton, 10 mi.; Clinton to U.S. 40 at Terre Haute, 15.9 mi.; Terre Haute to St. Rd. 154 at Hutsonville, Ill., 40.7 mi.; avg. fall per mi., 0.6 ft. Access— Lafayette, Attica, Montezuma, Clinton, Terre Haute, Hutsonville. No ptgs.

Wabash River—Sec. C: Sullivan, Knox, Gibson, Posey cos., 163 mi. from brdg. on St. Rd. 154 at Hutsonville, Ill., to Ohio River. Trips—brdg. at St. Rd. 154 at Hutsonville, Ill., to Merom, Ind., 7.2 mi.; Merom to Russellville, Ill., 25 mi.; Russellville to U.S. Hwy. 50 at Vincennes, Ind., 12.7 mi.; Vincennes to St. Francisville, Ill., 12.3 mi.; St. Francisville to St. Rd. 64 at Mt. Carmel, Ill., 21.0 mi.; Mt. Carmel to Crawleyville, Ind., 9.5 mi.; Crawleyville to U.S. 460 at New Harmony, Ind., 9.8 mi.; New Harmony to Maunie, Ill., 10.2 mi.; Maunie to St. Rd. 62 W. of Mt. Vernon, Ind., 9.5 mi.; St. Rd. 62 to Ohio River, 25 mi.; avg. fall per mi., 0.6 ft. Access—towns on river. Ptgs.—2 (1 above Mt. Carmel, 1 below New Harmony).

White River, E. Fork—Sec. A: Bartholomew, Jackson, Washington cos., 81 mi. from U.S. 31 brdg. at Edinburg to Sparksville.

Trips—Edinburg to Columbus, 16 mi.; Columbus to Azalia, 12.5 mi.; Azalia to dam N. of Seymour, 11.7 mi.; Seymour to Brownstown covered brdg., 17.4 mi.; Brownstown to Medora covered brdg., 10.6 mi.; Medora to Sparksville, 12.9 mi.; avg. fall per mi., 1.9 ft. Access—Columbus, Azalia, dam N. of Seymour, Brownstown, Medora, Sparksville. Ptgs.—2 (1 S. of Columbus, 1 N. of Seymour).

White River, E. Fork—Sec. B: Jackson, Laurence, Martin, Dubois, Daviess, Pike, Knox, Gibson cos., 174 mi. from Sparksville to Mt. Carmel, Ill. Trips—Sparksville to Tunnelton, 13.2 mi.; Tunnelton to Laurenceport, 4.5 mi.; Laurenceport to U.S. 50 Hwy. brdg. near Bedford, 12.1 mi.; U.S. 50 to Williams dam, 15 mi.; Williams dam to Shoals, 23.2 mi.; Shoals to Hindustan Falls, 13.4 mi.; Hindustan Falls to U.S. 231 brdg. near Haysville, 15.1 mi.; Haysville to St. Rd. 61 near Petersburg, 31 mi., Petersburg to Hazelton, 27 mi.; Hazelton to Mt. Carmel, 19 mi.; avg. fall per mi., 0.7 ft. Access—towns on river. Ptgs.—2 (1 at Williams dam, 1 at Hindustan Falls).

White River, W. Fork—Sec. A: Randolph, Delaware, Madison, Hamilton, Marion, Johnson, Morgan cos. 179.4 mi. source to Martinsville Brdg. near Paragon. Trips—source to McCullock Park at Muncie, 44.5 mi.; Muncie to Chesterfield brdg., 16.3 mi.; Chesterfield to St. Rd. 9 at Anderson, 7.8 mi.; Anderson to St. Rd. 13 at Perkinsville, 13.6 mi.; Perkinsville to Riverwood Dam, 10.4 mi.; Riverwood to St. Rd. 32 at Noblesville, 5.3 mi.; Noblesville to Broadripple dam, 19.9 mi.; Broadripple to U.S. Hwy. 40 at Indianapolis to St. Rd. 144 at Waverly, 20.6 mi.; Waverly to power-plant dam, 14.6 mi.; dam to St. Rd. 39 at Martinsville, 4.4 mi.; Martinsville to brdg. near Paragon, 10.2 mi. Best portion from Perkinsville to Paragon; avg. fall per mi., 3.2 ft. Access—towns along river. Ptgs.—8 (1 above Noblesville and 1 below, 1 above Broadripple and 1 below, 1 above Indianapolis and 2 below, 1 above Martinsville).

White River, W. Fork—Sec. B: Morgan, Owen, Greene, Daviess,

Pike, Gibson, Knox cos.; 179.3 mi. from brdg. S. of Paragon to Mt. Carmel, Ill. Trips—from brdg. S. of Paragon to Gosport brdg., 6.8 mi.; Gosport to McCormick's Creek St. Park, 9.8 mi.; St. Park to Spencer brdg., 2.5 mi.; Spencer to Freedom Brdg., 13.3 mi.; Freedom Brdg. to St. Rd. 157 at Worthington, 14.2 mi.; Worthington to St. Rd. 54 at Bloomfield, 9.7 mi.; Bloomfield to St. Rd. 58 near Elnora, 22.3 mi.; Elnora to St. Rd. 358 at Edwardsport, 20.6 mi.; Edwardsport to U.S. Hwy. 50 near Wash., 18.8 mi.; Wash. to St. Rd. 61 at Petersburg, 15.3 mi.; Petersburg to St. Rd. 56 at Decker, 23.9 mi.; Decker to Mt. Carmel, Ill., 22.1 mi.; avg. fall per mi., 1 ft. Access—towns on river. No ptgs.

Whitewater River: Fayette, Union, Franklin, Dearborn cos. 68.6 mi. Connersville to Lawrenceburg. Dangerous; experts only—fastest Ind. stream. Trips—St. Rd. 44 at Connersville to Laurel brdg., 13.2 mi.; Laurel to U.S. Hwy. 52 at Metamora, 5.8 mi.; Metamora to Brooksville, 11.2 mi.; Brooksville to St. Rd. 1 brdg. at Cedar Grove, 8.5 mi.; Cedar Grove to Harrison, O., 12.3 mi.; Harrison to Elizabethtown, O., 9.1 mi.; Elizabethtown to Ohio River, 6.2 mi.; Ohio River to Lawrenceburg, 2.3 mi. Best portion, Laurel dam to Ohio River. Avg. fall per mi., 2.7 ft. Access—Connersville, Alpine, Laurel dam, Metamora, Brooksville, Cedar Grove, Harrison. Ptg.—1 at Laurel dam.

(Credit for Indiana information—Dept. of Natural Resources, state of Indiana)

IOWA

Boone River: Webster City to the Des Moines River. Start—S. Bank, just below Millard's Brdg. (U.S. 60 crosses); 4.8-ft. drops per mi., muddy water; 1 hr. to Albright's Brdg.; banks hilly in spots; from Webster City to Belleville Brdg., 23 mi., 1 day, no ptgs. (Credit—*Iowa Canoe Trips*)

Des Moines River: Kalo to Lehigh, 11 mi., 3–4 hrs., slow current, no dams, no ptgs., most scenic part of river, some wading in low water. Access—Kalo, 6½ river mi. below Fort Dodge, 4 mi. S. from Hwy. 169 and 3 mi. through Ortho. Take-out—right downstream side above Lehigh Brdg. (Credit—*Iowa Canoe Trips*)

Iowa River: Alden to Liscomb, mostly shallow, slow current, sand and mud bottom except from Alden, 5 mi. above Iowa Falls to pt. below Eldora (deep, narrow valley, hard bottom, swift current, shallow). Large dam at Iowa Falls, below Alden ptg. right bank, steep path. Trips—Woods Hwy. 20 brdg. 1 mi. E. of Alden to Washington Hwy. 30 brdg. W. of Iowa Falls, 4¾ mi., 1 hr.; fast current, riffles; Iowa Falls to Crosser's Ford Brdg., 4 mi., 1¾ hrs.; Crosser's Ford Brdg. to Hughes Brdg., 5¼ mi., 1½ hr., watch out for throat-high barbed wire below Eagle City brdg.; Hughes Brdg. to Hardin City Brdg., 5 mi., 2 hrs.; Hardin City Brdg. to Steamboat Rock Dam, 6¼ mi., 3½ hrs., ptg., left bank; dam to Coal Bank Hill, 3 mi., 1¼ hrs. Take-out place—2 mi., ¾ hr. below, left bank, Pine Lake St. Park; Eldora to Indian Brdg., 18¼ mi., 6½ hrs., watch, for channel often crisscrosses river. (Credit —*Iowa Canoe Trips*)

Little Sioux: Linn Grove to Cherokee, 35½ mi., 2 days, top catfishing stream, 2-ft. drop per mi., slow current, narrow, no dams, no dangerous rapids, campsites scarce. Access—below main dam, Linn Grove, S.-side bank, take right channel at stream div. below Linn Grove, some logjams. Take-out—left bank, above Hwy. 39 brdg. and remains of old dam. Trips—Hwy. 10 brdg. to Cherokee Co. line, 1.9 mi.; co. line to Little Sioux access area, 2.7 mi.; Little Sioux to Nelson area, 1.5 mi.; Nelson to Martin area, 7 mi.; Martin to Barnes area, 3 mi. (Credit—*Iowa Canoe Trips*)

Raccoon River: Jefferson to Adel, 46¼ mi., 14 hrs., brdgs. far apart, no dangerous rapids, no dams, deep holes with sharp dropoffs. Access—S. of Jefferson near Hwy. 17 brdg., watch for fences across water. Trips—7½ mi., 2¼ hrs. to Squirrel Hollow Park. 2½ miles below, 1 hr. to Adkins brdg. 6½ mi. from here, 2 hrs. to Dawson Brdg. From Dawson Brdg. to Davey Hall Brdg. 5¾ mi. 2 hrs. 5–6 mi. beyond to hwy. brdg. S.W. of Minburn. From here to Garoutte Brdg., 4¼ mi., 1¼ hrs. On down to upper dam above Adelk, 4 mi., 1¼ hr. Trip can be extended 36½ mi. to Des Moines; 10¼ mi., 2 hrs. from Adel to Van Meter, ptg. Adel dam and powerhouse, 5 mi. more, 1 hr. to Walnut Woods St. Park; W. Des Moines Brdg., 4¼ mi., 1½ hrs. below Commerce Brdg., another 6¼ mi., 1½ hrs. to dam in park, Des Moines. Take out—right bank above dam, downstream from brdg. (Credit— *Iowa Canoe Trips*)

Red Cedar River: Ontario to Charles City, 4½ mi., 18½ hrs., excellent canoeing, good small-mouth bass fishing, no dangerous rapids, 4 easy ptgs., moderate current, good campsites, hard streambed. Access—E. bank, under brdg., Ontario. Trips—6¼ mi., 3½ hrs. to abandoned dam, no ptg.; 1½ mi., ½ hr. to mill brdg. and dam; ptg. here, right bank; dam to Hwy. S brdg., 1¼ mi., ¾ hr.; 5 mi., 1¼ hr. to W. Mitchell dam, ptg., left bank; dam to Iron Springs, 1¾ mi., ¾ hr.; Iron Springs to Hwy. 9 brdg., 1½ mi., ½ hr.; 1¼ mi., ½ hr. more to Spring Park Campsite; Campsite to Seeber Hwy. brdg., 1¼ mi., ½ hr.; 1¼ mi., ¾ hr. more to Sunny Brae Ctry. Club, ptg. footbridge; ¾ mi., ½ hr. more to Pierce Brdg.; Pierce to next brdg., 4½ mi., 2½ hrs.; next 4 mi., 1½ hrs. wild terrain to Fox Cottage and spring; 3½ mi., 2¼ hrs. to Floyd Brdg., Hwy. 218; Floyd to Charles City, 8 mi., 3 hrs. Take-out—right bank, 100 yds. above Main St. dam. (Credit—*Iowa Canoe Trips*)

Shell Rock River: Albert Lea to Nora Springs, 40 mi., 21 hrs.; Shell Rock River canoeable entire length, 100 mi., no information on 60 mi., shallow riffles, sand and limestone rubble bottom, open banks, 69 fences; from Albert Lea to Hwy. 65, flat marshland and meadowland, current not strong; past Hwy. 65 current faster, some rapids, waterfall, scenic country. Access—below dam, outlet of Albert Lea Lake, right bank, several brdgs., not more than 2 hrs. apart, most ½ hr. Take-out—below RR brdg. right bank, Nora Springs. (Credit—*Iowa Canoe Trips*)

Turkey River: Elgin to Garber, 34 mi., 2 days, narrow valley, rocky limestone bottom, 4 ft.–6 ft. rate of fall per mi., strong current, no dangerous rapids, dam at Elkader, some wading. Access —brdg. abutment, upstream side, left bank, Elgin. Trips—Elgin halfway pt., 18 mi., 5½ hrs.; Elkader to Garber, 5½ hrs. Ptg. —dam at Elkader, right bank, athletic field, 2 dams. Take-out— brdg. at Garber, right bank, below brdg. (Credit—*Iowa Canoe Trips*)

Upper Iowa River: Lime Springs to Kendalville, 24 mi., 14 hrs., beautiful stream, excellent small-mouth bass fishing, upper stretch shallow, riffles, sandbars. Best time—spring or early summer, deep holes, deep stretches, numerous fences. Access—1 mi. N. Lime Springs on rocky pt. below brdg. on right bank. Trips—Old Town dam to Foreston brdg., 3¾ mi., 2 hrs.; Foreston to Bronner's brdg., 4 mi., 3¼ hrs.; Bronner's to next brdg., 4 mi., 2¼ hrs., ptg. here around old dam on right bank; 5½ mi., 3 hrs. to Larkin brdg., left or W. channel goes around dam without ptg.; dam to good campsite, 2½ mi., 1½ hrs.; 1½ mi., ¼ hr. below Larkin brdg. to Daly's Flats brdg.; another mile, ½ hr. to Bigalk's brdg.; 2¾ mi., 1½ hrs. more to Clark's brdg.; 2½ mi., 1 hr. more to take-out place, right bank, above Kendalville brdg.; Kendalville to Decorah, 30 mi., 2 days, great scenery, swift current, sharp bends, pools and small rapids, 12 or more barbed-wire fences, some logjams, some wading. Access—N. side of river above brdg. over Hwy. 139 at Kendalville. Trips—Bluffton, halfway pt., 3 hwy. brdgs. and 1 suspension brdg. in first 7 mi., 3 hrs. below Kendalville; trout stream at Coldwater Creek; ¾ mi., ½ hr. below Coldwater Creek to hwy. brdg.; 2¾ mi. more, 1¼ hrs. to Bluffton Brdg., watch for fence under brdg.; 7 brdgs. below Bluffton, 1½ mi., ½ hr. to first, ½ mi., ¼ hr. more to Twin Brdg., largest rapids below Twin Brdg.; 5¼ mi., 1¾ hrs. to Waterfall from Twin Brdg.; Waterfall to Luther College, 6½ mi., 2¼ hrs., 4 brdgs. Take-out—above brdg., left bank, near Luther College.

(Credit—*Iowa Canoe Trips* and *A Guide to the Upper Iowa River*)

Volga River: Osborne to Garber, 12 mi., 7 hrs., a little river, not often canoed, flows through deep, narrow valley, high rolling hills, rock cliffs, sand, gravel, and rockbed, shallow, water level rises fast after rain, chocked with sand in lower stretches, wading necessary, dangerous in high water, good small-mouth bass fishing. Trips—put in left bank below Osborne brdg., 3¾ mi., 2¼ hrs. to Mederville brdg.; Mederville to Littleport, 4½ mi., 2¼ hrs.; Mederville to Elkport brdg. 7½ mi., 4½ hrs., ½ mile more to Garber brdg. Extended trip—Volga (8 mi. above Osborne brdg.) to Millville via the Turkey to pt. where Turkey enters Mississippi, 13½ mi., 4½ hrs. (Credit—*Iowa Canoe Trips*)

Wapsipinicon: Independence to Stone City, 50 mi., 24 hrs.; excellent fishing, some wading, 4 ptgs., parallels Cedar River, bottom sandy with some hard rock. Access—upstream from Hwy. 150 brdg. at Independence. Trips—6½ mi., 2½ hrs. to Old Iron Brdg.; Old Iron to Quasqueton Dam, 4½ mi., 1¾ hrs.; ptg. dam, right bank; dam to New Iron brdg., 6½ mi., 3¼ hrs.; New Iron to Troy Mills brdg. and dam, 3¾ mi., 1½ hrs., ptg., right bank; 9 mi., 4 hrs. more to 2 brdgs.; another 3½ mi., 1¼ hrs. to Central City brdg., ptg. dam below brdg., left bank; Central City to Jordon Grove brdg., 2¾ mi., 1¾ hrs.; 4 mi., 1½ hrs. more to Waubeek brdg.; 1½ hrs. below Waubeek, river narrows, logjams, ptg. left bank; Waubeek brdg. to Maetzold's brdg., 7½ mi., 5 hrs.; 2½ mi., 1¼ hrs. more to take-out. Take-out—right bank, above hwy. brdg., Stone City. (Credit—*Iowa Canoe Trips*)

Yellow River: Volney to the Mississippi, 18 mi., 9 hrs., beautiful, small stream, shallow, rocky bed, falls faster than other canoe streams, numerous rapids, hard on canoe, much wading, no dams, rapids not dangerous, fences, river rises rapidly after rain. Access —below brdg., left bank, Volney. Trips—1½ mi., 1 hr. to brdg.; 2 mi., 1 hr. to foot brdg.; brdg. to Hwy. 16 brdg., 1½ mi., 1 hr.; next 4½ mi., 2 hrs., good small-mouth bass, pools, and rapids; foot brdg. to next brdg., 1½ mi., ¾ hr. to take-out pt. Take-out —above Hwy. 13 brdg., right bank. (Credit—*Iowa Canoe Trips*)

KANSAS

Arkansas River: N.W. Bransom Run; Gray, Ford, Edwards, Pawnee, Borton cos.; from Charleston (near Garden City) to Wichita, 84 hrs.

Trip 1—Brdg. S. of Charleston to Dodge City, 16 hrs., sandy bottom, depth ranges from inches to several feet, poor fishing, no fast water, current 2–3 m.p.h., 2 ptgs.—diversion dam few miles E. of Ingalls and beaver dam E. of Howell. Obstacles—barbed-wire fences and felled trees E. of Howell. Some wading, good camping—cottonwood grove near Ingalls and cmpgrnd. at Cimarron (site of Indian raid by Dull Knife in 1878). (Credit—N. W. Bransom)

Trip 2—Dodge City to Ft. Dodge; 9 mi., 2 hrs. Put-in—City Park in Dodge City. Take-out—Coronado Brdg. near Ft. Dodge. Sandy bottom, some fallen trees. Ptg.—low-water dam near Ft. Dodge (can run with right water), good fishing, good camping sites, easy run.

Trip 3—Coronado Brdg. E. of Ft. Dodge to Ford, 14 mi., 5½ hrs., popular trip, sandy bottom, obstacles—old car bodies, may see deer.

Trip 4—Brdg. N. of Ford on Hwy. 154 to Hwy. 34 brdg., 8 mi., 2½ hrs. Obstacles—wire fences; some have electricity.

Trip 5—Hwy. 34 brdg. N. of Bucklin to St. Hwy. 183 brdg. S. of Kinsley, 35 mi., 11 hrs., ranch entry. No access for first 30 mi., seldom floated, excellent bow shooting of carp, several deer. Obstacles—fences and felled trees.

Trip 6—Brdg. 183 to Garfield, 18 mi., 6 hrs., farmland. Obstacles—fences and trees.

Trip 7—Brdg. S. of Garfield to Larned, 14 mi., 5 hrs., easy trip; Larned to Dundee, 18 mi., 6 hrs., 1 ptg.—diversion dam W. of Dundee.

Trip 8—Dundee to Raymond: Dale Y. Perkins Run, 35 mi.,

9½ hrs. Put-in—brdg. E. of Dundee. Take-out—Raymond. Lush growth on riverbanks, large trees, no fences, good campsites, sandy bottom, river wider here than at Dodge City. (Raymond was spot for holding cattle brought up trail from Texas for shipment to East.)

Trip 9—Raymond to Nickerson, Frank D. Dale Run, 35 mi., 9 hrs. Put-in—brdg. S. of Raymond. Take-out—brdg. S. of Nickerson. Sandy bottom, good campsites, no obstacles, good fishing.

Trip 10—Nickerson to Haven, John C. Burt Run, 30 mi., 8 hrs. Put-in—S. of Nickerson. Take-out—brdg. N. of Haven. River wider than above, several isles, right channel can be hard to find, sandy bottom, good campsites, good fishing, no obstacles.

Trip 11—Haven to Ridge Rd. Brdg. near Wichita, John C. Burt Run, 25 mi., 8 hrs. Put-in—brdg. N. of Haven. Take-out—E. side of Ridge Rd. Brdg., N. side of river. Wide river, very shallow, best time in spring or after rain, riverbanks low, good camping, cannot make run in low water.

(Credit—N. W. Bransom, Dale Y. Perkins, Frank D. Dale, and John C. Burt)

Caney River: Chautauqua Co.; Cedar Vale Dam to brdg. 1.5 mi., W. of Elgin, 20.6 mi., 14 hrs., many access pts., some wading over riffles, 2 dangerous rapids, 36 rapids—skill necessary, 10 other rapids, 3 small waterfalls—under 3-ft. drop, good campsites, best Mar.–June, avg. 4 ft.–5 ft. deep, catfish, bullhead, panfish, large-mouth bass. (Credit—James Nighswonger)

Lyons Creek: Dickinson, Geary cos.; brdg. ½ mi. S. of Lyons to brdg. ¾ mi. E. of Ureford, 20.7 mi., 13 hrs., no dif. rapids, many riffles, no dams, many access pts., many campsites, best spring–early summer, avg. 3 ft.–4 ft. deep, catfish, bullhead, panfish, others. (Credit—James Nighswonger)

Marais Dex Cygnes River: Miami Co.; brdg. ½ mi. E. of Osawatomie to S. end Miami Co. St. Lake, 20.2 mi., no rapids, few minor riffles, no ptgs., many campsites, avg. 4 ft.–5 ft. deep, catfish, large-mouth bass, panfish, others. (Credit—James Nighs-wonger)

Republican River: Cloud Co., from Concordia to Ames, 10 mi., 4½ hrs. Put-in—brdg. N. of Concordia. Take-out—at Ames where river bends S. near a paved rd., flat, wide, sandy bottom, soft sand, channel meanders, many sandbars, beautiful scenery, large trees, good camping. (Credit—Jay and Sandy Johnson, Jr.)

Spring River: Ottawa Co., Okla.; from Baxter Springs, Kan., below Dam to Oklahoma Rte. 10 and Twin Brdgs. at Park, Rte. 60, 24 miles, 2 days. Danger points—none. Dif. I–II. Obstacles—overhanging tree at end of Devil's Hollow. Ptg.—none. Dams—none. Limestone rock and gravel bottom, many campsites—private land; 1 access point—Promenade Brdg. at Rte. 10, beautiful stream and banks, history—Indians felt Devil's Hollow was an evil place; excellent fishing—bass. (Credit—John Helwic)

Verdigris River: Montgomery Co.; brdg. 2 mi. E. of Sycamore to brdg. 1½ mi. S. of Forty School, 20.4 mi. Limited access, several minor riffles, no major rapids, ptgs.—2 dams, 1 nav. dam, OK all year, 5 ft. avg. depth, scenic, gravel bars, small isles, catfish, bullhead, large-mouth bass, walleye, panfish. (Credit—James Nighswonger)

The following streams were also listed as desirable canoeing streams by Mr. George H. Mathews, planner, Planning Div., State of Kansas, Dept. of Econ. Development. Cottonwood River, Fall River, Kansas River, Mill Creek, Shoal Creek, and Spring Creek.

KENTUCKY

Kentucky has more free-flowing streams than any other state except Alaska. Canoeing on Kentucky's wild rivers is a rewarding but dwindling experience, as most streams are polluted by strip-mine acid, industrial waste, and sewage. Farm clearing and city sprawl have cut the list of wild rivers to a handful. Even the few rivers listed here are in danger of the Corps of Engineers' mark of progress, the dam.

The Red is destined to become a water-supply reservoir for the city of Lexington. The Big South Fork of the Cumberland is being studied for a possible hydroelectric dam site.

The Barren, Rolling Fork, Kentucky, and many other rivers in Kentucky may be used for canoe outings, but they lack the wilderness aspect of the rivers listed.

The best time to schedule canoe outings is from Apr. through June, although some streams may be floated year-round.

Check with local forest rangers about river conditions before planning an outing.

Cumberland River—N. Fork: USGS Wofford, Cumberland Falls, Sawyer, Dan Boone Natl. For., Redbird (near Williamsburg) to picnic area at Cumberland Falls State Park, 14 mi., starts in calm water, passes through shoals, ends in white water, wilderness, much wildlife, campfire permit needed. DANGER—falls below take-out pt., don't go beyond. Below falls at Cumberland Falls St. Park to Garrett's Dock in backwater of Lake Cumberland, 12 mi., most challenging run in Ky., narrow gorges, fast water, pools, lining may be necessary, study all rapids before running, private land. (Credit—Ron Stokeley)

Goose Creek: Clay Co.; Redbird Ranger Dist., Dan Boone Natl. For.; Rd. 421 to Rd. 66, 18 mi., 12 hrs., OK beginners, bass, cats, panfish, OK all season, ptg. 100 ft., slow flowing.

Greasy Creek: Bell Co., Redbird Ranger Dist., Dan Boone Natl. For. 12 mi., 8 hrs. Intermed. skill, ptg. 100 ft., run spring and fall, bass, cats, panfish, slow flowing.

Green River: USGS Mammoth Cave and Rhoda, Western Ky., 370 mi. long. Long pools broken by isles and shoals, excel. bass, crappie, catfish, and panfish, some muskie; Mammoth Cave Sec.

Dennison Ferry located where Hart-Edmonson Co. line crosses river to Houchins Ferry, 20 mi., obtain access and fire permit from Natl. Park Ser., beautiful trip, much wildlife, good camp-sites. (Credit—Ron Stokeley)

Jellico Creek: Whitley Co.; Williamsburg Ranger Dist., Dan Boone Natl. For.; Rd. 502 to Rd. 92, 6 mi., 10 hrs., slow flowing, ptg. 10 ft., run spring and fall, bass, cats, and panfish.

Kentucky River—Mid. Fork: Leslie Co.; Stanton Ranger Dist., Dan Boone Natl. For.; slow flowing, Rd. 421 to Rd. 257, 19 mi., 10 hrs., intermed. skill, ptg. 100 ft., bass, cats, panfish, run spring and fall.

Kentucky River—S. Fork: Owsley Co.; Dan Boone Natl. For., Redbird Ranger Dist.; Rd. 11 to Rd. 11, 9 mi., 8 hrs., intermed. skill, ptg. 100 ft., slow flowing, bass, cats, panfish.

Lake Cumberland: Pulaski Wayne cos.; Somerset Ranger Dist., Dan Boone Natl. For.; Rd. 1277 to Rd. 27, 30 mi., 16 hrs., lake travel, OK beginners, bass, cats, walleye, panfish, OK all year. Rd. 92 to Rd. 90, Stearns Ranger Dist., 45 mi., 20 hrs., experts only, no ptgs.

Licking River: Morgan Co.; Morehead Ranger Dist., Dan Boone Natl. For., Rd. 460 to Rd. 60, 54 mi., 2 days or 18 hrs., OK be-ginners, slow moving, no ptgs., muskie, catfish, panfish, OK all season. Rd. 460 to Rd. 985, 11 mi., 4 hrs.; Rd. 985 to Rd. 1274, 17 mi., 6 hrs.; Rd. 1274 to Rd. 60, 19 mi., 6 hrs.; Cave Run Dam will inundate upper part of Licking River soon, construction and clearing under way.

Little S. Fork River: Wayne, McCreary cos.; Stearns Ranger Dist., Dan Boone Natl. For.; Rd. 167 to Rd. 927, 32 mi., 30 hrs., slow flowing, experts only, ptg. 100 ft. bass, cats, walleye, panfish, OK all season.

Marsh Creek: McCreary Co.; Williamsburg Ranger Dist., Dan

Boone Natl. For.; Rd. 478 to Rd. 92, 10 mi., 10 hrs., slow flowing, intermed. skill, ptg. 500 ft., bass, cats, panfish, run spring and fall.

Red Bird River: Dan Boone Natl. For., Redbird Ranger Dist.; Rd. 66 to Rd. 11, 31 mi., 15 hrs., slow flowing, OK beginners, OK all season, ptg. 100 ft., bass, cats, panfish.

Red River: USGS Hazel Green, Pomeroyton, Slade, and Stanton. Powell, Wolfe cos.; Stanton Ranger Dist., Dan Boone Natl. For. River changes from white-water gorge section to shoals in Sky Brdg. sec. to calm river before meeting Ky. River; Rd. 746 to Rd. 213, 40 mi., bass, muskie, catfish; ptg. 800 ft., scenic, fast flowing, run in spring and fall, experts only in high water; gorge section, Rd. 746 to Rd. 715, 10 mi., rough sec., huge boulders, high cliffs, special danger falls at mouth of Calaboose Creek; Sky Brdg. sec., Rd. 715 to Rd. 77, 7 mi., OK in summer, River Sec., Rd. 77 to Rd. 213, 22 mi., 7 hrs., OK in summer, some private land— permission needed to camp. (Credit—Ron Stokeley)

Rockcastle River: USGS, Billows, Anno; Laurel, Pulaski cos.; London Ranger Dist., Dan Boone Natl. For.; Rd. 89 to Rd. 192, 34 mi., 24 hrs., experts only, ptg. 100 ft., bass, muskie, catfish, panfish, run spring and fall; Rd. 89 to Rd. 25 to Rd. 80, 12 mi., 6 hrs.; Rd. 8 to Rd. 192, 18 mi., 10 hrs., beautiful scenery. DANGER—narrows at end of run—ptg. on old logging road on right if necessary. Excel. fishing. (Credit—Ron Stokeley)

Rockcastle River—Mid. Fork: Jackson Co.; Berea Ranger Dist., Dan Boone Natl. For.; Rd. 89 to Rd. 25, slow flowing, OK beginners, 12 mi., 6 hrs., ptg. 100 ft., bass, catfish, panfish, run spring and fall.

Rockcastle River—S. Fork: Laurel Co.; Berea Ranger Dist., Dan Boone Natl. For.; Rd. 30 to Rd. 25, 13 mi., 8 hrs., OK beginners, ptg. 100 ft., run spring and fall, bass, muskie, catfish, panfish, slow flowing.

Roundstone Creek: Rockcastle Co.; Berea Ranger Dist., Dan Boone Natl. For.; Rd. 25 to Rd. 490, 8 mi., 6 hrs., slow moving, run in spring and fall, OK beginners, bass, catfish, panfish, ptg. 70 ft.

Russell River: See description under Virginia.

Sinking Creek: Laurel, Pulaski cos.; London Ranger Dist., Dan Boone Natl. For.; slow flowing, 10 mi., 6 hrs. OK beginners, no ptgs., bass, cats, walleye, panfish, run in spring and fall.

Station Camp Creek: Jackson Co.; Berea Ranger Dist., Dan Boone Natl. For.; Rd. 89 to Rd. 89, 11 mi., 8 hrs., OK beginners, ptg. 1,500 ft., run spring and fall, bass, catfish, panfish, slow flowing.

Sturgeon Creek: Owsley, Clay cos.; Berea Ranger Dist., Dan Boone Natl. For.; Rd. 587 to Rd. 399, 10 mi., 6 hrs., OK beginners, ptg. 100 ft., bass, muskie, catfish, panfish, run spring and fall, slow flowing.

LOUISIANA

Amite River: St. Helena and E. Feliciana par. From brdg. at La. 10 to La. 37 brdg., 7 hrs., OK year-round, some wading in low water, many sandbars, remote, nice trip, no partic. danger. (Credit —Michael Osborn)

Atchafalaya Basin (Bayou Plaquemine, Upper Grand River, Little Tensas Bayou, Atchafalaya River, Charenton Drainage and Navigation Canal, Bayou Teche): Iberville and St. Martin Par.; from Bayou Plaquemine in downtown Plaquemine to St. Martinville, 111 mi., 6 days. Semiwilderness area, thick fors., flood plain basin, much wildlife, incl. alligators, deer, bear, snakes; excellent fishing and hunting. Obstacles—many wide expanses of water to cross, danger in high winds, after start—60 mi. to next store, much paddling against current.

Trip 1—Bayou side of Plaquemine Loch to sandbars on Upper Grand River, 1 day, first 10 mi. down Bayou Plaquemine past Ind. Vil. and mouth of Gross Tete, then next 9 mi. E. on Upper Grand River to sandbars. Ptg.—E. Atchafalaya Basin levee (19 mi. from put-in—accessible by auto).

Trip 2—sandbars to Chicot oil field, 1 day (42 mi. from put-in), from sandbars to Little Tensas Bayou, down Little Tensas Bayou to Lake Mongoulois, down Lake Mongoulois to jctn. with Atchafalaya River, down Atchafalaya River to Chicot oil field (water and ice available here).

Trip 3—Chicot oil field to Charenton Beach, 1 day (60 mi. from put-in), continue down Atchafalaya River into Grand Lake, to Charenton Beach.

Trip 4—Charenton Beach to Jeanerette, 1 day (73 mi. from put-in), continue up Grand Lake to Charenton Floodgate. Ptg.—W. Atchafalaya Basin levee, on past ptg. into Charenton Drainage and Navigation Canal, continue in canal to jctn. with Bayou Teche, pass Ind. Res., pass plantation homes.

Trip 5—Jeanerette to Loreauville, 1 day (93 mi. from put-in), continue up Bayou Teche to New Iberia and on to Loreauville, historic sites—museum and plantation homes on this trip.

Trip 6—Loreauville to St. Martinville, 1 day (111 mi. from put-in), continue up Bayou Teche through Keystone Loch to St. Martinville. (Credit—*Canoeing in Louisiana* and Jim Evans)

Bogalusa Creek: Wash. Par. From brdg. at Par. rd. between St. Rds. 60 and 439 (about 1 mi. N. of Plainview on St. Rd. 60), to Cassiday Park in city of Bogalusa, 7 mi., 5 hrs., Dif. I–II, smooth water most of way, no white water, many fallen trees, low limbs, sandy bottom or rocky in swift shallows, muddy in slow, deep water, water level best in winter, best time is day after medium rain, low in summer, fishing fair (bass and bream), sewerage dumped nearer to Bogalusa, area occupied by Choctaw Indians before white man, arrowheads sometimes found on rocky beaches, don't drink water from creek, several beaches for camping, creek continues below Bogalusa to Pearl River but much pollution below Bogalusa. (Credit—Lou Major, Jr., Steve Major, and Bruce Busby)

Bogue Chitto River: Walthall Co., Miss.; Wash. Par., La. From U.S. 98 Crossing at Conerly, Miss., to Hwy. 437 at Enon, La., 44 mi.; moderately experienced canoeists, OK year-round except flood and drought. Put-in—U.S. 98 brdg., left side. Other access pts.—Hwy. 48, Miss., Hwy. 438, La. (poor access—not advised), Hwy. 38 W. of Clifton, boat ramp S. of Franklinton, Enon at Hwy. 437. Good fishing, swimming in spots, beautiful river. Start to Hwy. 438, 16 mi.; Hwy. 438 to Franklinton, 14 mi.; (Credit— *Canoeing in Louisiana*). Franklinton to Sun, Rick Norton's Run, 41 mi.; Franklinton to Enon, 18 mi., river forks 8 mi. below Franklinton but joins ½ mi. later, avg. current, 2 m.p.h. Put-in —public boat ramp at Franklinton on Hwy. 16 at N. end of Riverside Med. Cent.; Enon to Isabel, 9 mi. Put-in—rd. under Hwy. 437 brdg.; Isabel to Sun, 14 mi. Put-in—turn S. on gravel rd. at Isabel and go ¼ mi. to river. Camping—Five Lakes Cmpgrnd. 9 mi. below Isabel (pay facilities with showers). General information from Franklinton to Sun, beautiful river, mixed pines and hardwood, clean water, good swimming and fishing, fishing best to Isabel from June to winter—use artificial bait and flies for bream and bass, use trotline for catfish. Very little pollution, much wildlife, much solitude, local people helpful to canoeists. DANGER— from Dec. to Mar. floods are common, river can rise 9 ft. in 24 hrs.; Lower Bogue Chitto—below Sun, totally different from above, maze of sloughs and old lakes, should have guide, can paddle for day without seeing land. Put-in—Sun boat ramp (only good put-in); from ramp paddle S. in canal to river—1 mi. DANGER—1 mi. after reaching river, low-water dam, DON'T RUN—LIVES HAVE BEEN LOST HERE. Ptg. around dam, 100 ft., swamp beautiful but easy to get lost in, don't bother pigs in swamp (pigs belong to locals who don't like canoeists). (Credit —Michael Osborn and Rick Norton)

Calcasieu River: See description under Whiskey Chitto Creek in Louisiana.

Comite River: E. Feliciana, E. Baton Rouge par. From the Wilson-Clinton Hwy. in E. Feliciana Par. to Dyer Rd. in E. Baton Rouge Par.

Dugdemona River: Winn, Bienville, Jackson par. From Hwy. 4 to entrance into Little River.

Kisatchie Bayou: Natchitoches Par. In Kisatchie Natl. For. S. of Natchitoches, from Kisatchie Falls Rd. to Cypress Rd., 35 mi.; get maps from U.S. For. Ser., P.O. Box 2128, Natchitoches, La. 71457. DANGER—very dangerous in high water, most of river too shallow to canoe most of year, beautiful white-sand streambed, clean water. Start to Bayou Rd., 5 mi.; Bayou Rd. to Kisatchie Creed prim. camp, 2 mi.; Kisatchie Creed prim. camp to Longleaf Trail, 8 mi.; Longleaf Trail to Cypress Rd., 20 mi. (Credit—*Canoeing in Louisiana*)

Pushepatapa Creek: Wash. Par. From La.-Miss. st. line to its entrance into the Pearl River.

Saline Bayou: Natchitoches Par. within Kisatchie Natl. For.; Cloud Crossing Rec. Area to Old Salt Works near Goldonna, 10 mi., 6 hrs. Obstacles—fallen trees and logjams, snags and cypress knees, mosquitoes from May to Aug. Beautiful trip. Other trips—Old Salt Works to La. 156 brdg., 2 mi.; La. 156 brdg. to Saline Lake, 5 mi.; Bayou floatable Dec. to mid-July. (Credit—*Canoeing in Louisiana*)

Six Mile Creek: Vernon, Allen par. From its origin in Vernon Par. to its entrance into the Calcasieu River.

Spring Creek: Rapides Par. From Otis to Cocodice Lake in Rapides Par.

Tangipahoa River: Pike Co., Miss.; Tangipahoa Par., La. From

Chattawa, Miss., to Lake Pontchartrain, 39 hrs. Put-in—unnumbered st. hwy. brdg. 1 mi. E. of Chattawa, Miss., river not canoeable at low water, much wading except in high water. Other access pts.—Hwy. 27 near Osyka, Miss., Hwy. 38 near Kentwood, La., Hwy. 1057 near Tangipahoa, La., Hwy. 10 near Arcola, La., Hwy. 16 near Omite, La., Hwy. 40 near Independence, La., Hwy. 442 near Tickflaw, La., Hwy. 443; Chattawa to Osyka, 2 hrs., no good in low water, some wading always except high water, best spring and fall; Osyka to Kentwood, 5 hrs., picturesque, narrow channel, swift, deep, some logjams, good camping; Kentwood to Tangipahoa, 4 hrs., part of trip narrow river and deep, sandbars in part, good camping, swimming, and fishing. Tangipahoa to Arcola, 4½ hrs., OK year-round, many sandbars, some tricky spots, very good stretch; Arcola to Amite, 2½ hrs., nice sandbars, good pan fishing and swimming, good for beginners. Amite to Independence, 4 hrs., wide with sandbars, shallow in spots, good camping. Independence to Tickflaw, 2½ hrs., some sand beaches, slow-moving deep water. Tickflaw to Hwy. 443, 2½ hrs., slow, deep river, picturesque. Hwy. 443 to Pontchatoula Beach, 6 hrs., dull, power boats on river. Pontchatoula Beach to Lake Pontchartrain, 6 hrs., not recommended, marshy banks, power boats. (Credit—*Canoeing in Louisiana* and Michael Osborn)

Vermillion River: Lafayette and Vermillion par. From Beaver Park near Lafayette to New Flanders Rd. Brdg., 8 mi., 1 day. Put in—Amer. Leg. Home boat lndg. on Surrey St. N. of brdg. over Vermillion. Other access pts.—boat lndg. at Pinhook Brdg. (U.S. Hwy. 90 S.). Take out—Thibodeaux's shell yard. Distances—Amer. Leg. Home to Pinhook Brdg., 3 mi. Pinhook Brdg. to take-out—8 mi.; much pollution, slow river, many campers and fishermen. (Credit—*Canoeing in Louisiana*)

Whiskey Chitto Creek and **Calcasieu River:** Allen Par.; Mittie to Indian Village, OK for beginners, 29 mi. Put-in—La. 26 brdg. 1 mi. S.E. of Mittie. Other access pts.—Carpenter's Brdg. (take La. 410 S. of Mittie, turn left at jctn. with La. 1155, on to La. 1147, turn left to brdg.), pub. beach near southern Silica of La., Calcasieu Brdg. on U.S. 190. Take-out—turn right at Pentecostal

Church in Indian Village and on to river—small park there. Distances—Mittie to Carpenter's Brdg., 9 mi.; Carpenter's Brdg. to pub. beach, 11½ mi.; pub. beach to Calcasieu River Brdg., 1½ mi.; Calcasieu River Brdg. to Indian Village, 7 mi. Fishing—small-mouth bass. Other data—may see alligators, good campsites. (Credit—*Canoeing in Louisiana*)

The following trails were listed by the Louisiana Wild Life and Fisheries Commission as canoeable but very rough (many ptgs., etc.).

Bayou Bodcau: Bossier, Webster par. From the La.-Ark. st. line to Hwy. 157 in Bossier Par.

Bayou Dorcheat and **Lake Bistineau:** Webster Par. Hwy. 157 brdg. E. of Springhill to Lake Bistineau, 40½ mi., bald cypress swamps en route; through Cotton Valley oil field area the bayou is straight, below Cotton Valley oil field swampy, difficult to find course in swamp, excellent fishing. Hwy. brdg. 157 to Hwy. 2 brdg., 6 mi.; Hwy. 2 brdg. to Hwy. 160 brdg., 6½ mi.; Hwy. 160 brdg. to Hwy. 80 brdg., 18 mi.; Hwy. 80 brdg. to Hwy. 164 brdg., 8 mi; Hwy. 164 brdg. to Lake Bistineau, 2 mi. (Credit—*Canoeing in Louisiana*)

Bayou Sara: W. Feliciana Par. From the La.-Miss. st. line to its entrance into the Miss. River.

Bayou Teche: St. Martin Par. Breaux Bayou L'Outre: Union, Ouachita par. From the La.-Ark. st. line to its entrance into the Ouachita River. Breaux Brdg. to Evangeline Oak St. Martinville, 14 mi., 1 day; sluggish, meandering stream, semitropical growth. Put-in—behind Veteran's Home on La. 31 S. of Breaux Brdg. Other access pts.—Thibodeaux's shell yard in parks on La. 347, concrete launching ramp in Longfellow-Evangeline St. Park. Take-out—Evangeline Oak past brdg. in St. Martinville. Distances—start to Thibodeaux's shell yard, 6½ mi.; Thibodeaux's shell yard to Longfellow-Evangeline St. Park, 5½ mi., Long-

fellow-Evangeline St. Park to St. Martinville, 2 mi. (Credit—
Canoeing in Louisiana)

Black Lake Bayou: Red River, Winn, Bienville, Webster, Claiborne par. From the Webster-Bienville par. line to Hwy. 155 in Natchitoches Par.

Tchefuncte River: Wash., St. Tammany, Tangipahoa par. From its origin in Tangipahoa Par. to its entrance into Lake Pontchartrain.

Ten Mile Creek: Vernon, Allen par. From its origin in Vernon Par. to its entrance into Whiskey Chitto Creek.

Thompson Creek: E. Feliciana, W. Feliciana par. From the La.-Miss. st. line to the entrance of Karr Creek.

Tickflaw River: St. Helena, Livingston par. From the La.-Miss. st. line to its entrance into Lake Maurepas.

Trout Creek: La Salle Par. From Hwy. 8 to its entrance into Little River.

The additional following trails were listed by the State Parks and Recreation Commission as excellent canoe trails:

Amite River: E. Feliciana, St. Helena, E. Baton Rouge, Livingston par.

Bayou Bartholomew: Morehouse Par.

Bayou Chitto: Wash., St. Tammany par.

Bayou des Canes: Acadia, St. Landry, Evangeline par.

Bayou Dorcheat: Webster Par.

Bayou Ribolette: Grant, Rapides par.

Bayou Toro: Sabine, Vernon par.

Beckwith Creek: Beauregard, Calcasieu par.

Blind River: St. James, Ascension, Livingston par.

Calcasieu River: Vernon, Rapides, Allen, Jefferson, Davis, Calcasieu par.

Chappepeela: Tangipahoa Par.

Cocodrie Bayou: Concordia Par.

Corney Creek: Claiborne, Union par.

Fish Creek: Grant Par.

Hickory Branch: Beauregard, Calcasieu par.

Little River: Catahoula, Grant, LaSalle, Rapides par.

Mid. Fork of Lake D'Arbonne: Claiborne, Union par.

Pearl River: Wash., St. Tammany par.

Tangipahoa: Tangipahoa Par.

Whiskey Chitto: Allen, Vernon, Beauregard par.

According to the Thibodeaux Chamber of Commerce, "any bayou located around this area is ideal for canoe trails." They listed:

Bayou La Fourche

Bayou Teche

Grand Bayou

MAINE

Note: It is strongly recommended that you purchase and consult the *AMC New England Canoeing Guide* for further information.

A special word of thanks to Stewart Coffin, who generously shared his notes with me. These were collected over many years by a great canoeist.

Allagash Wilderness Waterway: A 92-mi.-long trail through the beautiful for. of northern Maine. The trip begins at Telos Lake and ends at W. Twin Brook. Many lakes, streams, and ponds are in the trail. It is 5 mi. across Telos Lake through Round Pond to Chamberlain Lake and 10 mi. from foot of Chamberlain to Lock Dam. A side trip for experienced canoeists is a 6-mi. trip with pole and paddle up Allagash stream 3 mi. W. of Lock Dam. Only canoes are permitted on Allagash stream and lake.

From Lock Dam take short ptg. along rte. for 12 mi. to Eagle Lake, then 2 mi. through thoroughfare and 5 mi. more of lake to Churchill Dam. A 9-mi. trip below dam through Chase Rapids to Umsaskis Lake, Chase Rapids famed for white-water canoeing takes experienced man in stream. From Umsaskis Lake to thoroughfare at Long Lake—5 mi. Another 5 mi. through Long Lake into 10-mi. run downriver to Round Pond, which is 3 mi. wide. An 18-mi. trip to Allagash Falls with ⅓-mi. ptg. and run of 8 mi. to W. Twin Brook. W. Twin Brook is end of Allagash Wilderness Waterway but many prefer to continue another 5 mi. to Allagash Village at confluence of St. John and Allagash rivers. It is 15 mi. downriver to St. Francis and 15 more to Fort Kent.

The most taxing stretch of water on the Allagash extends 9 mi. from Churchill Dam to Umsaskis Lake. Scenic climax of trip is 40-ft.-high Allagash Falls.

Campsites are designated and given on first-come basis. Excellent fishing for brook trout, togue, and lake whitefish.

Access—Road access to the waterway is limited, in general, to the Telos-Chamberlain area, Churchill Dam, Umsaskis Lake, and the Michaud Farm.

Telos and Chamberlain can be reached over three different rtes. via Greenville, Millinocket, or Patten.

From Greenville, one drives in a northerly direction to Ripogenus Dam, across the dam, and N. to Nesowadnehunk Lake Dam. From here it is approximately 23 mi. to the ranger station at Chamberlain brdg.

The route beginning at Millinocket proceeds N. toward Ripogenus Dam and, branching off at the entrance to Baxter St. Park, continues into the park, turning W. 6 mi. after crossing Nesowadenehunk Lake Dam. It is approximately 17 mi. from this turnoff to the ranger station at Chamberlain brdg.

Telos and Chamberlain can also be reached by traveling 50 mi. W. from Patten on Grand Lake Rd., across northern Baxter St. Park.

Umsaskis Lake is roughly 55 mi. W. of Ashland on the American Realty Road, and Churchill Lake about 23 mi. W. and S. of Umsaskis. The road is owned jointly by the Great Northern and International Paper companies. Great Northern charges a road fee for recreational use of the first part of the road. A permit is required for use of the road W. of Musquacook Lake, and must be obtained in advance from International Paper Company, Chisholm, Me. 04222, or picked up at the company office in Ashland.

Motorists en route to the Allagash can reach Greenville, Millinocket, Patten, Ashland, or Allagash Village via st. hwys. Greenville is on St. Rte. 6–15, Millinocket on Rte. 157 off Interstate 95. Patten is on Rte. 11 off Interstate 95, Ashland on Rte. 11, and Allagash Village on Rte. 161.

Private roads into the waterway are part of a larger system maintained entirely at landowner expense, designed for movement of for. products and fire equipment. Trucks and equipment have the right of way.

(Credit—Allagash Wilderness Waterway)

Aroostook River: Fly in to Chase, Millimagasset, or Millinocket lakes; Chase Lake and Munsungan Stream to Aroostook River. A guide is advisable. A 16-mi. trip with 1 ptg. (Munsungan Falls) can be run by experts, but has blind drop; 8½ mi.; scenic with continuous rapids Dif. I, II, Millinocket Lake, and stream to Aroostook River is 6 mi. with mixed smooth water and rapids. First couple mi. rough to outlet of Millimagasset Lake, a pretty lake—a good alternative or side trip, part of this trip for experts only.

Attean Lake: Trip—40 mi., 3 days, 2–4 ptgs., Jackman Wood Pond, Attean Lake, 1½ mi. ptg. to Holeb Pond and Stream, return to Jackman by Moose River, inquire directions to avoid falls.

Bagaduce River: Walker Pond to Castine, 15 mi., tidewater with coves, bays, etc. (check sluice under brdg. at N. Brookside before running; tide affects it markedly).

Baskahegan Stream: Carol to Baskahegan Lake, 12 mi.; mostly smooth, scenic, canoe during high water; med. high water only; 3 rips, 1 sharp; Baskahegan Lake and Stream to Mattawamkeag River, 24 mi. mostly smooth, 1–3 ptgs. (1 dam, 2 rapids).

Bear River: USGS sheets Old Speck Mtn., Bethel. Upper part above Screw Augar Falls too steep for canoeing, below falls some canoeable spots but river small with impassable drop—don't run. From N. Newry to brdg. in Newry, 6 mi., small river, steep drops first mi., ptg. or line—very dangerous ledge where Branch Brook enters from left under a brdg., some rapids below ledge with Dif. I, good current, wooded banks, clear water. (Credit—Stewart Coffin)

Belgrade Lakes Circle Trip: 32–41 mi., 2 days, smooth, scenic, 4 ptgs. N. Pond to Great Pond to Long Pond to Belgrade Stream to Messalonskee Lake to Oakland, a few miles from starting place.

Big Black River: Canadian crossing and private road access or from Rte. 24 in Quebec. Rte. 24 to St. John River, 30 mi.

Stretches of quick water with continuous rapids, some very rough. Guide service strongly urged.

Cabbossee Stream and Lakes: 41 mi., 2 days, smooth, pleasant, 4 easy ptgs. Torsey Lake to Maranacook Lake to Annahessacook Lake to Cabbosseecontee to Cabbossee Stream (through Pleasant Pond) to dam at Gardiner.

Carrabassett River: USGS sheets—Little Bigelow Mtn., Kingfield, Anson. Upper part good water run, Dif. I, II, in med. water, rocky stream, clear water, run early May; from Carrabassett to N. Anson, 31 mi.

    Trip 1—Carrabassett Village—not canoeable. Put-in—brdg. in Carrabassett or st. campsite, rapids continuous to Kingfield, long easy ones and short tough ones, don't run in high water. Take-out—1 ft. above Kingfield Dam.

    Trip 2—Kingfield to N. Anson, 20 mi. DANGER—1 impassable drop in E. New Portland and Falls in N. Anson, other parts combine quick water and smooth. Take-out—above E. New Portland; check carefully before canoeing. (Credit—Stewart Coffin)

Chain of Ponds: 5–7 mi., smooth, scenic, beautiful; 1 ptg. to N. Branch Dead River to Flagstaff Lake, 15 mi. mixed smooth and rapids, 2–3 ptgs. Flagstaff Lake to Long Falls Dam; 16 mi. mixed smooth and rapids with ptg. at Long Falls Dam. Continue to Grand Falls (through marsh to old log dam, out on left ¼ mi., hike to Grand Falls and return).

China Lake and **Stream:** To Sebasticook River near Kennebec River a few rapids in stream; 3–4 carries.

Chiputnecook Lakes: Grand Lake (east of Orient), Spednik Lake to Vanceboro, 36 mi. (much more available), mostly wild river area, river sec. past For. City, 1 ptg. (dangerous or impassable drop); St. Croix River below Vanceboro should be run only by well-experienced canoeists, most rapids Dif. III and IV.

Crooked River: Songo Pond (Rte. 5 below Bethel) to N. Waterford, 10 mi.; mixed smooth and rapids, scenic, canoe during high water; to Bolster's Mills, 25 mi.; 1 mi. steep rapids, then mostly smooth scenic combined with mixed smooth and rapids, some sharp rapids for 1¼ mi., and some ½-mi. stretches hard and intermediate; 2–3 ptgs. at impassable drops to Songo River, 22 mi. easier; 1 rapid, 2 ptgs. to Sebago Lake.

Crooked River: USGS sheets—Norway, Sebago Lake. From Songo Pond to Sebago Lake, 60 mi.

Trip 1—Songo Pond to N. Waterford. Put-in—Rte. 5 below Bethel, 10 mi. mixed smooth and rapids, scenic, canoe in high water only.

Trip 2—N. Waterford to Rte. 118 brdg., 11 mi. Put-in—N. Waterford sawmill, first mi. steep, then 3 mi. smooth with few small rapids to brdg. N. of Pappoose Pond, cliffs of 1 ft. 1 mi. below Pap Pond, then 3 mi. shallow to Iron Stringer Brdg., then 3 mi. slow and winding to 118 brdg.

Trip 3—Rte. 118 brdg. to Bolster's Mills, 14 mi. Nice, 1 day, first 4 mi. winding and slow, then sharp rapids to Sodom Brdg. DANGER—don't run first rapid. DANGER—impassable falls on this section, then shallow rapids to brdg., below Frost Corner smooth water at first, then dif. rapids, then quiet stretch, then intermed. rapids, then good current to town park above Ryefield brdg., then slow water to Bolster's Mills.

Trip 4—Bolster's Mills to Sebago Lake, 24 mi. Ptg.—dam at Bolster's Mills, dif. rapids below, then still water to Scribner's Mill. Ptg.—left at dam at Scribner's Mills, ½ mi. rapids below, then fair current to Ede's Mills. Ptg.—broken dam at Ede's Mills—left side, then fair current to Rte. 11 brdg., then 2 mi. to U.S. 302 brdg., last mile uninteresting, poor current, muddy, then 6 mi. to Sebago Lake, very crooked, slow.

(Credit—Stewart Coffin)

Cupsuptic River: USGS sheets—Cupsuptic. Sec. above Big Canyon is remote and uncanoeable; below Big Canyon to Big Falls, encircled by mtns., no information. Below Big Falls, 8 mi., good canoeing. Put-in—logging camp below Big Falls. Access—private rd. of Brown Paper Co., first mi. fast current with shallow rapids, can't canoe in late summer; next 3 mi. to brdg. below Camp Dorothy—good current, then 2 mi. slow current to Little Falls. Ptg.—Little Falls—¼ mi. on right side, then 2 mi. slack water to Rte. 16 and Cupsuptic Lake. (Credit—Stewart Coffin)

Damariscotta River and **Lake:** Circle trip, 50 mi., 3 days; Damariscotta Mills up lake, E. then S. through bay, ptg. 1½ mi. to Pemaquid Pond and River, to Pemaquid (ptg. here and at Bristol), Tidewater, cross John Bay (only experienced canoeists in favorable weather) to S. Bristol, upriver to starting place.

Dead River—N. Branch: OK into summer. Alt. put-in—Arnold Pond through Mud Pond through Horseshoe Pond, then down Horseshoe Stream to Chain of Ponds, 6 mi., run in high water only, see description of Horseshoe Stream. First 5 mi. after put-in on Chain of Ponds, pleasant, campsite on Chain of Ponds. Ptg.—small dam at end of Ponds, first mi. of N. Branch rapid and smooth, next mile mostly smooth, good current. Ptg.—small falls above right campsite, then 11 mi. smooth and rapids to Eustis. Line—log dam few mi. above Eustis, sharp pitches below dam. Take-out—lndg. in Eustis or ptg. around dam and continue into Flagstaff Lake. (Credit—Stewart Coffin)

Dead River—S. Branch: USGS sheets—Kennebago Lake, Stratton. Upper part from Rte. 16 brdg. at Dallas School through gorge, not recommended, first 2 mi. smooth, then small rapids near st. campsite, then gorge, might be run by expert, 2 ptgs. in gorge, mod. rapids for 3 mi. above Langtown Mill, next 6 mi. to brdg. mostly smooth. From Rte. 16 at Grant Farm Brdg. to Flagstaff Lake, 8 mi., first 4 mi. smooth with good current, rapids start 1 mi. above Lutton Brook, rapids of Dif. III for 1½ mi. to Nash Stream, riverbed mostly shallow, a few deep pools, banks heavily wooded, last 1½ mi. to Flagstaff Lake not as steep. Take-out—near third dirt rd. on right after entering Flagstaff Lake or continue to Rte. 27 brdg. to several pts. on lake. Obstacles—pulpwood in lake. (Credit—Stewart Coffin)

Dennys River: Meddybemps Lake outlet to Dennysville, 17 mi.; mixed smooth and rapids, scenic; 4 ptgs. (3 dams, 1 steep drop); several rips and short rapids.

Depot Stream: Guide service strongly urged. Canadian crossing and private-road access. Depot Mtn. to Big Black River, 10 mi.; fast water; 2 mi. rapids.

E. Machias River: A guide is advisable. Pocamoonshine Lake to E. Machias, 43 mi., much of it through wilderness, mixed (smooth and rapids), canoe during high water, 1 dam; several short rapids; not as dif. as the Machias River; run early.

Fish River—E. Branch: USGS sheets—Square Lake, Stockholm, Eagle Lake. Chain of Lakes trip, from St. Agatha at N. end of Long Lake to Frenchville, 1 long day, 10 mi. from put-in to Sinclair, then through short thoroughfare to Mud Lake, 2 mi. across Mud Lake, then 1 mi. through thoroughfare to Cross Lake, then 4 mi. down Cross Lake, then 1½ mi. through thoroughfare to Square Lake, 4 mi. across Square Lake and 3 mi. through thoroughfare to Eagle Lake, then down main Fish River to Ft. Kent, then down to Frenchville.

Fish River Lakes: From St. Agatha, Long Lake to Mud, Cross, Square, Eagle lakes to Fish River, 29 mi., plus much more lake paddling, smooth, can continue upriver to Fish River Lake, smooth to mostly smooth, scenic, canoe during high water, or to St. John River to Frenchville, 30 mi., a few miles from starting point (with 5 mi. of quick water, some sharp drops, 2 or more ptgs.).

Grand Lakes Chain: Extensive canoeing in lakes—Syslodobsis, Pocumpus, Junior, Senaggly, Pleasant, W. Grand, Big, and Grand Falls lakes—plus several smaller ones. Connecting carries to: Passadumkeag and Penobscot rivers; Machias River trip and St. Croix River.

Great Ossipee River: USGS sheets—Ossipee Lake, Kezar Falls;

Ossipee Lake to the Saco, 21½ mi.; Ossipee Lake to Kezar Falls, 15 mi., reach by paddling 2 mi. down the Bearcamp from Rte. 25. DANGER—lake wide and windy, aim toward Green Mtn. fire tower, outlet not easy to see, next 2½ mi. through bays to Effingham Falls. Ptg. right—into old sluiceway and on to quiet water, then severe rapid; rapid goes under Rte. 153 brdg., EXPERTS ONLY, then 4 mi. quiet water to E. Freedom, rapid under brdg. in E. Freedom, then 7 mi. slow water to Kezar Falls, unattractive. Ptg.—dam above brdg. at Kezar Falls and ½ mi. below, rapids between for ¾ mi., good run; Kezar Falls to the Saco, 6½ mi., carry 100 yds. to put-in, then 3 mi. rapids to brdg. Dif. II, dangerous in high water, then 2 mi. strong current and riffles to Cornish Sta. Brdg., then 2 mi. strong current to the Saco. Take-out—Cornish Sta. Brdg. (Credit—Stewart Coffin)

Horseshoe Stream: USGS sheets—Arnold Pond, Chain Lakes, Kennebago Lake, Stratton. From Horseshoe Pond to Chain of Ponds upper part of stream is shallow and rapid, lower part winding and obstructed. (Credit—Stewart Coffin)

Hudson Brook: See description under Mooseleuk Stream.

Kennebec River: Experts only. Carry Brook Eddy to the Forks, 9 mi. Continuous Dif. II, III rapids. WARNING: water level fluctuates quickly from shallow to dangerous. Check carefully before canoeing. Harris Generating Station has cmpgrnd.; permits are required. Forks to Caratunk, 9 mi. Continuous Dif. I. Some expert groups may wish to tackle E. Outlet of Moosehead Lake or the rapids below the dam at Indian Pond, but the outlet should be run only with thorough knowledge and checking pulp logs and flow rate (check with Kennebec Water Power Co., Waterville). Below Indian Pond: DON'T DO IT! River enters gorge, becomes impassable, with no way out.

Kennebago River: USGS sheets—Cupsuptic, Oquossuc; Kennebago Lake outlet to Kamankeag Brook, DON'T RUN UNTIL BRIDGE (½ mi. below BM 1566), dangerous rapids and gorge below outlet and power dams, first 6 mi.—don't run. Put-in—brdg., first mi. easy rapids below brdg., then 2 mi. good current to Kamankeag Brook, then slower current with winding river 4 mi. to Rte. 16 and lakes, nice early summer run, good scenery. (Credit—Stewart Coffin)

Kezar Lake: N. Lovell to Saco River, 17½ mi., smooth, 1 ptg. Little Androscoggin: Above W. Paris to S. Paris, 12 mi.; mixed smooth and rapids; 1–2 ptgs.; check carefully before canoeing the rapids at Snow's Falls; polluted below S. Paris; spring.

Kezar Lake—Nezinscot Branches: W. Sumner to Buckfield Spring.

Little Black River: Guide service strongly urged to St. John River, 27 mi., mixed smooth and rapids, check carefully before canoeing (private-road access), 1 ptg. maybe.

Little Madawaska River: USGS sheets—Caribou, Stockholm, Fort Fairfield; canoeable from Stockholm to jctn. with Aroostook River, 27 mi., sluggish, spruce and fir swamps. (Credit—Stewart Coffin)

Little Ossipee River: To Saco River, 31 mi.; continuous rapids, canoe during high water, scenic, some section for team of experts only. Early—by end of April. One of best in southern Maine.

Little River: USGS sheets—Berwick. From broken dam S. of Lebanon (in high water) to brdg. on Berwick–S. Lebanon Rd., 13 mi., first ¾ mi. shallow with good current to broken dam, then smooth water to brdg. on Little River Rd., then 5 mi. slow and winding to next brdg., this part swampy—many obstacles, best part starts at brdg., nice smooth water for 2 mi. after brdg., then ½-mi. rapids. Dif. II to Messenger Brdg. on Berwick–S. Lebanon Rd., then 1 mi. more rapids to next brdg., can't run in low water. DANGER—2 sharp pitches on rapids, then 1½ mi. smooth with riffles to broken dam—line on right, then ⅔ mi. to brdg. on Berwick–S. Lebanon Rd., take out here or continue to Salmon Falls River. (Credit—Stewart Coffin)

Little Spencer Stream: USGS sheets—Spencer, Pierce Pond. From Spencer Lake Dam to Spencer Stream, 3 mi., usually very low water, many carries, run in high water. (Credit—Stewart Coffin)

Lower Magalloway River: A guide is advisable. Aziscobos Dam to Umbagog Lake and Androscoggin River: Dif. III, IV; first 2 mi.

Machias River: USGS sheets—Mooseleuk Lake, Greenlaw, Ashland. Big Machias Lake to Aroostook River at Ashland, 1–2 days, 32 mi. Put-in—side rd. off American Realty Rd. from Ashland or Russell Crossing. First 7 mi. difficult rapids, next 5 mi. from Rowe Brook to N. Branch Camp—easy with good current and small riffles, then 6 mi. to logging dam—many obstacles—ptg. right, then 12 mi. below dam to brdg. on Garfield Rd. (first 3 mi. intermediate rapids, then flat water), old dam just above brdg.— lift over in shallow water. Take-out—at brdg. or go to Aroostook River. (Credit—Stewart Coffin)

Machias River: (Aroostook County) experts only. Big Machias Lake to Aroostook River, 32 mi., 1–2 days; mountainous, heavily forested, 2 ptgs.; continuous rapids, some fairly difficult. Third Machias Lake to Whitneyville, 51 mi.; experienced white-water canoeists only; 3–6 days. Check with St. Regis Paper Co. at Whitneyville about logs and pulp drives. Usual approach: Ptg. from Grand Lake or by road to third Machias Lake. The real white water begins below third Machias Lake with Dif. III and IV sections, 5–8 ptgs.

Macwahoc Stream: Macwahoc Lake to Molunkus Stream (at Macwahoc), 26 mi.; canoe during high water, some steep rapids.

Magalloway River: USGS sheets—Cupsuptic, Second Lake, Oquossoc, Errol; no public rds. in Parmachenee Wilderness. Put-in—public landing at end of driveway N. of Aziscohos Dam, 12 mi. paddle up Aziscohos. Campsites on lake, bear right at head of lake, paddle upriver 1 mi. to rapids—ptg. 1½ mi. around these, then paddle up 1 mi. to Parmachenee Lake, can paddle uplake and few more mi. upriver; below Aziscohos Dam—¼ mi. of horrible rapids—DON'T RUN, then 1 mi. tough rapids, best put-in—Rte. 16 brdg. at Wilson's Mills, good current for 2 mi., then slack water and swamp for 17 mi. to Unhagog Lake. Take-out—spots along Rte. 16. (Credit—Stewart Coffin)

Mattawamkeag River: Smyrna Mills to Pleasant Lake, 9 mi.; mixed smooth and rapids, scenic, canoe during high water, to Haynesville, 18 mi.; mostly smooth, to Wytopitlock, 21 mi.; mostly smooth, to Rte. 170 brdg., Kingman, 12 mi. out here heavy rapids downstream.

Mattawamkeag River—Fish Stream and W. Branch: Patten to Mattawamkeag Lake, 15 mi.; smooth, pleasant, good fishing to Haynesville, 18 mi., mostly smooth.

Millinocket Stream: USGS sheets—Millinocket Lake, Grand Lake Seboeis. From Millinocket Lake to Oxbow, 23 mi., 2–3 days, canoeable in high water. Put-in—Millinocket Lake—reach lake by plane or long ptg. from Penobscot headwaters; below lake—channel widens into pond, then few mi. of rough water; dead water above and below mouth of Millimagasset Stream. (Credit —Stewart Coffin)

Molunkus Stream: 35 mi.; 2 days, mostly wooded, 4–5 rapids. Sherman Sta. to Monardna, 10 mi. mostly smooth to Macwahoc, 13 mi.; mostly smooth to Kingman (2 mi. up Mattawamkeag River), 12 mi., mostly smooth.

Moose Pond: Rte. 202 to Saco River, 12 mi., smooth, 1 ptg. around 3 dams.

Moose River: Part of trip for experts only. One of best canoe-camping trips, with variety of choices: A guide is advisable from Skinner to Holeb, 12 mi.; continuous rapids, scenic, canoe during high water. A guide is advisable from Holeb to Jackman, 30 mi.; most smooth, scenic; check with ranger about falls; 2 ptgs. A guide is strongly urged from Jackman to Moosehead Lake, 31 mi.; smooth through Long Pond, 16 mi.; 2½ mi. rapids (Dif. I) out here; experts may ptg. dam and brdg.; 2½ mi. rapids, experts only, Dif. III and IV; 7 mi. Brassua Lake to dam; 3 mi. to Moosehead Lake.

Moosehead Lake: Greenville to N.W. Carry and return, 200 mi., 1–2 wks.; beware sudden squalls, strong winds, and power boats.

Mooseleuk Stream and Hudson Brook: USGS sheets, Mooseleuk Lake, Millinocket Lake, Grand Lake Seboeis. From Hudson Brook to Oxbow, 29 mi., 2 days, run in high water only; continuous rapids, Dif. I, with 1 sharp drop, sharp bends. Put-in—McPherson Brook Brdg. on American Realty Rd. from Ashland. Ptg.—canoes to Hudson Brook, then 2½ mi. to Mooseleuk Lake. Cross lake and ptg. around dam into Mooseleuk Stream, good current and little rapids all the way, sharp bends, wooded shores, 3 mi. below Boar's Head Falls to Aroostook River, continue down Aroostook to Oxbow. (Credit—Stewart Coffin)

Mousam River: USGS sheets: Berwick, Kennebunk, too many dams, not recommended. (Credit—Stewart Coffin)

Munsungan Stream: USGS sheets—Spider Lake, Millinocket Lake, Grand Lake Seboeis. From Chase Lake to Oxbow, 33 mi., 3 days, wilderness area, excellent fishing. Put-in—headwaters cannot be reached by car, access at Chase Pond (Is. Pond)—reach by rd. from Ashland, first 2 mi. stream blocked by cedar swamps, last 2 mi. are falls that can't be run, only mid. 4 mi. canoeable and only in high water, not a good canoe trail. Best pt. to start—fly in to Chase Lake, easy rapid leads to Munsungan Lake, then 5 mi. down lake to dam. Munsungan Lake Dam to Libby Camp, 10 mi., excellent run below dam, good current 1½ mi. to Munsungan Falls. Ptg.—Munsungan Falls—have been run by experts in high water. DANGER—worst drop around blind corner, remainder of rapids Dif. I–II, banks are forested, nice run; Libby Camp to Oxbow Lndg., 17 mi., 3 hrs. in high water, fast current, some riffles, current slow, 1 mi. to Lake Pomkeag Stream then increases again. Campsite—½ mi. on right below Lake Pomkeag Stream, below campsite river wide and less attractive. Obstacle—Basto Rips— has rocks in low water. Take-out—1½ mi. below Basto Rips to Oxbow Lndg. (Credit—Stewart Coffin)

Musquacook Stream: USGS sheets: Musquacook Lakes, Allagash Falls; a guide is advisable to Allagash River, 18 mi., 11–12 mi. of rapids, some must be lined, too low for canoeing after mid-June, very pretty white-water stream with ample water. Start—fifth lake, a good paper co. rd. from Ashland crosses stream above second lake, good camping on first and second lakes, authorized campsite on first lake at dam, carry over broken dam and into Horse Race Rapids, rapids too rough to canoe—line many stretches, then 3 mi. of good fast water, gets faster near Lower Horse Race Rapids, (1 mi. in length)—line in places, then 8 mi. to Allagash—rapids all the way but not difficult, stream enters Allagash at Musqua- cook dead water. (Credit—Stewart Coffin)

Narraguagus River: Deer Lake to Deblois, 23 mi., mixed smooth and rapids to Dif. III canoe during high water: Deblois to Cherryfield, 15 mi.; mixed smooth and rapids; 2 ptgs.; 8-mi. stretch Dif. I; another Dif. I, which needs scouting, maybe ptg.; out before town to avoid dams. May, June, or after heavy rains.

Nicatous Lake and Stream: To Passadumkeag River, 16 mi., mixed smooth and rapids, 3 rapids (1 sharp).

Old Stream: A guide is advisable (alt. easier start for Machias River trips), to Machias River, 17 mi.; 2–3 ptgs. or line.

Orange River: Rocky Lake to Whiting, 11 mi.; mostly smooth, 1 dam, 1 drop (maybe ptg.), and ½ mi. rapids. To Whiting Bay, 3 mi., connects with Denny's Bay; fairly protected tidal sec.

Ossipee Lake and River: Some rapids dangerous in high water, impassable in low. To Saco River mixed smooth and rapids, 17 mi., 2–5 ptgs. Spring.

Penobscot River: Mattawamkeag to Howland, 22 mi.; mixed smooth and rapids, 2 1-mi. rapids and 1 of 2 mi.; 1 ptg. (dam above Howland) to Old Town, 24 mi., smooth, pleasant. To Bangor the pollution and dams make it not worth the effort. Bangor to Sandy Point, 25 mi., strong tidal effects, waves from winds, unsafe for canoes beyond Sandy Point.

Penobscot River, E. Branch: Experts only, guide service strongly urged. Telos Lake to Grank Lake. Matugamon Dam, 24 mi., continuous rapids to mixed smooth and rapids, scenic, canoe during high water, a 9-mi. stretch of rapids, Dif. IV with 2 ptgs. For experts with ideal water. Run early, by mid-June. Usual start— Grand Lake Dam to Grindstone, guide service strongly urged, 40 mi.; not much opportunity for shooting rapids, but is a trip only for well-seasoned canoeists. Most drops are impassable, easy between, but heavy current can pull canoe into falls; 4–8 ptgs., some Dif. III–IV; for experts only, with favorable water. Attempt Whetstone Falls and below only under favorable conditions.

Penobscot River, W. Branch: Part of trip for experts only, guide service strongly recommended (can be traveled from Seboomok Lake to Ripogenus Dam, 59 mi., or even from the N. or S. Branch—i.e., from Big Bor or from Canada Falls Lake). Usual start—Big Eddy, 2 mi. below Ripogenus Dam to Norcross, 30 mi.; mixed smooth and rapids, with stretches of heavy rapids to Dif. IV, and spots dangerous even for experts; 3–7 ptgs.

Side trips—Up Debsconeag Lakes, mostly smooth, 3–4 ptgs. and/or Nahinakanta Lake and Stream, continuous rapids, scenic, canoe during high water; to Pemadumcook Lake; Pemadumcook to Jo Mary Lake; 3 ptgs., Togue Pond and Stream, Sandy Stream, Millinocket Lake and Stream, Shad Pond, Penobscot W. Branch, 23 mi., mixed smooth and rapids to smooth.

Piscataqua River—USGS sheets—Dover, York; not recommended for canoeing, a tidal estuary. (Credit—Stewart Coffin)

Piscataquis River: Blanchard to Guilford, 13 mi.; continuous rapids for first 8 mi.

Guilford to Howland, 47 mi., mostly smooth but 1 6-mi. stretch of continuous rapids with 1 mi. heavy rapids, steep banks. Check carefully before canoeing.

Pleasant River: Katahdin Iron Works to Brownville, 13 mi.; continuous rapids, canoe during high water, steep, declining to smooth, most smooth, last 6 mi. to dam at Brownville.

Rangeley Lakes: A guide is advisable, 45 mi., 3–4 days. Rangeley Lakes and River ptg. 1½ mi. or Dif. II to Mooselookmeguntic Lake, Cupsuptic Lake, Richardson Lakes, 2–3 ptgs. plus 8 mi. ptg. (trucking service available) to Umbagog Lake (can be reached from Aziscohos Lake).

Rapid River: USGS sheets—Oquossoc, Errol; for team of experts only. Lower Richardson to Umbagog Lake, 6 mi., Dif. III–V, check with Union Water Power Co. about flow. From put-in to lower dam, start below dam, then ½ mi. fast current and continuous rapids to pond in river; halfway before pond is curve called cemetery curve, less steep to pond, then 1 mi. paddling down pond to lower dam; from lower dam to Umbagog Lake, 3 mi., drop of 156 ft., 3–4 hrs. in canoe, can usually run lower dam, then first mi. has fast current and some rocky pitches; home of Louise Dickenson (author) on right, then short drop, then river leaves rd. and turns left with shallow rapid, next 1 mi. river drops 90 ft. in 4 severe rapids, approach with caution, can line on right, each rapid has long deep pool at foot. Smooth ledge below third rapid nice spot to rest; fourth rapid looks easy but is not, tough spot where it bends to right, then fast chute at end of fourth rapid, then another short steep pitch; after abandoned lumber camp, river continues in boulder-strewn rapids, known as Devil's Hopyard, then on to Umbagog Lake. (Credit—Stewart Coffin)

Saco River: Swan's Falls to Hiram, 33 mi.; 1–3 days, mostly smooth, pleasant, no ptg. (1 easy rip can be carried), wilderness canoeing close to populated area. Below Hiram, 44 mi. to ocean,

8–10 ptgs. around dams, dangerous or impassable rips and gorges, otherwise mostly smooth.

St. Croix River: Part of trip, experts only. A guide is advisable: Vanceboro to Kellyland, 33 mi., mainly rapids, only for well experienced to Dif. IV, 3 ptgs. (falls, dams), to Calais, 20 mi. (tidal below Calais); 3 ptgs. (falls, dams) to Dif. IV, logs to Woodland and below Woodland.

St. Francis River: Bean Lake to St. John River, 22 mi., combines lake, rapids, fast water; 1 ptg. or Dif. III rapid (can be dangerous), and some sharp drops.

St. John River: Wilderness trip, run before mid-June except on main river, OK till midsummer or later. In low water this trip is Dif. II with flat stretches between; in high water entire trip is swift, can have rapids of Dif. IV.

St. John River—Baker Branch: USGS sheets—St. John Pond, Baker Lake. From Baker Lake to jctn. with S.W. Branch. Put-in —Baker Lake, private rd., get permit from Int. Logging Corp., reach from Ste. Aurelie, Quebec. Another rd. from S., get permit from Great Natl. Paper Co., shallow water, rapid after rapid to Turner Brook, then deeper for several miles to St. Camille Rd. Brdg., then rapids rest of way.

St. John River—N.W. Branch: Daoquam to St. John River, 8 mi., put in at Daoquam For. Ser. camp in high water, then down Daoquam River 2 mi. and down N.W. Branch 6 mi. to main St. John. N.W. Branch to Allagash, 83 mi. USGS Beaver Pond, Clayton Lake, Seven Isles, Round Pond, Rocky Mts., Allagash. Dif. trip, many rapids, some very dif. rapids. LIVES HAVE BEEN LOST ON THIS TRIP. Fairly easy trip to Ninemile Brdg. with good current and rapids, then nice stretch to 7 Isles; below 7 Isles nice trip with mod. rapids till Priestley rapids. DANGER— rapids of Dif. IV before jctn. with Big Black River, then some tough rapids on stretch before Rte. 161. VERY DANGEROUS RAPIDS ON THIS STRETCH, can finish at Rte. 161 or go on.

From Allagash to Ft. Kent, unattractive, poor camping, some rapids with heavy waves; below St. Francis, river is broad and flat. From Ft. Kent to St. John, 285 mi.; to Edmundston, 19 mi.; good current, one long rapid at Fisk River Rapid 2 mi. below Kent, next 40 mi. to Grand Falls is deeper, river leaves Me. border and goes to ocean; need licensed guide to canoe in New Brunswick. DANGER—Grand Falls a dangerous gorge, cannot run, Reversing Falls at Bay of Fundy spectacular—impassable. (Credit—Stewart Coffin)

St. John River—S.W. Branch: Seldom canoed, no good access rd., similar to Baker, rapids for good distance above mouth, slow in middle part.

Salmon Falls River: USGS sheets—Newfield, Berwick, Dover. Flows from Great E. Lake S., forms border between Me. and N.H., good canoeing, upper part a strong brook, dams and flowage all the way below Milton Mills, become unattractive at Berwick-Somersworth, many large dams and much pollution. (Credit—Stewart Coffin)

Sandy River: USGS sheets—Rangeley, Phillips, Kingfield, Farmington, Norridgework, Anson; contains most quick-water canoeing of any river in western Me. From Small Falls to Kennebec River, 75 mi.

Trip 1—Small Falls to S. Branch, 7 mi., experts only, start at picnic ground below Small Falls in high water of mid-May, first mi. continuous rapids, Dif. III, then 1 mi. easier rapids to Rte. 4 Brdg., gauge marks on left upstream abutment. DANGER—below this brdg. is 1 mi. of easy continuous rapids, then 1 mi. hard rapids to Madrid, dangerous, then more hard rapids and impassable spot below Madrid Center, then easy rapids to narrow gorge 1 mi. below Madrid—pt. left 50 yds., can be run in med. water, dangerous always, below gorge is short run with continuous rapids to second Rte. 4 brdg. DANGER—keep extreme left under brdg.; just below is impassable drop, ptg. around drop, then 1,000-yd. gorge can be run but contains heavy drop, line on right river is small but can rise fast, then below gorge 1 mi. continuous mod. rapids to third Rte. 4 brdg.; at Rte. 4 brdg., S. Branch enters.

Trip 2—S. Branch to Phillips, 8 mi., beautiful water run, intermed., Dif. III, 1½ mi. from start Oberton Stream enters, good rest spot, river larger now, good into June, continuous rapids, not dif., heavy waves, some hard canoeing through Phillips, avoid by ptg. on side-rd. rte. ½ mi. above Rte. 142. Phillips to Strong, experts only, 9 mi., rapids to Dif. III, dif., fierce, 5–7 ptgs., weekdays are better because of dam control of water. Med. water only, for experts or well experienced. Strong to Farmington mostly smooth.

Seboeis River: Part of trip for experts only (alternate start for E. Branch trip, easier, less hazardous). Experts only from Snowshoe Lake to Grand Lake Rd., 11 mi., experts only to Dif. IV, 1 ptg. (dif.). Usual start—Grand Lake Rd. to E. Branch Penobscot, 17 mi. to Dif. II, ptg. with continuous rapids Dif. I.

Seven Mile Stream: E. Dixfield to Androscoggin River, 8 mi. Spring.

Sheepscot River: Part of trip for experts only. Montville to W. Branch, 18 mi., mixed smooth and rapids, canoe during high water, with sharp drops line or carry; 1–3 ptgs. Experts only. Below Sheepscot Pond for experts with favorable water. W. Branch—Palermo to Sheepscot River, mixed smooth and rapids, canoe during high water, 2 steep rapids, 1–3 ptgs. Coopers Mills to Wiscasset, 27 mi., mostly smooth but some very fast water, 2–3 rapids, 1 ptg., tide effects.

Spencer Stream: USGS sheets—Spencer, Pierce Pond, usually too low for canoeing by June 30, rises after rains; from Baker Pond to Dead River, 15 mi. Put-in—ptg. ½ mi. from end of dirt rd. to inlet of Baker Pond, paddle 1½ mi. down Baker Stream to Spencer Stream (see description of St. John River—Baker Branch), 2 mi. of pleasant quick water in Spencer Stream, then 3 mi. slack water to Spencer Dam (old logging dam with only foundation left),

5 mi. of rapids below dam to The Gut. Spencer Gut is narrow gorge, ½ mi. long, with high rock cliffs, many falls, and pools in Gut—don't run. Ptg. Gut—left ½ mi. over high ridge, good rapids below Gut, then hard rapids for 1 mi. to mouth of Little Spencer Stream, then easy rapids to Dead River. Alt. run—paddle down Little Spencer Stream. Put-in—Spencer Lake camps, then down Spencer Lake 5 mi. Ptg.—dam at Spencer Lake, then enter Little Spencer Stream (see description of Little Spencer Stream). (Credit—Stewart Coffin)

Sunday River: USGS sheets—Bethel. From large pool 2½ mi. above covered brdg. at Sunday River School to short connecting rd. 0.1 mi. above U.S. 2, 6 mi., beautiful, small, peaceful valley, crystal-clear water, best time first of May; first mi. steep and full of rocks, hardest pitch at start, rapids diminish after first mi. below covered brdg., few and easy rapids, river meanders, good current. (Credit—Stewart Coffin)

Swift River: USGS sheets—Rumford. Most of river too tough for canoeing, river rises and falls quickly, impassable in low water, dangerous if too high, experts only in high water, continuous rapids, at med. water put in just below gorge in Bryon, some sharp drops at first, then easier going for several mi. to Roxbury. Dif. I–II. Below Roxbury, at first too rough to canoe, then easy rapids 10 mi. to Rumford. DANGER—1 bad section just below Hale. (Credit—Stewart Coffin)

Wild River: USGS sheets—Bethel. Continuous severe rapids, Dif. V, only canoeable part is 2 mi. above Rte. 2, experts only, dangerous, don't run in high water. (Credit—Stewart Coffin)

Wilson Stream: Start below falls, 1½ mi. below Wilton, to Farmington Falls and Sandy River, 15 mi. mixed smooth and rapids to continuous rapids, 2–3 ptgs.

Wytopitlock Stream: (lake to Mattawamkeag River), 18 mi. mixed smooth and rapids, canoe during high water, with some continuous-rapids stretches, some steep.

MARYLAND

Antietam Creek: Wash. Co.; 10 mi. stone brdg. W. of Funkstown to Mill Dam Rte. 68, rapids, 3 or more canoes, white water, skilled only, 3 dams, ptg. first left side, strong current, scout ahead, before April 15 or after rain; 12 mi., Rte. 68 to town of Antietam, beautiful, fast water, OK beginners, small rapids, fallen trees, ptg. dam, 1 mi. from start, beginners end above Antietam—left. Fast water below, skilled only. (Credit—*Blue Ridge Voyages*)

Bennett Creek: From Little Bennett Creek to the Monocacy. Dif. I.

Big Pipe Creek: Rd. N. of Middleburg, Md., to Monocacy River; current 2½–4½ m.p.h. Dif. I.

Catoctin Creek: USGS—7½ Middletown and Point of Rocks, Md. From Rte. 17 to Rte. 464, 10 mi., run before mid-April or with wet spring till mid-May, beautiful, beginner's run, safe white water, 50 riffles, shallow, logjam below Lewis Mill, fences, may be logs in water. (Credit—*Blue Ridge Voyages*)

Monocacy River: USGS—7½ Buckeystown, Md.; "Sugar Loaf Mtn." From Rte. 355 to Rte. 28, before July 1, OK for beginners, easy riffles, 1 old mill dam near Buckeystown; riffles below dam require some skill. (Credit—*Blue Ridge Voyages*)

Potomac River: From Greenspring, W. Va., to Chain Bridge, D.C., 180 mi.
    Trip 1—Greenspring to Williamsport—USGS—W. Va., Old Town, PawPaw, Artemos, Belgrave, Great Cacapon, Cherry Run, Big Pool, Hedgesville, Williamsport. Cos.—Hampshire, Morgan, and Berkeley in W. Va. Dif. I–II, 76 mi., 2–3 days,

wide, flat river, some low ledges, easy rapids, good for beginners, can run all summer. DANGERS—Dam No. 6 at Great Cacapon, Dam No. 5 about 5 mi. downstream of Little Georgetown. Fish—panfish, small-mouth bass.

Trip 2—Williamsport to Dam No. 3, which is 1 mi. above Harpers Ferry, USGS—Williamsport, Hedgesville, Shepherdstown, Keedysville, Charles Town, Harpers Ferry. Cos.— Berkeley and Jefferson in W. Va. Dif. I–II, 41 mi., 2 days, river runs through shallow wooded gorge, good for beginners. DANGERS—Power Plant Dam ½ mi. below Williamsport, and Dam No. 4 about 15 mi. below Williamsport. Fish— panfish, small-mouth and large-mouth bass. Take-out—right side of 8-ft. dam 1 mi. above Harpers Ferry; river difficult below this pt.

Trip 3—Above Dam No. 3 to Knoxville—USGS—7½ ft. Harpers Ferry, Va., Md., and W. Va.; 7½ ft. Charles Town, W. Va.; 5 mi., Dif. Intermediate white water, beautiful gorge, long rapids, don't run in high water, waves can be 5 ft. in high water, don't run if there is no water release from dam. Put-in—Near John Brown Cave near Bakerton Rd., pass under RR brdg., turn right, then go 200 yds. on dirt rd. to river. Ptg.—Dam No. 3 on left side. DANGER—feeder canal near Dam No. 3.

Trip 4—Knoxville to Seneca, USGS—Harpers Ferry, Pt. of Rocks, Buckeystown, Waterford, Poolesville, Leesburg, Sterling, Seneca. Loudon Co. in Va., 39 mi., Dif. I–II, no partic. dangers, can run in summer, wide and picturesque river, slow-moving, beautiful. Fish–panfish, cats, bass.

Trip 5—Seneca to Great Falls Dam—USGS—Seneca and Rockville. Montgomery Co., Md., and Loudon Co., Va. Dif. I–III; 9 mi., wide, picturesque river, many isles. DANGER— old canal feeder Dam No. 2, which is ½ mi. down from Seneca. DANGER—rapids in Seneca Falls—not for beginners. Beginners—ptg. rapids to C&O Canal at feeder locks on Md. side. DANGER—Great Falls Dam—*Don't go below dam,* LIVES HAVE BEEN LOST HERE; take out above falls on left side. Fish—panfish, cats, and bass.

Trip 6—Great Falls to Brookmont Dam, "Potomac Gorge," USGS, Wash., D.C., and vicinity and Vienna and Falls

Church; 8 mi., Dif. III–V, spectacular scenery, heavy white water, put in below Great Falls, use Great Falls parking lot and ptg. down old C&O canal towpath. DANGER—opposite C&O canal lock where river goes down fish ladder, Dif. V–VI here, stay to right to avoid this spot. DANGER—entire gorge area at reading over 8 on Sycamore Isle gauge, heavy rapids and whirlpools in gorge. DANGER—Yeolow Falls and Stubblefield Falls, scout before running, don't run before reading description in guide books listed in credits.

Trip 7—Brookmont Dam to Chain Brdg., USGS Falls Church, Quadrangle, Wash., W.; 1¼ mi., Dif. III–VI, a big river within a narrow area, dangerous channel, run summer and fall with low water, white water, MANY LIVES HAVE BEEN LOST HERE, experts only and then in groups, read description in Randy Carter's book.

(Credit—*Canoeing White Water River Guide* and *Blue Ridge Voyages*. SPECIAL WARNING—Don't attempt sec. near D.C. before reading these books. The description in this book is not enough.)

Potomac River—N. Branch: See description under W. Va.

Savage River: Savage River Dam to Westernport, Md. This is one continuous 5-mi.-long Dif. IV–V rapids; dangerous. Dam 1 mi. below put-in, runnable at broken-out portion on left.

Wills Creek: See description under Pa.

MASSACHUSETTS

NOTE: It is strongly recommended that you purchase and consult the *AMC New England Canoeing Guide* for further information.

A special word of thanks to Stewart Coffin, who generously shared his notes with me. These were collected over many years by a great canoeist.

Assabet River: USGS sheets, Shrewsbury, Marlboro, Hudson, Maynard, Concord. From Westboro to Concord, 32 mi., polluted, mostly flat and unattractive.

Trip 1—Westboro to Hudson, 14 mi. Put-in—Crossing on Rte. 9, 5 mi. to dam. Ptg.—right side Northboro Dam, easy riffles below dam, river swift ¼ mi. below Northboro, Rob. Whittaker Co. mill below, can canoe under mill, then 1 mi. to Woodside Dam. Ptg.—left side Woodside Dam, riffle below running under mill—can be run, then swift water for ⅔ mi., then stream winds, many willows, then 1 mi. below Chapinville easy canoeing for 6 mi., 2 dams and much pollution at Hudson.

Trip 2—Hudson to Maynard, 9 mi., first few miles not attractive. Ptg.—Gleasondale Dam—left side, then nice trip to Maynard. Ptg.—dam 1 mi. above Maynard—left side, rapids below dam for 1½ mi.—can run in high water, bad trip through town, river polluted.

Trip 3—Maynard to Concord, 9 mi. Ptg.—Dam below Maynard—right side, swift water below dam. Ptg.—W. Concord dam—right side, swift current below and forested banks for 1 mi., river turns calm under RR brdg. Obstacles—large rocks in river near E. W. Emerson estate. (Credit—Stewart Coffin)

Bass River: USGS sheets—Dennis. From S. Yarmouth to N. shore and return, 1 day, pleasant trip. (Credit—Stewart Coffin)

Beaver Brook: See description under New Hampshire.

Boston Brook: N. Andover to Ipswich River, not recommended, poor scenery, many obstacles. (Credit—Stewart Coffin)

Canoe River: USGS sheets—Mansfield, Norton, Taunton. Above Rte. 123 brdg. not recommended, many obstacles. From Rte. 123 brdg. to Lake Sabbatia, first 2 mi. easy to Winnesonnet Pond, stream leaves pond S.E. corner, then long stretch through E. part of Great Cedar Swamp. Take-out—brdg. N. of Cranberry ponds or go few miles more to Lake Sabbatia N. of Taunton; lower river all sluggish. (Credit—Stewart Coffin)

Cape Cod Canal: Canoeing not allowed.

Charles River: USGS sheets—Franklin, Holliston, Medfield, Natick, Newton. Milford to Charles River Basin, 68 mi.

    Trip 1—Milford to W. Medway, 12 mi., first 4 mi. small stream, difficult, then 5 ponds past Bellingham. Ptgs.—easy carries around dams. Ptg.—W. Medway dam on right, canoe only in high water.

    Trip 2—W. Medway to Medfield, 12 mi., larger river than above, canoe any season. Ptg.—Medway dam, mild rapid below, dif. course past Medway, take left bank into Populatic Pond—outlet there, rapid at Rockville—run with ample water, boring trip.

    Trip 3—Medfield to S. Natick, 9 mi., beautiful, good picnic spot. Rocky Narrows—ptg. dam at S. Natick, may be canoes to rent near dam.

    Trip 4—S. Natick to Dedham, 11 mi., good current, nice scenery. Ptg.—Charles River Vil. Dam, may take ditch 1 mi. past Rte. 128 brdg.—canoeable in high water—cuts off 4 river mi.

    Trip 5—Dedham to Newton Lower Falls, 9 mi., 4 ptgs.—2 dams at Newton Upper Falls, left side, and 2 dams at Newton Lower Falls—ptg. left.

    Trip 6—Newton Lower Falls to Charles River Basin, 15 mi., many bays to Waltham, 2 ptgs.—Waltham and Watertown dams. DANGER—LIFE LOST BELOW WATERTOWN DAM, DANGER—Charles River Basin impassable in high wind; canoes can use lock in basin dam. (Credit—Stewart Coffin)

Chicopee River: not recommended, 12 dams in 18 mi., most water dead water, 1 mi. white water below dams at Red Bridge and N. Wilbraham. (Credit—Stewart Coffin)

Concord River: USGS sheets—Concord, Billerica, and Lowell.

From Concord to N. Billerica, 18 mi. DANGER—speedboats, best time spring and fall. Take-out—above N. Billerica dam on right side (in Talbot Mills); remaining 5 mi. to Merrimack unattractive. (Credit—Stewart Coffin)

Deerfield River: See description under Vermont.

Falls River: USGS sheets—Bernardston and Greenfield; too small to canoe above Bernardston. From below dam at Hoe Shop Rd. to falls, 3½ mi., run in high water, no rds. follow river, steep and frstd. banks, land posted on both sides, first mi. to Bascom Rd. mostly rapids, not dif. Ptg.—impassable ledge ¼ mi. below Bascom Rd. brdg., then good rapids below near Boy Scout camp, then small canyon, 1 mi. easy paddling to dam. Ptg.—dam on right, ½ mi. fast current, and not dif. rapids below dam. DANGER—go slow—rapids become waterfall just above brdg. Take-out—right side, last ¼ mi. to Connecticut River not canoeable. (Credit—Stewart Coffin)

Green River: See description under Vermont.

Housatonic River: USGS sheets—Pittsfield E., E. Lee, Stockbridge, Great Barrington, Ashley Falls, S. Canaan, Cornwall Ellsworth, Kent, Dover Plains, and New Milford; many dams, polluted. From Hinsdale, Mass., to the ocean, 152 mi., 6–8 days. Best part—Great Barrington to New Milford.

    Trip 1—Hinsdale to Lenox, 23 mi., impassable areas from Hinsdale to Dalton, dams in Dalton, then mostly flat, winding river.

    Trip 2—Lenox to Great Barrington, 25 mi., first 4 mi. to Lee —flat and not attractive. Ptgs.—dam ½ mi. below Lenox and 2 dams at Lee and 2 others between, several small rips between Lee and Stockbridge, swampy section. Ptg.—dam near S. Lee; in high water swamps to Glendale are fast and smooth. Ptgs.—2 dams below Glendale. DANGER—rapid below second dam, then river is like a lake for 1½ mi. to a dam—ptg. Ptg.—dam and rapids above Housatonic; don't run rapids below dam, then another lake to dam at Risingdale, then flat water 5 mi. to Great Barrington dam.

Trip 3—Great Barrington to Falls Village, 25 mi., smooth current most of way. 2 ptgs.—dam 1 mi. below RR brdg. W. of Canaan and 1 mi. above Falls Vil.

Trip 4—Falls Vil. to Kent, 19 mi., one of best runs in S. New England, steep frstd. hills, no dams. Put-in—right bank below powerhouse, rocky turn just below put-in, good rip at Cornwall with haystacks—starts above covered brdg.—look over first, then drop over ledge 1 mi. below, don't run rip or drop in high water, water level low on Sundays—may make run impassable. DANGER—in high water below W. Cornwall.

Trip 5—Kent to New Milford, 17 mi., first 5 mi. still water, rough ½-mi. rapid below Bulls Bridge Dam; to avoid rapid, paddle down 2-mi. canal to powerhouse and carry to river, below rapid current strong with rapids for 10 mi. to dam.

Trip 6—New Milford to Devon, 43 mi., slow current 3 mi. to dam at Still Water, river narrows below dam, then goes ¼ mi. through wild, steep gorge (Lovers Leap). Don't run in high water—hug E. bank in low or mod. water, from Still Water to mouth—good, fast summer run, lake near Sandy Hook from Stevenson Dam, 2 dams below Stevenson Dam, 16 mi. from Stevenson to Devon, tidewater below Derby. (Credit— Stewart Coffin)

Konkapot River: USGS sheets—Great Barrington, Ashley Falls; first 8 mi. very rough, sharp rapids at first, then mill site with ptg., then sharp drop—can be run, then second mill site with ptg., then sharp rapid through third mill site, then short ptg.—high dam (all in first mi.), then sharp drop under brdg. 3 mi. below Mill River, then ¼ mi. to falls on left where Umpachene River enters, then 4 mi. strong current and many rapids to Konkapot Vil., then 2 mi. to Southfield Rd. Brdg., river now fast stream, 4 more mi. to brdg. at Clayton, same strong stream below Clayton, 8½ mi. to Ashley Falls, last 4 mi. sluggish, 2 mi. below Ashley Falls to jctn. with Housatonic. (Credit—Stewart Coffin)

Martins Brook: USGS sheets—Wilmington, Reading, Salem,

Georgetown, Ipswich; Martins Pond to Street Station, ½ day, swampy ctry. after put-in for ¾ hr. to RR brdg. Ptg.—RR brdg. in high water, unattractive below RR brdg., swampy. (Credit— Stewart Coffin)

Merrimack River: See description under New Hampshire.

Millers River: USGS sheets—Winchendon, Royalston, Athol, Orange, Millers Falls, and Greenfield; Winchendon to Conn. River, 39 mi.

Trip 1—Winchendon to S. Royalston, 12 mi. Put-in—at brdg. below jctn. with branch—below sewage-disposal plant, polluted river, 5 mi. to next brdg., swampy, little current, OK trip if river not low.

Trip 2—S. Royalston to Athol, 8 mi., popular white-water run, continuing rapids. Intermed. Dif. III, run in April high water, don't run in flood. Put-in—right bank below mill site, broken dam ¼ mi. below put-in—can be run, heavy drop ½ mi. below second RR tracks, heaviest rapids—2 mi. below second RR brdg.—OK for experts, 3 dams in Athol—takeout on right above upper dam.

Trip 3—Athol to Erving, 11 mi., sec. not recommended, river flat, some rapids below Orange, broken dam at Erving Paper Mills—don't run, then smooth water to dam at Erving —can be run.

Trip 4—Erving to Millers Falls, 6 mi., called "Lower Millers," popular, white-water run, run late spring and after rains, most rapids Dif. II in low water, in med. water several spots require skilled canoeist, in high water dangerous. Put-in —brdg. on side rd. in Erving below dam, best water level is 1½ ft. below cement step on right brdg. abutment, don't run if water is up to this step, good stretch of rapids 1 mi. after put-in, then moderate rapids for 1 mi. to pt. above Farley Brdg., steep rapid at dam site, chute below old mill yard requires skill, then more rapids in next mi. DANGER— watch for power line over river—"The Funnel" is below it; ptg., don't run, river drops very fast, then shallow rapids in next mi., then chute with large haystacks near RR embankment, good beach on right, then a few more strong rapids, then long pond above large dam at Millers Falls Paper Co. Take out right bank.

Trip 5—Millers Falls to Conn. River, 2 mi., 3 dams in Millers Falls, then mod. rapids to jctn. with Conn. River at French King Brdg. (Credit—Stewart Coffin)

Namasket River: USGS sheets—Assawampset Pond, Bridgewater; unattractive, not recommended, first 2 mi. open swamp, then several dams through Middleboro, then wide shallow stream, then small rapids below millpond on N. side of town, then dead water to next brdg., then small rapid under last brdg. above Taunton River. (Credit—Stewart Coffin)

Nashua River: See description under New Hampshire.

Nissitissit River: USGS sheets—Townsend, Pepperell. From Bohannon Brdg. E. of S. Brookline to Pepperell, 7 mi., run in spring or after rains, some obstructions in first 2½ mi. to W. Hollis, then best part of river next 2½ mi. to Prescott St. brdg., good current, wooded banks, then 1½ mi. to dam in Pepperell, some shallow rapids, and long stretch of still water above dam. Take-out—left side and carry to rd.; rapids below dam dif.—can run in med. water, then ¼ mi. to brdg., no other take-out pts. to jctn. with Nashua River, ¾ mi. (Credit—Stewart Coffin)

N. River: USGS sheets—Colrain. Too steep to canoe above Mass.-Vt. line. From brdg. 1 mi. above Colrain to jctn. W. Deerfield River, 7 mi., first 2 mi. all rapids—not dif., ptg.— broken dam on right below Colrain, then rapids lessen for 1 mi. below iron brdg., then still water of dam past covered brdg. Ptg.— left around dam and mill at Griswoldville, river is polluted, then 2 minor rapids in next 2 mi. to Shattuckville, river narrows and small falls appear—ptg. left, then in short distance above high brdg. at Shattuckville—bad area, line this on right, then continuous rapids—intermed. dif. to Deerfield River. (Credit—Stewart Coffin)

Otter River: USGS sheets—Templeton, Winchendon. From Rte. 2 Brdg. near Gardner to Millers River, 10 mi. above Baldwinsville not good; put-in at Rte. 2 brdg., then fair current to Rte. 101 brdg., 1 carry around low brdg., then mod. current to broken dam above River St. Brdg., forested lift over 8-ft. dam, rapids below, fast but easy, then good current ½ mi. to another brdg., then slack water for ½ mi. to dam at Otter River Vil., paddle on canal to street, then 2 mi. to Baldwinsville, some rapids here, then below Rte. 202 brdg. lift around dam, then from below Baldwinsville to Miller River 2¾ mi., no hazards, fair current. (Credit—Stewart Coffin)

Palmer River: USGS sheets—Somerset, E. Providence. From upper of the two Rte. 44 crossings to head of millpond W. of Harris, 10 mi. Put-in at upper Rte. 44 crossing, small winding brook for 2½ mi. to a crossroad and old stone brdg., many obstructions in first mi., then ¼ mi. to another old stone brdg., quicker water, easier going, some small rapids, 1 mi. to dam in Rehoboth from old stone brdg., lift over dam, run sharp drop under brdg., then to mill on right bank, then again cross Rte. 44, then 1 mi. through meadows to old stone brdg. on a crossroad, then 1 mi. to crossing of Rte. 44 for third time, then 1 mi. sluggish, winding meadow stream to another stone brdg., then ½ mi. to another stone brdg. too low to go under, then 3 mi. through farmland to head of millpond W. of Harris. Trip not recommended, unattractive, can run only in high water.

Powwow River: See description under New Hampshire.

Quaboag River: USGS sheets—E. Brookfield, Warren, Palmer; above Warren, river is flat and marshy, from Warren to W. Warren mixed smooth and rapid, below W. Warren popular whitewater run, last sec. flat and industrialized. From W. Warren to Three Rivers, 17 mi.

   Trip 1—W. Warren to Fentonville, 9 mi., put in below dams in W. Warren, usually has good water through Apr. and into May, OK after rains, dark-colored water, good current and riffles for ¼ mi., then river goes under RR brdg., drops into steep chute 50 yds. long, passable but difficult, chute ends in small pond, at outlet river turns to right, passes under RR brdg., then ½ mi. continuous rapids, Dif. III, then suddenly comes to 3-ft. falls, study carefully before running, then in ½ mi. rapids less severe, take out at picnic area on Rte. 67 or on to Rte. 20 brdg. near Fentonville.

Trip 2—Fentonville to Three Rivers, 8 mi., mostly quick water, not as good as above, large dam 3 mi. below Rte. 20 brdg., slack water above dam at Three Rivers.

(Credit—Stewart Coffin)

Quinapoxet River: USGS sheets—Paxton, Worcester N., Sterling. Flows into Wachusett Reservoir, water supply for Boston, lower part posted against boating.

Salmon Brook: See description under New Hampshire.

Saugus River: USGS sheets—Boston N., Lynn. Canoeable from Rte. 1 brdg. to Lynn Harbor, freshwater marsh first mi., ptg. dam at Prankers Pond.

Shawsheen River: USGS sheets—Concord, Billerica, Wilmington, Lawrence; pleasant, smooth water, close to Boston. From Rte. 62 brdg. in Bedford to Ballardville, 1 day, start here in high water, above here is passable in high water but unattractive, below put-in is millpond and ptg. around dam, then rapids, then smooth water to Rte. 3 brdg., 1 mi., winding brook here, then 1 mi. to old Turnpike Brdg., then 2 mi. winding brook to Rte. 3A brdg., 3 mi. to Rte. 129 brdg., 2 mi. to Rte. 38 brdg., 3 mi. to Rte. 93 brdg., and 2 mi. to Ballardville, then carry around mill dam. Below Ballardville, river polluted, industrialized, not recommended, 2 dams in Andover, 2 2-ft. drops at Shawsheen, then river passes close to Lawrence and enters Merrimack. (Credit—Stewart Coffin)

S. River: USGS sheets—Shelburne Falls. From Conway to small iron brdg., 2½ mi., fast water, no hard rapids, run in spring, below Conway to high dam, ptg. right, take out at iron brdg.; below iron brdg., river enters wild gorge, no other take-out until

Stillwater Brdg. on Deerfield River, (Reeds Brdg. is gone), last 2 mi. to Deerfield extremely rough, 2 impassable falls, high dam and waterfall at a sporting camp, don't run. (Credit—Stewart Coffin)

Squannacook River: USGS sheets—Townsend, Shirley, Ayer. From W. Townsend to W. Groton, 11 mi., pretty stream, 1 short rapid, can be run or ptgs., run in high water, put in below W. Townsend Dam, then good current and light rapids to dam site. At Townsend after Rte. 119 brdg. and RR brdg. is 3-ft. cement dam, dangerous, ptg. right, then easy rapid at next turn, then stream is very scenic forested banks, obstructed by logs in low water, can take out at Broken Brdg. or continue through swamp to Harbor Pond, ptg. dam and mill at Townsend Harbor, then easy rapid, good current, good trip in high water, not good in low water. Run or ptg. rapid at broken mill dam, then 2 mi. more smooth to Townsend Rd. Take out here; below here not recommended. Ptg. right at dam at Vose, filthy river below; another dam at W. Groton. (Credit—Stewart Coffin)

Stony Brook: USGS sheets—Ayer, Westford; not recommended for canoeing—too many mills and dams.

Swift River: USGS sheets—Windsor Dam, Palmer. From Rte. 9 to jctn. W. Ware River, 1 day, nearly good flow of water first 4 mi. to Spring Rd. Brdg., pleasant, flat water, 1 obstruction at broken dam at W. Ware River Rd. follows valley on left, below Spring Rd. Brdg. 3 mi. of dead water to 12-ft. dam above Bondsville, no trespassing here, take out above. Below river flows through Bay State Dying and Finishing Plant, 3-ft. dam just below, after Rte. 181 brdg. Another dam and short rapid below, then 2 mi. to Jabisk Brook, another mill dam here—ptg., then 2 mi. of pleasant river to jctn. with Ware River, can paddle up Ware River ½ mi. to Rte. 181 brdg. (Credit—Stewart Coffin)

Taunton River: USGS sheets—Whitman, Bridgewater, Taunton, Assonet Large, sluggish river, badly polluted, industrialized; not recommended for canoeing. Below Auburn St. Brdg. no obstructions, 14 mi. until E. Taunton, then 6 mi. crooked, sluggish river to Taunton, tidewater below.

Tully River: USGS sheets—Royalston, Athol. W. Branch too small to canoe, E. Branch has dam at Rte. 32 brdg., put in 1 mi. below at Fryeville Rd. Brdg., first port is narrow, shallow, and rapid, run in high water, then 2 mi. slow water to broken dam just above Pinedale Ave., ptg. right, then fast current to Pinedale Ave. Brdg., then mostly slow water below, 2 mi. to The Millers at Athol. (Credit—Stewart Coffin)

Ware River: USGS Wachusett Mt., Barre, North Brookfield, Ware, Palmer. From Rte. 62 brdg. to Three Rivers, 45 mi.; current strong most of way, several rapids, water fairly clean, many ptgs. around dams, start down E. branch at Rte. 62 brdg., stream is small, many obstacles, at N. Rutland are 3 dams—ptg. each; then short rapid and strong current, ½ mi. to another dam, ptg. left; below are easy rapids, most canoeists skip this sec. and start at side rd. off Intervale Rd. ¾ mi. below N. Rutland; below are mod. rapids, passable only in high water, some brush jams, then 1½ mi. pleasant canoeing, mixed smooth and rapid to brdg. and millpond above New Boston, dam—ptg. left; strong current, scenic, the next 4 mi. to head of Barre Falls. CAUTION—land on left above the brdg. to avoid being swept into gorge, which begins below brdg., ptg. left ⅓ mi. to end of path, then down steep bank, put in just below lower dam abutments and above deep pool where river turns sharply right; below are 1½ mi. hard rapids, Dif. III, through a gorge, then river flattens out and meanders through marshes with good current 3 mi. to Rte. 122 brdg.; below is diversion dam of Metropolitan Water Commission, often little water below this dam, best in spring. DANGER—chute 200 yds. below the dam with large backwave in high water, can be lined down— left, then strong current and riffles to Powder Mill Pond and dam at White Valley, short but difficult ptg.—right; then fine hemlock woods, at S. Barre is difficult dam—ptg. 2 mi. by rd., put in below dam at Barre Plains, 10 mi. from dam to Gilbertville, longest stretch without dams, good current all the way, farm country, then at Gilbertville strong rapids, then good current 5 mi. to slack water above Ware, take out right at Greenville Park; if continuing on, ptg. by car around Ware, put in below the 3 dams; from Ware 10 mi. to Thorndike, fine canoeing with strong current, several riffles, 2 dams at Thorndike. DANGER—rapid below first dam, ptg. left; rapid below dam 2 not dif., then in 2 mi. the Swift and Quaboag rivers are joined to form the Chicopee River at Three Rivers. (Credit—Stewart Coffin)

Westfield River: Limited canoeing, much water flow variation, 12 mi. annual canoe race in April, approx. route N. of Huntington to S. of Montgomery; with adequate flow, area N. of race area may be run by experts, "wild river," then Chesterfield Gorge, start near Cummington. (Credit—Westfield River Watershed Association)

Weweantic River: USGS Plympton, Snipatuit Pond, Wareham. From Carver on S. Meadow Brook to S. Wareham, 16 mi., meadows, cranberry bogs, swamps, ptg. dam near Benson's Pond; ptg. dam at Tremont Pond; a flat-water trip (Credit—Stewart Coffin)

Williams River: USGS Stockbridge, State Line, Egremont, Great Barrington; not a good canoe stream, a few parts OK above Van Deusenville, dam at Rockdale Station. DANGER—gorge below this dam, don't run, last 3 mi. are best. (Credit—Stewart Coffin)

MICHIGAN

Au Sable River: Crawford, Oscoda, Iosco cos.; Grayling to Lake Huron, 180 mi., 2–3 wks., heavily canoed, excel. for beginners, water fairly fast. Take-out pts.—brdgs. every 10–15 mi. downstream: Grayling to Mio, 75 mi., 3–5 days; below Mio, water slow, 6 hydro. dams to ptg.

Au Sable River—S. Branch: Roscommon, Crawford cos.; M-76 brdg., 3 mi. N. of St. Helen to Roscommon, 35 mi., 2–3 days; wild ctry., crooked river, some jams. Take-out—3 brdgs. between M-76 and Roscommon, also 3 brdgs. from Roscommon N. to jctn. with main stream.

Au Train Waters: Alger Co.; 17 mi., 2 days. Put-in—head, Forest Lower Power Basin, go 6 mi., then move canoe overland 4 mi. to Lake Au Train, continue to Lake Superior, go along Lake Superior shore to Au Train Isle; bass, pike, perch, and trout.

Bad River: Saginaw and Bay cos.; 25 mi., 1–2 days. Through cities of Saginaw and Bay City to Saginaw Bay; apparently not a "bad" trip at all.

Bear Creek: Manistee Co.; 40 mi., 1–2 days. Wild ctry. from Potter's to Big Manistee. Access—Bond's Brdg. N.W. of Kaleva or other brdgs. Take-out—co. rd. at Big Manistee or on to Manistee; trout, salmon.

Belle River: St. Clair Co.; from roadside park on Gratiot Ave. (Rte. 25) 3½ mi. E. of Richmond to Marine City, take out at any brdg. crossing or public-access site in Marine City, farm ctry. with wooded and marshy areas, good small-mouth bass and N. pike fishing. (Credit—*Michigan Guide to Easy Canoeing*)

Betsie River: Benzie, Manistee cos.; Betsie Lake, 44 mi., 2–4 days. Ptg.—Brass Lake, Thompsonville dams, Homestead Dam (N. side), over M-22 brdg.; rainbow trout, pike, bass in stream; pike, bass, panfish in dam backwaters. Big Manistee River: Crawford, Missaukee, Kalkaska, Manistee cos.; 215 mi., 10 days; Deward Rd., Cameron Brdg. Rd., CH-612 crossing, or Manistee River Hunt Club off M-72 in Crawford Co. to N. end Manistee Lake; cedar swamps, many twists, 1–3 ft. deep, first 28 mi.; below M-66 brdg., water speeds till Hodenpyl Dam backwater; from Baxter to Harvey, 20 tortured mi.; downstream from Tippy Dam, 90 mi. wild ctry., 2-day trip. Ptg.—N. side, Hodenpyl Dam; N. side, Tippy Dam, ¼ mi.; trout in stream, walleye, pike, bass, panfish in backwater.

Big Sable River: Lake, Mason cos.; 35 mi., 2 days; co. rd. 669 brdg. in Lake Co. to Hamlin Lake, N. of Ludington; wild ctry., several brdgs. downstream; trout.

Black River: Gogebic Co.; check co. maps, 20 mi., 1–2 days; one of state's wildest rivers, experts only, expect worst, falls, rocky chasms; bottom—mud, sand, rock, no cut ptgs.; rainbow, brook trout.

Black River: Cheyboygan Co.; 45 mi., 3–4 days; Clark's Brdg. on upper Black River, N.W. of Black River Ranch to Cheboygan dam; experts only, logjams, swift water below dams, Crocket Rapids, 4 mi. below start, dangerous, canoeable. Ptgs.—Tower, powerhouse, put in below dam; dam 3 mi. below Tower; Alverno Dam, Van Buren Co.; 8 mi., 1 day; S. Haven, paddle up one side, back the other—lazy-day trip.

Boardman River: Grand Traverse Co.; 40 mi., 2–5 days. The Forks, 17 mi. from Traverse City over "The Old Supply Road" to consumer's Power Dam in Traverse City. Ptgs—2 lift-overs from Forks to Brown Brdg. Dam, ptg. on left at Brown Brdg. Dam, Keystone Dam ptg. and Boardman Hydro, 2 more dams before 1 at Traverse; trout in stream, perch, bass, pike in hydro ponds.

Brule River: Iron Co.; 47 mi., 2–3 days. From M73 brdg., 10 mi., S.W. of Iron River to Paint River jctn.; good canoe stream, few rapids, shallow rapids, 11½ mi. from start. Take-out pts.—brdg. near vil. of Scott Lake, then 3¾ mi. to Pentoga Brdg., then 3½ mi. to Rainbow Trail Brdg., then 3 mi. to Carney Dam, then 6½ mi. to U.S. 2-141 brdg., then 2 mi. to Conservation Dept. Rd. terminal, then 2½ mi. to Paint River jctn.; brook, rainbow trout.

Carp River: Marquette Co. From Deer Lake N. of Ishpeming off Co. Rd. 573 to old U.S. 41, E. of Negaunee, 8–10 mi., 1 day, ⅓ mi. ptg. around dam at E. end of lake, much marsh life in river, fish for perch and brookies, short rapids above take-out point. (Credit—*Michigan Guide to Easy Canoeing*)

Cass River: Tuscola and Saginaw cos.; 65 mi., 2–3 days; Cass City to jctn. of Saginaw River. Free of obstructions, numerous campsites; ptgs.—dams at Caro and Frankenmuth.

Cays River: Mackinac Co.; 20 mi., 1–2 days. From brdg. on M-123, 5½ mi., N.W. of Moran to St. Martin Bay; good canoeing, 1 short rapid below Platz Lake outlet; brook, brown, rainbow trout.

Chippewa River System: Mecosta, Isabella, and Midland cos.; 75 mi., 3–5 days. From N. Branch where it crosses Evergreen Rd.; S. of Osceola-Mecosta co. line to Pine River at Midland. Other access pts.—S. Branch at the Martiny Wildlife Flooding Project E. of Big Rapids; mainstream at dam at Barryton or several brdgs. downstream. Fish—trout as far as M2O in Isabella Co.

Cisco Chain: Gogebic Co.; up to 30 mi., 1–3 days; 15 lakes connected by channels. Start—Cisco Lake public-access site, go through entire chain, return same way. Panfish, bass, pike, walleye.

Clam River: Clare and Missaukee cos. From Falmouth Dam to Church Brdg. on Muskegon River, 19 mi., 2 days, beautiful trip, very few obstructions, scenery varies from rolling farmland to cedar swamps and hardwoods, clear water, a marginal trout stream, mostly private land along river, can take out at Pierre Rd., 10 mi. down from Falmouth. (Credit—*Michigan Guide to Easy Canoeing*)

Clinton River: Oakland Co. From Drayton Plains Nature Center off Hatchery Rd. to boat ramp at Dodge No. 4 St. Park, 7 mi., 4 hrs., small stream, pleasant, best in early spring, marshland, much waterfowl, trout and bass fishing fair in spring. (Credit—*Michigan Guide to Easy Canoeing*)

Clinton River—N. Branch: From 31 Mi. Rd. about 2½ mi. S.E. of Romeo to mouth of the Clinton at Mt. Clemens, 26 mi., 1–2 days, small stream, canoeable only in early spring or when river above normal, 1 dam to ptg. about midway between put-in and first brdg., take out at any brdg. downstream or at jctn. with Clinton, fair steelhead and brown trout fishing in spring, some N. pike, no camping facilities. (Credit—*Michigan Guide to Easy Canoeing*)

Escanaba River: Dickinson, Marquette, and Delta cos.; 55 mi., 8–14 days. W. Branch—access, 7 mi. N. of Ralph W. Branch Forest Cmpgrnd., gravel bottom, ptg. around rapids soon after start, another 1 mi. below Broken Back brdg.; trout. Main stream —access W. of Sands Sta., N. of Gwinn, where E. branch joins main ptg., rapids and small falls, 7 mi. to Gwinn, start after 10 A.M., catch outlet from Princeton Dam, trout to Boney Falls, then bass; 22 mi. from Boney Falls to take-out, no towns between. End—W. Gladstone Brdg., Co. Rd. 420.

Fence River: Iron Co.; 16 mi., 1–2 days. Access—14 mi., N.W. of town where woods rd. ends at river. Ptg.—Rock Dam, 3½ mi., below put-in; 7 mi. from put-in to co. rd. brdg.; trout upper reaches; walleye, northerns, bass, panfish lower.

Flat River: Montcalm, Ionia, and Kent cos. From Langston to Lowell Dam, 45 mi., 2½ days, runs through Langston and Flat River St. Game areas, small-mouth bass fishing fair to good. (Credit—*Michigan Guide to Easy Canoeing*)

Flint River: Lapler and Genessee cos. From Columbiaville to Mott Lake, 20 mi., 1–2 days, 6 mi. are through wildernesslike area; canoe concession and pick-up service on the river. (Credit —*Michigan Guide to Easy Canoeing*)

Ford River: Delta Co. From the brdg. on Co. Rd. E-2, public-access site at mouth of Ford River, 25 mi., 1–2 days, upper half of trip through rugged and remote country, some rapids on lower end of trip—not too dangerous, pretty ctry. (Credit—*Michigan Guide to Easy Canoeing*)

Fox River: Schoolcraft Co.; 15–20 mi., 1–3 days; Wagner Dam to Germfask. Access—12 mi. N.W. of Seney, ½-mi. shallow rapids below Wagner Dam, canoeable; brook trout; many take-out pts.

Huron River: Oakland, Washtenaw cos.; Proud Lake St. Rec. Area to Pte. Mouillee St. Game Area, 42 hrs.; 101 mi. Start— Proud Lake Rec. Area launching site.

Trip 1—Proud Lake to Kensington Metropolitan Park, 5½ hrs., 14 mi., 2 ptgs.—right side of brdg. and control dam below Proud Lake and right side of Milford Dam; 2 canoe rentals—near area headquarters, and in Isle Lake St. Rec. Area. Kensington Metropolitan Park office—635-1561, comb. river and lake canoeing.

Trip 2—Kensington Metropolitan Park to HCMA Canoe Camp Hudson Mills Metropark (above Dexter), 10½ hrs., 23½ mi. DANGER—fallen trees in forested areas, winds across Strawberry and Base Line lakes, rocky areas above and below Dexter Brdg.; 3 ptgs.—Kent Lake Dam, left side control dam at ptg. lake, left side rock barrier below ptg. lake dam. Canoe Rental—Isle Lake St. Rec. Area.

Trip 3—HCMA Camp to Ford Dam Brdg. Rd., 11½ hrs., 28 mi. DANGER—rapids at Delhi, steel post below Ypsilanti City Park, winds on Ford Lake; 9 ptgs.—left of Delhi rapids, RR brdgs. below Delhi, 200 ft. to right of Boston Dam Powerhouse, end of left channel of Argo Dam, to right of hidden underwater brdg. below Ann Arbor, right side of Geddes Dam, right side of Superior Dam, left side of Peninsular Dam, right side of Ford Dam, Canoe rental—Ann Arbor City Park.

Trip 4—Ford Dam Brdg. Rd. to Pte. Mouillee St. Game Area, 14½ hrs., 35½ mi., 3 ptgs.—right at Belleville Dam (French Lndg.) (aim for tall smokestack when portaging), right side of dam at Flat Rock through gate near factory, to right of submerged brdg. and rocky area below Flat Rock Dam. Take out—Pte. Mouillee St. Game Area.

(Credit—*Huron River Canoeing Maps*)

Indian River: Schoolcraft Co. 35 mi., 1–2 days; 6 mi. W. of Steuben to Indian Lake, no fast water, many take-out pts.; brook, brown, rainbow trout.

Inland Lakes Rte.: Emmet, Cheboygan cos.; 45 mi., 3 days; Conway to Lake Huron. Access—Conway Inn Dock, Conway, follow Crooked Lake shore, go out E. end to Crooked River, 5½ mi. to Burt Lake (good fishing in Burt). Long rte.—follow W. shore to N. then down to E. shore. Short rte.—turn right leaving Crooked River, cross to Poverty Bay, follow S. shore to Indian River, follow shore, don't cross open lake water, Indian River current fast, heavy boat traffic, leave Indian River, follow W. shore, Mullet Lake to Cheboygan River. Take-out—Mullet Lake Vil. or go on to Cheboygan through locks, end at Lake Huron.

Intermediate Chain of Lakes: Antrim Co., 60 mi., 4 days, Put-in —head of Six Mile, go N.W. to Ellsworth, turn S. through Six Mile, St. Clair, Ellsworth, Wilson, Benway, Hanley, Intermediate, Bellaire, Clam, Torch, Round (Skegemog), Elk Lakes, and rivers between; follow lake shores, not open water, use protected harbor at Alden if Torch Lake rough. Long rte.—turn N. around shore at Torch Lake, adds 35 mi. Shorter rte.—follow S. shore. Ptg.— Bellaire power dam; bass, pike, walleye, muskie, lake trout, trout.

Jordan River: Charlevoix, Antrim cos.; 15 mi., 1 day; Graves Crossing, 9½ mi., N. of Mancelona on M. 66 to E. Jordan; fast water, logjams, uninhabited; trout.

Kalamazoo River: Calhoun, Kalamazoo, Allegan cos.; 75–80 mi., 5–6 days. Homes to Lake Michigan. Start—Homes, S. of Albion; few dams, river slow and flat, bass in deep holes. Battle Creek to Allegan not recommended; Allegan to Saugatuck, interesting, good fishing below New Richmond; End—Saugatuck or go downstream to Lake Michigan.

Little Manistee River: Lake, Mason, Manistee cos.; 85–100 mi., 3–5 days; Lake Co. Rd. 669 brdg. to head of Hamlin Lake, N. of Ludington; several brdgs. between, wild ctry; trout.

Little Muskegon River: Mecosta, Montcalm, Newaygo cos.; 40 mi., 1–2 days: Blue Lake Dam to Croton Dam backwaters, Little Muskegon joins Muskegon: small stream, sand bass, fair trout fishing to Morley.

Looking Glass River: Clinton, Ionia cos. From Wacousta to Portland, 30 mi., 1–2 days, shallow. (Credit—*Michigan Guide to Easy Canoeing*)

Lower Platte River: Benzie Co. From Hwy. M. 22 Brdg. to Hwy. 168, 6 mi., 2–3 hrs., family canoeing, placid, nice scenery, water gets deeper after passing through Loon Lake. (Credit—*Michigan Guide to Easy Canoeing*)

Manistique River: Schoolcraft Co., 90 mi., 4 days. Main stream—start 9 mi. N. of U.S. 2 on M. 77 to brdg. End—brdgs. on M. Co. Rd. 77, P436; 3–4 days; wild, undeveloped ctry.; walleyes, perch; feeder streams, good side trips.

Manistique River—W. Branch: Start—W. Branch For. Cmpgrnd. Highwater truck trail, 15 air mi. N. of Manistique, 50 mi., 2 days, slow and fast water, perch and walleyes.

Maple River: Shiawassee, Clinton, Gratiot, Ionia cos.; 60 mi., 4–5 days. Ovid to Maple's jctn. with Grand River at Muir.

Menominee River: Dickinson, Menominee cos.; 100 mi., 1–2 wks.; big river, beautiful ctry., dams, few danger stretches, no towns on river from Niagara to Menominee. Start—Wis. side, U.S. 2-141 brdg. N. of Iron Mtn. Ptg.—Ford Dam, Kingsford, haul to Horserace Rapids, put in below, next ptg. is dam ½ mi., then 4 mi. to Kimberly Clark Dam, then 2 mi. to S. Portage Falls, then 7 mi. to Sturgeon Falls Power Dam, also ptg. Quiver Falls, then 6 mi. and Pemene Falls; northerns, walleyes, sturgeon, panfish, trout in feeder streams.

Michigamme River: Marquette, Dickinson, Iron cos.; 50 mi., 1 wk.; Champion to Menominee River. Trip—start Lake Michigamme, go to S. end of lake, river starts here, first part fast, dif., follow river to jctn. Brule and Michigamme. Ptgs.—300-ft. ptg. at Republic Dam. Way Dam, take out left shore. Hemlock Falls Dam, ¼ mi., right shore. Peavy Falls Dam, left shore. Tricky stretch water 12 mi. below Republic. Small-mouth bass, pike.

Muskegon River: Roscommon, Clare, Mecosta, Newaygo, Muskegon cos.; 227 mi., 1–2 wks.; Houghton Lake to Muskegon; mild stream, no danger rapids, some fast water. Trip—W. shore Houghton Lake through Deadstream Swamp above Reedsburg Dam, Hersey halfway pt., Big Rapids to Rogers Dam, 13 mi., Rogers to Hardy Dam, 16 mi., enter Croton Dam below Hardy, from Croton to Newaygo Dam, on to Bridgeton, 13 mi., on to Muskegon. Ptgs.—Rogers Dam, right side; Hardy Dam, W. side; Croton, right bank; Newaygo Dam, right side; bass, pike, rainbows, walleyes.

Muskegon River—W. Branch: Missaukee Co. From Young Rd. Brdg. to Kelly Rd. Brdg., 1 day, no "bad water," many beaver dams, many logjams, fine scenery; swampland and hardwoods, can take out at Hwy. M. 55 brdg., 7 mi. from M. 55 to Kelly Rd. Brdg. on Muskegon. (Credit—*Michigan Guide to Easy Canoeing*)

New River: Iron Co.; 14½ mi., 2 days; sand gravel bottom. Trip —12 mi. N. of Amosa on U.S. 141, then 1 mi. W. on Park Siding Rd. to brdg., pick-ups at Amosa and Crystal Falls, end at Paint River. Ptgs.—Chipmunk Falls, 8½ mi., from start; Snake Rapids, 11 mi., from start; excel. pike in wide waters.

Ocqueoc River: Presque Isle Co.; 30 mi., 2–3 days; Lake Emma to Ocqueoc Lake; several small lakes, swamps to high banks, forests to plains, mud, sand rock bottom, best May–June. Start— Lake Emma or brdg. ½ mi. W. of Millersburg. Ptg.—½ mi. falls at Ocqueoc; ½ mi. sandbar flats before Ocqueoc Lake. End— river crossing U.S. 23 or go down coast to Rogers City.

Ontonagon River: Ontonagon, Gogebic, Houghton cos.; W. Branch, 40 mi., 3 days. Start—13 mi. S. of Ontonagon, Norwich Rd., end Ontonagon. Ptg.—1 mi. Victoria Dam to powerhouse; lower river calm; bass, walleye.

S. Branch: 65 mi., 5 days. Start—N. of Thayer's off U.S. 2, Gogebic Cisco Branch; several mi. fast water; Ptg.—1 mi. Victoria Dam to powerhouse; end Ontonagon.

Mid. Branch: 30 mi., 2 days. Start—7 mi. W. of Watersmeet, off U.S. 2; fast water near Sylvania and Watersmeet, ptg. for novices, 10 mi. to more rapids then 3 mi. to more, ptg. Bond Falls, ½ mi., good trout. End—Bond Falls.

Mid. Branch from Agate: 50 mi., 3 days. Start—off Twnshp., rd. N. of Agate; many miles rapids, cross U.S. 45 at Military Hill; rock to sand bottom, rainbow, brown trout; main stream, brook trout—feeders. End—Ontonagon.

E. Branch: 60 mi., 2 days. Start—E. Branch at Kenton, fast stream, wild ctry., high banks, logjams, rocky runs, deadheads, joins main stream above U.S. 45; trout.

Otter River: Houghton Co.; 50 mi., 3–5 days. Start—brdg. gravel rd. 2¼ mi. N. Nisula, small stream, logjams; pass through Otter Lake to Sturgeon River, on to Portage Lake, Portage Lake canal to Portage Entry, N. Canal, or Torch Lake; trout, panfish, pike, walleyes.

Paint River: Iron Co.; 45 mi., 3–7 days; Gibbs City to mouth of Paint; sand gravel, rock bottom, cutover plains, swamps, mixed for. Trip—ptg. Hemlock Rapids 13½ mi. below Gibbs; 3½ mi. to take-out—put-in pt., C.H. 643 brdg.; then 9½ mi. to U.S. 141 brdg.; then 3½ mi., Crystal Falls Power Dam, line canoe or ptg. ½ mi., next pg. Little Bull Rapids Power Dam, E. shore, or take diversion canal to Peavy Pond; 2 mi. below Little Bull Rapids to Horserace Rapids ptg.; then ½ mi. to U.S. 2 and U.S. 141 access. Take-out—3½ mi. below Paint mouth at power dam in Wis.

Paw Paw River: Van Buren and Berrien cos.; 40 mi., 2 days. Start

—C.H. 681, between Hartford and Laurence; sand, gravel bottom. End—Coloma; pike, bass, panfish, trout.

Père Marquette River: Lake, Mason cos.; 100 mi., 4–7 days. Start —S.E. of Baldwin or M. 37 brdg.; many rapids, some tricky, especially Rainbow Rapids below Bowman's Brdg., ptg. S. side; logjams, overhangs, quick turns all frequent. Trip—below Walhalla go to Père Marquette Lake; trout.

Père Marquette River—Big S. Branch: Newaygo, Mason, Oceana cos. From 13-mi. rd. about 5 mi. W. of Bitely to Indian Brdg. on main branch, 25 mi., 2–3 days, oak hardwood hills and some cedar swamps, several access pts., most land publicly owned, many logjams, particularly after the public-access site 8 mi. south of Walhalla, excellent brown trout, especially in lower parts. (Credit—*Michigan Guide to Easy Canoeing*)

Pine River: Isabella, Montcalm, Gratiot, Midland cos.; 110 mi., 4–7 days. Start—near Remus; shallow, weedy in summer, several ptgs. around dams.

Pine River: Wexford, Lake, Manistee cos.; 70 mi., 3–4 days. Start—Skookum brdg., Lake Co., or Peterson brdg., M. 37; strong, often dangerous, experts only, no dams upper river, ptg. rough water. Take-out—S. side, 300-ft. ptg. where Pine joins Manistee, near Stromach Dam.

Pine River: Chippewa, Mackinac cos.; 30 mi., 1–3 days. Brdg. M. 48, W. of Rudyard, to St. Martin Bay. Alt. end—7 mi., from start, old U.S. 2; suitable for novices.

Platte River: 7 mi., 2 hrs. Start—Platte Lake outlet, or M. 22 brdg., above Platte Lake not good canoeing. Take-out—Lake Michigan.

Presque Isle River: Gogebic Co.; 93 mi., 4–6 days; wild river, rugged country; experts only; some cliffs; mud bottom in swamps, mostly rock. Put-in—E. of Marenisco, U.S. 2 brdg.; 4 falls here;

several ptgs. between U.S. 2 and M. 28 N. of M. 28, possible but many ptgs.; bass, trout, pike.

Raisin River: Lenawee Co.; 42 mi., 1–2 days. Start—Several brdgs. near Clinton. End—Deerfield; some wild stretches, some fishing.

Red Cedar River: Ingham Co. From Williamston Dam to MSU campus, 11 mi., 5–6 hrs., several access pts., at Zimmer Rd., Meridian Rd., Vanetta Brdg., Dobie Rd., and Okemos Rd., stop before low dam at MSU. (Credit—*Michigan Guide to Easy Canoeing*)

Rifle River: Ogemaw, Arenac cos.; 90 mi., 5–6 days. Start—Devoe Lake, 4½ mi. E. of Rose City; no dams or ptgs.; clear, fast water. Access—brdg. on Sage Lake Road north of Selkish; rough water 8 mi. below MSS brdg.; Forestman's camp to Omer, 45 mi., wild ctry. Take-out—several brdgs. or Saginaw Bay. Fish—bass, pike, panfish.

Saginaw River: Saginaw and Bay cos.; 25 mi., 1–2 days; industrial territory, along main hwys., through cities of Saginaw and Bay City to Saginaw Bay.

St. Joseph River: St. Joseph Co.; 60 mi., 2–4 days. Sturgeon Lake to Elkhart or Lake Michigan; fallen trees, farm ctry, good water all way. Ptgs.—dams at Sturgis, Constantine, Mottville, and Elkhart, Ind.; pike, bass, panfish.

St. Mary's River: Chippewa Co.; 40 mi., 3–7 days. Trip—start below Sault Ste. Marie, go around N. tip Sugar Isle through Lake George, follow coast to E. shore through Lake George, cross to E. shore of Neebish Isle, circle isle into Munuscong Lake, follow shore into Raber Bay, on to De Tour. Alt. rte.—start below Sault Ste. Marie, follow W. shore of Sugar Isle through Lake Nicolet then down to "Rock Cut": between W. shore Neebish Isle and mainland into Munuscong Lake, this rte. follows shore all way to De Tour. WARNING—St. Mary's River busiest in world, do not cross in front of freighter, do not hit wake broadside; freighters cannot move, you must; walleyes, northerns, bass, bluegills, perch (muskies in Munuscong Lake).

Shiawassee River: Shiawassee, Saginaw cos.; 65 mi., 2–4 days. Start—near Holly, peaceful river, several dams and ptgs.; fair fishing in backwater, bass, panfish, many take-out pts., clear water ends, Chesaning.

Sturgeon River: Baraga and Houghton cos.; 35 mi., 2–3 days. Start—1 mi. E. of Watton, M. 28, then 3 mi. N. on gravel to brdg.; week-long trip; several ptgs. before Prickett Dam, slower water—Prickett to Otter Lake; bass, trout, northerns, walleyes, panfish.

Sturgeon River: Sec. I—Baraga Co. DON'T RUN—a friend (George Demski) and I almost ran this before checking it out. Don't make that mistake—it will be your last. Above Prickett Dam, 10 mi. S. of L'Anse, is huge canyon filled with rapids and waterfalls.

Sturgeon River: Delta Co.; 15 mi., 1 day. Start—10 mi. N. of U.S. 2 Fed. Hwy. 13; follow river to Nakoma, other access pts.—4 mi. and 7 mi. N. of U.S. 2.

Sucker River: Alger Co.; 17 mi., 1 day. Start—Ask directions in Grand Marias to Old Whitewash Site, Sucker River, 6 mi. S.E. of town; some shallow rapids, not dangerous, many take-out pts.; brook and rainbow trout.

Tahquamenon River: Luce, Chippewa cos.; 63 mi., 1–2 wks. Put in McMillan, float 15 mi. first day, through willow marsh. Camp —6 mi. below Newberry brdg. on M. 123. Ptgs.—upper and lower falls; don't drink water; banks high, mud and sand bottom, June–July bad black-fly months, walleyes, muskies, rock bass, trout in feeders.

The Cut: Roscommon Co.; 10 mi., 1 day. Put in North Higgins Lake St. Park, N. side of Higgins; follow W. lakeshore to "The

Cut" between Higgins and Houghton Lake; on Houghton Lake follow either shore to take-out pts.

Thornapple River: Eaton, Barry, Kent cos.; 45 mi., 2–3 days. Hwy. M. 50 in Eaton Co. or M. 44 near Thornapple Lake to jctn. of Grand; Shallow, rocky during low water. Ptgs.—Irving Dam 12 mi. below Hastings, take out left bank; then 4 mi. to Midville Dam, right bank; then 5½ mi. to La Barge Dam left side; Ada Dam, left side. Old dam at Alaska canoeable in deepest part, rocks below Cascade Dam.

Thunder Bay River: Montmorency, Alpena cos.; 83 mi., 8–12 days. Lake 15 S.W. of Atlanta to Alpena; first 15 mi. shallow, med. fast; tricky rapids ½ mi. below Long Rapids, another 5 mi. beyond, then good water. Shortest rte.—N. shore, Seven Mile Pond. Ptgs.—Atlanta, short, S. side; Hillman Dam, short; 2 logjams below Hillman; Seven Mile Dam short; Four Mile dam short; trout, pike, bass.

Thunder Bay River—S. Branch: Alpena Co. From Hubbard Lake to Dam, 17 mi., 6 hrs.; no ptgs., through farmland and wild ctry., cmpgrnd. with water and toilets midway on trip, trout near headwater, bass, perch, and pike downstream. (Credit—*Michigan Guide to Easy Canoeing*)

Tittabawassee River: Gladwin Co.; 30 mi., 1–2 days; easy canoeing; 2 short ptgs., Secord and Smallwood dams; wild ctry. Put in, upper reaches; either mainstream or E. branch, 15 mi., N.W. Gladwin, near Ogemaw Co. line. Take-out—Wixom Lake or Edenville Dam; bass, pike, panfish.

Two-hearted River: Luce Co.; 25 mi., 2–3 days; experts only; ctry. wild and rolling, fast water, logjams. Start—High Brdg. For. Cmpgrnd. Co. Rd. 407, 23 mi. N. of Newberry. End— mouth; rainbow, brook trout.

Waiska River: Chippewa Co.; 7 mi., 1 day. Start—brdg. M. 28,

1¼ mi. E. of M. 221 jctn. End—Brimley St. Park; timbered ctry., high banks, slow current, good trip; perch, pike, walleyes.

White River: Oceana, Newaygo, Muskegon cos.; 60 mi., 2 days; Hesperia to White Lake at U.S. 31 brdg.; rocky bottom, some swamps, hairpin turns, ptrg. windfalls; trout, bass, panfish.

Whitefish River: Delta Co.; 12 mi., 1 day. Start—take Co. Rd. 509 (Whitefish For. Rd.) N. of Rapid River 12 mi., then ½ mi. W. on U.S.F.S. 2236 to E. Branch, Whitefish River. Take out U.S. 2 brdg.; no ptgs. in spring, short ones later on; brook trout, smallmouth bass, northerns, walleyes. (Credit for Michigan Information—*Michigan Canoe Trails, Michigan Guide to Easy Canoeing,* and *The Wild Rivers of Wisconsin, Upper Michigan and Northeastern Minnesota*)

MINNESOTA

Big Fork River: Koochiching Co.; Co. Rd. 29 brdg. or Dora Lake Lodge, to Laurell Indian Mounds below St. Hwy. 11 brdg., mixed rapids, ptg. Little American Falls—ptg. Lake Powell's Rapids—ptg. Lake Big Fork Falls—dam—ptg. lake. Selected access pts. —Start to Co. Hwy. 31 brdg., 9 mi.; Hwy. 31 brdg. to Co. Hwy. 14 brdg. 229, 28 mi.; Twn. brdg. 229 to Craigville, 11 mi.; Craigville to Mondo Cmpgrnds., 33 mi.; Mondo Cmpgrnds. to Big Fork Falls, 23 mi.; Big Fork Falls to Ben Lynn Lndg., 10 mi.; Ben Lynn Lndg. to Linford Brdg. Lndg.—Co. Hwy. 1, 24 mi.; Co. Hwy. 1 to St. Hwy. 11 brdg., 18 mi.

Boundary Waters Canoe Area: Cook, Lake, St. Louis cos.; 1 mi. acres of ptg.—linked lakes and streams, get free travel permit at Sup. Natl. For. office or from outfitters; beautiful, wild entry, wilderness, excel. fishing, maps a must.

Boy River: See description under Inguadona Canoe Tour.

Cannon River: Goodhue Co.; Hwy. 13 brdg. to Hwy. 61, 66.5 mi. Ptgs.—dam at Hwy. 3 brdg., dam at Dundos brdg., dam at Hwy. 19 brdg., dam below Lake Byllesby. Dif.—dam at Welch. DANGER—Lake Byllesby—motorboats—lack of access; in low water ptg. about Straight River; Cannon River jctn. and below Byllesby Dam to St. Hwy. 52 in low water; 4–5 small rapids. Start to Fariboult—Hwy. 11 brdg., 17.5 mi.; Fariboult to Northfield, 16.9 mi.; Northfield to Cannon Falls, 15.6 mi.; Cannon Falls to Hwy. 61 brdg., 16.5 mi.

Cascade River: USGS Two Harbors and Deer Park Lake; Superior Natl. For. From Hwy. 157 brdg. to Hwy. 45, 4.5 mi., Diff. II, 2 unrunnable falls halfway down—range between 10 ft. and 20 ft., some logs in river above falls, rapids Dif. II below falls. Don't run below take-out at Hwy. 45—many waterfalls. (Credit—*Whitewater, Quietwater*)

Cloquet River: St. Louis Co.; Hwy. 44 S. of Brimson to Brookston, 59 mi., mod. to treacherous rapids, wildlife inc. moose, good camping, run in high water, some lining in upper parts. DANGER —Isle Lake Res.—windy, below Isle Lake Dam—flow varies with release, motorboats, white water in lower parts, experts only ptg.

Isle Lake dam falls above Lake Alden; start to Lake Alden, 21 mi.; Lake Alden to ent. to Isle Lake Res., 6 mi.; 7 mi. through res.; Isle Lake Dam to Co. Rd. 8 brdg., 19 mi.; Co. Rd. 8 brdg. to Brookston, 6.8 mi.

Crow River—Mid. Fork: 90 mi. N.W. of Twin Cities, 12 mi. up and 12 mi. back, 65 mi. of shoreline, many bays and islands, small creeks, leisurely trip, OK family.

Crow River—N. Fork: Meeks, Wright cos.; St. Hwy. 22 near Litchfield to jctn. with Mississippi River, 90 mi., clear, narrow and fast-moving at start, pollution begins after 1 mi.—never stops, small rapids at first ptg.; dam near Hanover, dif. ptg.; ptg.—Bering Mill. Start to Co. Hwy. 2 brdg., 23 mi.; Co. Hwy. 2 brdg. to Co. Hwy. 7 brdg., 22 mi.; Co. Hwy. 7 brdg. to dam, 30 mi.; dam to end of trip, 14.5 mi.; several other access pts.

Crow Wing River: Morrison, Cass cos.; Nevis and brdg. 33 to dam below Hwy. 6, 88.2 mi.; Crow Wing Canoe Route—75 mi., good swimming, not dangerous, rapids, avg. waist deep, deep holes, many access pts., good camping; ptg.—2 dams in last 12 mi.; northern pike, walleye, black and rock bass, perch.

Des Moines River: Jackson Co.; Talcot Lake Dam to st. line, 53 mi., barbed-wire fences; ptg.—dams near Windom Rapids and Jackson, a few light rapids. Start to Hwy. 15, 12.5 mi.; Hwy. 15 to dam, 12.2 mi.; dam to Kilen Woods St. Park, 9 mi.; Kilen Woods St. Park to Jackson, 9 mi.; Jackson to st. line, 10 mi.

Inguadona Canoe Tour: Chippewa Natl. For. from st. public access on E. of Lover Trelipe Lake to Leech Lake, 23 mi.; from put-in at Trelipe Lake to Leech Lake, 23 mi.; from put-in at Trelipe Lake the trail goes downriver to Inguadona Lake, N. 2 mi. down the lake to the Boy River, then down the Boy to Boy and Swift Lake and on to Leech Lake; check For. Ser. map for recommended take-out place 3 mi. prior to Leech Lake; during last 3 mi. the river spreads into wide swamps with no high land accessible from river, no lndg. available until Sugar or Blackduck Point. Leech Lake can become very rough in a hurry; much wildlife, including bald eagle and osprey. (Credit—*The Inguadona Canoe Tour—Chippewa Natl. For.*)

Kettle River: Carlton, Pine cos.; Minn. 73 (poor access) to jctn. with St. Croix River, scenic, rapids, and long pools, good canoeing, white water—upper Kettle. DANGER—Hell's Gate Rapids, never run canyon in high water. Start to jctn. with Moose River, 13 mi., many rapids, low trees. Moose River jctn. to Hwy. 23, 14 mi., few rapids. Hwy. 23 to Kettle River dam, 6 mi., very dangerous, experts only, ptg. dam right; dam to St. Croix River, 3 short heavy rapids, whirlpool on bend, 20 mi.

Little Fork River: Koochiching Co.; Hwy. 53 brdg. at Cook to jctn. with Rainy River, 132 mi., wild entry, wildlife, incl. moose, excel. fishing—musky and walleye, some dif. rapids, logs and stumps in water below Nett Rapids. Start to Hananen's Falls, 16 mi., ptg.—S. bank. Falls to St. Hwy. 65 brdg. (Silverdale), 21 mi., small falls—can run, rapids. St. Hwy. 65 to Flat Rock Rapids, 67 mi.; Flat Rock Rapids to jctn. with Rainy River, 28 mi.

Minnesota River: S. Minnesota; Ortonville to Shakopee, 289 mi., very few rapids, some near Granite Falls, then Patterson Rapids (not dif.), heavily forested banks from Minn. Falls to N. Redwood, slow current; from Ortonville to Shakopee many snags and brush piles; ptg. Big Stone Dam on right; Granite Falls and dam —ptg. right; Minnesota Falls ptg. right. Many access pts., many historic sites.

Mississippi River: U.S. Hwys. 2 and 71 river crossing to jctn. with Rum River; 370 mi.; Lake Itasca to Lake Bemidji, semiwilderness, established as canoe rte.; Bemidji to Grand Rapids, ptg.— 4 dams, excel. fishing, 2 large lakes—Brainerd to Anoka, hills and plains, many towns. Ptg.—11 dams on river, some rapids, not partic. dif. DANGER—wind, motorboats; river dif. after Ball Club Lake, many isles, many collateral channels.

Moose River: Carlton Co.; Barnum to town of Moose Lake, 7 mi., can't run in low water. Access—Barnum Vil. Park.

Red Lake River: Polk, Red Lake cos. Small central dam between Lower Red Lake and Red Lake River to St. Hwy. 220 brdg., 164 mi., varies from wilderness to trash banks, rapids, and long, flat stretches. Start to dam—ptg. right, 12 mi.; dam to Thief River Falls, 46 mi.; ptg. Thief River Falls Dam left; Thief River Falls to St. Hilaire, 9 mi., some rapids; St. Hilaire to Red Lake Falls, 20 mi., many rapids, short pools, large boulders. DANGER—abandoned dam at Red Lake Falls; Red Lake Falls to dam—ptg. right 25 mi.; dam to Crookston Dam, 8 mi.; Crookston Dam to St. Hwy. 220 brdg., 44 mi., poor access between.

Rice River: Chippewa Natl. For., Marcell, Minn. From the public-boat access on Clubhouse Lake to vil of Bigfork, 18 mi., no ptgs. but some carries over beaver dams may be impassable after June 30, partic. between Cameron Lake and brdg. on For. Rd. 2181, check with Ranger Sta. in Marcell about water level, much wildlife; this trip is combination of river and small lakes, available campsites. (Credit—The Rice River Canoe Tour—Chippewa Natl. For.)

Root River: Houston, Fillmore, Olmstead cos. Brdg. on old Hwy. 5 to slough at end, 82 mi., seldom over 3 ft. deep, some deep pools, no serious waterfalls, several rapids. Chatfield to Lanesboro, 22 mi., some rapids; Lanesboro to Rushford, 20 mi., some rapids; Rushford to Houston, 12 mi., fast water, few rapids; Houston to Hokah, 16 mi.

Rum River: Mille Lacs, Anoka, Isanti cos. Wayside Park, N. of Hwy. 95 brdg. in Princeton to Anoka Dam, 68 mi., variety of scenery, upper part wild with much wildlife; ptg. St. Francis old dam and brdg.—rough rapids. Start to St. Hwy. 47 brdg.—W. Point, 15 mi.; Hwy. 47 to Cambridge Park, 17 mi.; Cambridge to St. Francis, 17 mi.; St. Francis to Anoka Dam, 19 mi.

St. Croix River: See description under Wisconsin.

St. Louis River: Carlton, St. Louis cos. Undeveloped campsite by Ford Fairlane Taconite Plant off Co. Rd. 16 to Cloquet, 91 mi., scenic, riffles in upper end, some dif. rapids, much wildlife, good fishing. Start to Co. Rd. 436, 25 mi., some rapids; Fl. City Park to Paupores Resort, 10 mi., severe rapids; Paupores Resort to Cloquet, 26 mi.

Snake River: Aitken, Kanabec, Pine cos. Hwy. 65 to Co. Rd. 18, 77 mi.; McGrath to Mora, 38 mi., some of most dif. rapids in st., skilled only, many rapids, beaver dam, old logging dam; Mora to Pine City Dam, 28 mi., 2 days, easy, safe, a few rapids; Pine City to St. Croix River, 11 mi., fast run in high water, shallow in low water—maybe some wading, many rapids and pools. (Credits—See sources listed in back. Particular credit to *Minnesota Voyageur Trails, Whitewater, Quietwater,* and *The Wild Rivers of Wisconsin, Upper Michigan and Northeastern Minnesota*)

MISSISSIPPI

Beaverdam Creek: Perry Co., De Soto Natl. For. Hwy. 308 to Block Creek, 8 mi., narrow, winding, overhanging trees, clear with brownish tint water. (Credit—*Black Creek Float Trip*—De Soto Natl. For. and G. W. Wasson)

Black Creek: Perry, Stone, Forrest cos., De Soto Natl. For. Bog Creek Lndg. to Old Alexander Brdg., 42 mi., 42 hrs., most obstacles have been removed, some submerged logs; Big Creek Lndg, to Moody's Lndg., 12 mi.; Moody's Lndg. to Janice, 10 mi.; Janice to Fairley Brdg., 11 mi.; Fairley Brdg. to Old Alexander Brdg., 9 mi. (Credit—*Black Creek Float Trip*—De Soto Natl. For. and G. W. Wasson)

Bogue Chitto River: See description under Louisiana.

Little Sunflower River: This river is the western bdry. of Delta Natl. For. for ⅔ of river's length, separates farmland from for., runs through Natl. For. for 6 mi., poor canoeing, nearly dry in summer, mudbanks, no designated campsites on river, camping allowed only in designated sites. (Credit—Stephen R. Rickerson)

Tchoutocabouffa River: Harrison Co., De Soto Natl. For. F.S. Rd. 421 access to F.S. Rd. 403 crossing, approx. 2 mi., submerged logs and stumps, logjams, wildlife incl. alligators (please help protect—endangered species); good fishing—bass, catfish. (Credit—*Black Creek Float Trip*—De Soto Natl. Forest and G. W. Wasson)

Tuxachanie Creek: Harrison Co., De Soto Natl. For. F.S. Rd. 402 to F.S. rds. 419 and 439 crossing, approx. 7 mi., submerged logs and stumps, logjams, wildlife incl. alligators (please help protect

—endangered species); good fishing—bass, catfish; add. access—F.S. Rd. 413. (Credit—*Black Creek Float Trip*—De Soto Natl. For. and G. W. Wasson)

MISSOURI

Bear Creek: 9.7 mi., Hwy. P. brdg. to Sac River; Dif. I, II, brdg. Access—Hwys. P and M.

Beaver Creek: Douglas, Taney cos.; 41.4 mi.; St. Hwy. 76 brdg. 8 mi. S.W. of Ava to St. Hwy. 160 brdg. Access—several brdgs.; 1 ptg.—Rome Dam, ptg. right; may be some wading.

Big Creek: 17 mi.; St. Hwy. 49 brdg. S.E. of Annapolis to St. Francis River. Other access—Hwy. N. brdg., brdg. in Sam A. Baker St. Camp, 2 mi. S. of Brunot, old brdg.; read description of St. Francis River before canoeing.

Big Piney River: Texas, Pulaski, Phelps cos.; 77 mi.; Dog's Bluff Access Pt. at St. Hwy. 17 to Gasconade River jctn.; Dif. I, II. Access—several brdgs. and fords. Dams—low rock dam at Fort Leonard Wood (possible danger here), concrete dam and ptg. right at Fort Leonard Wood; good fishing.

Big River: St. François, Washington, Jefferson cos.; 83.2 mi; mouth of Turkey Creek to Meramec River. Dif. I. Access—several brdgs; 4 ptgs.—Morse Mill Dam, ptg. right; Cedar Hill Brdg. and Mill Dam, ptg. left; Dam—68.9 mi. downstream, ptg. right; Byrnes Mill Dam, ptg. right.

Big Sugar Creek: Elk River, McDonald Co.; 43.7 mi.; Hwy. 90 brdg. at mouth of Trent Creek to Okla. st. line. Dif. mostly II; some over. Access—several brdgs. and fords; ptg.—dam 35.8 mi. from start, some fast water.

Black River: Reynolds, Wayne, Butler cos., 88.3 mi.; St. Hwy. 21 brdg. above Centerville on W. fork to U.S. Hwy. 60 brdg. in Poplar Bluff; Dif. I, II. Access—several brdgs.; 1 ptg., Clearwater Dam, ptg. left.

Black River—E. Fork: 4.9 mi.; Taum Saulk Creek to jctn. with main river. Other access—St. Hwy. 21—49 brdg. Dif. I, II.

Black River—Mid. Fork: 9.4 mi.; Hwy. J Brdg. near Black River to jctn. with W. Fork, 1 ptg. over concrete ford. Dif. I, II.

Bourbeuse River: Gasconade, Franklin cos.; 107.6 mi.; St. Hwy. 19 brdg. to jctn. with Meramec River. Dif. I. Access—low-water brdg. Hwy. 19, Tea brdg., Hwy. H brdg.; St. Hwy. 155 brdg; Hwy. UU runs parallel to river, U.S. Hwy. 50 brdg., Hwy. 50 and 66 brdgs., I—44 brdg., brdg. 1 mi. N.E. of Moselle.

Bryant Creek: Douglas, Ozark cos.; 40½ mi.; St. Hwy. 14, Rippee Wildlife Area to Corps of Engineers cmpgrnd. at Tecumseh. Dif. I, II. Relatively wild stream, obstacles in creek, some fast riffles. Access—several brdgs. and other pts.

Bull Creek: Christian, Taney cos.; 9.5 mi.; brdg. 3.5 mi. N. of Walnut Shade to St. Hwy. 76 brdg. Access—put in St. Hwy. 148 brdg. at Walnut Shade, St. Hwy. 76. Falls 4.9 mi. below start; channel to left avoids falls. Good fishing—small-mouth and large-mouth bass.

Cedar Creek: 18.3 mi.; Ivy brdg. (Hwy. K) to Sac River. Dif. I, II. Brdg. access—Hwy. K, St. Hwy. 39, Co. Rd. 54.

Center Creek: Jasper Co.; 26.5 mi.; S. of Carthage to brdg. 2 mi. W. of Belleville. Dif. II and III. Rocky rapids, tricky runs, brush, overhanging limbs. Access—many brdgs.; 2 ptgs.—Old Mill Dam 9.1 mi. downstream, concrete dam 10.2 mi. downstream.

Courtois Creek: Washington, Crawford cos.; 21.2 mi.; Brazil low-water brdg. between Hwy. Y and Palmer to jctn. with Huzzah

Creek. Dif. often II, sharp turns, obstructions, narrow channel. Brdg. access—St. Hwy. 8, 2 low-water brdgs.; some fast water.

Crane Creek: 8.2 mi.; Hwy. CC brdg. 3 mi. S. of Hurley to James River. Access—4 brdgs.; no dams.

Current River: Dent, Shannon, Carter, Ripley cos.; 139 mi.; Montauk St. Park to Currentview. Dif. I, sometimes II. Float throughout yr.; seldom freezes, in normal water a very safe river. Access —several brdgs.

Eleven Point River: Oregon Co.; 49 mi.; Thomasville to Mo.-Ark. st. line; Dif. I, II. Some rapids, 7 access pts., no dams.

Finley Creek: 18.9 mi.; St. Hwy. 125 brdg. below dam at Lindenlure Lake to James River. Access—several brdgs. Ptg.—U.S. Hwy. 65 brdg. and mill dam at Ozark, dam at Riverdale.

Flat Creek: Barry, Stone cos.; 24 mi.; brdg. S. of Jenkins to St. Hwy. 173 brdg. Dif. I, II. Some rapids, no dams.

Gasconade River: Wright, Laclede, Pulaski, Phelps, Maries, Osage, Gasconade cos.; 253.1 mi. Dif. I, seldom II. St. Hwy. 38 brdg. E. of Hartville to Missouri River. Access—many brdgs.; some fast riffles; some logjams; no dams; safe family river.

Grand Auglaize Creek: Camden, Miller cos.; 13.8 mi.; low-water brdg. 1.8 mi. up from Hwy. A brdg. to brdg. at end of "Glaize Arm" of Lake of Ozarks. Dif. I, II. Access—Hwy. A, Toronto, plus start and finish pts.; no dams. Kentucky bass, white bass.

Huzzah Creek: Washington, Crawford cos.; 23.4 mi.; Hwy. V brdg. S.E. of Davisville to Meramec River. Dif. often II, sharp turns, obstructions, narrow river. Access—Hwy. V, Davisville, low-water brdg., N.E. Huzzah Settlement, Harper Ford Brdg., St. Hwy. 8 brdg., Scotia brdg. (possible ptg.).

Indian Creek: Newton, McDonald cos.; 27.9 mi. Dif. II, III, brush, logs, fast turns. From Hwy. D Brdg. (spring or high water) to Elk River. Access—many brdgs., 2 ptgs.—Mill Dam at McNatt, concrete slab ford 24.5 mi. below start, ptg. right.

Jacks Fork River: Texas, Shannon cos.; 44.6 mi.; Hwy. Y low-water brdg. to ferry landing ¾ mi. below Little Shawnee Creek and Current River jctn. Dif. I, II. One of the wildest, most scenic Mo.-Ozark streams. Some wading, 6 access pts., no dams, upper section good fly fishing.

James River: Greene, Christian, Stone cos.; 61.7 mi.; St. Hwy. 125 brdg. to St. Hwy. 148—13 brdg. at Galena. Dif. I, a few places on upper river III due to obstructions. Access—many brdgs., 3 ptgs. —dam 12 mi. below start, rapids 20 mi. below start, low-water brdg. 2.5 mi. S. of Battlefield; good fishing.

Little Niangua River: Hickory, Camden cos., 34.3 mi.; first low-water brdg. above Hwy. 54 (high water only) to Hwy. J Brdg. Dif. I, II. Brdg. access—Hwy. 54. Hwy. F, Hwy. P, Hwy. J. Rocky riffles; no dams. Fishing good—small-mouth and large-mouth bass, perch, sunfish, bluegill, crappie, walleyes, cats.

Little Piney: 18.3 mi.; Yancy Mills to Gasconade River jctn. Dif. I, II. Brdg. access—rd. connecting Hwys. T and 63, rd. connecting Hwys. T and CC, Newburg Brdg., U.S. Hwy. 66; no dams.

Little Sac River: 24.8 mi. S.E. of Aldrick to Sac River. Dif. I, II. Brdg. access—Hwy. 123, Hwy. C, Hwy. T.

Little St. Francis River: 15 mi.; Hwy. 72 to main river; ptg. paved ford 9 mi. below start. Other access—Hwy. 72 and Hwy. T brdg. Read description of St. Francis River before canoeing.

Little Sugar Creek: 7.9 mi.; Hwy. 90 brdg. N.E. of Jane to Elk River. Other access—Griffin Ford, Hwy. K brdg.; 1 ptg.— Havenhurst Dam, ptg. left; falls below dam too shallow to run.

Maries River: Osage Co.; 28.5 mi.; brdg. on Koelztown–Freeburg rd. to Osage River. Dif. I, II. Brdg. access—Hwy. T, U.S. Hwy. 63, N.E. of Westphalia, Hwy. 50.

Meramec River: Dent, Crawford, Phelps, Franklin, Jefferson, St. Louis cos.; 191.4 mi.; brdg. at Short Bend to Mississippi River. Dif. I, seldom II. Access—several brdgs.; ptg.—1 dam, 13.4 mi. from start.

Mineral Fork of Big River: 13.8 mi.; Hwy. F brdg. to Big River. Other access—St. Hwy. 47; no dams.

Moreau River: Moniteau, Cole cos.; 61.4 mi.; Rockhouse brdg., N. Moreau Creek, 5.5 mi. S. McGish, Hwy. 50 to Missouri River. Dif. I, except high water. Access—several brdgs. and other pts.; no dams; good bass fishing.

Niangua River: Dallas, Laclede, Camden cos.; 79.5 mi.; St. Hwy. 32 brdg. 4 mi. E. of Buffalo to mouth of Bank Branch. Dif. I, II; some rocky riffles. Access—many brdgs. and other pts.; ptgs.— Tunnel Dam (may not be canoeable farther downstream). DANGER—powerhouse below Tunnel Dam and power-line crossing; good fishing river.

N. Fork River: Douglas, Ozark cos.; 49.5 mi.; Hwy. HH brdg. to Corps of Engineers cmpgrnd. below Bryant Creek jctn. Dif. I, II, some III in high water. Access—several brdgs. and other pts.; rocky riffles. DANGER—don't approach the falls broadside or the wooden low-water brdg. on extension of Hwy. KK to Hwy. H access; Dawt Brdg. dangerous in high water. Ptg. Dawt Mill Dam.

Osage Fork of Gasconade River: Webster, Wright, Laclede cos.; 57 mi.; Hwy. 22 near Rader to Gasconade jctn. Dif. I, II; some logjams. Access—10 brdgs.; no dams; good fishing.

Pomme de Terre River: Polk, Hickory, Benton cos.; 70 mi.; Sunset Brdg. S.E. of Bolivar to Little Pomme de Terre River. Dif. I. Access—many brdgs.; ptg.—Pomme de Terre Res., 17 mi.

Roaring River: Barry Co.; 5.8 mi.; below falls in Roaring River St. Park to Hwy. 86 brdg. Dif. II, very little III. Sometimes exciting depending upon flow. Access—3 brdgs., 1 ford; no dams

Rock Creek: Barry Co.; 3.5 mi.; jctn. E. Fork and Rock Creek to Hwy. F. Dif. II, III. Normally almost dry creek; white water after rains; barbed wire; use caution; no dams.

Sac River: Dade, Cedar, St. Clair, Polk cos.; 100.5 mi. Hwy. U brdg. S.E. of Dadeville to Osceola Dam. Dif. I, II. Dams—2: Hulston Mill, Caplinger Mills (ptg. right). Access—several brdgs.

St. Francis River: St. François, Madison, Wayne, Iron cos.; 78.6 mi. Hwy. H brdg. 3 mi. S. of Farmington to U.S. Hwy. 67 brdg. at Greenville; run during high or mod. high water; some wild, dangerous areas. Dif. I to III but some IV and possibly V in flood; dense willow thickets; rapids, experts only. Access—brdgs. and other pts.; no dams; check carefully before canoeing.

Shoal Creek: Newton Co.; 42 mi. Below mill dam at Ritchey to old brdg. site on S. side of lake 2.5 mi. above jctn. of Shoal Creek and Spring River. Access—many brdgs.; 6 ptgs.—Old Mill Dam near Hwy. E brdg. (4 mi. below put-in), low dam 11.7 mi. below start, low dam 13.6 mi. below start, U.S. Army Dam 14.6 mi. below start (ptg. on path), rifts at Redings Mill 30 mi. below start, Grand Falls Dam. Dif. II, III; some rapids, obstructions, falls.

South Moreau Creek: 13.8 mi. Dif. I except high water. Hwy. AA brdg. S. of Russellville to jctn. with Moreau Creek. Brdg. access— Hwy. AA, McCann; low water—Hwy. D, Taylor, Hwy D; no dams.

Spring River: Lawrence, Jasper cos.; 62.8 mi. Williams Creek near low-water brdg. 3 mi. W. of Mt. Vernon to brdg. 2 mi W. of Belleville. Dif. II, sometimes III; some rapids, obstructions. Access —several brdgs.; 2 ptgs.—Morrow Mill Dam and brdg. dam at Hwy. 66—ptg. right; 3 danger pts.—old mill dam 13.6 mi. downstream from start, 40 mi. downstream river divides before Old Quaker Mill—left channel dangerous, old mill dam at Galesburg.

Swan Creek: Christian, Taney cos.; 21.2 mi. Hwy. 125 brdg. at Garrison to Hwy. 76 brdg. Dif. normal water I, II; high water II, III. Access—5 brdgs.; rapids in high water; good fly fishing.

Tavern Creek: Miller Co.; 34 mi. Hwy. 42 brdg. 2 mi. N.W. of Iberia to Osage River. Dif. I, II. Brdg. access—St. Anthony 2 mi. N.W., Hwy. A (2 pts.). Low-water brdg. adjacent E.–W. co. rd.; low-water brdg. mouth of Brush Creek, St. Elizabeth, Hwy. 52; Conservation Comm. brdg. near Osage River.

Turnback Creek: 16 mi.; Dilday Mill site upstream, Hwy. K brdg. to Sac River; Dif. I, II. Brdg. access—Hwy. K, Antiok, St. Louis, San Francisco RR, S. Greenfield, Hwy. O, Hwy. 160.

Weaubleau Creek: St. Clair Co.; 20.1 mi. Low-water brdg. 3 mi. S.W. of Gerster to Osage River. Dif. I, II, III; logs and brush. Access—several brdgs.; no dams. Fish—small-mouth and large-mouth bass, sunfish, perch, bluegills.

(Credit—*Missouri Ozark Waterways*)

MONTANA

Beaverhead River: Clark Canyon Dam to Pipe Organ hwy. brdg.; water not too fast, meanders, brushy banks; other parts canoeable but irrigation diversion headgates, cross fences.

Big Blackfoot River: Lincoln to Bonner, Hwy. 200 parallels most way; upper end to Helmville hwy. brdg. slow; lower end, Clearwater River to MacNamarra's Landing, large boulders, faster. Mid–late June upper area; early July–fall, lower end.

Big Hole River: Below Divide Dam to brdg. near Twin Brdgs.; deep holes, good fishing.

Bitterroot River: 80 mi.; pleasant, leisurely, nonhazardous; lower part, fences and irrigation dams, access from ctry rd. brdgs.; E. and W. branch canoeable; rainbow, whitefish, browns.

Clark Fork River: 180 mi.; Deer Lodge to Flathead River; scenic. After July 1 to late fall; Hwy. 10A and 10 parallel most of way. Good fishing—brown, rainbow trout, whitefish, Dolly Varden.

Dearborn River: Hwy. 287 brdg. to jctn. with Mo., low after mid-summer—not recommended. Rainbow, brown, excellent fishing.

Flathead River: Main; above Flathead Lake not hazardous, beautiful, excellent fishing. Columbia Falls to Flathead Lake, many access pts. Dolly Varden, cutthroat, whitefish, Kokanee snag fishing.

Flathead River—N. Fork: originates British Columbia, beautiful, apparently canoeable, good fishing.

Flathead River—S. Fork: bad spots, Black Bear to Meadow Creek, ask locals first; wilderness, inaccessible country.

Jefferson River: entire length canoeable, several brdgs. and other access pts.

Kootenai River: Accessible all length. Star Rte. 37 on U.S. Rte. 2. DANGER—Kootenai Falls area between Troy and Libby; don't run. Other trips OK through rugged country. Libby Dam will kill 50 mi. of stream, excellent fishing—whitefish, cutthroat, Dolly Varden, ling, sturgeon.

Marias River: excellent trip, Tiber Dam to jctn. with Mo. near Loma, private access pts. between. Excellent fishing—northern pike, catfish, sauger, goldeye.

Missouri River: Upper 3 forks or Trident to Townsend, Trident to

Toston Dam, 1½ days, ptg. dam. Old Toston hwy. brdg. to Townsend, end—fish and game access or Can Ferry Res. below Townsend, Hwy. brdg. below Holten Dam at Craig to pts. downstream. River level varies quickly, hwy. parallels, trout fishing good at times, Fort Benton to Fred Robinson Brdg., 160 mi., wild, catfish, sauger. DANGER—rattlesnakes along bank. Access pts. between Ft. Benton and Ft. Peck Res.: (1) brdg. off W. end of U.S. 87; (2) ferry at Loma near mouth of Marion River; (3) ferry at Virgelle; (4) Ophis Ferry from Big Sandy on N.W. and Winnefred to S.E.; (5) brdg. on U.S. 191.

Smith River: Ft. Logan Fish and Game access to co. rd. between Cascade and Eden, scenic, Indian paintings and caves, near wilderness, excellent camping, several fences, small creeks enter with good fishing.

Sun River: Hwy. 289 between Augusta and Chateau to Vaughn, good till mid-August. Brown, rainbow, whitefish.

Swan River: Not hazardous, mosquitoes, logjams, several ptgs., hwy. parallels.

Yellowstone River: Entire length canoeable. Yellowstone Park line through Yankee Jim Canyon above Livingston, hazardous, experts only. Livingston to Billings, some hazards, low div. weir in S. Channel, 4 mi. below Springdale; below Billings, many dangerous structures, ask locals; inexperienced should put in below mouth of Yankee Jim Canyon, ptg. large irrigation div. near Huntley—don't run; river is swift. Gardiner to take-out pt. above Yankee Jim Canyon deep and fast with large boulders at first, long riffles past Corwin Springs, take-out isles before Yankee Jim Canyon. River divides often in following trips; Carbella to Emigrant, 15 mi.; Emigrant to Carter Brdg., 23 mi.; Carter Brdg. to Springdale, 27 mi.; through McAdous Canyon; Springdale to Big Timber, 18 mi.; Big Timber to Reed Pt., 25.5 mi.; Reed Pt. to Columbus, 18 mi. (protruding logs short distance before Columbus); Columbus to Laurel, 29.4 mi.; Laurel to Billings E. Brdg., 20 mi.; Billings E. Brdg. to Huntley, 12 mi. (dam near

Huntley); Huntley to Pompey's Pillar, 20 mi.; Pompey's Pillar to Custer, 29 mi. (ptg.—1 dam); Custer to Myers, 16 mi. (ptg.—1 dam, left channel).

(Credit—*Montana's Popular Float Streams* and Vern Craig)

NEBRASKA

Big Blue: Beatrice (Hoag Brdg.) to Riverside Park, 13 mi. Popular Run, longer trips to Holmesville, Barenston, Marysville, Kansas, and on to Turtle Creek Res. First 50–60 mi. of river too shallow for canoeing. (Credit—*Canoeing in Nebraska*)

Blue Creek: apparently OK from Crescent Lake to McConaughy. (Credit—Nebraska Game and Parks Commission)

Calamus River: Brown, Loup, Garfield cos. Hwy. 7 S. of Ainsworth to Burnell, 48 mi., 3–4 days, no ptgs., excel. campsites (need landowner permission).
Trip 1—Hwy. 7 to Hwy. 183, 33 mi., 1½ days.
Trip 2—Hwy. 183 to Burnell, 15 mi., 1 day. Best time May, June, Sept., Oct. (Credit—*Canoeing in Nebraska*)

Dismal River: Hooker, Thomas, Blaine cos. Hwy. 97 S. of Mullen to Dunning, 50 mi., some fast water near Hooker-Thomas co. line, mostly sand bottom, no ptgs., no obstacles, some trout fishing in gravel pits S. of Neb. St. For., good campsites, geyser 12 mi E. of Hwy. 97, Indian artifacts along stream. Hwy. 97 to Hwy. 83 S. of Thedford, 28 mi., 1½ days. Hwy. 83 to Dunning, 22 mi., 1½ days, stream shallow in summer, some wading. (Credit—*Canoeing in Nebraska*)

Elkhorn River: Cuming, Dodge, Washington, Douglas cos. From West Point to Two Rivers St. Rec. Area, 4–5 days, best in spring. Trip 1—West Point to Dead Timber St. Rec. Area, 18 mi. Trip 2

—Hooper to Arlington, 22 mi. Trip 3—Arlington to Q St. Brdg., 22 mi. Trip 4—Q St. Brdg. to Two Rivers St. Rec. Area. Take-out—Hwy. 6 brdg., go past jctn with Platte. (Credit—*Canoeing in Nebraska*)

Gorden Creek: lower ½ to ⅔ canoeable to jctn. with Box Butte River. (Credit—Nebraska Game and Parks Commission)

Harlan Co. River: below Harlan Co. Res. to st. line. (Credit—Nebraska Game and Parks Commission)

Little Blue River: approx. ⅔ to st. line. (Credit—Nebraska Game and Parks Commission)

Logan Creek: approx. ½, lower to jctn. with Elkhorn River. (Credit—Nebraska Game and Parks Commission)

Loup River: entire length to mouth jctn. with Platte River. (Credit—Nebraska Game and Parks Commission)

Medicine Creek: below Harry Strunk Lake to jctn. with Republican River. (Credit—Nebraska Game and Parks Commission)

Middle Loup River: halfway above jctn. with Dismal River to jctn. with S. Loup River. (Credit—Nebraska Game and Parks Commission)

Missouri: Unchanneled stretch from Yankton, S.D., to Ponca (popular). Take-out—Ponca State Park; towboats not a hazard in this area. DANGER—Channelized area S. from Sioux City due to towboats and other hazards. (Credit—*Canoeing in Nebraska*)

Niobrara River: Cherry, Brown, Rock cos. Rte. 97 S. of Nenzel to Rte. 183 N. of Bassett, 90 mi., 7 days. Rte. 97 S. of Nenzel to Consumer's Public Power Dam E. of Valentine, 34 mi., 3 days; ptg.—Con. Pub. Pow. Dam, trout fishing in spring-fed creeks (Schlagel, Fairfield, Plum, and Long Pine). Dam to Rte. 183 N. of Bassett, 56 mi., 4 days, 2 rapids; fishing—catfish. Fred Thomas Run, 3½ mi. E. of Valentine. Start—Brdg. into Valentine Wildlife Refuge. Access pts.—4 downstream brdgs. or rugged Rocky Ford White-water Crossing (considered best trail in Neb.). From Ft. Niobrara Refuge Brdg. to Brewer Brdg., 8 hrs.; 20 mi. Start to Buffalo Brdg., 1 hr.; Buffalo Brdg. to Berry Brdg., 1½ hrs.; Berry Brdg. to Allen Brdg., 2½ hrs.; Allen Brdg. to Brewer Brdg., 2½ hrs. Sandy bottom, scenic part—90-ft. Smith Falls ¼ mi. up Smith Creek, some rocky white water, Pine Ridge scenery. (Credit —Fred Thomas and *Canoeing in Nebraska*)

N. Loup River: From Hwy. 83 brdg. past Halsey Natl. For. to Dunning (popular).

N. Platte River: Lincoln Co. Hershey to Cody Park in N. Platte, 18 mi., 4–5 hrs., much wildlife, many isles, banks and bottom mostly sand; clear water. (Credit—*Canoeing in Nebraska*)

Platte River: Dawson, Buffalo cos. From Cozad to Elm Creek, 60 mi., 2–3 days, some wading—last few mi., other parts—good current, no partic. obstacles, good camping, deer, other wild game. Elm Fork to Odessa, Buffalo Co.—not recommended. DANGER —diversion dam, headgates. (Credit—Explorer Post 179)

Trip 1—Buffalo Co. Odessa to Gibbon Brdg., 17 mi., 1 day, leisurely trip, sandy bottom, many isles, land is private. Odessa to Kearney, 10 mi., Kearney to Minden Interchange Brdg., 7 mi.; side trip—1–2-mi. hike from RR brdg. to Ft. Kearney Rec. Area, safe river, much wildlife. Canoeing possible from Kearney to Grand Isle, some barbed-wire fences. (Credit—Fred Thomas)

Trip 2—From Columbus to the Missouri, 100 mi., 4–5 days, great camping, st. cmpgrnds., sandbars. Columbus to Fremont, 48 mi., 2 days. Hwy. 79 brdg. to Hwy. 77 brdg. near Fremont, Neb., 7 hrs., 10–12 mi.; good family trip, OK for novice, no white water. Put-in—1½ mi. south of N. Bend, Neb., many sandbars and small islands, channel twists often, shallow, channel hard to follow, prairie scenery—some trees, wildflowers, bluffs, corn fields, RR brdg.—halfway pt. Take out—Hwy. 77, wildlife, catfish, panfish, best in spring, late spring, and early fall. From Fremont to Two Rivers, 23 mi., 1 day. From Two Rivers to Louisville Lakes, 15 mi., 1 day.

From Louisville Lakes to Plattsmouth, 14 mi., 1 day. All runs best in spring; from June to Aug. canoeing poor above Columbus, water diverted for irrigation. (Credit—Pete Wegman)

Plum Creek: approx. ⅔, lower to jctn. with Box Butte River. (Credit—Nebraska Game and Parks Commission)

Red Willow Creek: below Hugh Butler Lake to jctn. with Republican River. (Credit—Nebraska Game and Parks Commission)

Republican River: Red Willow, Furnas, Harlan cos. From McCook to Harlan Co., 70 mi., 3–4 days, sandbanks, not polluted.
    Trip 1—McCook to Cambridge, 27 mi.
    Trip 2—Cambridge to Oxford, 33 mi.
    Trip 3—Oxford to Harlan Co. Res., 18 mi.; below Harlan Res. water level unpredictable due to flow from dam.
    (Credit—*Canoeing in Nebraska*)

Snake River: Has some white-water stretches; portion that borders National For. S.W. of Valentine is ideal canoe trail. (Credit—*Outdoor Nebraskaland*)

S. Loup River: almost all to jctn. with Mid. Loup River. (Credit—Nebraska Game and Parks Commission)

Verdigre Creek: approx. ½, lower, to jctn. with Box Butte River. (Credit—Nebraska Game and Parks Commission)

NEVADA

Bruneau River: Begins in Humboldt Nat. For., flows N. few mi. and enters Ida., branches join 25 mi. N. of Nev. line then join E. Fork 50 mi. N. to become Bruneau River; Bruneau River continues 30 mi. more into Strike Res. and Snake River; first 60 mi.

(Bruneau, Jarbridge, and W. Fork) flow through canyon 200 ft. deep at Nev. line and 1,000 ft. at a pt. 10 mi. S. of town of Bruneau Hot Springs; from this pt. to Strike Res., slow, muddy through ranch ctry.—canoeing OK here but dull. Trips from Nev. line have been tried in rubber rafts, couldn't make it, too many rocks and rapids, had to walk 7 days through canyon; canyon walls vertical, banks of river infested with rattlesnakes. (Credit— Paul Riffice)

Bruneau River—W. Fork: Same data as Bruneau River.

Jarbridge River: Same data as Bruneau River.

Lake Tahoe: 28 mi. of shoreline on Nev. side, 42 mi. on Cal. side. Access—Nev. Beach cmpgrnd., Cave Rock boat lndg., Sand Harbor Beach. DANGER—rough water and motorboats; good to outstanding fishing.

Truckee River: USGS Tahoe, Tahoe City; from Wadsworth for 10 mi. downstream, 1 day, OK intermed., desert scenery, much birdlife, need permission from Tribal Council, Nixon, Nev.; no fishing; can go on to Nixon at Pyramid Lake, 2 days. (Credit— *Canoeing Waters of California*)

NEW HAMPSHIRE

NOTE: It is strongly recommended that you purchase and consult the *AMC New England Canoeing Guide* for further information.

A special word of thanks to Stewart Coffin, who generously shared his notes with me. These were collected over many years by a great canoeist.

Ammonoosuc River: USGS sheets—Mt. Washington, Whitefield, Littleton, Moosilauke, Woodsville; from Twin Mtn. to Woodsville.

40 mi., good white-water river; run from mid-May till June 1, possible to put in near Bretton Woods Hotel but not recommended due to falls and rapids below.

Trip 1—Twin Mtn. to Pierce Brdg., 7 mi. Put-in—½ mi. above Twin Mtn., hard drop after put-in, good current and easy rapids to Trout Brook, strong rapids past Trout Brook at pt. where river turns left. DANGER—dif. rapids ¼ mi. above Pierce Brdg.

Trip 2—Pierce Brdg. to Littleton, 11 mi., rapids tame down past brdg. followed by slow water; ptg.—power dam 2 mi. below Pierce Brdg. Take out right side, below dam ½ mi. dangerous rapids through gorge—EXPERTS ONLY, also bad rapids for ½ mi. below powerhouse, have canoes taken from dam to Maplewood Brdg.; below Maplewood Brdg. 2 mi. rapids to Wing Rd. Brdg.; below Wing Rd. Brdg. 2 mi. easier rapids. DANGER—Alderbrook Rapids—look for 2 cabins on right bank above rapids—stop on left bank abreast second cabin to scout rapids. DANGER—Railroad Rapids, below Alderbrook Rapids, high RR embankment on right, keep to far right of Railroad Rapids; below Railroad Rapids —mod. rapids. Take-out—side rd. 1 mi. above Littleton Dam.

Trip 3—Littleton to Woodsville, 22 mi. Ptg.—Littleton Dam on right, 1½ mi. easy rapids (Dif. II) below dam. DANGER —falls near Littleton Main St. Brdg. Ptg.—falls left side, below falls—mixed smooth and rapids (Dif. II) to Lisbon, then 6½ mi. of smooth and small rapids, Dif. I–II, to Bath, then 4½ mi. smooth water to Woodsville; check for dams in Lisbon and Bath.

(Credit—Stewart Coffin)

Ashuelot River: USGS sheets—Lovewell Mt., Bellows Falls, Keene. From Ashuelot Pond to Hinsdale, 52 mi.

Trip 1—Ashuelot Pond to Gilsum, 12 mi. Too rough to canoe until Marlow, below Marlow 2 mi. of still water, then dif. narrow chute, then more rapids. Ptg.—dam 3 mi. below Marlow—left side. Ptg.—old dam 2 mi. below other dam, run with ample water only. Dif. IV run. Ptg.—2 dams at Gilsum, right side. DANGER—take out before stone arch brdg. on Rte. 11—bad gorge below.

Trip 2—Gilsum to Keene, 15 mi. Put-in—below gorge, then 4 mi. rapids, Dif. II, to Shaws Corner, run early in season to mid-Apr., river turns to left with strong rapid at Shaws Corner, then ¼ mi. below turns left with sharp pitch over ledge—don't run, next 2 mi. river flattens. Ptg.—Surry Mtn. Flood Control Dam, stream meanders below dam, wider, deeper.

Trip 3—Keene to Ashuelot, 21 mi. Ptg.—left of old dam at Keene, current slow below Keene, not too polluted, winding river. Ptg.—left side dam at S. Swanzey, below dam river placid until ½ mi. below Westport Brdg., broken dam there —can be run, then river quiet for 7 mi. to Winchester. Ptg.— left side dam at Winchester, still water below for 2½ mi. to Ashuelot.

Trip 4—Ashuelot to Hinsdale, 4 mi., severe white-water run, Dif. IV–V, river drops 220 ft., 6 dams with rapids between, very dangerous, heavy pollution, not recommended. (Credit —Stewart Coffin)

Ashuelot River—S. Branch: USGS sheets—Monadnock, Keene, for 2 mi. above Webb, can be run but is steep and dif. Lower part —put-in below dam and millpond in E. Swanzey to jctn. with main Ashuelot, 7 mi., good current, few rapids. (Credit—Stewart Coffin)

Baker River: USGS sheets—Rumney, Plymouth; Warren to Plymouth, 27 mi.

Trip 1—Warren to W. Rumney, 11 mi. Put-in—brdg. on crossroad at N. end of Warren, first drop rough and fast with few obstructions. Alt. put-in—brdg. 1 mi below town where Oak Hill Brook enters, next 2 mi. continuous rapids Dif. II, river broader near Wentworth, mod. rapids, good current. Ptg.—Dam at Wentworth—left, then 6 mi. to Rumney, easy and pleasant, clear water, wooded banks.

Trip 2—W. Rumney to Plymouth, 16 mi., 3 mi. down to Rattlesnake Mtn., below Rattlesnake Mtn. river is wider and not as deep. Alt. take-out—Rte. 25 between Rumney Depot and W. Plymouth, sluggish river beyond. Baker enters Pemigewasset River after Rte. 3 brdg. N. of Plymouth. (Credit—Stewart Coffin)

Bearcamp River: USGS sheets—Mt. Chocura, Ossipee Lake; upper part exciting white-water run, mod. Dif. II, run in high water near end of Apr.; from Bearcamp Pond to Ossipee Lake, 16 mi.

Trip 1—Bearcamp Pond to S. Tamworth Dam, 5 mi., meadow brook below outlet of Bearcamp Pond until Bennett Corners; below Bennett Corners, wide brook for ⅔ mi., then heavy rapids ⅛ mi. long, then sharp pitch—can run both in high water, then smooth water, then very sharp pitch, then rd. meets right bank, then tough rapid above brdg. at S. Tamworth. Ptg.—high dam at S. Tamworth.

Trip 2—S. Tamworth to Whittier, 2 mi., much action in this part of river, continuous rapids, dangerous rapid above iron brdg.—can be run; bad rapid—⅛ mi. above Whittier brdg., last rapid on river. Whittier to Ossipee Lake, 9 mi., no more rapids, river spreads out. Take-out—Rte. 16 or go 1 mi. more to Ossipee Lake. (Credit—Stewart Coffin)

Beards Brook: Joins N. Branch of Contoocook River below power plant, run in high water, several areas of Dif. III. (Credit —Stewart Coffin)

Beaver Brook: USGS sheets—Manchester, Lowell; W. Derry to Collinsville, 25 mi., forested sides, good current, several small rapids; best time—Apr.

Trip 1—W. Derry to Kendall Pond, 4 mi., can start S. of W. Derry near sewage plant—a smelly put-in, not a good place to start, good current halfway, then slows down. Ptg.—sharp drop at brdg. at outlet.

Trip 2—Kendall Pond to Pelham, 14 mi., 1 day, nice trip, winding with OK current at first, some jams, then stream slows down. Ptg.—old 15-ft. dam at cider mill; best part of trip starts at Rte. 128 brdg., fast water and small rapids, forested banks, 1½ mi. to Rte. 111 brdg., then ½ mi. to old Rte. 111 brdg., then 1 mi. to Rte. 128 brdg. near N. Pelham. DANGER—1 mi. to broken dam-line on left side, then pass under Castle Hill Rd. Brdg., then ⅓ mi to brdg., no rapids below but fine current, 2 mi. to old wooden brdg., then 1½ mi. to small cement dam—OK to run, then ⅔ mi. to Brdg. St. DANGER—don't go under brdg. in high water; take out here.

Trip 3—Pelham to Collinsville, 7 mi., all slow water, twisty, last 3 mi. not good.

(Credit—Stewart Coffin)

Bellamy River: USGS Dover. From dam in Madbury to S. end of Dover, 7 mi., shallow rapid ⅓ mi. long below dam—not good in low water, then good current and many small rapids, 3 mi. to Manchester Rd. Brdg., lower river—not attractive, few small rapids, much brush, logjams, tidewater from Bellamy Mill to tidewater in S. end Dover—not recommended. (Credit—Stewart Coffin)

Blackwater River: USGS sheets—Mt. Kearsarge, Penacook, Concord. From Cilleyville to Contoocook River, 29 mi., several ptgs., impassable chutes, run Apr.–May.

Trip 1—Cilleyville to W. Salisbury Brdg., 9 mi. Put-in—at Cilleyville where river forks. DANGER—Don't put in at Rte. 11 brdg.—dam and rapid below. Alt. put-in—brdg. on old rd. at foot of rapid, run to Andover, nice with small rapids; past Andover 3 mi. slow current, marshy ponds past U.S. 4 crossing. Dif. rapid at W. Salisbury, then short way to brdg. and broken dam.

Trip 2—W. Salisbury Brdg. to Snyders Mill, 15 mi., not recommended. Ptg.—bad rapids below broken dam, then leisurely 8 mi. to Salisbury. Take-out—dirt rd. N. of Littles Hill before Webster Dam, dangerous gorge below dam—Don't run, avoid next 3 mi. DANGER—1 mi. below Sweets Mill Gorge, line the drop here, slack water below drop for 1 mi. until brdg. DANGER—Impassable chute above brdg.—ptg.

left, next ½ mi. pleasant to Dingit Corner. Don't canoe beyond Dingit Corner—too steep.

Trip 3—Snyders Mill to Contoocook River, 5 mi. Put-in—from Rte. 127 on right bank ¼ mi. below brdg. at Snyders Mill, little current. Take-out—brdg. at 4 mi. pt. or 1 mi. more to Contoocook River.

(Credit—Stewart Coffin)

Cocheco River: USGS sheets—Alton, Berwick, Dover. From Farmington to dead water 1 mi. N. of Rochester, first 1½ mi. easy to brdg., fine current, easy rapids, same kind of river 6 mi. more to next brdg., then 1 mi. to RR brdg., then smooth water to Rochester. Take-out—Rte. 11 N. of Rochester; several dams in Rochester, 2 dams at Gonic, heavy pollution, more dams through Dover, not recommended below Rochester. (Credit—Stewart Coffin)

Cockermouth River: USGS sheets—Cardigan, in high water can be canoed from Groton to Newfound Lake, 3 mi. (Credit—Stewart Coffin)

Cold River: USGS sheets—Bellows Falls, from S. Ackworth to Cold River Vil., 11½ mi., popular, white water, Dif. II, run in med.-high water in mid-Apr. Put-in—below gorge below S. Ackworth, some sharp drops, partic. 1½ mi. above Vilas Pool. Take-out—Vilas Pool above Alstead, 2 dams here. Alstead to Cold River Vil., 6 mi., fast water, short strong rapid below Alstead Brdg., then fast water with some obstacles, ptg. Take-out—on right above Drewsville Brdg. DANGER—high waterfall and canyon under brdg.; below waterfall to Cold River Vil. no obstacles. Take-out—brdg. at Cold River Vil. or continue to Conn. River. (Credit—Stewart Coffin)

Connecticut River: Canadian border to Mass. line. Fast, rough, and dangerous in spring flood waters. After May 1, usually safe for careful canoeist. Not suitable for drinking or swimming. Obtain fresh water at homes and picnic areas along banks. Ptgs.—13 dams—information on marked ptg. routes avail. from Lebanon,

N.H., office of New England Power Co. Start—Canaan, Vt., on Canadian border. Above this pt. canoeing limited, turbulent in spring and shallow after mid-summer. Canaan to Colebrook, N.H., good conditions, several canoeable rapids soon after start. Colebrook to former Lyman Falls Dam, good conditions for 3 mi., then fast for 3 mi. Swift water called "Hoe in the Woods"— use care, sharp bend in river, and 100-yd.-long chute above Lemington, ½ mi. above Columbia River Brdg. followed by 3-mi. stretch of calm water then 2 mi. of fast water. A series of 4 or 5 log piers located downstream called "The Gorge," canoe to N.H. side and inspect. Rainbow trout in area. Former Lyman Falls Dam to Bloomfield, Vt., 26 mi., large boulders below falls. Bloomfield to Gilman, Vt., 3-mi. rapids below Bloomfield, good trout fishing in Guildhall, Vt. Ptg. Northumberland Dam (Wyoming Dam), canoeing good below dam, 6 mi. below dam U.S. Rte. 2 crosses river, warm-water fishing good here. Gilman to Moore Dam, long ptg. at Gilman Dam, possible to carry, enter backwaters Moore Res. below dam, watch for strong winds, ptg. Moore Dam; Moore Dam to Comerford Dam to McIndoes, 7 mi., canoeing excellent, ptg. at McIndoes not dif. on Vt. bank; McIndoes to E. Ryegate, 4 mi., no dif., easy ptg. at E. Ryegate; Ryegate to Newburg, some fast water below dam, E. shore best channel, river widens 4 mi. below dam, river twists from Wells River to Newburg Vil., shallow in late summer. Newburg to Wilder Dam, deepens and current slacks, Piermont Brdg. 2 mi. below Bradford, then 2 mi. to "Bugs Isle," deep, winding river from Bradford to Wilder Dam; fishing excel. below Hanover, warm-water species, easy ptg. at Wilder Dam on N.H. side. Wilder Dam to Bellows Falls, 44 mi., use care below dam, water shallow at jctn. of White and Connecticut rivers. DANGER—10 mi. below jctn. keep to right side of river, be ready to beach. Very dangerous rapids in Hartland, IN LOW WATER RAPIDS MAY NOT BE HEARD UNTIL TOO LATE, *LIVES HAVE BEEN LOST HERE*. Ptg. rapids, right side of river, below rapids canoeing easy to Bellows Falls, 9 mi. from Cheshire Toll Brdg. to Bellows Falls, ptg. Bellows Falls to Mass. st. line, slow water 32 mi., beautiful ptg. on Vt. side at Vernon Dam, follow ptg. trail, 6 mi. from dam to Mass. st. line, easy canoeing. (Credit—*Canoeing on the Connecticut River*)

Contoocook River: USGS sheets—Monadnock, Peterborough, Concord, Penacook; above Peterborough usually too low to canoe. From Cheshire Pond to Penacook, 64 mi.; Cheshire Pond to Peterborough, 7 mi. Put-in—near outlet of pond 1 mi. E. of E. Jaffrey on Rte. 202, all rapids to Peterborough, nice white-water run; Dif. II, run spring. DANGER—2½ mi. below start—Dangerous gorge below wooden brdg. Ptg.—gorge above wooden brdg. Take-out—brdg. above Noone or continue down millpond to dam. Ptg.—dam, 1 mi. more to Peterborough; Peterborough to Hillsboro, 24 mi., mostly slack water, 2 dams in Peterborough, dam at N. Vil., 10 mi. from dam to Bennington. Ptg.—first dam at Bennington—ptg. all 4 dams and rapids below. DANGER—don't run rapids below dams, then 13 mi. to Hillsboro, river slow and meanders. Take-out—above Hillsboro; rapid at site of upper Hillsboro dam, then slack water. Ptg.—dam under Rte. 149, dif. ptg. here. Hillsboro to Henniker, 8 mi., rapids below Hillsboro dam not dif. DANGER—2½ mi. of rapids Dif. IV (½ mi. below Rte. 202 brdg.), don't run these rapids in high water, LIFE HAS BEEN LOST HERE, more heavy rapids downstream, rapids end above dam in W. Henniker. Ptg.—right at W. Henniker Dam. DANGER—poison ivy here, short rapid below dam, not dif., then 1 mi. flat water to Henniker. Obstacle—broken dam below stone arch brdg., can be run on right in med. water. Ptg.—small dam ¼ mi. farther down; Henniker to Penacook, 25 mi., nice trip to W. Hopkinton flood-control dam, ptg. left—W. Hopkinton flood-control dam. Ptg.—power dam below—left side, then 5 mi. flat water to dam at Contoocook Vil., then 8 mi. smooth to Riverhill; 3 dams —Contoocook Park and Penacook, last 2 mi. not good canoeing. DANGER—severe rapid below dam in last stretch. (Credit— Stewart Coffin)

Contoocook River—N. Branch: only last 1½ mi. canoeable. Put-in—below power plant on Rte. 9, good current when generator runs, then slow current to jctn. with main river. (Credit—Stewart Coffin)

Cow Pond Brook: See Salmon Brook in New Hampshire.

Dead Diamond River: No canoeing, logging road from Hell Gate to Diamond Gorge is closed to public. (Credit—Stewart Coffin)

Ellis River: USGS sheets—N. Conway; from Jackson to the Saco, 4½ mi., hard rapids all the way, run in med.-high water. Ptg. or take-out—2 mi. below Jackson where river turns W. under Rte. 16 brdg.—high dam and gorge below, dif. ptg., rest of trip all rapids but not as tough as above. Take-out—U.S. 302 brdg. or on into the Saco. (Credit—Stewart Coffin)

Exeter River: USGS sheets—Hampstead, Mt. Pawtuckaway, Exeter, Dover. From Rte. 121A brdg. N. of Sandown to Great Bay, 40 mi. Run in high water, then short paddle to Lilly Pond; go across pond, pass under rd. at pond outlet, then easy rapids to dam above brdg. Ptg.—dam, then ½ mi. below to another dam —ptg., then another brdg., river below enters a swamp, then 2 brdgs. in next 3 mi., then 3 mi. of twisting river to brdg. in S.E. Chester; below brdg. river nears Rte. 102 at side-rd. brdg., quick water and riffles below with one small rapid, to iron brdg., then river loops to Fremont; last mi. is backwater of dam. Ptg.— Fremont Dam, below dam 1½ mi. to log dam, then 1½ mi. to Rte. 111A brdg., then 3 mi. to Rte. 107 brdg. Ptg.—from Rte. 107 brdg. around 2 dams, short rapid below dams, then poor river to Brentwood. Ptg.—3 dams at Brentwood, lowest dam destroyed —can be run, then 2 mi. good rapids, to next brdg., broken dam at brdg., 1 mi. riffles below broken dam, then 2 mi. flat water to next brdg., then 1 mi. strong rapids below brdg. Don't run in low water—to Rte. 111 brdg., sharp rapid at Rte. 111 brdg., also short way below brdg.—sharp rapid, then flat water to RR brdg., rapid below RR brdg., then 2 mi. to Rte. 108 brdg., then 3 mi. to Exeter Dam. Ptg.—Exeter Dam, below Exeter 1 mi. of salt marsh to Great Bay; last part also called Squamscott River. (Credit— Stewart Coffin)

Great Ossipee River: See description under Maine.

Israel River: USGS sheets—Mt. Washington, Whitefield; from Jefferson to Lancaster, 14 mi.

   Trip 1—Jefferson to Riverton, 9 mi., easy trip, some easy rapids, hot in summer.

   Trip 2—Riverton to Lancaster, run before June 1, tree-lined banks, rapids most of way. DANGER: steep rapids halfway, 2 broken dams above Lancaster. Take-out—second old dam site, rapids go on through town, small dam below brdg. (Credit—Stewart Coffin)

Lamprey River: USGS sheets—Mt. Pawtuckaway, Dover; some canoeing above Raymond but too many obstacles; unattractive from Raymond to Epping, 8 mi. dams and back flowage, not good run. From Epping to Newmarket, 21 mi.

   Trip 1—Epping to Wadley Falls, 9 mi., best part of river, mostly quiet, winding river, woods and pastureland, ptg.—Wadley Falls.

   Trip 2—Wadley Falls to Newmarket, 12 mi., good current through pasture, some hemlock banks, 4 mi. to brdg. near Lee, ⅛ mi. rapid below brdg.—rough in high water, then 1 mi. to short rapid—rough in high water—then smooth water to iron brdg. at Wiswalls Falls. Ptg. dam, then 1 mi. to Packers Falls, rapids here—danger in high water—ptg. left, below falls flat and uninteresting for 3 mi. Take-out—left bank at Newmarket above dam, below Newmarket Dam—2 mi. to Great Bay. (Credit—Stewart Coffin)

Lovell River: Too small, too steep, canoeable only last mi. into Ossipee. (Credit—Stewart Coffin)

Mad River: USGS sheets—Plymouth; too steep to canoe; Hardy Brook to Campton Pond, don't run in high water, must line several spots before Smarts Brook, next 2 mi. to Chickenboro Brook almost as bad, steep chute and pool below Goose Hollow Brdg., last 2 mi. all rapids. Take-out—sec. of pond that goes to River Rd., last 2 mi. through Compton to jctn. with Pemigewasset—not worth the trouble. (Credit—Stewart Coffin)

Magalloway River: See description under Maine.

Merrimack River: From Franklin to Newburyport, 109 mi.; Franklin to Manchester, 49 mi., Put-in—right bank below high school, first 2 mi. fast water with Dif. III rapids, then some sandbars, current OK, 16 mi. to Penacook, 3 mi. below Penacook to Sewallis Falls—ptg. dam and rocky stretch below, then 12 mi. to Gowens Falls Dam—ptg. right by transformer enclosure, then easy paddling 7 mi. to Hooksett Dam–ptg. right, then 9 mi. to Amoskeag Falls Dam at Manchester. Take out above Manchester; Manchester to Newburyport, 60 mi., can run rapids below dam at Manchester, keep to right bank, then 20 mi. to Nashua with 5 sharp rapids—keep to right bank on first 3, slow water from Nashua to Lowell. Dif. ptgs. at dams in Lowell and Lawrence, last falls in Haverhill, tidewater below Haverhill. (Credit—Stewart Coffin)

Nashua River: USGS sheets—Fitchburg, Shirley, Clinton, Ayer, Pepperell, Milford, Manchester. Fitchburg to Nashua, 47 mi.
Trip 1—N. Branch—Fitchburg to Lancaster Commons, 15 mi., many dams, heavy pollution, nicer below N. Leominster, good current, several small rapids.
Trip 2—Main River—Lancaster Commons to Nashua, 32 mi., no rapids, polluted water, ½ mi. ptg. left at E. Pepperell Dam. Ptg. right—broken dam of Ronnells Mills below Pepperell, little current beyond this pt., forested banks, dif. right ptg.—upper dam at Nashua, take out here, last mi. to Merrimack not good. (Credit—Stewart Coffin)

Newfound River: USGS sheets—Holderness, not recommended, dangerous, impassable rapids, 4 dams in 3 mi. (Credit—Stewart Coffin)

Otter Brook: USGS sheets—Monadnock, Keene. From along Rte. 9 above Branch Rd. Brdg. to Rte. 12 Brdg., 8 mi., experts only, white water, run in high water, best in Apr., after Branch Rd. Brdg. ¼ mi. to small brdg., gauging sta. beyond, small cement dam here—can run spillway, then river flattens, nice run to large dam, ptg. is steep here, below dam 150 yds. fast water, then rapids, Dif. III, next 4 mi., then becomes slack water after high stone RR brdg. until cement dam, paddle through break in right flange of dam to small pool, then mild rapids 1½ mi. to Rte. 12 brdg. Take out at brdg. or continue down the Ashuelot, lower part through Keene unattractive, river here called The Branch. (Credit —Stewart Coffin)

Peabody River: Flows N. out of Pinkham Notch, too steep to canoe.

Pemigewasset River: USGS sheets—Franconia, Plymouth, Holderness, Penacook. Main Pemigewasset River begins in Profile 2 Lake and is joined by E. Branch at N. Woodstock. Banks ruined by tourist development, polluted from Lincoln to Livermore Falls.

Trip 1—from N. Woodstock to Livermore Falls, 24 mi., mostly fast current, mod. rapids, Dif. II, with dangerous waves; 1 hr. from put-in to Woodstock, run with care— broken dam above covered brdg. in Woodstock, there is a brdg. below W. Thornton and at W. Campton, 5 mi. below W. Campton river goes under RR brdg. and enters gorge, take out above here to avoid ptg. at Livermore Falls, bad rapids below falls, *don't run.*

Trip 2—from Plymouth to Franklin Falls Dam, 30 mi., put in at Plymouth, 3 mi. below Livermore Falls, strong current, no rapids, 5 mi. to Rte. 3 brdg., then fair current to New Hampton, then slack water 4 mi. to hydroelectric dam above Bristol, very bad rapids below dam through Bristol Gorge to brdg., then no bad rapids, good current to Hill, then smooth water to Franklin Falls Dam; still water below dam to dam in Franklin, then rapids through Franklin to the Merrimack. (Credit—Stewart Coffin)

Pemigewasset River—E. Branch: USGS sheets—Franconia; beautiful river not good for canoeing, many dangerous rapids, Dif. V, has become a popular run for covered craft. (Credit—Stewart Coffin)

Piscataqua River: See description under Maine.

Piscataquog River: Main Piscataquog not good for canoeing, many dams, pollution buildup. (Credit—Stewart Coffin)

Piscataquog River—S. Branch: USGS sheets—Peterborough, Milford, Concord; not canoeable after mid-Apr.

Trip 1—Francistown to dam at foot of Cochrane Hill, 7 mi., put in just below Francistown, this sec. not good, first mile meanders with many beaver dams. Just above first brdg. on Francistown–Mt. Vernon rd. is a tough rapid, run only in high water, then short way to hard drop under small brdg., then next 2 mi. flat and rapid, broken dam below small brdg., a dif. rapid here, then pond, at end of pond is dangerous gorge under a small brdg., don't run, ptg. left and put in at small pond, then combination of flat and rapid to old paper mill site, look for high brick chimney, dangerous spot here, don't run, then small rapids to small dam at Cochrane Hill, ptg. dam, best part of river below dam.

Trip 2—from brdg. below dam at Cochrane Hill to Goffstown, nice white water, good rapids to dam near N.H. 13 Brdg., ptg. right, then another dam in New Boston Vil., ptg. right, then river is polluted, there is a good run ½ mi. below The Vil. called The Broken Dam, then easy rapids for several mi., most canoeists take out at brdg. near gravel pit 4 mi. below New Boston, 2 more mi. with good current, and small rapids to Goffstown.
(Credit—Stewart Coffin)

Saco River: USGS sheets—Crawford Notch, N. Conway, Ossipee Lake, Fryeburg, Kezar Falls, Sebago Lake, Buxton, Kennebunk, Biddeford, Portland. Popular canoe trail, usually has good water into May, Upper Saco down to Bartlett is dif. white-water run, Lower Saco from Bartlett to Conway easier, last 80 mi. to sea is popular summer trip.

Trip 1—The Upper Saco—from footbrdg. on the Davis Path to brdg. in Bartlett, 9 mi., experts only. DANGER—can rise quickly, soon after put-in river enters gorge at Notchland, ptg. right along RR, then below gorge 1 mi. very hard rapids with bad drop and quick turn at end, next 2½ mi. to RR brdg. dif. rapids, many boulders, then ½ mi. below RR brdg. are bad rapids with blind right turn, line on right, then ½ mi. of continuous rapids to hwy. at Sawyer Rock, next 2½ mi. to iron brdg. in Bartlett not as rough, dif. spot under RR brdg.

Trip 2—Lower Saco—generally broad with gravel bottom, many quick bends, best water in early May, strong current, nearly all rapids, nice scenery, from iron brdg. in Bartlett to covered brdg., 6 mi., watch for fallen trees, dangerous in high water, rapids 200 yds. above covered brdg. From covered brdg. to brdg. in N. Conway, 7 mi., OK for white-water instruction, strong rapid ½ mi. below Rte. 302 brdg. and strong rips for several mi.

Trip 3—Below N. Conway, valley broader, many washed-out banks; from N. Conway to Conway, 9 mi., mostly fast current, short rapid above Conway Brdg.—not dif., below Conway Brdg. ½ mi. is a sharp rapid, in ½ mi. more another strong rapid, run with caution, in another 1 mi. a long steep drop for ⅓ mi. with heavy waves. Rte. 302 brdg. is 3 mi. below Conway, then RR brdg. is another ⅛ mi., then good current to Fryeburg, from RR brdg. to Fryeburg, 7 mi., 3 mi. below Fryeburg is dam at Swans Falls with rapids.

Salmon Brook: USGS sheets—Ayer, Pepperell, Tyngsboro. Small stream; can be run in high water from E. Groton to Nashua, no rapids, many short ptgs. around dams and other obstacles, start at Knops Pond in Groton, down Cow Pond Brook to Massapoag Pond, below stream is larger, less ptgs., passes through woods, farmland and swamp to Nashua, then not good for canoeing, take out at Everett Hwy. Brdg. (Credit—Stewart Coffin)

Salmon Falls River: See description under Maine.

Silver Brook: USGS sheets—Ossipee Lake, also called W. Branch, flows from Silver Lake to Ossipee Lake, 6 mi. Nice trip, several rapids—not dif.—most in upper half, run in spring only.

Smith River: USGS sheets—Cardigan, Holderness; upper half almost flat, rest of river steep and fun; Crafton Center to Profile Gorge, 24 mi.

Trip 1—Crafton Center to Rte. 104 Brdg., 14 mi., a small stream to Grafton, more current after Grafton, not good canoeing at first, 5 mi. below Grafton to Fords Crossing, banks become forested, in next 7 mi. river passes under Rte. 4 at Danbury and another brdg. on side rd., then winds through flat ctry. to brdg. on side rd. and upper Rte. 104 brdg.

Trip 2—Upper Rte. 104 Brdg. to Profile Gorge, 10 mi., dam just below Rte. 104 Brdg., carry right, then smooth for 1 mi. to second Rte. 104 brdg., don't park cars here, gauging marks on left brdg. abutment, then less than 1 mi. to heavy rapids, Dif. IV, rapids are continuous 3 mi. to S. Alexandria, can't run in low water, dangerous in high water. Steep sec. just above third Rte. 104 brdg., another bad spot at brdg. in S. Alexandria. Below S. Alexandria river leaves rd. and goes 4 mi. through pretty wooded valley, rapids Dif. III, gradually diminish, then brdg. on side rd. near Willow School, good current, sandy bottom. Then below brdg. banks not as pretty, some obstructions, in 2 mi. come to small rapid, then falls at old brdg. site, carry over an isle. DANGER—take out in 200 yds. on left, above high cement brdg., gorge is under brdg., not runnable, Profile Falls just below Rte. 3A brdg., reach by good footpath, below gorge river enters Merrimack.

(Credit—Stewart Coffin)

Soucook River: USGS sheets—Gilmanton, Soucook. From brdg. ⅔ mi. above Pearls Corner to the Merrimack at Concord, 1 day, pleasant, good current, run in high water, small stream, shallow, to brdg. on dirt rd., then 2½ mi. twisty, slack water halfway to dam at Loudon. From brdg. in Loudon carry right area past a rapid, then 3 mi. to brdg. on N.H. 106, good current, then 1 mi. below N.H. 106 is dangerous rapid, ptg. or line right, then 1 mi. good current to brdg., then 2 mi. to brdg. on U.S. 4, then another brdg. on Horse Corner Rd., then 3 mi. to brdg. at French's Brook, strong current, a few rapids, then slower current next 2 mi. to brdg. on N.H. 106, then 3 mi. strong current to brdg. on U.S.

3, gauge mark on right bank abutment downstream, below—1 sharp rapid, many long rips, U.S. 3 no place to take out, not recommended. (Credit—Stewart Coffin)

Souhegan River: USGS sheets—Peterboro, Milford, Manchester. From Greenville Hydro. Station to Merrimack, 27 mi.; fine white water, run upper part only in high water, experts only, rapids less harsh downstream, lower river nice smooth water, not good in low water, early spring best time.

Trip 1—Greenville Hydro. Sta. to Wilton, 7 mi., small stream, steep, full of boulders, Dif. IV, OK in high water, many ledges shortly after start, scout first, then steep rapids to Rte. 31 brdg. (alt. put-in spot), then 2 mi. below to dif. chute around big boulder; after steel brdg. near W. Wilton, rapids less dif., 1 mi. to old concrete brdg. and Rte. 101 brdg., then river turns to right, dif. rapids here through boulders, ends in large drop, don't run this drop, below is mill pond, 3 dams in Wilton, dif. rapid full of boulders just below first dam.

Trip 2—Wilton to Merrimack, 20 mi., ptg. around Wilton by car, put in below factories; short, steep rocky sec. just below last dam, usually too shallow to run, then rapids Dif. II for 1 mi. below Wilton, river smooths out past steel brdg., then wanders to Milford, fair current, some riffles, no take-out pts. between steel brdg. and Milford. Ptg. dam in Milford, put in on left below second dam, then a few small rapids, then fine flow to Rte. 122 brdg., 2 mi. to Amherst–S. Merrimack Rd. brdg., then 2 mi. more of same, then 1 mi slow water, then some short rapids and steep spot at Indian Ledge, can run upper rapids, ptg. ledge and rapid below, then easy paddling, 2 mi. to covered brdg. at Turkey Hill (most people take out here), then ⅔ mi. below brdg. to short, easy rapid, then 1 mi. flat water, then falls ahead—series of 3 falls—Wildcat Falls, ptg. on left, then ½ mi. to pond at Merrimack Vil. DANGER—area under Everett Turnpike Brdg., below dam river joins Merrimack. (Credit—Stewart Coffin)

Squam River: not a good canoe stream, from Squam Lake to the

Pemigewasset River, lakes caused by dams, stretch of bad rapids below each, don't run. (Credit—Stewart Coffin)

Squamscott River: See Exeter River in New Hampshire.

Stony Brook: USGS sheets—Peterboro, Milford, from Rte. 31 Brdg. below S. Lyndeboro to Wilton, 4 mi., tough run, not recommended, many rocks in river at first, then ptg. dam by the RR, then becomes very dif., hwy. runs beside stream, ptg. dam above Wilton. (Credit—Stewart Coffin)

Suncook River: USGS sheets—Gilmanton, Suncook. Above Pittsfield not good canoeing, many dams, shallow rapids, mill ponds; from Pittsfield to brdg. W. of Short Falls, 1 day, run in mid-Apr., put in on left ⅓ mi. below Pittsfield Center, 3 mi. to Websters Mills, fast current, then 1 mi. above Websters Mills rapids increase, last ¼ mi. to brdg. at Websters Mills is hard rapid—can be dangerous, then continuous rapids of intermed. dif. under brdg. and down past large isle, then 1½ mi. less dif. rapids and flat water to brdg. at N. Chichester. From N. Chichester to Epsom Sta., 3 mi., slack water, not much fun, 1 mi. below Epsom brdg. is sawmill, channel goes to left, take out on right and carry around dam, then rapid water. Then river is quiet, then 1 mi. fast water, then 2 mi. easy stretch to brdg. W. of Short Falls. (Credit —Stewart Coffin)

Swift Diamond River: USGS sheets—Errol. Small river, in wild ctry., run in spring, probably too low by June, hard trip in high water. Put-in—rd. off Rte. 26 that parallels Courser Brook—at S. Valley Brook Rd. crosses Swift Diamond and joins a rd. that runs length of river—start here or ½ mi. up rd.; after put-in 1½ mi. easy rapids to dam, ptg., then ptg. 2 falls below dam, then 3 mi. rapids, can be run, then next mi. has very dif. areas—line or ptg. Then ptg.—Ellingwood Falls, then 2 mi. mod. rapids, then last mi. to jctn.—hard rapids, ptg.—bad drop—DON'T RUN. Takeout—on left after jctn. with Dead Diamond.

The Branch: See description of Otter Brook.

NEW JERSEY

Alloway's Creek: Salem Co. Lakes at Alloway and river to Hancock's Brdg., interesting, canoeable. (Credit—*Exploring the Little Rivers of New Jersey*)

Batsto River: Trips—Hampton Gate to Quaker Brdg., spring, 8 mi., campsite at Lower Forge. Quaker Brdg. to Batsto, 3½ hrs. Quaker Brdg. to Green Bank, 7 hrs. Batsto to Green Bank, 3 hrs. Excel. canoeing. (Credit—*Exploring the Little Rivers of New Jersey* and *Canoeing in New Jersey*)

Canal Feeders: Trenton; Mercer Co. Parallels Delaware River from Trenton to Lambertville, 25 mi., good canoeing. (Credit— *Exploring the Little Rivers of New Jersey*)

Cohansey Creek: Cumberland Co., tidal stream through marshlands, lower part like Cape Cod, not usually canoed. Above city park in Bridgeton is "Raceway," good canoeing, paddle from reaches of "Northwest Passage" to Sunset Lake, beautiful. (Credit—*Exploring the Little Rivers of New Jersey*)

Cooper River: Camden Co., S. of airport and through park, interesting few mi. (Credit—*Exploring the Little Rivers of New Jersey*)

Cross State Canoe Rte.: 8 days, 63 mi.
> *Day 1*—Put in Rancocas Creek at jctn. of Del. River (Delanco, N.J.), go through Burlington Co. to jctn. of N. and S. branches, take S. branch, camp at Eayrestown.
> *Day 2*—Canoe to jctn. of Friendship Creek (below Vincenttown), camp at Retreat, several logjams.

Day 3—Canoe on Friendship Creek to Presidential Lakes (Rte. 70), rough going.

Day 4—Continue to Lake at Girl Scout Camp, ptg. on sand rd. to Rte. 532.

Days 5 and 6—Put in at tributary of Batsto River and continue S. to Carranza Rd., very nasty going (good luck).

Day 7—Carranza Rd. to Batsto, first 2 hrs. hard work, opens to popular canoe rte., camp at Crowley Lndg.

Day 8—Canoe on Mullica River to Chestnut Neck Marina. First and last day, tidal water, no danger areas but thick swamps, go in spring or fall, mosquitoes terrible. (Credit—Eigil Hansen and Jon Smith)

Crosswicks Creek: Burlington Co., 14 mi. above Crosswicks to Delaware River, last few mi. through tidal marshes. (Credit—*Exploring the Little Rivers of New Jersey*)

Delaware River: NOTE—streamflow characteristics (given in roman numerals) apply to the Delaware River only and do not conform with the International Scale of River Dif., as published in The American White Water Affiliation Safety Code. Under no circumstances should the Delaware River Basin Comm. classifications of the Delaware River rapids be applied to streams elsewhere. Stream rapid conditions under various classifications on the Delaware River Basin Comm. maps are substantially less hazardous than under the corresponding classifications of the American White Water Affiliation.

Delaware River: Hancock, N.Y., to Trenton, N.J., approx. 200 mi., 10–14 days, description divided into 10 secs. (17 mi.—1 day ea.), listed under N.Y., Pa., and N.J.

Sec. J—Lambertville, N.J., and New Hope, Pa., to Trenton. Dif. I–VI, many pools, otherwise mostly II–III, some IV, 1 Dif. VI at Lambertville Wing dams, very dangerous, ptg. or line, 1 Dif. V at Scudders Falls. Access—Lambertville—Delaware River Power Boat Association, free, Yardley-Pa. Fish Comm., free parking, Morrisville-Delaware River jctn. Toll Brdg. Comm., free; small-mouth bass, panfish, blue black herring, alewife, shad, white

perch, some striped bass. DANGER—Lambertville-New Hope Wing dams at mi. 148 (0.7 mi. down from old Lambertville-New Hope Brdg.). LIVES HAVE BEEN LOST HERE.
(Credit—*The Delaware and Outdoor Recreation*)

Delaware and Raritan Canal: Runs parallel to Millstone River, connects the Delaware to Raritan River, owned by state, 45 mi. long, 75 ft. wide, 8 ft. deep. Start trip from Titusville, Lambertville, or Washington Crossing at 2 pts. off U.S. Rte. 1 N. of Trenton, U.S. Rte. 1 on S.-bound lane between Bakersville and Clarksville, hwy. crosses canal (private land). From N. lane of U.S. 1 turn right on Carnegie Rd. (Petry Storage Co.). Ptg.—before lock at Kingston S. of Lake Carnegie Dam, carry to N. side of Rte. 518, west bank, short ptg. at Griggstown Lock. End—10 mi. lock N. of Zarepath. (Credit—*Exploring the Little Rivers of New Jersey* and *Canoeing in New Jersey*)

Flat Brook: Sussex Co., canoe from headwaters near Layton in spring floods, during summer only parts S. of Wallpack Center. (Credit—*Exploring the Little Rivers of New Jersey*)

Great Egg Harbor River: Berlin to Lake Lenape possible. Start trip—St. Pol. barracks Rte. 73, tough trip to Penny Pot, Hospitality branch also tough from N.W. of Penny Pot to main river, most popular trip from Teakwood Dam at Penny Pot to Mays Lndg. on S. end Lake Lenape, 8 hrs., tidewater and winds below Mays Lndg.—dif. (Credit—*Exploring the Little Rivers of New Jersey* and *Canoeing in New Jersey*)

Hackensack River: few mi. of canoeing, no canoeing on Oradell Res., put in below New Milford, canoe to Hackensack, tidewater trip, canoe during high tide only; commercial traffic below Hackensack. (Credit—*Exploring the Little Rivers of New Jersey*)

Laurence Brook: Middlesex Co., res. S. of Dans to Raritan River, canoe through lake and down brook. (Credit—*Exploring the Little Rivers of New Jersey*)

Manasquan River: Monmouth Co., pt. on Rte. 4 to Brielle, some carrying and wading, beyond Brielle tide and wind dangerous, attractive stream. (Credit—*Exploring the Little Rivers of New Jersey*)

Maurice River: Malga at jctn. Rte. 40 and Rte. 47 to Millville, 20 mi., 1–2 days. Tidewater and salt marsh below Millville—not recommended. (Credit—*Canoeing in New Jersey*)

Millstone River: Cranbury to Princeton, 8 mi., runs parallel to Del. River and Raritan Canal; river enters Lake Carnegie W. of U.S. Rte. 1 at Princeton; ptg. at N. end of lake crossing Rte. 518; re-enter N. of dam at Rocky Hill. Princeton to Bound Brook—jctn. of Raritan River, 15 mi.; high and low water make trip difficult. (Credit—*Exploring the Little Rivers of New Jersey* and *Canoeing in New Jersey*)

Mullica River: Launch at Goslen Pond, N.E. of Atsion Lake or at lake. Campsite—Goslen Pond, campsite and cabins, Atsion Lake. Trips—Batson to Green Bank, 3 hrs.; Atsion to Pleasant Mills, 8 hrs.; Pleasant Mills to Green Bank, 3 hrs.; excellent canoeing. (Credit—*Exploring the Little Rivers of New Jersey* and *Canoeing in New Jersey*)

Musconetcong River: only few mi. canoeable. Trips—through canal to Waterloo; upstream for 1 mi. on lake at Saxton Falls, 1 mi. through vil. of Bloomsbury.

Navesink River: Monmouth Co., W. of Red Bank to little pond (several mi. good canoeing); continue into Swimming River. (Credit—*Exploring the Little Rivers of New Jersey*)

Oswego River: E. of Wading River, launch at Oswego Lake S. end of Pa. St. For., Oswego meets Wading near Harrisville. S. of Harrisville, tidewater, no canoeing. Scenery—wild, cedar swamps, cranberry bogs, historical sites. Trips—Oswego Lake to Harrisville, 4 hrs.; Speedwell to Godfrey Brdg. (on Wading), 7 hrs.; Godfrey Brdg. to Rte. 563, 1½ hrs.; Speedwell to Rte. 563, 8 hrs.; Speedwell to Harrisville, 9 hrs.; Speedwell to Wading River Brdg., 11 hrs.; Harrisville to Wading River Brdg., 3½ hrs. (Credit—*Canoeing in New Jersey*)

Passaic River: second longest in N.J.; best canoeing over 35 mi., Millington Singac, 2 days, spring and fall best, hazardous during floods, numerous wildlife, particularly birds, slow-moving river, canoe either direction. Recommended trip—few mi. E. Millstone to Singac or turn N. to Ramapo at jctn. of Passaic S. of Mt. View.

Paulins Kill: River turns and twists around hills; Stillwater to Columbia, spring, some parts canoeable anytime, 6 mill dams on river, dangerous below dams at Marksboro and Hainesburg. 1 mi. white water above Hainesburg, second drop dangerous. (Credit—*Exploring the Little Rivers of New Jersey*)

Pequest River: Warren Co. run from Pequest to Del. in spring. (Credit—*Exploring the Little Rivers of New Jersey*)

Rahway River: Union Co., quiet stream, winds in big loops through Cranford, popular with canoeists. (Credit—*Exploring the Little Rivers of New Jersey*)

Ramapo River: Fine weekend canoeing, spring and fall, high water. Start—1 mi. S. of Suffern, N.Y., near jctn. Rte. 202 and Rte. 17; from here to Mt. View, 20 mi., couple low dams N. of Pompton Lake, 1 ptg. at outlet to lake, some white water, camping, fishing, Ramapo Water Gardens; may continue trip to Little Falls or W. to Millington, follow Passaic, S.E. (Credit—*Exploring the Little Rivers of New Jersey*)

Rancocas River: From headwaters Rancocas to Brown's Mills to Mt. Holly, 25 mi., pretty ctry., water amber but clear, abundant wildlife, river free from obstructions; not suitable for canoeing beyond Mt. Holly. (Credit—*Exploring the Little Rivers of New Jersey* and *Canoeing in New Jersey*)

Rockaway River: Morris Co.; Dover to res. at Boonton, narrow and swift through Dover, slows and spreads past town, beautiful. (Credit—*Exploring the Little Rivers of New Jersey*)

Raritan River: Trip starts High Brdg., Clinton, Flemington jctn. or 3 brdgs. River OK early spring to late fall from Flemington jctn. except in draught; N. and S. branches meet near Rte. 567 crossing to form Raritan; 10 mi., exciting canoeing, N. Branch, spring, Whitehouse to jctn. of branches; Flemington jctn. to Somerville, 16 mi., fine trip; Somerville to New Brunswick, 10–12 mi., end trip outskirts of Trenton via Millstone, Lake Carnegie, Del. and Raritan Canal, several days, end 30 mi. from start. (Credit—*Exploring the Little Rivers of New Jersey* and *Canoeing in New Jersey*)

Saddle River: Bergen Co., shallow, many small dams, lower part unattractive, canoeable in spots for mi. or so. (Credit—*Exploring the Little Rivers of New Jersey*)

Shrewsbury River: Monmouth Co., 6–7 mi., little stream, upstream toward Tinton Falls. (Credit—*Exploring the Little Rivers of New Jersey*)

Stony Brook: Mercer Co. head of Carnegie Lake and up brook for leisurely afternoon. (Credit—*Exploring the Little Rivers of New Jersey*)

Toms River: From Thomson Brdg. Rd. to bay, 13 hrs.; Thomson Brdg. Rd. (1.3 mi. W. of jctn. of Rtes. 527 and 528) to Rte. 528, ½ hr., some liftovers, much brush—may need clippers and small saw; ample parking at Thomson Brdg. Rd. Beaver between Thomson Brdg. Rd. to Rte. 528, landowner reacts violently toward canoe groups. Rte. 528 to dirt rd. brdg. off Rte. 528 (turn off Rte. 528 to S. at Jackson Township Municipal Bldg., go past elementary and high school to brdg.—ample parking, local swimming hole), 1¾ hrs. Swimming hole to Meadowbrook Vil. Retirement Community, 1 hr. (also an access at st. game farm). Meadowbrook Vil. Retirement Community to Bowman Rd., 40 min., good camping at Bowman Rd. Bowman Rd. to Rte. 547 at

Whitesville, 3½ hrs., no interm. access pts. Rte. 547 to Rte. 70, 1¾ hrs., good parking at Rte. 70; Rte. 70 to Rte. 571 at Pleasant Plains, 1½ hr. (access also at Camp Albocondo, private with reasonable rates; for rates call owner, Hugh Clayton, 201-349-4079, free for Boy Scouts and Girl Scouts), good take-out area at municipal parking lot at bus terminal in Toms River, some liftovers en route and low trees, some underwater snags, popular rte. Rte. 571 to bay, some overhanging trees, poison ivy along entire trail. (Credit—Murray Hill Canoe Club)

Wading River: E. of Batsto, N.–S. course, parallel Rte. 563. Wading River begins in Chatsworth but is too small for canoeing to Speedwell. (Credit—*Exploring the Little Rivers of New Jersey* and *Canoeing in New Jersey*)

Wallkill River: Sussex Co., winding and narrow till it crosses N.Y. st. line, not recommended. (Credit—*Exploring the Little Rivers of New Jersey*)

NEW MEXICO

Chama River: 30 mi., El Vado Dam to Abiquiu Dam; fences; avg. 15 ft. drop per mi., water level erratic, wild entry. Dif. III. Dam to Christ of Desert Mtn. Monument, 20 mi.; Abiquiu to jctn. with Rio Grande, 30 mi. Dif. II–III; dams, fences; water level varies.

Gila River: St. Hwy. 527 to Mogollon Creek, 45 mi., Gila Wilderness Area, Mar. and Apr. of wet years only, 20 ft. per mi. drop, min. of 200–300 cfs. necessary.

Rio Grande River: 150 mi., Manassa Brdg. on Col., 142 to Cochite Dam; Col. 142 to Lobator Brdg., Dif. I, easy, novice. Lobator Brdg. to Lee Trail, 24 mi., wild, canyon, ptg. out 220 vertical ft., no rd. in canyon, Dif. II. Lee Trail to jctn. with Red

River, Dif. VI, experts only, seldom run, deep canyon, ptg. in and out. Red River to Arroyo Hondo, Dif. III, experts only, deep canyon, no rds. in canyon, ptg. in 800 vertical ft.; Arroyo Hondo to Taos Jctn. Brdg., wild, experts only, deep and narrow canyon, no roads in, Dif. V. Taos Jctn. Brdg. to Pilar, Dif. I, novice, 2 short Dif. II rapids. Pilar to Rinconada, Dif. IV, experts only, white water. Rinconada to Otowi Brdg., 39 mi., Dif. I, easy, several ptgs.—dams, obstacles—junk, OK novice; Otowi Brdg. to Cochite Dam, 23 mi., Dif. III–IV, wild entry, experts only, most popular white water in New Mexico. (Credit—C. Carnes and J. H. Fretwell)

San Juan River: From Aztec Brdg. on St. Rd. 173 below Navajo Res. to Blanco Brdg. on St. Rd. 17, approx. 11 mi., fast water, may be light rapids in spots, excel. fishing. DANGER—water very cold; possible to float from farther upstream but access can be problem; area from dam to Simon Canyon restricted for flies and lures only, limit of 4 fish, none under 15 in.

NEW YORK

Adirondack Rtes.

Blue Mountain Lake Sec.: 19 mi., 1 day, 2 mi. ptg.; 8th Lake Camp to Blue Mtn. Lake. Trip—8th Lake to Raquette Lake through Brown's tract inlet, 2½ mi. Cross Raquette Lake from Raquette Lake Vil. up Marion River to ptg. 6 mi. Dam at foot of Utowana Lake, through Utowana, Eagle, and Blue Mtn. lakes, 7 mi. Ptgs.—N. end 8th Lake, 1.1 mi.; old RR brdg. on Marion River to dam, ½ mi.

Fulton Chain Sec.: 18 mi., 1 day, 1.7 mi. ptg.; Old Forge to 8th Lake campsite. Trip—Old Forge, down mid. branch Moore River 1½ mi. to 1st Lake, through 1st Lake to 2nd Lake to 3rd Lake, 4½ mi.; 3rd Lake to 4th Lake, across 4th Lake, 5½ mi. to inlet into 5th Lake (small pond), through

5th Lake to 6th, 7th, and 8th lakes. DANGER—heavy motorboat traffic between 1st and 4th lakes; high winds make lakes dangerous. Ptgs.—between 5th and 6th lakes, .7 mi.; between 7th and 8th lakes, 1 mi.

Long Lake Sec.: 14 mi., 1 day, no ptg., head of Long Lake to foot of lake. Trip—head to Long Lake Vil., 4½ mi.; Vil. to lake foot, 9½ mi.

Paul Smith Sec.: "Rte. of 7 carries," beautiful trip; through series of ponds from Saranac Inn to Paul Smith's; 3¼ mi. ptgs.; from Paul Smith's to Lake Kushaqua; ¼ mi. ptg. to Church Pond, to Osgood Pond, to Lake Lucretia, to 1 mi. ptg., to Rainbow Lake, then down Saranac River to Lake Kushaqua to N. end of lake.

Raquette Lake Sec.: 17 mi., 1 day, 1¾ mi. ptg., 8th Lake camp to Forked Lake Dam (outlet). Trip—8th Lake to Raquette Lake through Brown's tract inlet, 2½ mi.; through Raquette Lake past Tioga pt., through outlet bay, to Forked Lake and through to Raquette River, down Raquette River to Forked Lake Dam, ½ mi.; Buttermilk Falls, .1 mi.; rapids below falls, ½ mi. Forked Lake Dam—hire truck here. DANGER—rounding Bluff Pt. on windy day.

Saranac Sec.: (A) 12 mi.; 1⅓ mi. ptg.; 1 day; Axton through Upper Saranac Lake to Fish Creek Pond campsite. (B) 16¼ mi.; 1½ mi. ptg.; Axton to Ampersand Dock boat livery, E. end Lower Saranac Lake. (C) 14¼ mi.; 1½ mi. ptg.; Axton to Tom's Rock Leanto, lower Saranac. (D) 10 mi., 1 day; Tom's Rock Leanto to Saranac Lake Vil. via Saranac River. (E) 10 mi., ¾ mi. ptg.; 1 day; Fish Creek Bay to Fish Creek Ponds to Little Square Pond via small stream, then via another stream to Floodwood Pond, then into Rollins Pond, then return to Fish Creek Pond through Whey and Square ponds; 3 ptgs. ¼ mi. Floodwood to Rollins Pond; ⅛ mi. Rollins to Whey Pond; ¼ mi. Whey to Copperas Pond. (F) 10 mi.; 2 mi. ptg., 1 day. Fish Creek Pond up Spider Creek to Follensby Clear Pond, ptg. ⅛ mi. to Pollywog Pond, then ptg. ¼ mi to Floodwood Pond, return to Little Square Pond, ¼ mi. ptg. to Follensby Clear Pond, ptg. ⅛ mi. to Green Pond. (G) 10 mi.; 1 mi. ptg.; 1 day; Hoel Pond through

Turtle and Slang ponds, ¼ mi. ptg. to Long Pond, ¾ mi.
ptg. to Fleetwood Pond, back to Saranac Inn by rtes. E or F.
Tupper Lake Sec.: 24 mi., 2 days; Axton to Head Tupper
Lake. Trip—down Raquette River 18 mi. to foot, Big
Tupper; foot to head, Big Tupper Lake, 6 mi.; N. loop near
Hwy. 30 may be dif., take cutoff at Trombler Clearing leanto
(8 mi. from Axton). DANGER—Tupper Lake on windy
days, Underhill Rapids on N. loop, Raquette River.
(Credit—*Adirondack Canoe Routes*)

Allegheny River: W. of vil. of Mill Grove to st. line, 54 mi. Dif.
II–III. Rattlesnakes in ear near end, narrow chute near Tunung-
want Creek, some tricky rifts. Mill Grove to Olean, 7 mi.; Olean
to Salamanca, 23 mi.; Salamanca to N.Y.-Pa. line, 24 mi. Good
small-mouth bass fishing.

Ausable River: Essex, Clinton cos. Ausable Forks to Keeseville,
14 mi. Dif. II–V. DANGER—stop 3 mi. above Keeseville—dam
below, mostly fast water, experts only in spots, dangerous rapids
in spots. Don't run below dam, dangerous rapids, waterfall. Ausable Forks to Clintonville, 6 mi., Clintonville to end, 8 mi.

Ausable River—E. Branch: Essex Co. Keene to Ausable Forks,
18 mi. Dif. II–V. Keene to Upper Jay, 7 mi., shallow, dam above
Upper Jay. Upper Jay to Jay, 3 mi., mixed calm and rapids, 1 low
dam, ptg. falls. Jay to Stickney Brdg., 5 mi., low dam, fairly
smooth. Stickney Brdg. to Ausable Forks, 8 mi., tight squeezes,
rough. Upper Ausable, impassable rapids, falls.

Ausable River—W. Branch: Essex Co. Brdg. 1 mi. N.E. of ski
jump to monument on Rte. 86, 7 mi. Dif. II–V. DANGER—falls
at destroyed dam, 1 mi. below Rte. 86 brdg., ¼ mi. bad rapids—
skilled only. Ptg.—bad rapids; Lower river falls, cascades, rushing
torrent, don't run.

Batten Kill: Washington Co. Vt.-N.Y. st. line to Center Falls, 23
mi. Dif. II–IV. DANGER—old dam with rapids. Ptg.—right side
of E. Greenwich Dam. Start to Rte. 22 brdg., 13 mi.; Rte. 22

brdg. to Center Falls, 10 mi.; beyond Center Falls, many dams and falls, many ptgs.

Beaver Kill: Sullivan, Del. cos. Roscoe to E. Branch, 17 mi. Dif. III–V. Drop 16–30 ft. per mi., run in high water, no dams or obstructions, scenic, several dif. spots in first 8 mi.; Roscoe to Horton, 9 mi.; Horton to E. Branch, 8 mi.

Beaver River: Herkimer, Lewis cos. Mostly too steep, some canoeing between Croghan and Black River, 9 mi.; dams and falls between Beaver River flow and Croghan.

Bennett Creek: Steuben Co. Fast, shallow, barbed-wire fences, unnavigable shoals, not recommended.

Black Creek: Genesee, Monroe cos. Brdg. 1 mi. E. of Pumpkin Hill to Genesee River, 33 mi. Dif. I–V. Brush at start, fallen trees, dam—Churchville. DANGER—broken dam with rapids, some swampland. Start to Churchville, 13 mi.; Churchville to Genesee River, 20 mi.

Black River: Lewis Co. Below Lyons Falls to Carthage, 49 mi. Dif. I–III. Polluted, little current, some wading; obstacles—old wire and old dam. Below Carthage, falls, dams, bad rapids; start to Glenfield, 11 mi.; Glenfield to Bushe's Lndg., 9 mi.; Bushe's Lndg. to Rte. 26A brdg., 11 mi.; Rte. 26A brdg. to Carthage, 18 mi.

Boreas River: From brdg. at Rte. 28N (about 15 mi. from N. Creek) to spot near jctn. with Hudson River, less than full day trip, white water, can be a terror in high water, high water is when Hudson is 6 ft., 9 in., better when Hudson gauge reads about 5 ft. Shortly after put-in is steep and tricky staircase (a semi-waterfall in high water), then river becomes quiet, then 4 mi. of continuous rapids; scout rapids before running. (Credit—David Binger)

Bouquet River: Essex Co. Fast, many ptgs., falls, dams, bad rapids and ledges, not recommended.

Buffalo Creek: Erie Co. Much wading, lining necessary, bad ledges, tricky rapids, may be OK in high water.

Butternut Creek: Onondaga Co. 1 mi. below Jamesville to Chittenango Co., 18 mi. Dif. II–III. Pollution, logjams, low brdgs., low dams, not recommended. Start to N.Y.C. RR brdg., 8 mi.; RR brdg. to Chittenango Co., 10 mi.

Butternut Creek: Otsego Co. New Lisbon to Unadilla River, 21 mi. Dif. II–IV, many ptgs. Some obstacles—fallen brdg., logs, low dams, barbed-wire fences, not recommended.

Canandaigua Outlet: Ontario, Wayne cos. Canandaigua Lake to Lyons, 38 mi., Dif. I–IV, many washed-out mill dams, 5 dams intact, bad rapids below, some washed-out dams, shallow rapids, steep banks, barbed-wire fences. Best sec. below Manchester, light rapids, some wading in low water. Start to Littleville, 9 mi. (3¼ mi. to ptg. from Littleville to Manchester); Manchester to Phelps, 13 mi.; Phelps to Lyons, 16 mi.

Canaseraga Creek: Livingston Co. W. Sparta Sta. to Graveland Sta., 22 mi., fast current in high water, few rifts; many beaver dams in lower sec.

Canisteo River: Steuben Co. Brdg. 2 mi. N.W. of Canisteo to Tioga River, 45 mi. Dif. II–IV. Few logjams, rattlesnakes. Ptg.— old dam (3 ft. high), some rifts. Start to Adrian, 10 mi.; Adrian to Cameron, 11 mi.; Cameron to Rathbone, 9 mi.; Rathbone to Addison, 9 mi.; Addison to Tioga River, 6 mi.

Cassadaga Creek: Gerry to Levant, 10 mi. Dif. II–III. Mild stream, 1 small riffle.

Catatonk Creek: Tioga Co. Spencer to Owego Creek, 22 mi. Dif. II–IV. Spencer to W. Candor, 6 mi., sharp turns, river divides— right branch blocked with dam, left branch sharp drop around turn, 3 ptgs. W. Candor to Candor (first dam), 6 mi., white water, fast current, ptg. dam. Candor to Owego Creek, ptg.— dam, fast, pretty.

Cattaraugus Creek: Cattaraugus Co. Rte. 16 brdg. to Lake Erie, 44 mi., exciting, canyons. Dif. I–V, hazardous spots, don't run— high water, some bad rapids, line or ptg., some fences, some trees in water, mostly shallow, scout rapids. Start to Rte. 219 brdgs., 14 mi.; 219 brdg. to Zoar brdg., 20 mi.; Zoar brdg. to farmlands 1 mi. below outlet of S. Branch, 8 mi.; Rte. 20 brdg. to Lake Erie, 2 mi.

Cayuta Creek: Chemung, Tioga cos. Brdg. 1 mi. below Smartwood to Susquehanna River, 23 mi. Dif. III–IV, fast, many rifts, some wading, few fallen trees, obstacles—E. Waverly, 7 mi. E. Waverly to Susquehanna River, 3 mi.; brown trout, bass.

Chadakoin River: Chatauqua Co. Levant to Conewango Creek, 11 mi. Dif. III. Fair current, logjam.

Champlain Canal—Lake George Trip: 90 mi. Start—Fort Ann, Hwy. U.S. 4; 2 locks on way to Whitehall via canal to Lake Champlain (good side trip here into S. Bay for pike, panfish, bass). Down the lake to Ticonderoga, 2 mi. ptg. to Lake George, S. down Lake George to head at beach. DANGER—winds on Lake George, good fishing.

Charlotte Creek: Delaware Co. Brdg. 1 mi. below Fergusonville to Susquehanna River, 19 mi. Dif. III–V, skilled only, 2 ptgs. Obstacles—fallen brdg. and logjams, heavy rapids, 40 ft. per mi. grade in spots. Start to Davenport Center, 9 mi.; Davenport Center to W. Davenport, 4 mi.; W. Davenport to Susquehanna River, 6 mi.

Chemung River: Steuben, Chemung cos. Painted Post to Susquehanna River, 43 mi. Dif. II–III, many isles. Ptg.—Elmira Dam.

Start to Elmira, 19 mi.; Elmira to Wellsburg, 8 mi.; Wellsburg to Susquehanna River, 16 mi.

Chenango River: Chenango, Broome cos. Earlville to Susquehanna River, 75 mi. Dif. II–IV, mild, easy white water, best water below brdg. at Chenango Forks. Ptg.—Binghamton Dam. Earlville to Sherburne, 8 mi.; Sherburne to Norwich, 15 mi.; Norwich to Oxford, 11 mi.; Oxford to Greene, 17 mi.; Greene to Chenango Forks, 9 mi.; Chenango Forks to Susquehanna River, 15 mi.; Colgate Univ. to Binghamton, good trip, beautiful, few short ptgs. around riffs, good fishing, bass, pickerel, panfish.

Cherry Valley Creek: Otsego Co. Middlefield to Susquehanna River, 19 mi. Dif. II–IV. 3 mi. of white water, some obstructions, fast current. Middlefield to Westville, 10 mi.; Westville to Susquehanna River, 9 mi.

Chittenango Creek: Madison, Onondaga cos. Stuart to Oneida Lake, 35 mi. Dif. I–V. Stuart to Upper Brdg. at Chittenango, 4 mi.; skilled only, fast, exciting, 40 ft. per mi. drop. Upper Brdg. at Chittenango to N.Y.C. RR brdg., 5 mi., fast, snags and fallen trees; RR brdg. to Bridgeport, 21 mi., meandering river, smooth current. Bridgeport to Oneida Lake, 5 mi.

Claverock Creek: Columbia Co. Claverock to Stottville, 11½ mi., Dif. II–V, logjams, 3-ft. dam past Rte. 23 brdg. DANGER—ledges near Stockport.

Cohocton River: Steuben Co. Brdg. 2 mi. above Avoka to Chemung River (Painted Post), 34 mi. Dif. II–IV. Fast, easy rifts, some white water, debris in channel below RR brdg. at Coopers Plains. DANGER—gap between old dam 1 mi. above Painted Post. Start to Bath, 12 mi.; Bath to Campbell, 13 mi.; Campbell to Chemung River, 9 mi.

Cold River: Below Long Lake, off Raquette River to right, (Adirondack rtes.); 1 mi. upriver to Calkins Creek; wild, rugged, canoeable at certain stages, good fishing.

Conewango Creek: Chautauqua Co. Conewango Valley to N.Y.-Pa. line, 31 mi. Dif. I–III. Mostly slow, straight course, 3 mi. of easy rifts from Rte. 17 to Kennedy, no partic. dangers or obstructions. Start to Kennedy, 10 mi.; Kennedy to brdg. W. of Freusburg, 15 mi.; Freusburg to N.Y.-Pa. line, 6 mi.

Delaware River: NOTE: Streamflow characteristics (given in Roman numerals) apply to the Delaware River only and do not conform with the International Scale of River Dif., as published in the American White Water Affiliation Safety Code. Under no circumstances should the Delaware River Basin Commission classifications of the Delaware River rapids be applied to streams elsewhere. Stream rapid conditions under various classifications on the Delaware River Basin Commission maps are substantially less hazardous than under the corresponding classifications of the American White Water Affiliation.

Delaware River: Hancock, N.Y., to Trenton, N.J., approx. 200 mi. 10 to 14 days. Description divided into 10 17-mi. secs. (1 day ea.), listed under N.Y., Pa., and N.J.

   Sec. A: Hale Eddy, N.Y., on W. Branch to Long Eddy, N.Y., on Delaware River, also short section of E. Branch, jctn. E. of W. branches marks bdry. of Catskill Mts. Dif. I–IV. Hale Eddy to Equinunk, I–III; Equinunk to Long Eddy, 2 Dif. IV areas mostly II and III. Access areas—W. Branch—2 privately owned N. and S. of Hancock Brdg. Tent and trailer space here—charge. Hancock access area below jctn. of E. Branch and main branch. Buckingham access—owned by Pa. Fish Comm.—free, off 191 above Equinunk 2–3 mi. Equinunk access—charge, Long Eddy access—2 private, charge in Long Eddy. Brown and rainbow trout, walleye, small-mouth bass, shad in deep pools, May–June. DANGER—eel weir 1½ mi. down from Lordsville, N.Y. brdg.

   Sec. B: Long Eddy, N.Y., to Narrowsburg, N.Y. Similar to Sec. A but has very hazardous pt. downstream from brdg. at Skinners Falls. DANGER—eel weir just below Skinners Falls; also deep pool (113 ft. or more) below Narrowsburg brdg., river fairly narrow, min. ptgs. even in low water. Dif.

I–IV. Long Eddy to Hankins I–IV. Hankins to Callicoon I–V, mostly III, swift V rapids below Callicoon brdg., Callicoon to Cochecton mostly III, Cochecton to Narrowsburg mostly II–III with IV at Skinners Falls. Access areas—Long Eddy—2 private in Long Eddy, charge. Hankins access—1 private in Hankins, charge. Callicoon access—1 private, charge. Cochecton access—N. of Damascus–Cochecton brdg., free. Narrowsburg access (N.Y.)—future. Small-mouth bass, walleye, shad in lower half.

Sec. C: Narrowsburg, N.Y., to Barryville, N.Y. Drops precipitously through series of riffles and rapids separated by short, mod. deep pools. Most remote and least developed sec. of river from Hancock to Trenton. Dif. I–V, Narrowsburg to Lackawaxen mixed I–IV with 2 areas of V. Lackawaxen to Barryville II–IV. Access areas: Narrowsburg (Pa.), Pennsylvania Fish Comm., free; Narrowsburg (N.Y.)—future. Lackawaxen—near mouth of Lackawaxen—charge. Barryville—private N. of brdg.—free; Barryville—N.Y. Dept. of Cons.—future; water suitable for swimming in Sec. C. Shad, small-mouth bass, walleye, rainbow and brown trout, fallfish. DANGER—eel weirs 2 mi. below Narrowsburg brdg. and 1 mi. down from Barryville Shohala Brdg.

Sec. D: Barryville, N.Y., to Port Jervis, N.Y. Mod. deep section with pools, riffles, and rapids, outstanding area for canoeing. Dif. I–V, 2 areas Dif. V, first near intersec. of Mongaup River, second where river narrows approx. 2 mi. above Port Jervis. Access area—one of least accessible secs., Bob's Beach on W. bank near Milford—Montague Brdg.; Barryville—private and future public. Small-mouth bass, shad, walleye, panfish, fallfish. DANGER—eel weirs 7 mi. up from Mongaup River and ¾ mi. below Erie-Lackawanna Brdg.

Sec. E: Port Jervis, N.Y., to Dingman's Ferry, Pa. At Port Jervis river changes from short pools and many riffles to series of pools of mod. length, fewer riffles and more gentle descent, slower travel than above, will be impounded as part of Tocks Isle Res. in future. Dif. I–IV, several III and IV. Access areas—Bob's Beach, take Rte. 209 S. of Milford, Pa.; Milford Brdg.—S. of brdg. on N.J. side, charge; Dingman's

Brdg. (Pa.)—charge; Dingman's Brdg. (N.J.)—undeveloped. Small-mouth bass, panfish, walleye. (Credit—Delaware River Basin Comm.)

Eighteen Mile Creek: Niagara Co. Rte. 104 brdg. to Olcutt, 11 mi. Dif. I–III, shallow rifts, ptg.—Newfane Dam, Burt Dam (no-trespassing signs), some wading.

Ellicott Creek: Erie Co. Hwy. 324 to Tonawanda Creek, 13 mi. Dif. I–IV.

Esopus Creek: Ulster Co. Allaben to Saugerties, 41 mi. Dif. I–V. Scenic, upper Esopus—experts only. Don't run in very high water. Allaben to Phoenicia, 4½ mi., 15–100-ft. drop per mi., very dif., rough chutes, bad rapids. Mt. Pleasant to Boiceville, 4 mi., ptg.— Ashokan Res.; brdg. 2 mi. up from Marbletown to Rte. 28 brdg., 12 mi., deep gorge, ptg.—falls, fences, several easy rifts. Rte. 28 brdg. to Glenerie Falls, 9½ mi., ptg.—dam. Glenerie Falls to Saugerties, 6 mi., rocky ledges, river widens, dam at Saugerties.

Fall Creek: Tompkins Co. Malloryville to Varna, 15 mi. Dif. II–V, scenic deep ravines; lower part—continuous rapids. Malloryville to Freeville, 4 mi., easy rifts, fallen trees, ptg.—Freeville Dam (low), Freeville to Etna, logjam, some white water. Etna to Varna, 6 mi., steep, continuous rapids, skilled only, barbed wire, logs, sharp turns, white water. Don't go beyond Rte. 392—dangerous beyond.

Fall Stream: Hamilton Co. Inlet to Piseco Lake, to Valley Lake; brdg. near Piseco for 6 mi. downstream. Dif. I–II. Placid brook, remote entry; fair fishing—pickerel, perch.

Fish Creek: Hamilton Co. Westdale to Barge Canal; 38½ mi. Dif. II–IV. Westdale to Camden, 6 mi., rapids at first, then fast current. Ptg.—Camden dam; 3 mi. below Camden to E. Branch, 12½ mi., rough rapids below dam, then good current but no rapids to mill dam. Ptg.—McConnellsville Dam; below dam fine canoeing, rapids, fast and heavy current. E. Branch to Barge

Canal, 20 mi., isles, complex channels, good current; good fishing, bass, walleye.

Fish Creek: Saratoga Co. Outlet of Saratoga Lake to Victory Mills, 10 mi. Dif. I–V. First 3 mi. wide and without current. Ptg. —dam above Grangerville, rapids below dam mixed with smooth. DANGER—broken dam.

Fishkill Creek: Dutchess Co. Hopewell to Groveville, 13 mi. Dif. II–IV. Ptgs.—Hopewell, Glenham, Groveville dams, low footbrdg. and cable, some rifts.

Five Mile Creek: Steuben Co. Bean's Sta. to Cohocton River, 13 mi., not recom. Dif. II–IV. Muck clogs, logjams, rifts, last part very fast, barbed wire.

Flint Creek: Ontario Co. Brdg. across flood channel to Orleans, 22 mi. Dif. II–IV. Start to Gorham, 5 mi., 2 small dams, rocky ledges below dam at Gorham. Gorham to Flint, 9 mi., fast, smooth current below second dam, barbed wire, rough spots, ptg. 3-ft. dam. Flint to Seneca Castle, 4 mi., experts only, quick turns, white water.

Genegantslet Creek: Chenango Co. Smithville Flats to Rte. 12, 14 mi. Dif. III–IV. White water, narrow, fast, shallow in spots, quick turns, barbed wire, brushy.

Genesee River: Allegany, Wyoming, Livingston, Monroe cos. Wellsville to Rochester, 132 mi. Dif. I–V. Wellsville to Portageville, 57 mi., intermed. dif., exper. canoeists, brushy in spots, logs, many rapids, ptg. Belmont Dam. End—brdg. 2 mi. above Rte. 245 brdg., falls beyond Rte. 245 brdg. Ptg.—Portageville to St. Helena, falls, rapids, canyon, no canoeing. St. Helena to Mt. Morris Flood Control Dam, fast, dangerous in high water, cross currents, heavy rifts, inaccessible in parts. Mt. Morris to Rochester, 63 mi., mostly slack current, high banks, barbed wire.

Grass River: St. Lawrence Co.; Canton to St. Lawrence River, 44 mi. Dif. I–IV. Long, easy stretches, a few dif. rapids, impassable ledges and falls between Chamberlain and Louisville. Ptg.—dam near Massena.

Great Chazy River: Clinton Co. Foot of Ledges, 1 mi. below Mooers to Lake Champlain, 21 mi. Dif. I–IV. Upper and lower parts monotonous, mid. section exciting, some heavy rapids. Ptg. —3 dams, some lining necessary.

Honeoye Creek: Ontario, Livingston, Monroe cos. Rd. brdg. 1 mi. W. of Allen's Hill to Genesee River, 21 mi. Start to Rte. 20 brdg., 9 mi., light current at first, white water last 2 mi. Ptg.—to Sibleyville. Sibleyville to Genesee River, fast, smooth run. Ptg.— Rush Dam, mostly slack water after dam, some riffles.

Hoosic River: Rensselaer, Washington cos. Vt.-N.Y. st. line to Valley Falls, 30 mi. Dif. II–IV. Start to Hoosick Falls, 13 mi., fast current, east rift, some brush and fallen trees. Ptg.—Hoosick Falls. Hoosick jctn. to Valley Falls, 17 mi. Ptg.—bad stretch between falls and jctn. Ptg.—Johnsonville power dam.

Hudson River: 243 mi. North River to George Washington Brdg. Dif. I–V. Above Hodley, beautiful trip to Stony Point and beyond depending upon water level. Fair fishing—bullhead, panfish.

Indian River: Jefferson, St. Lawrence cos. Brdg. 2 mi. below Antwerp to Oswegatchie River, 67 mi. Dif. I–IV. Start to Phila., 6 mi., slow, narrow, ptg. Phila. dam and falls. Brdg. 2 mi. below Phila. to Theresa, 15 mi., shallow—rocky rifts, slow current, ptg. 2 dams in Theresa. Theresa to Rossie, 24 mi., meanders, little current. Rossie to Oswegatchie River, 22 mi. Bass, pickerel.

Ischua Creek: Cattaraugus Co. Brdg. on 5-mi. rd. to Hinsdale. Dif. III–IV. Skill necessary, sharp turns, many rifts.

Johnson Creek: Orleans Co. Lyndonville to Lake Ontario, 14 mi. Dif. I–IV. Rapids.

Kayaderosseras Creek: Saratoga Co. Rd. E. from Porter Corners to Saratoga Lake, 28 mi. Dif. I–V.

Trip 1—Start to first dam at Rock City Falls, 9 mi., deep, slow, few easy rapids, barbed wire. Ptg.—2 dams at Rock City Falls.

Trip 2—Rock City Falls to Factory Vil., 8 mi., easy rapids, mixed with still water, fallen trees.

Trip 3—Factory Vil. to Ballston Spa, 2 mi. Ptg—1 dam at Ballston Spa; experts only.

Trip 4—Swimming pool at Ballston Spa to Saratoga Lake, 13 mi., light ripples, slack current, excellent for beginners. (Credit—C. H. Grose)

Kinderhook Creek: Columbia Co. Chatham Center to Stuyvesant Falls, 14 mi. Dif. II–III. Ptg.—low dam and dams at Valatie.

Kunjamuk Creek: Hamilton Co. Moffitt Beach State Campsite on Sacandaga Lake near Speculator (Hwy. 8) through inlet to Lake Pleasant; E. to Sacandaga River outlet, soon branching left upstream into the Kunjamuk to Elm Lake. Dif. I–II. Light riffles. Ptg.—destroyed brdg., some drops, beaver dams, fair fishing.

Limestone Creek: Onondaga Co. High brdg. to Butternut Creek, 10 mi. Dif. II–V. First ½ mi. rough rapids, sharp turns. Ptg.—dam below Fayetteville brdg. and dam near end, jams—require carry.

Little Salmon River: Oswego Co. Rte. 11 brdg. to Lake Ontario, 14 mi. Dif. II–IV. Run high water only. Ptg.—dams below Mexico.

Little Salmon River: Franklin Co. S. Bombay to river jctn. at Ft. Covington, 16 mi. Dif. II–IV. Barbed wire, some lining and wading.

Livingston Creek: Columbia Co. Mt. Ross to Bingham Mills, 17 mi. Dif. II–IV. DANGER—falls near Elizabeth brdg., strong currents, rifts, narrow channel.

Mohawk River: Delta Dam to loop near E. Canada Creek, 51 mi. Dif. II–IV. Start to Rome, 6 mi., some strong rapids, fallen trees, nice run. Rome to Oriskany Creek, 9 mi., unpleasant, green slime, poor canoeing. Oriskany Creek to Utica, 13 mi., high banks, very few rifts, uninteresting. Utica to Frankfort, 13 mi., pollution, fair current. Ptg.—dam near Frankfort; Herkimer to Jackson, 5 mi., mild rifts, good current. Loop near E. Canada Creek, 5 mi.

Moodna Creek: Orange Co. 1 mi. W. of Washingtonville to Orrs Mills, 14 mi. Start to Salisbury Mills, 7 mi., 3-ft. dam in Washingtonville and one 2 mi. below; Salisbury Mills to Orrs Mills, 7 mi. Ptg.—high dam and gorge, white water below Mountainville, shallow ledges.

Moose River—Mid. Branch: Herkimer Co. Dif. I–II. Old Forge to dam below Thendara, 4½ mi., meanders, mostly smooth, 1 small pitch.

Moose River—N. Branch: Herkimer Co. Lake Rondaxe to Mid.

Branch, 13 mi. Dif. I–II. Ptg.—1 small dam, mostly slow, ¼ mi. rapids—may need to line.

Mud Creek: Steuben Co. Bradford to Savona, 14 mi., wild area, many beaver dams, 1 shallow pitch near Savona.

Nanticoke Creek: Broome Co. Maine to Susquehanna River, 13 mi. Dif. II–IV. Some sharp turns, light rifts, pretty, slow current at end, snags.

Neversink River: Sullivan, Orange cos. Rte. 55 brdg. to Port Jervis, 34 mi. Dif. II–V. Start to Fallsburgh, 8 mi., rifts, fallen trees, fast, 3 dams at Fallsburgh. Fallsburgh to Bridgeville, 10 mi., fast deep-wooded ravines, no partic. dangers. Ptg.—first few miles below Bridgeville. Oakland Valley to Rose's Pt., 6 mi., steep, white water, some lining. Rose's Pt. to Port Jervis, 10 mi., fast but easy, some heavy waves at jctn. with Basher Kill.

New York City: 80 mi., 5 days. This trail described in *Sports Illustrated,* Nov. 22, 1971. Trip:
> *Day 1*—Hutchinson River in Bronx across Long Island Sound to Queens and back to Bronx.
> *Day 2*—Bronx shore back to Queens.
> *Day 3*—Queens down East River to S. Manhattan.
> *Day 4*—Explore Brooklyn coast, paddle and ptg. to Jamaica Bay.
> *Day 5*—Through marshes S. of Queens. Unusual ptgs. through city; obstacles—tides, rocks thrown from Queensboro Brdg.; heavy pollution in places, some wild birds, possible to canoe under LaGuardia Airport runway on this trip. (Credit—*Sports Illustrated*)

Niagara River: Erie, Niagara cos. Lewiston to Youngstown, 6 mi. Dif. II.

Nine Mile Creek: Onondaga Co. Brdg. near Marcellus Sta. to Onondaga Lake, 11 mi. Dif. II–III. Submerged logs, fallen trees, low stone brdg., low dam above Camillus, dam at Ambay.

Nissequoque: Town park on Landing Road to Sound in Suffolk Co., L.I.; excellent trip, time with tides.

Normanskill: Albany area; 4–6 mi., down to New Scotland Ave. brdg. Fishing fair—bass, eels, chubs.

Oatka Creek: Livingston, Monroe cos. Brdg. W. of Pearl Creek to Genesee River, 31 mi. Dif. I–IV. Start to Le Roy, 14 mi., fast, narrow, fallen trees, 1 fast narrow chute, shallow rifts. Ptg.—Le Roy Dam, dam at Rte. 5, and unnavigable cataracts below. Ft. Hill to Mumford, 8 mi., good rapids at first, fast current. Mumford to Genesee River, 9 mi. DANGER—mill at Wheatland Center, some exciting rocky rapids; logs and debris.

Olean Creek: Cattaraugus Co. Hinsdale to Allegheny River. Dif. II–III. Fast, sharp turns.

Oneida Creek: Oneida Co. Oneida Castle to Oneida Lake, 19 mi. Dif. I–III. Line—low dam below start, fallen trees.

Oswegatchie River: St. Lawrence Co. High Falls to Ogdensburg, 87 mi. Dif. I–V. Start to inlet above Cranberry Lake, 15 mi., wild. Ptg.—steep rapids between inlet and Wanakena. Wanakena to Cranberry Lake, 9 mi., clear, slow current, beaver dams. Ptg.— Cranberry Lake to Vil. of Wegatchie. Wegatchie to Elmdale, 12 mi. Access—Hwy. 3, 5 mi. W. of Wanakena; fair to good trout fishing.

Otsego Creek: Otsego Co. Mt. Vision to Susquehanna River, 20 mi. Dif. II–IV. Mt. Vision to Laurens, 6 mi., many snags, barbed wire, fast run above Laurens; Laurens to W. Oneonta, 8 mi., logjam, barbed wire, shallow pitch. Oneonta to Susquehanna River, 6 mi., good current, pleasant.

Otselic River: Chenango, Cortland, Broome cos. Otselic to Tioughnioga River, 46 mi. Dif. I–V. Rte. 80 brdg. to S. Otselic, 10 mi., narrow, meanders, logjams, fast rifts, sharp turns. Ptg.— 4-ft. concrete dam near St. Fish Hatchery; barbed wire, dangerous, not recommended. S. Otselic to Cincinnatus, 12 mi., many riffles, logjams. Cincinnatus to Willet, fast current, logjams. Willet to Upper Lisle, 10 mi., little rifts. Upper Lisle to Tioughnioga River, 7 mi., strong current, flat water. Ptg.—Fed. Whitney Pt. Dam.

Ouleout Creek: Delaware Co. Rte. 7B brdg. below N. Franklin to Susquehanna River, 19 mi. Dif. II–IV. Fast, long stretches mod. white water. Ptg—E. Sydney dam, barbed wire.

Owego Creek: Tioga Co. Ritchford to Susquehanna River, 25 mi. Dif. II–IV. Much barbed wire in hazardous spots, fallen trees. Ptg.—broken dam and 2 dams near Owego, not recommended.

Owego Creek—W. Branch: Tioga Co. W. Newark to main creek, 6½ mi. Dif. III. Fast, sharp turns, several carries, fallen trees, shallow shoal.

Ramapo River: Orange Co. Suffern to Oakland, 10 mi., ideal fast water for novice, 2 low dams. Oakland to Pompton River, dam at Pompton Lake, mild current below dam. DANGER—poisonous snakes in Suffern area.

Raquette River: (see also Adirondack rtes.)

Sec. A: 13¼ mi., 1 day, 1¼ mi. ptg. Long Lake foot to Raquette Falls ptg., 6 mi.; foot of falls to Axton, 6 mi.; 1 ptg. —Raquette Falls.

Sec. B: 18 mi., 1 day; Axton to foot Big Tupper Lake, N. loop near Hwy. 30 may be dif., take cutoff at Trombler Clearing Leanto, 8 mi. from Axton, watch Underhill Rapids on N. loop.

Sec. C: lower Raquette River from N. end Raquette Pond to Colton, Potsdam, Norwood, and St. Lawrence River; many dams, falls, rapids.

Rondout Creek: Ulster Co. Napanock to Hudson River, 38 mi. Dif. I–V. Start to Kerhonkson, 8 mi., fallen logs, fast current, divides into several rough channels. Kerhonkson to High Falls, 15½ mi., sluggish in spots, some rough spots, fast with easy rifts past Alligerville. Ptg.—dam and falls. High Falls to Wallkill River, 6 mi., skilled only. Ptg.—unnavigable gorge above Rosendale and Lafever Falls Dam; Wallkill River to Hudson River, ptg. dam, fast water.

Sacandaga River: Algonquin Lake dam to Northville, 17½ mi. Dif. I–V. Start to Sacandaga campsite, 2½ mi., some rough rapids, good current. S. campsite to Northville, 15 mi., low dam at campsite, heavy rapids at first, then 5 mi. of rapids, good current.

Sacandaga River—E. Branch: Foxlair to rd. above falls (don't land at brdg.—it's located over the falls), 10 mi. Dif. II–V. Challenging, steep, among forests and hills, easy at first, fast and furious in canyon, heavy rapids, hazardous in high water, second gorge most dif., experts only, stop above Griffin Falls.

Sacandaga River—W. Branch: Hamilton Co. First brdg. N. of

Arietta to Shaker's Pl., S.E. of rd. from Caroga to Piseco, 10 mi. Dif. II–III. Some wading, brush; end—near quarry and shallow rapids; lower part very steep and dangerous, experts only.

St. Regis River: St. Lawrence Co. Above Santa Clara to St. Lawrence River, 29 mi. Dif. I–IV. Start to Santa Clara, 6 mi., calm water. Ptg.—Santa Clara to Sanfordville; brdg. 1 mi. below Sanfordville to Winthrop, 6 mi., fast, easy, 1 heavy rift; ptg. Winthrop to 2 mi. above Helena; above Helena to Hogansburg, 8 mi., no partic. dangers. Hogansburg to St. Lawrence River, ptg.— Hogansburg dam, slack water after rapids below dam.

Salmon Creek: Monroe Co. Parma Center Rd. to Lake Ontario. Dif. I–IV. 10 mi., continuous light riffles, brush pile, low concrete brdg.

Salmon River: USGS quads.—Pulaski, Richland, Orwell; 1½ mi. E. of Altmar to Selkirk Lighthouse at mouth of Lake Ontario, 16 mi. Start near Sloperville Rd. Take out Selkirk Lighthouse. Trip: Avoid during heavy runoff, canoes have been lost on this run, summer water too low, run when reservoir gates are open. Contact Niagara Mohawk Power Control for information in Salmon River Res. Phone 315-474-1511; river with gates open is Grade III, river drops 284 ft., is polluted, between put-in and brdg.—exciting rapids. W. of brdg. river is fast with small rapids; between Pineville Brdg. and I 81 brdg. are two ledges, 1½ mi. above Pulaski, and immed. after RR brdg. is hairpin turn and whirlpool —stay to left, from whirlpool to 2 mi. below Pulaski—good Grade III run, keep to right of isle and avoid standing waves before Pulaski Brdg.; ½ mi. below Pulaski Brdg. is Black Hole hairpin turn—deep and fast, still water 2 mi. above Lake Ontario; scenic, take bailer. (Credit—Victor G. McNett)

Salmon River: Franklin Co. Westville Center to Ft. Covington, 10 mi. Dif. I–V. Some heavy rapids, ledges, sharp plunge under brdg., then easy rapids.

Sandy Creek: Monroe Co. 272 brdg. at Kendall Mills to N. Hamlin, 13 mi. Dif. I–III. Continuous riffles, 1 barbed-wire fence.

Sangerfield River: Madison Co. N. Brookfield to Chenango River, 23 mi. Dif. II–IV. Many carries, logs, beaver dams, white water between 2 brdgs. near Hubbardsville, barbed wire. Ptg.—Poolville Dam; last 3 mi. fast current.

Saranac River: Franklin, Essex, Clinton cos. Whey Pond to dam 5 mi. below Morrisonville, 80 mi. Dif. I–V. Whey Pond to Fish Creek Pond, 10 mi. F. C. Pond to Rte. 3 brdg., 9 mi. Rte. 3 brdg. to Saranac Lake Village, 12 mi. Saranac Lake Village to W. end Franklin Falls Res., 12 mi., mostly slow, ½ mi. of rapids, too shallow in summer. W. end Franklin Falls Res. to E. end of Union Falls Res., 8 mi. Ptg.—Union Falls Dam to Clayburg or Riverview; N. branch Riverview to Clayburg, 5 mi., fast current, east rifts. Clayburg to High Falls, 6 mi., easy rifts at first. DANGER—ledges below 2 Redford brdgs.—ptgs., then rifts to High Falls Dam—ptg. Ptg.—rapids and falls below dam. Moffitsville brdg. to Caryville, 10 mi.; first 2 mi.—skilled only, fast, ptg.—3 dams. below Kent Falls to dam 5 mi. below Morrisonville, fast, continuous rifts. *See* also Adirondack Rtes. in New York.

Schenevus Creek: Otsego Co. Brdg. near Schenevus Sta. to Susquehanna River, 14 mi. Dif. II–V. Some barbed wire, snags, short tricky pitches, several rough turns.

Schoharie River: Montgomery Co. Lexington to Mohawk River, 48 mi. Dif. II–V. Lexington to Prattsville, 9 mi., skilled only, very

steep, fast. DANGER—weir 1 mi. above Prattsville—ptg. Ptg.—
Prattsville to N. Blenheim. N. Blenheim to Middleburg, 15 mi.,
exciting, heavy rapids, skilled only. Middleburg to Esperance, 18
mi.; fast, easy between Breakabeen and Schoharie, sluggish after
Schoharie. Ptg.—Esperance to Mill Pt. Mill Pt. to Mohawk River,
6 mi., steep rapids at first, one 3-ft. drop, lower part calm.

Schroon River: Warren Co. Vil. of Schroon Falls to Hudson
River, 40 mi. Dif. I–IV. Start to N. end Schroon Lake, 10 mi.,
light rifts, beautiful, wild entry, too shallow part of yr. Schroon
Lake N. end to Schroon Lake S. end, 9 mi., heavily populated.
End of Schroon Lake to Rte. 8 brdg.; marshes, forests, little cur-
rent to dam, ptg. to 1 mi. S. of Riverbank to Warrensburg, 14 mi.,
1 powerful S. turn, slack current. Ptg.—2 dams at Warrensburg.
Lower Warrensburg dam to Hudson River, 1 mi., nice trip.

Seely Creek: Chemung Co. Wells to Chemung River, 10 mi. Dif.
II–IV. Attractive, small stream, exciting turns, fallen branches,
good current, rifts.

Shawangunk Kill: Orange, Ulster cos. Burlingham to Wallkill
River, 22 mi. Dif. II–IV. Burlingham to Pine Brush, 7 mi., may
be too shallow, dams at Burlingham, 3 mi., below and at Pine
Brush. Pine Brush to start of eastward bend, 12 mi., pleasant,
mostly easy, fast, some rifts. E. Bend to Wallkill River, 3 mi.,
skilled only, fast white water; dam—1 mi. above Ganahcote.

Susquehanna River: Cooperstown to Chesapeake Bay, 420 mi.
Dif. I–V. Cooperstown to Oneonta, 37 mi., dam 1 mi. down, meanders, fallen trees, snags, pitch at Phoenix Mills. Ptg—Portlandville dam, skill required on fast water below dam. Ptg.—2 concrete dams after Portlandville. Oneonta to Windsor, 55 mi., slack
to fast current; at Unadilla the right channel leads to dam—go
left, mostly flat water, rough pitch near brdg. at Center Vil. Windsor to Susquehanna, 12 mi., narrow. Susquehanna to Binghamton,

25 mi. Ptg.—dam 1 mi. after Susquehanna, 1 rough turn 1½ mi. above Great Bend Brdg., mostly flat water. Binghamton to Owego, 25 mi., river widens. Owego to Sayre, Pa., mostly smooth, few mild rifts; Sayre to Chesapeake Bay, 247 mi.

Ten Mile River: Dutchess Co. Wassaic to Housatonic River, 18 mi. Dif. II–V. Wassaic to Dover Plains, 6½ mi., some rocky runs, then fast, smooth current. Ptg.—Dover Plains Dam; Dover Plains to Housatonic River, 11½ mi., skilled only, some rough runs, rough rapids.

Tioga River: Steuben Co. Rte. 15 brdg. over Cowanesque River, to Cohocton River, 16 mi. Dif. II–III. Pleasant, fast, mild white water.

Tioughnioga River: Cortland, Broome cos. Jctn. of E. and W. Branch to Chenango Forks, 36 mi. Dif. II–IV. No dams, fast current, OK for novices.

Tonawanda Creek: Genesee, Niagara cos. Attica to Niagara River, 88 mi. Dif. II–IV. Attica to Alexander, 5 mi., fine run, rifts, gravel shoals, unobstructed. Alexander to Batavia, 12 mi., poor run, many carries. Batavia to Airville, 15 mi., fast current. Ptg.—E. Pembroke and N. Pembroke dams, some rough rapids, many rifts. Ptg.—Indian Falls and rapids. Rte. 267 brdg. to Rte. 93 brdg., 13 mi., wild entry, rough corkscrew turn, weir 2 mi. down, debris, narrow spot. Rte. 93 brdg. to Barge Canal, 29 mi., high banks, forested, carry—1-ft. dam below Middleport; jctn. of river and Barge Canal to Niagara River, 14 mi.

Unadilla River: Madison, Otsego, Chenango cos. W. Edmeston to Susquehanna River, 51 mi. Dif. II–IV. Partly fast, fairly easy run, some barbed wire, destroyed dams with fast water, trash in stream, easy rifts. Start to S. Edmeston, 10 mi. S. Edmeston to New Berlin, 7 mi. New Berlin to S. New Berlin, 12 mi. S. New Berlin to Mt. Upton, 11 mi. Mt. Upton to Susquehanna River, 11 mi. For several mi. above Unadilla Forks from pt. on Hwy. 413, still water; good trout and pickerel fishing.

Upper Mohawk: 5 mi.; Delta Dam to Rome; start Westerville, Hwy. 46; good current. Good fishing in Delta Lake—bass, walleye.

Wallkill River: Orange, Ulster cos. Brdg. above Papakating Creek to Rondout Creek, 79 mi. Dif. I–V. Ptg.—2 dams and gorge, mostly slow, some rifts, white water near end. Start to Liberty Corners, 9 mi. Liberty Corners to N. Hampton, 23 mi. N. Hampton to Montgomery, 12 mi. Montgomery to Shawangunk Kill, 14 mi. Shawangunk Kill to New Paltz, 8 mi. New Paltz to Rondout Creek, 13 mi.

Wappinger Creek: Dutchess Co. Salt Pt. to New Hamburg, 23 mi., run in high water, Dif. I–V, fast, fallen trees, some rough rapids. Ptg.—3 dams. Start to Pleasant Valley, 5 mi. Pleasant Valley to Rockdale, 3 mi. Rockdale to Man brdg., 4 mi. Man brdg. to Wappinger Falls, 9 mi. Wappinger Falls to New Hamburg, 2 mi.

W. Canada Creek: Oneida, Herkimer cos. Trenton Falls to Mohawk River, 32½ mi. Dif. II–V. Skilled only. Start to Poland, 8½ mi. DANGER—sudden release from dam, wild spots, fast. Ptg.—2 mi. Poland to Newport, 4 mi., rough rapids. Newport to Middleville, 8 mi. Ptg.—Newport Dam, unsafe rapids below, heavy rapids after put-in. Middlefield to Mohawk River, 12 mi., long, fast rapids. DANGER—boulders, white water, gravel bars; trout.

Wharton Creek: Otsego Co. Edmeston to Unadilla River, 14 mi. Dif. II–III. Pleasant, shallow spots, barbed wire, fallen trees, mixed smooth and easy rifts. Ptg.—dam 2 mi. from end.

Willomemoc River: Sullivan Co. Below Livingston Manor to jctn.

with Beaver Kill at Roscoe, very attractive, intermed. white-water stream.

Wood Creek: Oneida Co. Last brdg. on Canada Creek to Barge Canal, 10 mi. Dif. II–III. Sandy bottom, high banks, a few light rifts, brush piles, low brdg., barbed wire, shallow in spots.

(Credit for majority of information about N.Y. trails— Lawrence I. Grinnell)

NORTH CAROLINA

Brice Creek: Craven Co. Croation Natl. For. Brdg. access on dirt rd. S. of Less Brdg. to Brice's Creek boat ramp, 5 mi. Good fishing.

Dismal Swamp Traverse: See description under Virginia.

French Broad: USGS Rosman, Brevard, Pisgah For., Horse Shoe, Skyland, Ashville, Weaverville, Leicester, Marshall, Spring Creek, Hot Springs, Paint Rock, Neddy Mt., New Port. From Rosman on Rte. 64 to Rte. 411, 126 mi. Dif. I–IV.
> *Trip 1*—Rosman to Ashville, 55 mi. Dif. I–II, no partic. dangers.
> *Trip 2*—Ashville to below Hot Springs, 40 mi. Dif. IV–VI. DANGER—3 dams, a bad rapid, Class VI, whirlpool, dif. trip.
> *Trip 3*—Below Hot Springs to Rte. 411 near New Port, 31 mi. Dif. I–II. No partic. dangers, flat, quiet. (See description under . Tennessee.) (Credit—*Canoeing White Water River Guide*)

Green River: USGS Cliffield, Saluda. From S. of Hendersonville near Saluda to brdg. at head of Lake Adger, 12 mi. Dif. II–III, small river, no partic. dangers, scout Corky Rapid. (Credit— *Canoeing White Water River Guide*)

Laurel Creek: White water, experts only, high waters.

Little Tennessee: USGS Franklin, Alarka, Wesser, Judson. From Iotla, 4 mi. N. of Franklin to Lake Fontanna below U.S. Rte. 19 brdg., 23 mi. Dif. II–IV. No partic. dangers; when Lake Fontanna is low watch out for the bad rapid 2 mi. above Rte. 19 brdg.; run all summer. (Credit—*Canoeing White Water River Guide*)

Nantahala River: USGS Hewett, Wesser. From below power plant above Nantahala to Nantahala Falls, 8 mi. Dif. IV–V. DANGER —Nantahala Falls, don't run, small, fast, cold; run when power plant is operating. (Credit—*Canoeing White Water River Guide*)

Oconaluftee River: USGS Great Smoky Mountain Natl. For. Park. From Smokemont through Cherokee to Bryson City, 25 mi. Dif. III–IV.
> *Trip 1*—from Smokemont to Cherokee, 9 mi. Dif. IV. Very small river, many twists and turns, tight places, not for beginners.
> *Trip 2*—Cherokee to Bryson City, 16 mi. Dif. III. DANGER —30-ft. dam about 7 mi. above Bryson City. (Credit— *Canoeing White Water River Guide*)

Pigeon River: USGS Clyde and Hepco. From Clyde on Rtes. 19–23 to Waterville Lake, 15 mi. Dif. II–IV. DANGER—rapids at old wood dam about ½ mi. above Waterville Lake. Slow-flowing river, polluted. (Credit—*Canoeing White Water River Guide*)

Raven Fork River: USGS Great Smoky Mt. Natl. For. Park. From 7 mi. above Pioneer Structures to Cherokee, 8 mi., Dif. III–V. Very fast, run in spring or after rain, white water. (Credit —*Canoeing White Water River Guide*)

Toxaway River: USGS N.C.–S.C., Reid, S.C.–Salem. From the Narrows of the Toxaway to Rte. 11 Hwy. brdg., 9 mi. Dif. II–IV. Many rapids, fast river, over boulders, wilderness, clear water, run all summer, scout rapids before running. (Credit—*Canoeing White Water River Guide*)

Tuckaseigee River: USGS Glenville, Big Ridge, Cullowhee, Greens Creek, Whittier, Bryson. From Glenville Power Plant to Bryson City, 42 mi. Dif. I–IV.

   Trip 1—Glenville Power Plant to Cullowhee, 12 mi. Dif. I–III. DANGER—12-ft. dam above Cullowhee brdg.; pt. right.

   Trip 2—Cullowhee to Dillsboro, 10 mi. Dif. I–II. DANGER —12-ft. dam above Dillsboro.

   Trip 3—Dillsboro to Bryson City, 20 mi. Dif. III–IV. DANGER—heavy rapids, partic. in gorge 1 mi. below Sylva; polluted below Dillsboro. (Credit—*Canoeing White Water River Guide*)

White Oak River: Onslow Co. Croation Natl. For. Haywood Lndg. to Swansboro, 12 mi. Good fishing.

NORTH DAKOTA

Little Missouri Public-use Area: New canoe trail, Little Missouri Bay to Lost Brdg., no ptgs., canoe on Garrison Reservoir, 22 mi. From Hwy. 22, Lost Brdg. W. through Theodore Roosevelt Park, N. and S. unit, canoeable high water only.

Little Missouri River: USGS Theodore Roosevelt Natl. Mem. Park —Watford City NL 13-3, Dickinson NL 13-6. Bowman, Slope, Billings, McKenzie, and Dunn cos. Federal land maps N. and S. of McKenzie-Billings county line—available from U.S. For. Ser.

   Trip 1—Between N. and S. units of Theodore Roosevelt Natl. Mem. Park, 120 mi.

   Trip 2—Continue on from Long Brdg. on Rte. 85 to Lost Brdg. on Rte. 22, 2 days. Information regarding both trips— ice generally breaks up by early April; May and June normally best months, contact park headquarters in Medora for information on river condition, low water in much of yr.

means many ptgs., much wading, remote country, no guide service available, plan for extremes in temp., no sources of drinking water, many good campsites in cottonwood groves, private land on much of trip, need camp permit for nondesignated sites on public land. Fish—catfish, goldeyes, and sauger.
(Credit—*Little Missouri River Float Trips*—U.S. For. Ser.)

Missouri River: Canoeable according to N.D. Park Ser. Trips—Riverdale to Bismarck most popular canoe rte. in N.D. Bismarck to Oahe Dam, experts only. Mo. River N. of Garrison Dam, dangerous, poor canoeing, big water.

Red River: Entire length or eastern border canoeable according to N.D. Park Ser. Best part Grand Forks to Winnipeg.

Snake Creek: Near Riverdale to Devils Lake Diversion Project; future canoe trail except for tunnels.

Wakpoa Game Management Area: 2 marked canoe trails; semiwilderness area, Turtle Mts., N. Cent. N.D.
Trip 1—Put in along Laird Lake Hwy.; follow trail 1½ mi. to Hooker Lake, ¼ mi. ptg. here.
Trip 2—Start at public boat ramps on Lake Upsilon, canoe through Upper Walker Lake and into Lower Walker Lake, short ptg. to channel into Lake Laird, through Rames Lake and Isle Lake, short ptg. into Hooker Lake, 4 mi., marked with signs. Fish—Lake Upsilon, pike; Gravel Lake, trout.

OHIO

Cuyahoga River: 56 mi. Burton to Granger Rd., Cuyahoga Co. Experienced canoeists start St. Rte. 168 S. of Burton; inexperienced start below rapids near Hiram. Access—hwys. 4–6 mi.

apart, 6 ptgs.—rapids near Hiram, Lake Rockwell (closed to boating), Munroe Falls, Cuyahoga Falls, Peninsula Dam, Brecksville Dam. Good bass fishing S. of Mantua.

Great Miami River: 140 mi. Few mi. below Indian Falls to Corps of Engineers, 3½ mi. from the Ohio. No dangerous water, some wading in summer. Access—every few mi. Ptg.—dams at Quincy, Sidney (2), Troy, Piqua, Steele Dam N. of Dayton, Chautauqua Dam, Hydraulic Dam below Franklin, Middletown Dam S.W. edge of Franklin, hydraulic dam 4 mi. N.E. of Hamilton, 1 N. edge of Hamilton. Small-mouth bass fishing good in upper river.

Little Miami River: 95 mi. Clifton to Cincinnati; dangerous rapids and falls in gorge S. of Clifton; 4 dams—1 near Waynesville, 3 dams between Fort Ancient and Hamilton Co. line; other short ptgs.

Maumee River: Oakwood to Maumee, 81 mi. Start—Defiance Power Dam head on Auglaize River. Ptgs.—Defiance Power Dam, 1–2 mi., Independence Dam, Grand Rapids Dam and rapids below, 4 mi. from Missionary Hill to Maumee, rapids on river. Canal bypasses Independence Dam and Grand Rapids Dam.

Mohican, Walhonding, Muskingum rivers: 162.9 mi. Mohican St. For. near Loudinville to Marietta; very scenic; good fishing; safe canoeing for amateur; some fast water. Dams—10 on Muskingum River, at Devola, Lowell, Beverly, Lake Chute, Stockport, McConnelsville, Rakeby Lock, Philo, Zanesville, Ellis; 2 on Walhonding, at Six Mile and Mohawk; 1 on Mohican, at Brinkhaven.

Portage Lakes System: Summit Co. Chain of lakes; short ptgs. part of old Ohio-Erie Canal system. Trip—Start at Portage Lakes, use part of the canal and the Cuyahoga River, arrive at Lake Erie.

Sandusky River: 65 mi. Upper portion of river not good for canoeing, lower 65 mi. good, good squirrel and waterfowl hunting.

Dams—1 above Upper Sandusky, 2 above Tiffin and 2 below, 1 below Fremont. Access pts.—several hwy. crossings; good small-mouth bass, rock bass, channel cat, bullhead, crappie, white bass.

(Credit—most information from *Ohio Canoe Adventures*)

OKLAHOMA

Barren Fork: Cherokee Co. Crystal-clear, quick-moving water, some ptgs. in low water, flow subject to rapid change.

Blue River: Blue, Okla., to sec. rd. brdg. S. of Bokchito, 7 mi., 6 hrs. Put-in—antique iron truss brdg. S. of Blue on gravel section rd.; river width, 15 ft.–25 ft., current ½ m.p.h., mudbanks, many stumps, snags, and logjams, heavily wooded banks, many wild birds, many snakes (water moccasin—take care around logjams), several difficult ptgs. around logjams—take rope, many campsites, very little civilization, no rapids. (Credit—Hans Weichsel)

Cimarron River: Canoeable, can be tricky, watch for whirlpools and eddies.

Flint Creek: Cherokee Co. Crystal-clear, quick-moving water, some ptgs. in low water, flow subject to rapid change.

Glover River: McCurtain Co. RR brdg., no ptgs., some rapids.
  Trip 1—Upper Forks of Glover to Arkansas Crossing, 2.2 mi., 5–6 hrs. DANGER—small falls, large rocks, best time mid-April to June 1 and mid-Sept. through Oct.
  Trip 2—Glover Boy Scout Camp to Meat Hollow, 4.3 mi., 8–9 hrs., best time same as Trip 1. DANGER—small falls, good fishing, large rocks in river.
  Trip 3—Low-water brdg. at Glover to RR brdg., 5.2 mi., 10 hrs., good fishing, lots of logjams, best time same as Trips 1

and 2, can make trip in lower water; other float trips rough—not often floated. DANGER—snakes; John Dunagan can tell you about them, as he was bit on Glover. (Credit—John Dunagan and Jim Jones)

Illinois River: Adair, Cherokee cos. St. Hwy. 59 brdg. N. of Watts to Carters Lndg.—start of Tenkiller Res., 71.6 mi., easy flowing, scenic, several stretches mild rapids, camping areas. Excel. fishing—small-mouth and large-mouth bass, cats, white bass, walleye, sunfish.

Kiamichi River: Excellent float trip; no other information.

Little River: McCurtain Co. Bogalge Crossing (1.2 mi. float on Mt. Fork) to Ashillintubble Crossing, 6.6. mi., 10 hrs., no ptgs., no partic. danger, some narrow rapids with logjams on Mt. Fork sec. Best time—June–Oct. Fair to good fishing, some rapids. (Credit—Jim Jones)

Mountain Fork River: McCurtain Co. 34.7 mi. total, Beachtone to Bogalge Crossing, no ptgs.
> *Trip 1*—Beachtone to Smithville, 11.2 mi., 18 hrs., rapids, small falls, large rocks.
> *Trip 2*—Smithville to Eagle Fork, 4.2 mi., 8 hrs., large rocks, small falls, rapids.
> *Trip 3*—Eagle Fork to Narrows, 4.6 mi., 10 hrs., large rocks, small falls, rapids.
> *Trip 4*—Re-Reg Dam to Jones Lndg., 7.3 mi., 11 hrs., large rocks, small falls, rapids.
> *Trip 5*—Hwy. 70 brdg. to Bogalge Crossing, 7.4 mi., 11 hrs., rapids. Good fishing on all trips. Trips 1–3, small-mouth bass; Trips 4–5, large-mouth bass. Best time—mid-April to mid-June, Trips 1–3; mid-April through Oct., Trips 4–5. (Credit—Jim Jones)

Spring River: See description under Kansas.

OREGON

Clackamas River: Upper sec., from backwaters of Cazadero Dam to Three Lynx Powerhouse, experts only. Lower sec. from McIver Park to Willamette River, 20 mi., 4 hrs., OK intermed. canoeists, best with 1,500–5,000 cfs. on Clackamas gauge; some blind channels and overhanging limbs in low water. Best time May 15–July 15, many minor rapids, no major rapids, several access pts.

Deschutes River—Lower Part: Sherman, Wasco cos. From Hwy. 216 brdg. to U.S. Hwy. 80 N. brdg. (Columbia River), 40–45 mi., 2 days; no open canoes, no beginners. Put-in—¼ mi. downstream of Hwy. 216 brdg. Rapids each ½ mi., 3–10 m.p.h. current between rapids, approx. 10 Dif. II–III rapids, Dif. IV rapids midway and toward N. end. Ptg.—Dif. VI rapid 1¼ mi. S. of Columbia River. LIVES HAVE BEEN LOST HERE, last rapid ½ mi. S. of Columbia River, Dif. III on left side of isle, slow water with logs and brush on right side; no pollution, good camping, rock/sand bottom, seasonal water—high in spring, low late summer and fall. In canyon most of trip, river 60 ft.–200 ft. wide. Good fishing. (Credit—Paul Riffice)

Deschutes River—Upper Part: From public boat ramp where Hwy. 26 crosses river near Warm Springs to Sherara Falls, 53 mi., 2 days, experts only, very dif. for open canoes, best with 3,000–5,000 cfs. at Pelton Dam gauge, 14 major rapids. Alt. put-ins—cmpgrnd. near Trout Creek, mouth of Warm Springs River and S. jctn. on E. side. DANGER—Sherara Falls—don't run; take out on left above falls.

Grande Ronde River: From Minam Cmpgrnd. to Troy, 45 mi., 1 day, OK intermed. canoeist, 4 major rapids—can line or ptg., best time June 15–July 15, good camping. CAUTION—rattlesnakes. (Credit—*Oregon River Tours*)

John Day River: From Service Creek to Clarno, 48 mi., 1 day, OK intermed. canoeist, Apr. and May best months, good campsites. CAUTION—poison oak, remote ctry., 3 major rapids—can run all. Access pts.—St. Hwy. 19 brdg. at put-in, Twickenham Brdg., Clarno Brdg.—St. Hwy. 218 at end. (Credit—*Oregon River Tours*)

McKenzie River: From Blue River to Leaburg, 18 mi., experts only, run with 1,500–5,000 cfs. on Vida Gauge, covered boats only, many minor rapids, nine major rapids. CAUTION—LIVES HAVE BEEN LOST ON THIS STRETCH, scout all rapids before running, can line or ptg. rapids. May through mid-Nov. best months. (Credit—*Oregon River Tours*)

N. Santiam River: From Packsaddle Park to Stayton, 26 mi., 4 hrs., experts only, run with 1,500–5,000 cfs., white water, run Mar.–Aug., not for open canoes. DAGER PTS.—Spencer's Hole and rapids under Mill City Brdg.—scout before running.
   Trip 1—Packsaddle Park to Mill City Brdg., 8 mi., Spencer's Hole on this stretch. Take-out—right before Mill City Brdg.
   Trip 2—Mill City Brdg. to Stayton Brdg., 18 mi., 2 major rapids, last one is 6-ft. dam—dangerous high water. Above backwaters of Detroit Dam too difficult for open canoe. Sec. below Big Cliff Dam—don't run—very dangerous.
   (Credit—*Oregon River Tours*)

Owyhee River:
   Trip 1—from Duck Valley to Three Forks, has been run, experts only, no other data.
   Trip 2—from Three Forks to Rome, 32 mi., experts only, at least 6 major rapids, ptg. or line these, runnable only short time of yr.
   Trip 3—from Rome to Lake Owyhee, 52 mi., remote ctry., experts only, run with 1,000–4,000 cfs. on Rome gauge, better to run at high stage than at low stage, run in May, some-

times OK in June. Put-in—old Steel Truss Brdg. at Rome, much wildlife, birdlife, Indian petroglyphs, many campsites and springs, flows through beautiful Owyhee Canyon on this stretch. Dif. take-out; take out at reservoir with lake paddling or special permission to take out at Hole in the Ground Ranch.

Rogue River: Curry, Josephine, Jackson cos. Finley Bend to Agness, 55 mi., white water, large rapids, submerged boulders, shallow water. Ptg.—Rainie Falls, experts only, no open canoes. Applegate River to Robertson Brdg., 8 mi., 6.7-ft. drop per mi.; no other information. Robertson Brdg. to Copper Canyon, 62 mi., 11.7-ft. drop per mi.; no other information. Copper Canyon to Lobster Creek, 14 mi., 3.1-ft. drop per mi. Steelhead, salmon, cutthroat, rainbow, eastern brook, German brown; Lower Rogue suitable for novice.

Sandy River: From Dodge Park to Dabney Park, 13 mi., experts only, can extend trip to Lewis and Clark Park near U.S. Hwy. 80N., dif. rapids for 3 mi. below Dodge Park, Scout-Pipeline Rapids—most dif. area, at high water—no open canoes, run Mar.–June; above Sandy River Diversion Dam, has been run in kayaks, experts only, very dangerous. DANGER—dam has no warning; dif. ptg. at dam.

Snake River: From Hells Canyon Dam to Grande Ronde River, 78 mi., experts only, run with 9,600 to 12,000 cfs. at Hells Canyon Dam, deepest gorge in North America, many dangerous and major rapids, don't run in open craft, strong waves, standing haystacks, first 17 mi. worst. DANGER—poison ivy and rattlesnakes.

S. Santiam River: From Foster Dam to Waterloo, 14 mi., 4 hrs., OK novices, farm ctry., some wading, no major rapids, minor rapids, 1,000–3,000 cfs. best. DANGER—falls below Waterloo Co. Rd. Brdg.; take out well before this brdg. (Credit—*Oregon River Tours*)

Umpqua River: From town of Umpqua to Bullock Brdg., 24 mi. Combination of smooth and rapids; some rapids can swamp or destroy a canoe; after put-in 7 minor rapids, then concrete brdg. (Tyee Access Rd. Brdg.), then 2 minor rapids, then gravel bar, then minor rapids, then major and minor rapids. Take right channel around isle before Bullock Brdg., rd. parallels river all the way. Best time Apr.–June, OK for intermed. canoeists, run with 2,000–5,000 cfs. (Credit—*Oregon River Tours*)

Willamette River: Dexter Res. to Columbia, 203.8 mi. Upper river swift, alt. white water and pools, large deltas of many channels, isles, backwaters, gravel bars, few houses, strong current. Near Salem, broad wooded banks, swift; heavy urban and ind. development begins at Oregon City Falls; Corvallis to Portland, motorboats; much wildlife and fishing; Dexter Res. to Springfield Brdg., 18.5 mi., 8 hrs., some overhanging trees, few fast chutes, some rapids, submerged logs, some easy white water. (Credit— Richard I. Bonn)

PENNSYLVANIA

Allegheny River: Warren and Forest cos. W. Pa. above Franklin normally canoeable from Port Allegheny till June 1, from Olean till June 15, from Warren till Aug. 1. Good canoeing from Kinzua Dam to mouth of Tionesta Creek, 41 mi.; a succession of eddies separated by riffles in upper part, minor rapids, many isles, fast water, OK for novice. CAUTION—current deceiving under RR brdg. 2,000 ft. below Kinzua Dam, can pull you into pillar of the brdg.; camping between dam and Warren on isles. Distances— Kinzua Dam to Warren, 6.6 mi.; Warren to Cloverleaf Camps, 17 mi.; Cloverleaf Camps to mouth of Tionesta Camp, 22 mi. (Credit—*Canoeing in Kinzua Country*)

Baab Creek: USGS Morris and Cedar Run. From Morris Brdg. to

Blackwell (short way up Pine Creek), 7 mi., Dif. II, beautiful, road parallels stream, polluted by mine acid, no fish, run till mid-Apr., windfalls, sharp bends, tight going. (Credit—*Select Rivers of Central Pennsylvania*)

Bald Eagle Creek: Clinton and Centre cos. Source to Milesburg, moving water; Milesburg to Blanchard, slack water; rest, moving water.

USGS Port Matilda, Julian, Bear Knob, Bellfonte, Mingoville. From Port Matilda to Mt. Eagle, 25 mi., beautiful, partly wilderness.

> *Trip 1*—From Port Matilda to Julian, 8 mi., Dif. I+, narrow, brushy, windfalls. CAUTION—water level cable 1 mi. below Port Matilda; don't run in high water.
>
> *Trip 2*—Julian to Milesburg, 10 mi., long flat stretch, windfalls. Dif. I.
>
> *Trip 3*—Milesburg to Mt. Eagle, 6 mi., windfalls. CAUTION—multiple arched brdg.—run left in low water, last part slack water.

(Credit—*Select Rivers of Central Pennsylvania*)

Beaver River: Beaver and Lawrence cos. Mahoning River brdg. ½ mi. above jctn. with Shenango to first brdg. Beaver Falls; some easy riffles, wooded mudbanks; 1 hazard—wing dam, stick to wall, avoid power intake currents; few access pts. between Beaver dam; backwater from Connoquenessing Creek to end; motorboats near dam; Newcastle to Wampum, 11 mi. (Credit—*Canoeing Guide to Western Pennsylvania and Northern West Virginia*)

Beech Creek: Clinton and Centre cos. Kato to halfway, good white water; remainder moving water. USGS Snoe Shoe S.E., Howard and Beech Creek. From Kato to Beech Creek, 22 mi., run at 7.5 ft. on gauge in Monument, some mine pollution.

> *Trip 1*—Kato to Orviston, 12 mi., most of trip flat and meandering, some isles, rapids of Dif. II in last third of trip, some windfalls.
>
> *Trip 2*—From Orviston to Beech Creek, 10 mi., pretty, clear

water, rapids Dif. II mixed with deep pools, some windfalls in side channels. (Credit—*Select Rivers of Central Pennsylvania*)

Big Nescopeck Creek: N.W. of Hazleton, rough and exciting most of the way, used as a training stream for new canoeists, has some dangerous spots. (Credit—Max Gardner)

Black Moshannon Creek: Clearfield Co. Dif. white water all the way, danger.

Blacklick Creek: From Wehrum-Heshbon, 2 rapids near Heshbon, otherwise flat, flowing water. From Heshbon to Josephine, run in covered canoes, at 5.3 ft. extremely dif.—experts only, about 5 ft. reading good for rafting. (Credit—*Canoeing Guide to Western Pennsylvania and Northern West Virginia*)

Brandywine River: Chester, Delaware cos. W. Branch, 1 long day, some riffles, pleasant, intermed. canoeists, high water only. Lenape to Rockland, Del., 1 day, novices, some riffles, pleasant. Rockland to Wilmington, 1 day, skilled only, mixed smooth and rapids, 9 dams, can run 2 or 3 at med. to high water, 3–4 rapids.

Brokenstraw Creek: Warren Co. From brdg. at Rte. 426 E. of Corry to Allegheny River, 25 mi. Dif. II–III. Canoe before June 1, has good fast water, sharp turns.

   Trip 1—Put-in to Rte. 27 brdg. at Garland, 12 mi., creek meanders through dense woodland after put-in, some logjams, can be exciting in high water, good trout stream, very scenic. CAUTION: Low-hanging cables across creek between Spring Creek and Garland.

   Trip 2—Rte. 27 brdg. to Allegheny, 12 mi., nice 1-day trip, open terrain, farm ctry. (Credit—*Canoeing in Kinzua Country*)

Buffalo Creek: Armstrong, Butler cos. 1 day, 19½ mi., W. Winfield to Freeport, tricky parts, strong current till May 1, pretty, good white water. Casselman River: Somerset Co. Md. line to Garrett, moving water; Garrett to 1½ mi. from end, good white water; last 1½ mi., moving water.

Buffalo Creek: USGS Mifflinburg, Lewisburg. From side rd. along stream near Mifflinburg to side rd. from airport near Lewisburg, 12 mi. Dif. I. Run till early May or after rain, farming country, locals not friendly to canoeists, some windfalls, some riffles, meandering; can extend trip to Buffalo Cross Rds. Brdg. (third brdg.), very remote, much birdlife, below Buffalo Cross Rds. Brdg., slow, relaxing. CAUTION: low dam almost 2 mi. below Buffalo Cross Rds. Brdg. (Credit—*Select Rivers of Central Pennsylvania*)

Chartiers Creek: Allegheny, Washington cos. 18 mi., upstream half, moving water; downstream half polluted, unattractive.

Chest Creek: USGS Hastings and Westover. From Patton to Westover, 11 mi. Dif. IV. Wilderness, some windfalls, acid pollution from mines. Don't run in open boats in high water. Last few mi. are Dif. I. (Credit—*Select Rivers of Central Pennsylvania*)

Chester Creek: Del. watershed, 1 long day, mixed smooth and rapids high water only.

Clarion River: Clarion, Jefferson cos. Millstone to Cooksbury, 15 mi., good trip, easy riffles, motorboats on Piney Dam Backwater, water flow varies, call 814-226-9610, Clarion, Pa., for flow information, ptg. Piney Dam. Cooksburg to Mill Creek, 11.8 mi., swift current. Callensburg to Parken, 17 mi., right water cond. only (Credit—*Canoeing Guide to Western Pennsylvania and Northern West Virginia*)

Conemaugh River: Westmoreland, Indiana, Cambria cos. S. Fork to Johnston, 10.2 mi. Dif. II. New Florence to Blairsville, 17 mi.; Tunnelton to Saltsburg, 5.5 mi. Start—below dam, under old stone arch brdg.; polluted at Johnston. DANGER—20-ft. drop around sharp bend on S. Fork to Johnston trip, can't be run.

(Credit—*Canoeing Guide to Western Pennsylvania and Northern West Virginia*)

Conestoga Creek: Lancaster Co. 2 days, smooth, pleasant, novice.

Conewango Creek: Warren Co. From Riverside Rd., N.Y., to Allegheny River, 16 mi., usually good canoeing year-round, put-in is 2 mi. S. of Frewsburg, N.Y.

    Trip 1—Put-in to Rte. 62 brdg. at Akelyey, 5.5 mi., swampy bottom land and placid water.

    Trip 2—Rte. 62 brdg. to Allegheny River, 10 mi. CAUTION: old pipe across river below brdg. at Russell. CAUTION—old dam 1 mi. below brdg. near st. hosp. and 4.8 mi. below Russell, dam can be run but not by beginners, shoal below dam. CAUTION—breached dam at N. Warren, ptg. dam just N. of Pa. Ave. Brdg. near beauty school parking lot, then short distance to Allegheny River. (Credit—*Canoeing in Kinzua Country*)

Connoquenessing Creek: Butler, Beaver cos. Zelienople to Frisco, 15.5 mi., easy riffles, quiet, pretty, canoe till June 15. Several ptgs. —dams, not dangerous. Below Frisco, dangerous, experts only, large rocks, ledges, rapids, steep drops, no access pts. between Wurtemburg and Beaver River. Access Rte. 488 brdg., Wurtemburg. Frisco to Wurtemburg, 2 mi.; Wurtemburg to Beaver River, 5.5 mi. (Credit—*Canoeing Guide to Western Pennsylvania and Northern West Virginia*)

Delaware River: From Hancock, N.Y., to Trenton, N.J., 129 mi.

    Trip 1—Hancock to Callicoon Brdg., 31 mi., excel. scenery, put in at private access at St. Rte. 97 Brdg. on Pa. side of W. Branch Delaware River, river winds between high slopes, several short rapids, and long stretches of still water.

    Trip 2—Callicoon Brdg. to Lackawaxen River jctn., 28 mi. Dif. I–III. Excel. scenery. Put-in—brdg. at Callicoon, N.Y. DANGER—8½ mi. below Callicoon Brdg. at Skinners Falls Brdg., heavy rapids at Skinners Falls—don't run in high water; Skinners Falls may be run by experienced canoeists with closed decks or kayaks in normal water.

Trip 3—Bushkill Creek jctn. to Belvidere, N.J., via Delaware water gap, 30 mi. Dif. I–II. Excel. scenery, put in at Bushkill Creek jctn., first 3½ mi. deep canyon, then many isles appear. After Brodhead Creek jctn. is Delaware water gap; this part is deep with river flowing among bldrs., easy rapids after gap. DANGER—1½ mi. below Belvidere Brdg.—Foul Rift Rapids—don't run. This is for experts in covered craft only; all others leave river at Belvidere Rte. 79 brdg.

Trip 4—Riegelsville Brdg. 4 mi. below Milford, N.J. Take left channel around isles. DANGER—below isles is brdg. at Pt. Pleasant, then Lumberville dams—these are 2 low walls that form V-shaped dam; ptg. dams on Pa. side, put in below next brdg.; from here to New Hope many isles; take left channel around isles.

Trip 5—New Hope to Trenton, 12 mi., good scenery, put in below Union Paper Mill Dam, this is almost 1 mi. below New Hope; first brdg. below New Hope is called Washington Crossing Brdg., put ashore 1 mi. below brdg. DANGER—Scudder's Falls—for experts in closed craft only, then below Scudder's Falls river becomes tidewater; not good canoeing below.

(Credit—*Canoe Country Pennsylvania Style* and Delaware River Basin Comm.)

Elk Creek: USGS Millheim. From top of gap above Millheim to Coburn, 4.6 mi. Dif. II+. Some windfalls, ptg. dam under Rte. 45 in Millheim; below Millheim Dif. II. (Credit—*Select Rivers of Central Pennsylvania*)

Fishing Creek: USGS Millheim, Madisonburg, Beech Creek. From second brdg. up from Lamar on rd. to Tylersville, to Lamar Brdg. at fish hatchery S. of Rte. 64, 5 mi. Dif. II+. Beautiful stream, much affected by rainfall, high waves in high water, wading in low water, windfalls, many clogged channels. CAUTION—small dam for fish hatchery below rd. brdg. after green footbrdg., then CAUTION—diagonal ledge—run left. (Credit—*Select Rivers of Central Pennsylvania*)

Fishing and Catwissa creeks: Schuylkill, Columbia cos. 1 day wholly smooth; novices.

French Creek: Venango, Crawford cos. Utica to Franklin, 9.5 mi., excel. canoeing, wooded, mudbanks, some obstacles, easy riffles. Cochranton to Utica, 8.2 mi. (Credit—*Canoeing Guide to Western Pennsylvania and Northern West Virginia*)

French Creek: Bucks, Montgomery cos. Perkiomen-Unami brdg. to Schwenksville, 5 days, mixed smooth and rapids, high water only, skilled. Schwenksville to Schuylkill N.E. brdg., 1 mi., not recommended, many carries, high water only.

Gifford Run: See Mosquito Creek in Pennsylvania.

Honey Creek: See description of Kishacoquillas Creek in Pennsylvania.

Juniata River: Huntingdon, Mifflin cos. Little Juniata River, 1 day, mixed smooth and rapids, skilled. Frankstown branch, 1½ days, some riffles, very attractive, intermed. canoeists. Raystown branch, 2½ days, smooth, novice. Main stream, Alexandria to Susquehanna, 5 days, smooth, very attractive, novice.

Juniata River—Raystown Branch: Bedford, Huntingdon cos. Run before mid-June; Everett to Saxton, no information, has been run; Saxton Dam to Entriken Brdg, 11 mi., no information Entriken Brdg. to Fink Brdg., 13 mi., good trip, good fishing, deer, clear water. Fink Brdg. to Hawn Brdg., Raystown Dam upstream from Hawn Brdg., backwater to Fink Brdg.; 2-day trip—Saxton Dam to Fink Brdg.; new dam will ruin trip. (Credit—*Canoeing Guide to Western Pennsylvania and Northern West Virginia*)

Kettle Creek: Potter, Clinton cos. 1 day; smooth, intermed. canoeists, ptg.—Alvin C. Bush Dam.

Kishacoquillas Creek: USGS Burnham. From Reedsville Brdg. on Honey Creek to old Rte. 322 Brdg. in Lewistown, 7 mi. Dif. II+. Trash polluted, run in spring or after heavy rain, best rapids in first part of trip, best rapids begin below second brdg. of New Rte. 322. CAUTION—broken dam below old Rte. 322 Brdg.—run right. Ptg.—low-water brdg. ¼ mi. below first dam. Ptg.—dam in Burnham. (Credit—*Select Rivers of Central Pennsylvania*)

Kishiminetas River: Armstrong Co. 1 day; Conemaugh River below Old Central Dam to Salina, pretty, easy riffles. Salina to Apollo, poor trip, easy riffles, industry along banks. Saltsburg to Salina, 6.7 mi. (Credit—*Canoeing Guide to Western Pennsylvania and Northern West Virginia*)

Lackawaxen River: From Prompton to Delaware River, 32 mi., excel. white-water stream, run until late Apr. or mid-May.

    Trip 1—Prompton to Hawley, 15 mi. Dif. I–II. Scenery good, put in U.S. 6 and 106 brdg. CAUTION—scout before running, there are two dams on this sec.; can't spot dams from river. Take out—St. Rte. 590 brdg., at Hawley.

    Trip 2—Hawley to Delaware River, 17 mi. Dif. I–III. Good scenery, scout rapids before running. DANGER—powerhouse just above Kimble Brdg.; when gates are open there is a high standing wave, steepest rapids in lower part of this trip—run in high water only. Take-out—right shore directly beyond Delaware River jctn.

(Credit—*Canoe Country Pennsylvania Style*)

Laurel Hill Creek: Somerset Co. From brdg. on rd. between New Centerville and Trent to Ursina, 17 mi. Dif. III. Clean, wilderness —white water, OK intermed.

    Trip 1—New Centerville Rd. Brdg. to Rte. 653, 6 mi., stream needs lots of water to run, first mi. flat, then dangerous ledge (really a waterfall), then another ledge.

    Trip 2—Whipkey's Dam to Ursina, 11 mi. Dif. III. Fast running at first. CAUTION—dif. ledges halfway, then long wooded isles, then flat water. Put-in—below brdg. just down from Whipkey's Dam. Take-out—second covered brdg. 1 mi. above Ursina.

(Credit—*Canoeing Guide to Western Pennsylvania and Northern West Virginia* and *Select Rivers of Central Pennsylvania*)

Lehigh River: Carbon, Luzerne, Northampton, Lehigh cos. From Francis E. Walter Res. to Northampton, 61 mi., experts only, kayaks or closed canoes only, many obstructions in water, run in late Apr. or early May, water conditions change fast due to dam.

Trip 1—From Francis E. Walter Res. to Rockport, 20 mi. Dif. I–IV. Experts only, excel. scenery. Put-in—St. Rte. 113 Brdg. W. of Stoddartsville. CAUTION—put in below Stoddartsville Falls—these are just below old abandoned brdg. Ptg.—dam 6½ mi. below St. Rte. 115 brdg., below dam are rapids with bldrs. and jagged ledges; 6 mi. below Bear Creek Dam are remnants of old dam at White Haven; below this are rocky shelves—run in high water only. White Haven Brdg. is next, then steep and complex rapids on to Lehigh Tannery, where high brdg. crosses river; below this brdg. take left channel, complex rapids at this pt.; vil. of Rockport is 7 mi. below Lehigh Tannery Brdg.

Trip 2—From Rockport to Jim Thorpe, 16 mi. Dif. II–III. Good scenery, below Rockport rapids are more dif., river is steeper, very dif. when water is not high. S. of Penn Haven jctn. is RR brdg. and then footbrdg., then just below is wild sec.—"Glen Onoko," rapids drop over staircase and eroded ledges for more than 1 mi., below this rapid and past two RR brdgs. is Glen Onoko ravine, then another steep rapid, then river leaves canyon, then another RR brdg., then town of Jim Thorpe, then remnants of old dam. Take-out—on left under Rte. 903 brdg.

Trip 3—From Jim Thorpe to Northampton, 25 mi. Dif. I–III. Good scenery, put in below St. Rte. 903 Brdg. in Jim Thorpe, river immediately enters deep canyon with easy rapids. CAUTION—bend at first RR brdg.—a concrete retaining wall here. Near Weissport is second RR brdg. and steep rapid. CAUTION—low dams at Treichler's and

Laury's stations—short ptgs. Take-out—St. Rte. 329 brdg. (Credit—*Canoe Country Pennsylvania Style*)

Licking Creek: Westmoreland Co. Start below small dam along Rte. 30. End dam backwater, cold water, swift current, riffles, not attractive, high water only. Ligonier to Kingston Dam, 6.9 mi. Dif. II, III. (Credit—*Canoeing Guide to Western Pennsylvania and Northern West Virginia*)

Little Juniata: USGS Spruce Creek, Alexandria. From Tyrone up from Rte. 350 Brdg. to Barree Brdg., 14 mi., polluted, run with high flow.

> *Trip 1*—Tyrone to Spruce Creek, 8 mi. Dif. I+. Several rapids when river is high. CAUTION—rapids near end. CAUTION—concrete pipe first part of trip. DANGER— don't take side channels along isles. DANGER—4-ft. waterfall in side channel along isle above Union Furnace.
> *Trip 2*—Much like Trip 1, good rapids throughout. CAUTION—first rapids below Barree.

(Credit—*Select Rivers of Central Pennsylvania*)

Little Pine River: USGS English Center, Waterville. From English Center to Waterville, 12 mi., clean, beautiful, relaxing. Dif. I–III. From low dam down—easy riffles, sharp bends, and some windfalls. Ptg.—Little Pine Dam—keep away from Spillway, 3 rapids of Dif. III below dam. Take-out—on Pine Creek ½ mi. below Little Pine in Waterville, run until late Apr., 2½ ft. min. level at dam, 3 ft. min. at English Center. (Credit—*Select Rivers of Central Pennsylvania*)

Loyalsock Creek: Lycoming and Sullivan cos. From Lopez to Montoursville, 55 mi.

> *Trip 1*—Lopez to Forksville, 19 mi. Dif. II–III. Excel. scenery. Put in at St. Rte. 487 brdg. in Lopez. First part of run above U.S. Rte. 220 possible only in high water; U.S. 220 is more common put-in; 2 mi. below U.S. 220 are "The Haystacks," Dif. IV–VI. Ptg. on right; then 2 mi. to access pt., then from here to World's End St. Park, 6 mi. of Dif. III–IV, worst rapid is in S. bend 1 mi. below Sportsman's Park— approach with caution, scout from right shore, especially lower half of this rapid. CAUTION—low brdg. in upper end

of park. CAUTION—low dam just below St. Rte. 154 brdg. in the park. Take-out—St. Rte. 87 brdg., read river gauge on right bank at Loyalsockville (4 ft. is low; 4.5 ft.–5 ft. med.; above 5.5 ft. is high).

Trip 2—Forksville to Montoursville, 36 mi. Dif. I–II. Excel. scenery; first 9½ mi. to Rte. 87 brdg. is white water, can have high waves. CAUTION—low dam 3 mi. below Forksville, then below dam are channels between isles—can be tricky. Below Hillsgrove rapids become spaced out, less dif., many access pts. in downstream sec., lower sec. not as steep. (Credit—*Canoe Country Pennsylvania Style*)

Lycoming Creek: Lycoming Co. 2 days, some riffles, intermed.

Mahoning Creek: Jefferson, Indiana, Armstrong cos. Brdg. N. of Valier to brdg. jctn. with Little Mahoning, 1 day, pretty, easy riffles, till June 15. Putneyville to Mahoning Furnace, swift, quick drop at first, no rapids, till June 15. Valier to Lake Mahoning Creek, 12 mi. Mahoning Dam to Rte. 66, 11.5 mi. (Credit—*Canoeing Guide to Western Pennsylvania and Northern West Virginia*)

Mahoning River: Lawrence Co. Flat water, too dirty and warm, not good canoeing. (Credit—*Canoeing Guide to Western Pennsylvania and Northern West Virginia*)

Maiden Creek: 1 long day, some riffles, fair scenery, novice.

Meeker Run: See Mosquito Creek in Pennsylvania.

Monongahela River: 132 mi., Allegheny, Washington, Beaver, Greene, Fayette cos. Poor canoeing, locks, dams, heavy barge traffic, industry. Stretch near Ten Mile Creek, OK. Navigable from mouth at Pittsburgh to Fairmount, W. Va., but not good.

Moshannon Creek: Centre, Clearfield cos. Wilderness Stream, acid-iron pollution from abandoned coal mines. From Winburne to Karthaus, 25 mi.

Trip 1—Winburne to Peale, 10 mi. Dif. I–II. Good scenery. Put-in—small rd. brdg. at Winburne. Take-out—Peale Brdg. on small dirt rd. between Grassflat and Moshannon. Sec. starts easy, with better rapids in last half.

Trip 2—Peale to Karthaus, 15 mi. Dif. II. Good scenery. Put-in—Peale Brdg. Take-out—W. Branch at Rte. 879 brdg. at Karthaus. First 3 mi. relatively easy, remainder of trip nearly continuous Dif. II, no still water till mouth of Moshannon at Miller's Landing, then 3 mi. of easy paddling on W. Branch to Karthaus.

(Credit—*Canoe Country Pennsylvania Style*)

Mosquito Creek: Devil's Elbow, Pottersdale, and Karthaus. From Gifford Run on Lost Run Rd. off Rte. 879 to Karthaus Brdg. along RR brdg., 11 mi. Dif. II–III. Beautiful, wilderness-like in upper part, below jctn. with Gifford Run and Mosquito Creek are good rapids, windfalls, stream must be high to run. Can put in at Meeker Run 4 mi. up on Mosquito from Gifford Run; narrow, many isles, many windfalls. (Credit—*Select Rivers of Central Pennsylvania*)

Muddy Creek: York Co. From put-in immediately S. of steel girder brdg. on Rte. 74 (S. bank) 4 mi. S. of Rte. 327 to dirt rd. at Susquehanna River, 4.5 mi., 3 hrs. Dif. II–IV. DANGER— impassable gorge 1.5 mi. from put-in, ptg. right side, large bldrs. there, the bottom is rock and gravel, then mud near end of trip, little pollution, water level good in winter but very high in spring. Access pts.—upper-stretch brdg. on rural road crosses; no access pts. downstream, also two vertical cliffs; scenery outstanding—fors. and gorge. DANGER—Dif. IV rapids are 1.3 mi. from put-in, don't take this trip in open boat at low to med. water. Excel. trout fishing. Helmet and lifejackets necessary. (Credit— David H. Sloan)

Nesamining Creek: 1½ days, skilled only, high water only, some riffles.

Nescopeck Creek: USGS Sybertsville, Berwick, Nuremberg. From

Rte. 93 brdg. to second brdg. down, 5 mi. Dif. III. Wilderness, some trash, can usually be run when Lehigh is too high; at high water—mostly waves; at low water—rocky; first rapids need high water to run; below camp ⅔ way down are large waves. (Credit —*Select Rivers of Central Pennsylvania*)

Neshannock Creek: Neshannock Falls to Hottenbaugh Run, 7 mi., 2 rapids, skilled canoeists only; first—entrance to gorge at Neshannock Falls—RR track abutments; second—rapids in gorge; fallen trees and great scenery in gorge ¾ mi. long; rest of stream —fast water, gravel bottom, mudbank. Start—covered brdg. above Neshannock Falls. (Credit—*Canoeing Guide to Western Pennsylvania and Northern West Virginia*)

Octararo Creek: Lancaster, Chester cos. Some riffles, mixed smooth and rapids, very attractive, intermed.

Oil Creek: Venango, Crawford cos. Centerville to Titusville, 12 mis., high water only, fallen trees. Dif. I. Titusville to Rouseville, 12 mi. Dif. I. Wilderness area, 2 mi. below start dif. in low water. Start—Drake Well Park in Titusville or Rte. 27 brdg. End—Rynd Farm Brdg., Rte. 8; below to mouth, pollution. (Credit—*Canoeing Guide to Western Pennsylvania and Northern West Virginia*)

Penns Creek: USGS Millheim, Beavertown, Hazelton, Mifflinburg, Middleburg, Sunbury, Lewisburg. From Coburn Rocks to brdg. off Rte. 204 N. of Selinsgrove, 48 mi. Dif. II. Beautiful, clean, heavily fished. Run with 2.6 cfs. at Coburn Brdg. and 3.8 cfs. at second RR brdg.

 Trip 1—Coburn Rocks to Weikert, 15 mi. Dif. II. Windfalls, rapids, and waves near Poe Paddy St. For. and Park. Scout before running.

 Trip 2—Weikert to Glen Iron, 33 mi. Dif. II. CAUTION— rapid that turns sharp left against steep right bank—has large waves, then long stretches of flat water with riffles and low rock dams, best sec. from New Berlin to Kratzville—very scenic, remote, much wildlife.

(Credit—*Select Rivers of Central Pennsylvania*)

Pennsylvania Canal: Check locally for water; novice.

Pine Creek:

Trip 1—Lycoming, Tioga cos. Ansonia to Tiadaghton, white water, Grand Canyon of Pa.! Tiadaghton to mouth, moving water. Ansonia to Cedar Run, ½ day, mostly rapids, skilled only, very attractive scenery. Cedar Run to Susquehanna, 2 mi., some riffles, pleasant, intermed., some wading in low water.

Trip 2—Tioga, Potter, Lycoming cos. Flows through Grand Canyon of Pa., white water, run until May, great scenery. CAUTION—don't run alone, too dangerous for lone canoe. From Ansonia to Waterville, 48 mi. Dif. I–II. Creek follows bend around Mt. Tom and then goes into canyon, entrance has long and easy vortex, then easy riffles, then shoals and small isles, channel shifts from side to side, creek leaves gorge at Blackwell. Take-out—jctn. of Little Pine Creek on left side at Waterville. (Credit—*Canoe Country Pennsylvania Style*)

Raccoon Creek: Beaver, Washington cos. Lake to mouth, moving water, 15 mi.

Red Bank Creek: Clarion and Jefferson cos. 1 day, 16 mi.; New Bethlehem to Lawsonham; good current; riffle past Lawsonham Brdg. (called Buttermilk Falls) till July 1, steep banks, small dam near Rtes. 28 and 66 brdg. Lawsonham to Rimer, 5½ mi. Dif. I. (Credit—*Canoeing Guide to Western Pennsylvania and Northern West Virginia*)

Sinnemahoning Creek: 2 days, smooth with some riffles, intermed., spring canoeing on Driftwood branch.

Slippery Rock Creek: Lawrence Co. White water, beautiful; 2 dam ptgs.—Kennedy Mill, McConnell's Mill, ptg. left; line or ptg. some rapids; early spring no good, waves; after June 15 no good. Dam—Heinz Camp, downstream of first brdg. beyond Breakneck Brdg. ptg. right. Rte. 173 to Kennedy Mill, 14.5 mi.; Kennedy Mill to McConnell's Mill, 3 mi., Dif. III–IV. McConnell's

Mill to Breakneck Brdg., 1 mi., Dif. III, Breakneck to Wurtemburg, 7.4 mi., Dif. II. (Credit—*Canoeing Guide to Western Pennsylvania and Northern West Virginia*)

Stony Creek: USGS Windber and Johnstown. From covered brdg. on dirt rd. W. off rd. to Shanksville from Kantner to Kring, 24 mi. Dif. II–IV.

Trip 1—Covered brdg. ¾ mi. from Shanksville to brdg. on rd. W. out of Lambertsville, 4 mi. Dif. IV. Lots of water needed, 4–4½ at Holsopple gauge. DANGER—high levels from Shanksville to covered brdg.; below brdg. rapids start fast. CAUTION—sharp right bend with brush dam—scout before running, then series of steep ledges and rapids, Dif. IV, then easier stretch, then rapids, Dif. IV, near end. CAUTION—2 big holes at base of long, straight drop.

Trip 2—Kantner to Holsopple, Dif. II, 12 mi., steepest part at first, then flattens out.

Trip 3—Holsopple to Kring, 8½ mi. Dif. III–IV. Can be fast and wild; first rapid 1 mi. below Holsopple is very dif., then 2 more very dif. rapids and many lesser ones. Ptg.—Border Dam on left. CAUTION—pipe and large ledge below dam—take left, then Dif. II–III on downstream.

(Credit—*Canoeing Guide to Western Pennsylvania and Northern West Virginia* and *Select Rivers of Central Pennsylvania*)

Susquehanna River: Bradford, Wyoming, Lackawanna, Luzerne, Columbia, Montour, Northumberland cos. From Wysox to Holtwood Dam.

Trip 1—Wysox to Laceyville, 29 mi., good scenery, OK for canoeing till early June, mostly slow-flowing. Put in—St. Rte. 187 brdg. access at Wysox. Take out—Laceyville Brdg. (second hwy. brdg.).

Trip 2—Laceyville to Tunkhannock, 25 mi., good scenery, OK most of summer. Put in at Laceyville Brdg., many bends in river, mostly slow-flowing, good campsites. Take out—U.S. Rte. 309 brdg. (third hwy. brdg. below Laceyville).

Trip 3—Bloomsburg to Northumberland, 25 mi., fair scenery, mostly slow-flowing, good for novice, many isles, good campsites. Can leave at jctn. of N. Branch and W. Branch, arrange for pickup at St. Rte. 61 brdg. at Northumberland.

Trip 4—Sunbury to Harrisburg, 25 mi., mostly slow-flowing, some swift-flowing, good scenery. Put-in—hwy. brdg. S. of Sunbury, islands divide course into 2 or 3 channels. CAUTION—McKee Half Falls about 18 mi. below Sunbury, can be easily run, good campsites.

Trip 5—Halifax to Harrisburg, 25 mi., mostly slow-flowing, some swift, good scenery. Put in at Halifax, don't run in low water, several small eroded ledges of Dif. I in this section. Take-out—shallow lake formed by sanitation dam in Harrisburg.

Trip 6—Columbia to Holtwood Dam, 18 mi., mostly slow-flowing, excel. scenery. Put-in—below Intercounty Brdg., Rte. 462 at Columbia. Ptg.—Safe Harbor Dam, 10 mi. below Columbia on E. shore just above powerhouse. Ptg.—Holtwood Dam. Take-out—E. shore and carry by car to access on W. shore below Norman Wood Brdg., can extend trip 30 mi. to tidewater at Havre de Grace, Md., with ptg. at Conowingo Dam.

(Credit—*Canoe Country Pennsylvania Style*)

Susquehanna River—N. Branch: Northumberland, Montour, Wyoming, Luzerne, Bradford, Columbia cos. Sayre to Wilkes-Barre, 6 days, some riffles, very attractive, intermed. Wilkes-Barre to Shamokin Dam, 4 days, some riffles, pleasant, novice. Shamokin Dam to Md. st. line, 6 days, smooth, some riffles, intermed., canoeists. Ptg.—5 dams, Harrisburg, York Haven, Safe Harbor, McCall's Ferry, Conowingo.

Susquehanna River—W. Branch: Clearfield, Cambria, Clinton, Lycoming, Union cos. From Clearfield to Williamsport, 107 mi. From headwaters to jctn. with main branch is magnificent canyon.

Trip 1—Clearfield to Frenchville Sta., 28 mi. Dif. I–II. Excel. scenery. Put in—¼ mi. down from U.S. Rte. 322 brdg. at Clearfield. CAUTION—low dam near eastern part of town, leave river on left bank at boat-launch area, carry along hwy., and put in below dam; at Shawville Brdg. the river enters deep canyon, mod. white water. Take out—old hwy. brdg. at Frenchville Sta.

Trip 2—Frenchville Sta. to Karthaus, 17 mi. Dif. I–II. Excel. scenery. Put in at hwy. brdg. at Frenchville Sta.; river flows through canyon, many rapids. CAUTION—Moshannon Falls begins opposite Karthaus RR tunnel. Stop above fall area, scout falls, can run falls on left side of river then move to center of falls. Run with water level 2.67 and 2.35 on Karthaus gauge. Polluted. Call Mr. Howey, AM3-4365, Frenchville Sta., for information. Can take out at St. Rte. 879 brdg. at Karthaus.

Trip 3—Renovo to Lock Haven Dam, 30 mi., excel. scenery. Put in at St. Rte. 144 brdg. at Renovo, OK novice, runs through canyon-like gorge to Lock Haven.

Trip 4—Lock Haven to Williamsport, 32 mi., fair scenery, OK novice. End in Williamsport or go on 41 mi. to jctn. with main branch. CAUTION—low dam near Williamsport and Lewisburg—ptg. both.

(Credit—*Canoe Country Pennsylvania Style*)

Swatara Creek: Lebanon, Dauphin cos. 2 days, smooth, some riffles, OK novice.

Tionesta Creek: Warren Co. From brdg. at Farnsworth Brdg. Rd. to Tionesta Dam, 45 mi.

Trip 1—From brdg. at Farnsworth Brdg. Rd. to Kellettville, 30 mi. At high water trip can start where Farnsworth Rd. crosses; otherwise start at brdg. at Weldbank, Tiona, Sheffield, Lynch or Mayburg; very nice scenery, may not be able to canoe after June 1 due to water level.

Trip 2—Kellettville to Tionesta Dam, 15 mi., pleasant trip.
(Credit—*Canoeing in Kinzua Country*)

Tobyhanna Creek: Monroe Co. ½ day, mixed smooth and rapids, very attractive, intermed. canoeists.

Trail to Ohio River: (A) From Lake Erie at Erie to Waterford,

15 mi., ptg. Waterford via French Creek to Allegheny River at Franklin, on to Pitt., then down Ohio River past mouth to Beaver River to Ohio; no serious obstructions, ptg. dams. (B) Leave French Creek at Conneaut outlet, on to Conneaut Lake, ptg. ½ mi. to Pymatuning Res., then down Shenango and Beaver rivers to Ohio River. Ptgs.—dams, spring run.

Tulpehacken Creek: 1 long day, some riffles, pleasant, high water only, intermed. canoeists.

Turtle Creek: Allegheny, Westmoreland cos. 6–12 mi. upstream from mouth, moving water; remainder downstream polluted, unattractive.

Wallenpaupack Creek: S. Fork and W. Branch; Lackawanna, Pike cos. 1 day on S. Fork, mostly rapids, very attractive, high water only, experts only; ½ day on W. Branch, mixed smooth and rapids, pleasant, high water only, skilled canoeists. DANGER—S. Fork, dangerous falls 1–1¼ mi. beyond second brdg. after Greentown, fast, deep drop.

White Deer Creek: USGS Williamsport and Allenwood. From side rd. off main rd. (6 mi. above White Deer) to White Deer, 6 mi. Dif. II. Run in spring or after heavy rain, several windfalls, small stream, sharp drops, tricky currents; first 3 mi. are best. (Credit—*Select Rivers of Central Pennsylvania*)

Wills Creek: USGS Fairhope and Hyndman in Pa. and Evitts Creek and Cumberland in Md. From Fairhope, Pa., to Ellerslie, Md., 14 mi. Dif. II–V. Experienced canoeists only, fast-flowing, steep, runs through gorge, beautiful, some trash at end.
    Trip 1—Fairhope to Hyndman Rte. 96 brdg., 5.5 mi. Dif. IV–V. Experts only, first mi. Dif. III, then continuous rapids, Dif. IV. DANGER—yo yo rapids, run right or in middle. DANGER—Wall Rapids—below yo yo—go to right. Scout rapids before running; last mi. Dif. III.
    Trip 2—Hyndman to Ellerslie, Md., 8.6 mi. Dif. II–III.

Steepest part at first, easy water at end of trip; 1.5 mi. below put-in stream branches with isles, take main channel. CAUTION—heavy waves in parts of trip. CAUTION—waves below Rte. 96 brdg., then Dif. II to end.

(Credit—*Select Rivers of Central Pennsylvania*)

Yellow Breeches Creek: Cumberland Co. 2 days, smooth, pleasant; novice.

Youghiogheny River: Fayette, Westmoreland, Somerset cos. Large, powerful river, fine white water, adequate water spring through fall. Don't run when too high. From Confluence to McKeesport, 75 mi.

Trip 1—Confluence to Ohiopyle, 12 mi. Dif. I–II. Excel. scenery. Water level critical, max 4 ft. at Confluence gauge. Put-in—St. Rte. 281 brdg. on W. side of Confluence, then river enters deep canyon, rapids have many bldrs. and sharp ledges, don't run alone, no access on this stretch. DANGER —leave river at St. Rte. 381 brdg. near Ohiopyle (first hwy. brdg.), Ohiopyle Falls are below brdg. Don't run, approach to brdg. can be tricky, stay close to right shore, take path along right side to spot below falls.

Trip 2—Ohiopyle to Stewarton, 6½ mi. Dif. III–IV, excel. scenery. Put in at sand beach below Ohiopyle Falls; river then curves to right around Ohiopyle Loop, 6 major rapids are on the loop, first and last ones most dif., can take out after loop by carrying up steep trail on right side at end of last rapid; after the loop less dif. for couple of miles, then Dif. IV, 6 major and minor rapids in 1 mi., scout. Take-out at Stewarton is steep trail on right and hard to see from river. DANGER—this stretch for experts only—no open canoes; water level of 2½ ft. means Dif. IV rapids, above 4 ft. means Dif. V.

Trip 3—Stewarton to S. Connellsville, 11 mi. Dif. I–III. Excel. scenery. First rapid most dif., scout this and next rapids before running. No open canoes, rapids become less dif., last part into S. Connellsville almost flat. Take-out—left

side at a water works about ¼ mi. past a footbrdg. and about
100 yds. above dam; don't get near dam.

Trip 4—Connellsville to McKeesport, 46 mi. Dif. I. Good
scenery. OK novice.

(Credit—*Canoe Country Pennsylvania Style*)

PUERTO RICO

"Puerto Rico has several hundred streams and about 20 river
systems. Because of the mountainous and steep topography of our
island, only the lower portions (a few miles) of the larger streams
would be at all usable for canoes.

"In view of the fact that the slow-flowing portions of the
streams may have schistosome, a water-borne parasite that causes
bilharzia in man, we do not believe that it is advisable at this time
to publicize our rivers for canoe trips."

Charles Romney-Joseph
Asst. Sec. of Agriculture
Puerto Rico

RHODE ISLAND

Pawcatuck River and **Wood River:** According to the state of
Rhode Island, Dept. of Natural Resources, there are relatively few
opportunities in Rhode Island for extensive canoeing. The best
river for this purpose is the Pawcatuck; 3 long trips possible: (1)
Start at One Hundred Acre Pond in W. Kingston, go through
Thirty Acre Pond into Cepufet River to Worden Pond, then down
Pawcatuck to Westerly or Watch Hill. (2) A shorter trip starts in
the village of Usquepaug down Queens River into Pawcatuck. (3)
Long trip—start in Exeter at Rte. 165 in Arcadia Mgmt. area,
float down Wood River to the Pawcatuck through Barkerville,

Wyoming, Hope Valley, Woodville, and Alton (ptg. over dams necessary at each). On the Pawcatuck, ptgs. at Kenyon, Shannock (2), Carolina, Burdickville, Bradford, Potter Hill, White Rock, and Westerly. Public boat lndg. and launching sites shown on Dept. Natural Resources map; 2 overnight camp areas in Carolina and Burlingame mgmt. areas. Large-mouth bass, pickerel, white perch; catfish, trout at Watchaug Pond and Wood River, trout fishing from Arcadia St. Mgmt. area to Pawcatuck River. Hunting: jump shooting for waterfowl, gray squirrels. (Credit—Pawcatuck River and Wood River)

Pawtuxet River: Heavily dammed and industrialized, not recommended. (Credit—Stewart Coffin)

SOUTH CAROLINA

Chattooga River: Oconee Co. Russell brdg. to Earles Ford, 7 mi., 3–4 hrs., OK beginners. Dif. I–III, most rapids Dif. II. Shallow at first, novice. Ptg.—Big Shoals; river above and below this stretch for experienced or experts.

Chauga River: Oconee Co. Sumter Natl. For. Access pts.—S.C. Secondary 290 (Stumphouse Rd.) and numerous F.S., st., and fed. hwys. to Hartwell Res.; total, 20 mi. DANGER—waterfalls, bad rapids—don't run, submerged bldrs. Ptg.—4 waterfalls and 4–6 shoals, challenging trip for middle to advanced beginners. Trout in upper reaches, fair to good bass in lower sec.

SOUTH DAKOTA

James River: 500 river mi., 3 in. per mi. drop, meandering, good canoeing. Fisher's Grove State Park area popular, too low to canoe in drought.

Little White River: Rosebud Indian Reservation, Bennett, Todd, Mellette cos. Todd Co. line to White River, 115 mi., 3 days; canoeable any season, beautiful, good campsites. Todd Co. line to Spring Creek School, 20 mi., swift, some rapids, some fallen trees, 20–40 ft. wide. Spring Creek School to Ghost Hawk Park, 20 mi., "Crazy Horse Canyon," beautiful canyon, very winding river, swift current, rd. parallels section most of way, very little litter. Ghost Hawk Park to Hwy. 18, 10 mi., 5 hrs., sandbars, about same as upstream, beautiful. Hwy. 18 to brdg. near Ring Thunder community, 15 mi., poor canoeing, few rapids, swift and winding, many fallen trees, slow canoeing. Ring Thunder community to Hwy. 40, 25 mi., 6½ hrs., long runs of beautiful rapids, grassy banks, 60–80 ft. wide, exciting white water, in high water. DANGER—power dam 100 yds. down from Hwy. 40 with bad take-out. Hwy. 40 to White River, 25 mi., no information, appears to have white water; watch for fences on river. (Credit—Dean Norman)

TENNESSEE

Beaver Creek: Knox Co. 23 mi., I.S. 75 brdg., near Powell to Melton Hill Lake; Dif. I, II. Easy trip, pleasant, floods danger, brush overhanging fences. Ptg.—Coward Mill Dam, last 1½ mi., some rapids and riffles.

Blackburn Fork: Mid. Tenn., Highland River, Jackson, Overton cos. Hwy. 86, a natural gorge river area, first 1½ mi. for experienced canoeists only, floatable, Dec.–June, accessible below falls for collapsible craft only. (Credit—*Canoeing in Tennessee*)

Brimstone Creek: USGS Helenwood. Probably canoeable for 12–15 mi. (Credit—C. E. Cosgrove)

Buffalo River: Lawrence, Lewis, Wayne, Perry, Hickman, Humphreys cos. Henryville Brdg. to mouth, 177 mi., sharp turns, some overhang, some hazardous shoals, 18 access pts., beautiful, good camping, best Apr.–Nov., gravel bars, unpolluted. Bells Brdg. (Hwy. 13 crossing on way to Waynesboro) to Hwy. 13 crossing below Flatwoods, 15 mi., or to Slinks Shoal, 10 mi. from Bells Brdg., sharp turns, overhanging limbs, small game, good current, some rapids, bass, catfish.

Caney Fork River: Below Center Hill Dam. Good easy trip; trout, bass.

Clear Creek: USGS Campbell Jctn., Isoline, Jones Knob, Twin Bridge, Hebbertsburg, Lancing. From gravel rd. near Pugh Cemetery N. of Campbell Jctn. to jctn. with Obed River, 49 mi. Dif. II–IV.

Trip 1—Campbell Jctn. to U.S. 127 brdg., 20 mi., gradient 12 ft.–15 ft. per mi. Dif. I–II. Canoe in high water only, run with 2,000–5,000 cfs. on Oakdale gauge.

Trip 2—U.S. 127 brdg. to rd. brdg. at White (Witt) Creek, 20 mi., wild canyon, no auto access, small rocky, some parts are sheer-wall canyon, many rapids Dif. I–II, starting 8 mi. below U.S. 127, extending for 2 mi., then 2 mi. of rapids Dif. III–IV, then 1-mi.-long pool, then rapids Dif. II mixed with pools, then DANGER—about ¾ mi. above White Creek is 8-ft. falls, Dif. IV–V, has blind approach, very dangerous.

Trip 3—White Creek to jctn. with Obed River, 9 mi., steep canyon, scenic, powerful river, rapids Dif. I–II to Jette Brdg., below Jette Brdg. Dif. II–III to Lilly Brdg., wild canyon, rocky. DANGER—the last 1½ mi. after Lilly Brdg., Dif. II–IV. Ptg.—2 waterfalls, impressive canyon, gradient 45 ft. per mi., clear and clean water, no access at river jctn., must go on down Obed River. Needs 1,300–3,000 cfs. from Jette Brdg. to Lilly Brdg. and 750–1,500 cfs. from Lilly Brdg. to Obed River. (Credit—C. E. Cosgrove)

Clear Fork River—N. Prong (also called W. Prong): USGS Grimsley, Burrville, Rugby, Honey Creek. From brdg. on gravel rd. 6 mi. E. and N. of Grimsley and U.S. 127 to jctn. with New

River, 33 mi., small rocky stream, gravel bed, small bldrs. in river, wild canyon, scenic. Dif. I–III.

Trip 1—Put-in to Gatewood Brdg., 6 mi., first 3-mi. gradient is 13 ft. per mi., Dif. I rapids, river goes under ledge at 1 pt. —barely headroom, then next 3 mi. to Gatewood Brdg. 7 ft. per mi. drop, quiet with some riffles and light rapids. Jctn. with S. Prong is 1½ mi. above Gatewood Brdg., flow doubles, run with 2,000–2,500 cfs. on Stearns gauge at S. Fork.

Trip 2—Gatewood Brdg. to Peters Brdg., 6½ mi., gradually deepening but gentle canyon, wild country, some rapids Dif. I–II, near midpoint, more rapids ½ mi. above Peters Brdg., several long quiet stretches on this trip, run with 1,200–1,500 cfs. on Stearns gauge at S. Fork.

Trip 3—Peters Brdg. to Brewster Brdg., 6 mi., quieter than above, long pools, scattered Dif. I rapids, scenic cliffs, same gauge readings as above trip.

Trip 4—Brewster Brdg. to Burnt Mill Brdg., 10 mi., canyon gets deeper, rockier, gradient 13 ft. per mi., first 3 mi. gentle with few easy rapids, then 2 mi. above Whiteoak Creek Dif. II rapids, very scenic around Whiteoak Creek, below jctn. there are rapids Dif. I and short pools, same gauge reading as above.

Trip 5—Burnt Mill Brdg. to jctn. with New River, 4 mi., gradient is 22 ft. per mi., first half has rapids Dif. I–II, last half some tough rapids Dif. III, old dirt rd. comes to far side of jctn. through private property, run with 1,000–2,500 cfs. at Stearns gauge at S. Fork.

(Credit—C. E. Cosgrove)

Clinch River: E. Tenn., Claiborne, Granger, Hancock cos. Access pts.—U.S. Hwy. 25 E., St. Hwys. 33, 66, and 94. OK novice, pastoral countryside, year-round floating. (Credit—*Canoeing in Tennessee*)

Collins River: E. Tenn., Highland, River, Warren, Grundy cos. Access pt.—St. Hwy. 56, OK novice, pastoral countryside, year-round canoeing, low flow during July, Aug., Sept., and Oct. (Credit—*Canoeing in Tennessee*)

Conasauga River: E. Tenn. Polk Co. Access pts.—U.S. Hwy. 411 and For. Ser. rds., experienced canoeists only, natural wilderness-type river, not floatable during Aug., Sept., and Oct. (Credit—*Canoeing in Tennessee*)

Cumberland River—S. Fork: 36 mi., Honey Creek to St. 9a brdg., rugged, wild, spectacular, canyon, some dif. stretches, flow varies. Honey Creek to Leatherwood Ford Brdg., 7 mi., first 5 mi. most dangerous, sharp drops and turns, narrow, Dif. III–IV, Dif. I and II last few mi. Leatherwood to John Smith Pl., 3½ mi., Dif. I–II, to "falls." "Falls"—Dif. IV–V rapids, ptg. right bank, wild rapids below falls. John Smith Pl.–Tenn.-Ky. st. line, 12½ mi., Dif. I–III. St. line to St. 92 brdg., most Dif. I–III, Devils Jump: 1 mi. after strip mine, Dif. III–IV. DANGER—ptg. E. bank; wild, many rapids; below St. 92, Lake Cumberland; small-mouth bass: Indian cliff dwellings in canyon. (Credit—Ron L. Stokes and C. E. Cosgrove)

Daddy's Creek: USGS Grassy Cove, Dorton, Ozone, and Hebbertsburg. From U.S. Hwy. 127 Brdg. at Big Lick to jctn. with Obed River, 40 mi. Dif. I–VI.

Trip 1—U.S. Hwy. 127 Brdg. to Meridian Brdg., 13 mi. CAUTION—may be dam at St. Hwy. 28 brdg., gradient averages 21 ft. per mi., rocky course, rapids of Dif. II, shallow but wild canyon, run with 2,000 cfs. on Oakdale gauge.

Trip 2—Center Brdg. to Antioch Brdg., 8 mi.; wild, shallow canyon continues, rapids Dif. I, first third of trip and last third, some Dif. II rapids in last third of river, run with 2,000–5,000 cfs. on Oakdale gauge.

Trip 3—Antioch Brdg. to jctn. with Obed, 9 mi., very dangerous sec., no access for over 6 mi. below Antioch Brdg. except for trail, avg. 34 ft. per mi. gradient, at Yellow Creek—cove in the canyon with mild water 1 mi., then canyon narrows, this is wild stretch, unrunnable parts with dif. ptg., Dif. can be V–VI.

Duck River: a doomed river, soon to be killed by 2 dams, better go now. Manchester to Sowell Mill Brdg., 14½ mi. Manchester to

Normandy, 18½ mi., best sec., scenic, farmland and woodland, exciting rapids, fast water stretches; low water—late summer and fall. Put-in—Powers Brdg. End—Normandy Brdg. Other secs.— Dement Brdg. to Mullings Mill Brdg., 7½ mi.; Mullings Mill Brdg. to Sims Brdg., 19 mi.; Sims Brdg. to Warner Brdg., ruined by industrial pollutant, avoid. Warner Brdg. to Hopkins Brdg., 18½ mi. Hopkins Brdg. to Hardison's Mill, 20 mi. Hardison's Mill to Howard Brdg., 22 mi. Howard Brdg., 22 mi. Howard Brdg. to Sowell Mill Brdg., 9½ mi. Sowell Mill Brdg. fair access, some difficulty. Good fishing, small-mouth bass, rock bass, black perch, redeye, sunfish, cats. (Credit—*Float Trip Guides for Duck River, Tennessee*)

Elk River: Middle Tenn., Giles, Lincoln, Franklin cos. Access pts.—U.S. Hwys. 31, 431, 231, St. Hwys. 7, 10, 50, 130, 16. OK novice, year-round canoeing, pastoral countryside, low flow during Aug., Sept., and Oct. (Credit—*Canoeing in Tennessee*)

Emory River: USGS Gobey, Lancing, Camp Austin, Harriman. From Mahan to Watts Bar Lake, 47 mi.

  Trip 1—Mahon to County Rd. Brdg. off U.S. a7 N.W. of Wartburg on Lancing Rd., 12 mi., very small first few mi., hardly enough water to float on at first, quick runoff, not too scenic, rapids Dif. II in first few mi., then river peaceful to Lancing Rd.

  Trip 2—Lancing Rd. to Camp Austin Brdg., 14 mi., river changes rapidly, wild canyon to jctn., avg. gradient 25 ft. per mi., rapids Dif. III–IV, at jctn. river flow increases, below jctn. are moderate rapids Dif. I–II with pools; just below Nemo brdg. is Dif. III rapid; rapid of Dif. II–III at Camp Austin Brdg.

  Trip 3—Camp Austin Brdg. to Watts Bar Lake, 21 mi., river becomes quieter as Oakdale is neared, after Oakdale brdg. are 3 mod. rapids Dif. I–II, then some mild rapids into backwater of Watts Bar Lake, scenic. (Credit—C. E. Cosgrove)

French Broad River: USGS Hot Springs, Paint Rock, Neddy Mt.,

Newport. From Barnard, N.C., to Douglas Lake, Tenn., 45 mi., Dif. I–IV. Barnard to Hot Springs most dif. part—experts only.

Trip 1—Barnard to Stackhouse, 5½ mi., wide and shallow, series of rocky rapids and small ledges, Dif. I–II, then deep canyon is ahead, rapids more severe and close together, Dif. III–IV, 40 ft. per mi. fall in 1½ mi. to Sandy Bottom, steepness and tough rapids continue to Stackhouse, in canyon there are large waves, huge bldrs., tough ledges, and many chute gaps; experts only.

Trip 2—Stackhouse to U.S. 70 brdg., 5 mi., Dif. I–III, old dam at Stackhouse—stay left, then ½ mi. of rapids, Dif. II–III, then Laurel Creek joins. Then river changes, shallow and straight for 2 mi. with riffles and rapids, Dif. I, then river disappears in mt. gate ahead—watch for large white-rock formation like a castle on mt., at foot of mt. is steep rapid with high waves, don't take right channel—blocked by falls. Then river widens and shallows with many isles, Dif. I for ½ mi., then more small isles and bad rapid—The Falls—don't run, very dangerous, then river narrows and RR brdg. crosses river, then river widens again, shallow and fast to Hot Springs.

Trip 3—U.S. 70 brdg. at Hot Springs to Paint Rock, 8 mi. below brdg. ½ mi. of rapids, Dif. I–III, heavy waves near narrow bend, then next 8 mi. river is straight, wide, and peaceful, some Dif. I rapids, then gradient steepens with rapids Dif. III, then 2 mi. of lesser gradient and rapids Dif. I, then last mi. before Paint Rock has many big isles.

Trip 4—Paint Rock to Bridgeport Brdg., st. line at Paint Rock; below Paint Rock are more rapids, Dif. I–III, 17 mi., several ledges and runnable gaps before Del Rio Brdg. After Del Rio Brdg. the valley ends, mts. close in, rapids begin, rocky rapids below Del Rio Brdg., Dif. II–III, many spots that often swamp canoes, large waves.

Trip 5—Bridgeport Brdg. to U.S. 411 brdg., 6 mi., river still swift, farm ctry., river wider, rapids mostly Dif. I, scenic, wooded hills; below U.S. 411 brdg., backwater of Douglas Lake reached quickly, can be current to Pigeon River.

(Credit—C. E. Cosgrove)

Harpeth River: Mid. Tenn., Dickson, Cheatham, Davidson, Williamson cos. Access pts.—I 40, U.S. Hwys. 70, 431, and 31, St. Hwys. 49, 1, and 106. OK novice, year-round floating, low flow during Aug., Sept., and Oct., pastoral countryside. (Credit— *Canoeing in Tennessee*)

Hatchie River: W. Tenn., bottomland stream, catfish.

Hiwassee River: Polk, Bradley cos.; 20 mi. Put in below Appalachia Powerhouse, good camping, deep holes, some wading in low water, trout.

Holston River: E. Tenn., Knox, Jefferson, Grainger, Hawkins, Sullivan cos. Access pts.—U.S. Hwys. 11E. and 11W., St. Hwys. 1, 92, 66, and ctry. rds. OK novice, pastoral countryside, year-round floating. (Credit—*Canoeing in Tennessee*)

Laurel Creek: USGS Hot Springs; Laurel Creek empties into Spring Creek, a rough white-water stream, experts only, run in high water only. (Credit—C. E. Cosgrove)

Little Emory River: USGS Petros, Elverton; Morgan Co. From Coalfield to Hwy. 61, 10 mi. Closed canoes and kayaks, experts only. Don't run in flood, dangerous. Put-in—across a field from a dirt rd. on N.W. side below Pleasant Grove Church, narrow, rocky, brushy, creek, rapids. Dif. II. Then watch for steep bank where blacktop rd. approaches on a large horseshoe bend, below is steep grade, gradient 60 ft. per mi., dif. rocky chutes, much brush and windfall, no good stop areas, all parts Dif. II–IV, rapids, there is a 5-ft. falls—don't run, then footbrdg. Then steep grade continues with rapids Dif. II–III, more windfalls, then after 1 mi. canyon widens, then brdg. near Christmas is passed. Then river is milder, riffles and Dif. I rapids. After second U.S. 27 brdg. is backwater of lake; above Coalfield rivers start as separate forks, scenic but don't run, waterfalls, rocky beds. (Credit—C. E. Cosgrove)

Little Pigeon River: E. Tenn. Sevier Co. Access pts.—U.S. Hwys.

411, 441, St. Hwy. 13. OK novice, pastoral countryside, year-round floating. (Credit—*Canoeing in Tennessee*)

Little River: E. Tenn. Blount Co. Access pts.—U.S. Hwy. 411, St. Hwy. 13. OK novice, pastoral countryside, year-round floating. (Credit—*Canoeing in Tennessee*)

Little Tennessee River: 35 mi., Fort Loudon Dam to brdg. below Chilhowee dam; 1 ptg. Chilhouse Dam. first 20 mi. best trout section.

New River: USGS Fork Mt., Duncan Flats, Norma, Huntsville, Helenwood. From Fork Mt. to jctn. with S. Fork, 55 mi.
Trip 1—Fork Mt. to 116 Brdg. at Ligias Fork Jctn., 10 mi., can be exciting in high water. Dif. III, 38 ft. per mi. gradient first 4 mi. then next 6 mi. have 11 ft. per mi. gradient, rocky stream, mountainous.
Trip 2—Ligias Fork to Smoky Jctn., 9 mi., needs high water to run, first 4 mi. narrow and brushy with overhanging trees, then gradient steepens and there are rapids Dif. II, then river is easier, narrow canyon before Smoky Jctn.
Trip 3—Smoky Jctn. to Norma, 6 mi., narrow valley, semi-wilderness in canyon, 8 ft. per mi. gradient.
Trip 4—Norma to Winona, 8 mi., flows through another gorge, easy going.
Trip 5—Winona to U.S. 27 brdg., 13 mi., easy river continues, another gorge, 2 county-rd. brdgs. on this section.
Trip 6—U.S. 27 brdg. to jctn. with New River, 9 mi., most dif. part, wilderness. Below Silcott Ford, river enters canyon, wild, rugged, gradient reaches 27 ft. per mi., many dif. rapids of Dif. III, deep canyon. Take-out—primitive rd. on private property on N. Bank at jctn.
(Credit—C. E. Cosgrove)

Nolichucky River: E. Tenn. Greene, Washington cos. Access pts. —St. Hwys. 70, 35, 107, and 81. OK novice, pastoral countryside, year-round floating. (Credit—*Canoeing in Tennessee*)

N. Whiteoak Creek: USGS Honey Creek. Start former site of Zenith, scenic, deep canyon, rugged, suitable for canoeing, no other information. (Credit—C. E. Cosgrove)

Obed River: USGS Crossville, Isoline, Fox Creek, Hebbertsburg, Lancing. From Lake Holiday near Crossville to jctn. with Emory River, 38 mi. Dif. II–VI.

Trip 1—Lake Holiday to Bishop Brdg., 3 mi., small creek, shallow, run with 2,000 cfs. on Oakdale gauge.

Trip 2—Bishop Brdg. to Adams Brdg., 10 mi., over 30 ft. per mi. gradient, wild canyon, first 2 mi. have rapids Dif. I, then third mi. has rapids Dif. II–IV, then next 3 mi. Dif. II–VI, some unrunnable spots, roughest section of the river very dif., very dangerous, experts only. Below sharp left turn at Bob Creek Jctn. river is Dif. I–II, then more gentle to Adams Brdg., run with 2,000–5,000 cfs. at Oakdale gauge.

Trip 3—Adams Brdg. to Potter Ford Brdg., 4 mi., avg. gradient of 10 ft. per mi., steep part in middle, bldr. rapids. Ptg. Small river, wild canyon, scenic, trail along river, run with 2,000–5,000 cfs. at Oakdale gauge.

Trip 4—Potter Ford Brdg. to Daddy's Creek Jctn., 12 mi., peaceful for 1 mi. with rapids, then Dif. I–II to lower Potter Ford, then from lower Potter Ford to Daddy's Creek—hold on, steep, rocky, wild canyon, unrunnable parts, experts only, rapids Dif. III to Obed Jctn. Then rapids Dif. III–IV, very dif., very dangerous to mouth of Clear Creek, then ½ mi. rapids Dif. II–III, then quiet pool, then more rapids Dif. II, then much milder to end—Dif. I, run with 650–1,500 cfs. on Oakdale gauge between Clear Creek and end.

(Credit—C. E. Cosgrove)

Ocoee River: E. Tenn., Polk Co. Access pts.—U.S. Hwys. 64, 411; OK novice, pastoral countryside, floatable only below Parksville Lake. (Credit—*Canoeing in Tennessee*)

Powell River: Above Norris Lake, canoeable but no information.

Red River: Mid. Tenn., Montgomery, Robertson cos. Access pts.

—St. Hwys. 11 and 76. OK novice, pastoral countryside, low flow during Aug., Sept., and Oct. (Credit—*Canoeing in Tennessee*)

Roaring River: Mid. Tenn. Highland Rim, Jackson, Overton cos. Access pts.—St. Hwy. 136 and co. rds. Experienced canoeists only. Roaring River is a natural gorge area. First 2 mi. strictly for experienced canoeists, floatable only from Dec. to June, dangerous in high water. (Credit—*Canoeing in Tennessee*)

Sequatchie River: E. Tenn., Cumberland, Plateau, Marion, Sequatchie, Bledsoe cos. Access pts.—I 24, U.S. Hwy. 72, St. Hwys. 27 and 28. OK novice, pastoral countryside, year-round canoeing, low July–Oct. (Credit—*Canoeing in Tennessee*)

Spring Creek: USGS Spring Creek, Hot Springs, Paint Rock, Neddy Mt., and Newport. From Barnard, N.C., to Douglas Lake, Tenn., 41 mi.; river drops about 550 ft. in 40 mi., canyon segment from Barnard to Hot Springs for experts only; read gauge at Newport—above 1,200 cfs. is minimum level, at 3,000–4,000 there are difficult standing waves, above 10,000 don't run.

Trip 1—Barnard to U.S. 70 brdg., 9 mi. Reach river from blacktop rd. that leaves U.S. 70 at Walnut and goes to Barnard Brdg.; river wide and shallow here, Dif. I–II for 1½ mi., then narrow valley closes and deep canyon is ahead, rapids become more severe and closer, Dif. III–IV, steep gradient and complex rapids continue to Stackhouse. Remains of old dam at Stackhouse, stay in left channel. After dam there is ½ mi. rapid, Dif. II–III, then Laurel Creek enters from N., then river suddenly changes, becomes shallow and wide for 2 mi. with good current and riffles, small ledges and rapids Dif. I, then look for large white-rock formation ahead, there is a steep rapid at foot of this mt., then river widens and shallows for ½ mi., then look for group of isles, severe rapids below known as The Falls—very dangerous, then river calms down (Dif. I–II) to U.S. 70 brdg.

Trip 2—U.S. 70 Brdg. to Del Rio Brdg., 18 mi., ½ mi. of rapids, Dif. I–II, then rapids Dif. III with dangerous waves, then next 8 mi. river follows rd., river peaceful with Dif. I rapids, then at pt. where mountains close in there are rapids Dif. III, then 2 mi. of riffles and Dif. I rapids, look for colored cliff—Paint Rock; this is end of quiet stretch. Next 3 mi. rapids Dif. I–III, then steep ledges and runnable gaps, Dif. II–III. River remains fast with small ledges to Wolf Creek Brdg., then river swift but easy to Del Rio Brdg.

Trip 3—Del Rio Brdg. to U.S. 411 brdg., 14 mi.; below Del Rio Brdg. a left bend indicates end of valley and start of rapids Dif. II, then below very narrow pt. is ledge called The Falls—take right side, bad spot in middle of The Falls, the narrow mt. gap is 3 mi. long with some severe rapids and large waves, many canoes are swamped here, then wide rocky rapid alongside Huff Isle, then Bridgeport Brdg. below, river remains swift, farm ctry., rapids mostly Dif. I, to U.S. 411 brdg. Below 411 brdg. is backwater of Douglas Lake. (Credit—C. E. Cosgrove)

Tellico River: In Cherokee Natl. For. in E. Tenn., 5 mi., run 2½ hrs.; after heavy rain this is Dif. III–V. Avg. gradient over 50 ft., covered boats only, road follows river all the way, experts only. (Credit—Georgia Canoeing Association)

White Creek: USGS Twin Brdgs., Hebbertsburg, tributary of Clear Creek, joins Clear Creek 9 mi. above jctn. with Obed. Canoeable with adequate flow from Twin Brdgs. S. of Deer Lodge to jctn. with Clear Creek, 7 mi., wild and narrow canyon, gradient 20 ft. per mi., clear and clean water, rapids Dif. I–II. (Credit—C. E. Cosgrove)

Whiteoak Creek: USGS Rugby and Honey Creek. From Matthews Brdg. to Burnt Mill Brdg. on Clear Fork River, 16 mi. Put-in—on a ctry. rd. W. of Glenmary, flows through shallow wooded gorge, after White Oak Brdg. on St. Rd. 52 river goes into gorge, gradient is 20 ft. per mi. in parts, some Dif. II–III rapids, no access at jctn., must canoe on to Burnt Mill Brdg. (Credit—C. E. Cosgrove)

TEXAS

Angelina River: Jasper Co. in E. Tex. near city of Jasper, from Sam Rayburn Dam to B. A. Steinhagen Res., 24 mi. Access— S.H. 63 and Farm Road 2799, 75–150 ft. in width. Angelina Natl. For. borders river on W. bank on upper end, banks heavily vegetated, beautiful scenery, good fishing, black bass, catfish, white sandbars, normally adequate water for floating, clean water, takes on green color downstream. (Credit—*Texas Waterways* and *Texas Rivers and Rapids*)

Big Cypress Bayou (Creek): Marion Co., N.E. Tex., from Lake-o-the-Pines Dam to Caddo Lake St. Park, 34 mi., narrow from dam to Jefferson but very wide below Jefferson, murky color, usually enough water for floating, steep banks, heavily vegetated. Access —U.S. Hwy. 59, F.M. Rd. 134, S.H. 43. Canopylike cover in upper portion, swamplike in lower part, popular stream for canoeing. (Credit—*Texas Waterways*)

Big Sandy—Village Creek: Polk, Hardin cos. in E. Tex., from Alabama-Coushatta Indian Res. to Neches River, 69 mi. Access pts.—8 rds. cross this section, river is 20–30 ft. in width, sufficient water level at all times, small stream, but a major drainage for Big Thicket, very scenic, very popular canoe trail. (Credit—*Texas Waterways*)

Blanco River: Blanco, Hays cos. in central Tex near San Marcos, from F.M. 165 to San Marcos, 60 mi., 30–50 ft. in width. Access —11 rds. cross river in this section, several small low-water diversion dams, fed by springs, crystal-clear water, river often shallow, OK for canoeing after rain, homesites along the river at first; overall a scenic river. (Credit—*Texas Waterways*)

Boggy Creek: Houston, Leon cos. Boggy Creek enters Trinity 8 mi. above Hwy. 21, possible to canoe upstream some distance from Trinity. Access may be possible from private rd. near Cairomiss.

Brazos River: 1,210 total river mi., much canoeable. River starts on high plains, ends at Gulf of Mexico at Freeport; 7 dams at present, 23 total planned. DANGER—Brazos Falls below Waco—opposite Marlin, low-water causeway in same area; co-ordinate trips below Possum Kingdom and Whitney dams with water release. St. 16 brdg. below Possum Kingdom Dam to Hwy. 281 brdg., 1½ days, novice OK, long pools broken by small rapids, good camping, 1 brdg. between some wading low water. Good fishing—catfish, bass, panfish.

Colorado River—Highland Lakes: Burnet, Travis, Llano cos. 150 mi., 5 dams, runs near LBJ ranch, mostly dam backwater, motorboats, annual Explorer Scout canoe race. Austin to Columbus popular run. "Weichsel's Run," Flat Rock to Gorman Falls, 2½ hrs., remote ctry., deer. Access—½ mi. upstream from Bend, Texas, to old cable suspension brdg. Murky red stream, fast water with good rapids and standing haystacks, exciting, submerged bldrs., beautiful waterfall, cave behind waterfall, real thrill when river is above normal; waterfall follows mi. of bluffs alternatively on either side.

Concho River: Tom Green, Concho cos., W. central Tex., from San Angelo to Colorado River, 65 mi., 30–40 ft. in width, muddy-looking below San Angelo, normally shallow, OK for floating but has many shallow areas. Access—8 rds. on this section, several small low-water dams, passes through rolling hills and semi-arid ranch and farmland, mesquite, elm, willow, peron, yucca, and cacti on sides, flows through semi-arid land. (Credit—*Texas Waterways*)

Curry Creek: Kendall Co. The wide stream channel of Curry Creek is navigable for about 1 mi. upstream, then the creek changes from a placid hollow to a series of pools and falls. Looks like E. Texas bayou with Spanish moss and palmettos. Access from Guadalupe River below Curry Creek Canoe Camp. (Credit —*Pathways and Paddleways*)

Denton Creek: Tarrant, Dallas cos. Above Lake Grapevine there are a few mi. of canoeable water with some riffles, pleasant, easy, OK beginners, best in spring. Below Lake Grapevine—from outlet to jctn. with Trinity River, 1 day, easy, some rapids first ¼ mi., Dif. II, then a few spots with riffles rest of trip, mostly smooth, some trash in lower end, some logjams, some barbed wire, little civilization much of trip, much birdlife, some wildlife, deep holes. Fishing—fair for catfish, bream, some bass, long haul to put in below dam, don't run in flood.

Devils River: Val Verde Co. in W. Tex. near Del Rio. From S.H. 163 to Amistad Res., 44 mi., width 10–10½ ft., clear and clean water, said to have enough water for floating all year but this seems doubtful. Access—no rds. except for occasional ranch rd., arid ranchland, hills, bluffs, and mesas, becomes canyonlike as river flows downstream, many Indian pictographs. Rapids—numerous and exciting, Dolan Falls (can find no one who has been on this river so don't know anything about these falls)—take care. (Credit—*Texas Waterways*)

Frio River: Uvalde Co. From Rd. 1050 to end of Garner St. Park. Put in—low-water brdg. at Rd. 1050. Take out—first low-water brdg. below St. Park or in St. Park. Trip—too much wading; beautiful, clear, cold water; best sec. in St. Park boundaries with 3 nice runs; private property and barbed-wire fences above and below park; runs in park OK for beginner training. Some fishing—small panfish. Not a good trip unless visiting park.

Garcitas Creek: From Hwy. 616 S. of Victoria near La Salle to mouth of creek, 6 mi. Put in at brdg. at Hwy. 616, there are no rds. leading to mouth of creek, necessary to canoe back up the river or canoe 2½ mi. across the flats of Lavaca Bay to rd. that goes E. to the bay from Six Mile Community on Rd. 1090. Don't cross the flats on a windy day. (Credit—Don Purinton)

Guadalupe River: Kerr, Kendall, Comal, Coldwell, Gonzales, De-Witt, and Victoria cos. From St. Hwy. 27 brdg. to Gulf Coast, 430 mi., many brdgs., several dams, popular river, flows through beautiful ctry., no detailed information on upper river above Sultenfuss Crossing, landowners very touchy, not recommended—canoeists have been shot at and hauled into court on parts of Guadalupe above Canyon Lake. Trips 1–4 best in spring and fall.

Trip 1—Sultenfuss Crossing to Bergman Crossing, 3½ mi., river drops 20 ft., reach by turning N. at Bergheim from F.M. 46, then 7 mi. to river, 11 rapids on this sec.—first 4 are Dif. I, then Dif. IV—"The Rockpile"—can be dangerous, then 4 rapids of Dif. I–III, then Dif. III–IV rapid called "Dog Leg."

Trip 2—Bergman Crossing to Spechts Crossing, 9 mi., river drops 60 ft., 2 canoe camps on this sec., 22 rapids on this stretch, mostly Dif. I–III, 1 rapid of Class IV.

Trip 3—Spechts Crossing (Silver Spring Crossing) to Ranch Rd. 311, 5½ mi., river drops 32 ft., 11 rapids, mostly Dif. I–III, 1 Dif. IV with waterfall near right bank—this is about 50 yds. below U.S. 281 Brdg.; go to left of small cypress tree to miss waterfall.

Trip 4—Ranch Rd. 311 Crossing to Rebecca Creek Crossing, 4.5 mi., river drops 31 ft., 11 rapids, 3 are Dif. IV–V. DANGER—Mueller Falls and Rust Falls, Rebecca Creek Crossing above last rapids before deadwater of Canyon Res., reach from N. off U.S. 281 or from S. off F.M. 46 onto Ranch Rd. 311; parking space here.

Trip 5—Canyon Dam to New Braunfels, 22 mi., very good trip, several ptgs. at low-water dams, for experts only in high water—above 600 cfs., several rapids—some dangerous. DANGER—rapids below Bear Creek, these are Dif. V. DANGER—rapids below Waco Springs, these are Dif. V. DANGER—Gruene Crossing in high water, no passage under brdg., ptg. instead, take out at Cypress Bend Park.

Trip 6—New Braunfels to Gonzales, no information, not generally considered a good stretch, dams on this stretch.

Trip 7—Gonzales to Hockheim, 38 mi., 3–4 days, scenic, no particular danger, no rapids, some wading, fair fishing, camping in Gonzales City Park, good campsites along way—on private land, no access pts. on this stretch, OK for beginners. Take out at 183 brdg. N.W. of Hockheim.

Trip 8—Hockheim to Hwy. 87, no data.

Trip 9—Hwy. 87 to Thomaston Crossing, 24 mi., 2–3 days, sandbars, few small rapids, private land along both sides, many long, quiet pools.

Trip 10—Thomaston Crossing to Victoria Hwy. 59, 27 mi., 2–3 days, 1 serious rapid about 9–10 mi. after put-in—ptg. or line, can be run but dangerous, a few riffles beyond this, later on channel becomes tricky, stay to left, headwinds, sandbars for camping.

Trip 11—Victoria to Seadrift, 129 mi. Don't canoe below Victoria, many logjams, power-generating plant makes water poor for canoeing. From Victoria Park to Swinging Brdg., 66 mi.; from Swinging Brdg. to Tivoli Brdg., 45 mi.; from Tivoli Brdg. to Seadrift, 18 mi.

(Credits—*Texas Rivers and Rapids,* Vols. I and II; *Pathways and Paddleways; Texas Waterways*)

Keechi Creek—Lower: Houston, Leon cos. Canoeable upstream some distance from jctn. with Trinity; no other information.

La Vaca and Navidad rivers: From Hwy. 59 near Edna to Hwy. 616 where rivers join together. Many farm rds. cross these rivers, no stretch more than 7 mi. (Credit—Don Purinton)

Lampasas River: Lampasas, Burnet, and Bell cos. in central Tex. near Temple.

Trip 1—Kempner to Youngsport, 34 mi., width 30–40 ft., flows over limestone, sand, and gravel. Access—U.S. 190 at Kempner and 6 farm rds., divides river into secs. of 1–12 mi., 4 small towns along banks, high, steep-banked, small picturesque bluffs, tree-lined banks, very scenic, many rapids when river is on a rise, normally has low flow of water, some wading. Stillhouse Hollow Res. located immediately below Youngsport.

Trip 2—Stillhouse Hollow Dam to Little River, 17½ mi., width 30–40 ft., depends upon flow from Res. for good canoeing, releases of 200–300 cfs. necessary. Access S.Y. 35 and 5 farm rds. cross this sec., divides river into secs. of ½ to 4 mi., some wading. Trespassing can be a problem on both secs. of this river; heavy vegetation in lower end. (Credit— *Texas Waterways* and Roy Douglas)

Leon River: Coryell Co. in E. central Tex. near Waco. From Gatesville to Lake Belton, 46 mi., slow-moving river, muddy banks, normally sufficient water for floating. Access—7 rds. cross river in this sec., small scenic river, particularly scenic around Mother Neff St. Park; thickly vegetated banks, some wading. (Credit—*Texas Waterways* and *Texas Rivers and Rapids*)

Little River: Bell, Milam cos. in E. central Tex. From town of Little River to Gause, 102 mi., muddy-looking water, slow-flowing, width 30–50 ft., deep water in river. Access—12 rds. cross this sec., longest distance between rds. is 23 mi., muddy and steep banks, flows through flat terrain and rolling hills, Sugarloaf Mt. is landmark on lower portion. Catfish, bass, and bream. Not all rds. make good access pts.—some are on private land; check with *Texas Rivers and Rapids.* (Credit—*Texas Waterways* and *Texas Rivers and Rapids*)

Llano River: Kimble, Mason, Llano cos. in central Tex. From Junction to Lake LBJ, 104 mi., width 30–300 ft. fed by springs, flows over limestone, when is on rise there are dangerous rapids, has sufficient water for float at all times, very shallow in spots. Access—13 rds. cross, distances between rds. 3–19 mi. picturesque cliffs, very scenic, can be dangerous in lower portions, large boulders in lower area.

Long King Creek: USGS Blanchard, Camilla, Livingston; Polk and San Jacinto cos.; canoeable with normal precipitation, canoe up from Trinity, no other data. Probably can canoe down from Rd. 1988 near Goodrich.

Medina River: Bandera Co. in S. central Tex. From city of Medina to Lake Medina, 28 mi., width 30–40 ft., clear and clean water, spring-fed river, low during dry weather, usually has enough water for float trips. Access—6 rds. cross from Medina to Bandera but only 1 from Bandera to Lake Medina. Free-flowing stream above Lake Medina, small dam at Bandera City Park, cedar and live oak-covered hills, very scenic, no dangerous rapids between Bandera to Medina, some wading in spots. Don't run in high water—the river has white water, good fishing, some rapids below Bandera, dangerous when river is high, otherwise OK, much posted land. (Credit—*Texas Waterways* and *Texas Rivers and Rapids*)

Neches River—Sec. A: Anderson Co.; "Douglas Run." Blackburn Crossing Dam to Channel Dam, 30 mi. Blackburn Crossing Dam to St. Hwy. 175, 4 mi., 4 hrs., some brush, good flow, 1 long slough with very little current, no particular dangers. St. Hwy. 175 to a wooden brdg., Carry Lake Crossing, 9 hrs., some brush, no particular dangers. Carry Lake Crossing Brdg. to St. Hwy. 79, 6 hrs., very brushy in places. St. Hwy. 179 to Channel Dam, 7 mi., 4 hrs., access via entry rd. on W. bank, very brushy in low and high water. Ptg.—Channel Dam or run in high water. (Credit— Roy Douglas)

Neches River—Sec. B: Jasper Co. McGee Bend 15-ft. quad. From Quarry at end of rd. going W. off U.S. 69, turn right 1 mi. N. of Neches River Brdg. to Bouton Lake Cmpgrnd. (Angelina Natl. For.), 17 mi., 7 hrs., easy trip, much still water. Obstacles— waterfalls 4 ft. high approx. 4 mi. down from Hwy. 69 brdg. (at low water), old brdg. and pipeline 2 mi. down from waterfall, many mosquitoes, large rocks when river cuts ledges in banks, 1 ptg.—river to Bouton Lake (1,200 ft.), sandy silt and gravel bottom, very little pollution. Campsites—Bouton Lake, white sandbars and beaches halfway (at low water), heavy seasonal fluctuations. Other access pts.—Ft. Teran Rd. below brdg., Quarry, Gaging Sta., thick forests on sides, some high bluffs. History— Fort Teran. Fishing—bass in clearer water and in Bouton Lake. Rapids—below Ft. Teran (could be bad in high water), below quarry (small), below old brdg. pilings (small). DANGER—old brdg. pilings and waterfalls. Other distances—18 mi. from Ft.

Teran to Bouton Lake Cmpgrnd.; 7½ mi. from Gaging Sta. to Bouton Lake Cmpgrnd. This run would be interesting *only* during low-water conditions. (Credit—John and Amye Kelsey)

Paluxy River: Hood and Sommerville cos., map No. 112 by Tex. St. Hwy. Dept., Planning Div., Austin, Tex. Paluxy, Tex., to Brazos River, 23 mi., 1 day. Put-in—brdg. at Farm Rd. 204 outside Paluxi, Tex. (at E. edge of Tolar turn left on Farm Rd. 201, go 5 mi. to Farm Rd. 204, turn right, then 4 mi. to river), OK for canoeing in spring or after rain, must be 25 ft. wide below brdg. for OK canoeing. Alt. put-in—Hwy. 205 brdg., take old Hwy. 205 near ranch-style home to low-water brdg.; if water covers drain pipes in center of brdg., canoeing should be OK. If water is over low-water brdg., trip can be dangerous. Trip—first 6 mi. below Paluxi easy paddling, some sand and gravel bars, picturesque and remote; beyond dump by pecan tree are easy riffs and shoals, good campsites. River passes Girl Scout camp with mild rapids in area. Girl Scout camp is halfway to low-water brdg. at Hwy. 205; below Girl Scout camp river is challenging with many ledges; 1 mi. below Girl Scout camp to Lanham Mill Ford; 1 mi. below Lanham Mill Ford to Dinosaur Valley, look for huge prints in rocks; from Dinosaur Park to Hwy. 205, several rapids, can be run with sufficient water; below Hwy. 205, interesting scenery, small canyon and bluffs. Use Hwy. 67 as access in emergency only. DANGER—barbed-wire fences across river ½ mi. below Hwy. 67, can take out at Glen Rose City Park or continue on to Brazos. Take-out—turn up Brazos River 1 mi. to Rainbow Brdg. or go 7 mi. downstream on Brazos to Scanlon's Camp (fee charged). (Credit—Hans Weichsel)

Pecos River: Pecos, Crockett, Terrell, and Val Verde cos.; USGS Sonora and Del Rio. From Sheffield to U.S. Hwy. 90 to brdg., 115 mi.

> *Trip 1*—from Sheffield to F.M. 1865 near Pandale, 55–60 mi., no access rds., first 20 mi. shallow. After Independence Creek enters the river there should be adequate water, some wading in this sec., desert scenery, no particular dangers.
> *Trip 2*—from F.M. 1865 to U.S. Hwy. 90, 60 mi., cliffs on

either side get larger as stream goes S., good campsites, wilderness trip, 4–6 days, beautiful, best time from Oct. to Mar., combination of low water with lots of wading to very fast white water with rapids, no access. Only way out is downriver or walking across desert. DANGER—flash floods, rapids in canyons; rapids become increasingly more dangerous downstream. Indian pictographs in canyons. Take out—old U.S. 90. This trip for experts only.
(Credit—M. M. Harman, *Texas Rivers and Rapids,* and *Texas Waterways*)

Pedernales River: Blanco, Hays, and Travis cos. in central Tex.
Trip 1—Johnson City to Pedernales St. Park, 12–17 mi., kayaks only, shallow, rocky, waterfalls in St. Park.
Trip 2—Pedernales about 3 mi. above Hwy. 71, beautiful scenery, many rapids. DANGER—rapid ½ mi. above 962 crossing, can be strenuous trip. Take-out—fishing camp below Hwy. 71 brdg.; unpolluted river.
(Credit—*Texas Rivers and Rapids* and *Texas Waterways*) .

Pine Island Bayou: Hardin and Jefferson cos. in E. Tex. From F.M. 770 crossing to Neches River, 54 mi. Access pts.—5 rds. that divide river into segments ranging from 6 mi. to 21 mi., river about 30 ft. wide, murky-looking water, heavily forested, good flow of water except in dry periods, no dams, flows through heart of Big Thicket, area is swamplike, many cypress trees, many endangered species of plants in area, extremely scenic. (Credit—*Texas Waterways*)

Rio Grande River: Presidio to Langtry; beautiful, great, Colo. Canyon, 2 days. Start—the Anvil or Davit Rocks, 24 mi., W. of Lajitas Hwy. 170. End—Lajitas (don't miss; no other pt. till past Santa Elena Canyon); many rapids, swift, ideal trip. Santa Elena Canyon, toughest trip in Big Bend Nat. Park experts only, high water, intermed. low or normal water. Start—Lajitas Trading Post, 2 days, ¾ mi. to main river, 11 mi. to canyon entrance, rapids to entrance, in canyon cross currents, hidden rocks, undercut walls, strong current. DANGER—rockslide, suck holes, blind

alleys, huge blders. Ptg. or line rockslide, Tex. side; below Santa
Elena, narrow mostly smooth. End—Terlingua Creek jctn. Maris-
cal Canyon, 1–2 days. Start—Ponterra or Talley Ranch, few
minor rapids before canyon; canyon deep and narrow; 2 dif. spots
in canyon—rockslide (go left side) and "Old Swimming Hole"—
line in high water. End—Solis gravel bar. San Vincente and Hot
Springs Canyon, 1 day; tame, 2 rapids only. Start—Solis Ranch.
End—Tex. to Boquillas, Mexico, ford. Boquillas Canyon, 2 days,
OK for novice, no bad rapids, no danger spots. Start—Tex. to
Boquilla, Mexico, ford. End—cable footbrdg. at U. J. Adams
Ranch-Stillwell crossing. Rugged lower canyons, 5 days–1 wk.,
wilderness, many tough rapids, some ptgs.; ¾ of trip continuous
canyon, swift. Start—Adams Ranch at Stillwell crossing. End—
Langtry. Emergency exit—signal border patrol plane with mirror.
(Credit—Bob Burleson)

Sabine River: Wood, Upshur, Gregg, Harrison, Panola cos.;
Mineola to Toledo Bend Res. Mineolas to Crow, 11 hwy. mi., no
particular hazards, some old wooden and concrete brdgs., wooded
banks; Crow to Gladwater brdg., ? dist., wooded, no oil derricks
and platforms in water, very little civilization, interesting sec.
Longview-Kilgore Hwy. 259 to new I 20 to Hwy. 149 brdg., several mi. (5 plus), ranch entry. Hwy. 149 to Hwy. 43 brdg.
HAZARDS—massive rock crossing (short shoals—run with caution), Rocky Ford (5-ft. falls in low water—don't run), Watson
Shoals (large steel cables cross river before shoals), white sandbars, wooded banks, much small game. Hwy. 43 brdg. to head of
Toledo Bend, ? mi. Black Shoals below brdg. run. Toledo Bend is
huge lake—ptg. or check with Sabine River Authority. Below
Toledo Bend—navigable to mouth.

San Antonio River: Originates in city of San Antonio, several
flood-control dams in Bexar Co. and in city, low stream flow in
upper reaches; logjams and sandbars in Wilson, Karnes, Goliad,
Refugio cos.

San Bernard River: Wharton, Fort Bend, and Brazoria cos. in
S.E. Tex. From F.M. 442 to Church Hill Brdg., 48 mi., 30–100

ft. in width, sandy-color water, normally shallow in extreme upper sec., flow gets heavier nearer gulf. Access—8 rds. cross river, 1–17 mi. between access pts., banks heavily vegetated, 1 low-water dam between F.M. 1301 and St. Hwy. 35, no other dams, scenic flat to gently rolling hills, many springs along rivers, site of hand-operated Hinkle's Ferry along this sec., relatively under-developed. (Credit—*Texas Waterways*)

San Gabriel River: Williamson, Milam cos. in E. central Tex. From Georgetown to Little River, 78½ mi. Access pts.—11 roads, longest stream sec. between is 12 mi., 30–40 ft. in width, murky-looking water, flows through Circleville and Laneport after Georgetown, flows through farm and dairy ctry.; 1 dam in George-town, no dams below. Banks of river heavily vegetated, some outcroppings of limestone in parts, some small rapids and fast water, usually sufficient water for floating. (Credit—*Texas Waterways*)

San Marcos River: San Marcos to jctn. with Guadalupe, 90 mi.; 7 dams, many logjams between Luling and Gonzales, low-water brdgs. Rapids but not great white water. Start to Martindale Dam, 21 mi. Martindale to Staples Dam, 12 mi. Staples to Fentress Brdg., 12 mi. Fentress Brdg. to Luling Hwy. 90, 23 mi. Luling Hwy. 90 to Luling Dam, 9 mi. Luling Dam to Palmetta Park, 20 mi. Palmetta Park to Gonzales 90A brdg., 21 mi. Popular float stream, particularly in spring. Access pts. controlled; check with hwy. patrol for legal access pts.

Sulphur River: Canoeable over most of its length, many rd. cross-ings for access, no other information. (Credit—Don Purinton)

Trinity River:
> *Trip 1*—In Dallas—From Hwy. 75 to Mallory Brdg. Rd., 21½ mi.; from Hwy. 75 to S. Loop 12, 3 mi., lies within city limits, surprising amount of wildlife, city development hidden by trees, polluted water, don't swim or fish; from S. Loop 12 to Dowdy Ferry Rd., 9½ mi., winds through nice flood-plain for.; from Dowdy Ferry Rd. to Belt Line Rd., 5 mi., about

same as previous stretch; from Belt Line Rd. to Mallory Brdg. Rd., 4 mi.; 2 nice wooded elbows in this stretch.

Trip 2—From Mallory Brdg. Rd. to Hwy. 34, 23 mi. Distance from put-in to old Navigation Lock, 2½ mi. (ptg. here), to nice wooded area on right 5.8 mi., to Parson's slough on left 11½ mi., to Old Navigation Lock (ptg. here) 13½ mi.; to E. Fork of Trinity on left, 14½ mi.; to Red Oak Creek on right, 17½ mi.; to Old Navigation Lock and abandoned RR grade (ptg. here), 21 mi.

Trip 3—From Hwy. 34 to Hwy. 85, 19 mi.; several med.-sized for. areas on right side.

Trip 4—From Hwy. 85 to Trinidad (Hwy. 31), 38 mi.; the last 11 mi. of this trip can be used as separate trip or cutoff to make trip only 27 mi. To reach access go N. out of Trinidad on 274 to Cedar Creek Res. overflow ditch, turn around, and go back S. and take first rd. to right—this is a co. rd. and passes within 50 ft. of steep riverbank, private property, no camping, many springs along this stretch, good catfishing, big gar, many birds.

Trip 5—From Hwy. 31 to Hwy. 287 will be partially flooded by Tenn. Colony Dam, 18 mi., can divide into 2 trips since Cedar Creek dumps into Trinity 7 mi. downstream from Hwy. 31. Access to Cedar Creek from Hwy. 1677 S. of Trinidad access is 1½ mi.

Trip 6—From Hwy. 287 to Catfish Creek, 35 mi. Tenn. dam will cover this; this is a beautiful sec.

Trip 7—From Catfish Creek to Hwy. 79, 26 mi.

Trip 8—From Hwy. 79 to Hwy. 7, 50 mi. Access pts.—5 mi. downstream of Hwy. 79 from co. rd. going E. out of Oakwood; all other accesses on private land, can find by asking along Hwy. 592 on W. side of river or Hwy. 227 on E. side out of Copeland.

Trip 9—From Hwy. 7 to Hwy. 21, 33 mi. Several side creeks and canyons worth exploring. Accesses to break this trip up can be found by asking along Hwy. 811 or Hwy. 132. Can canoe up Boggy Creek, which is 8 mi. above Hwy. 21. Lower Keechi Creek also canoeable for some distance upstream; several creeks below Boggy Creek have canyons at mouths.

Falls Canyon is at mouth of small creek 5 mi. above Hwy. 21.

Trip 10—From Hwy. 21 to Lake Livingston, no data.

Trip 11—From Lake Livingston to Hwy. 59, 10 mi., 3 hrs., USGS Blanchard, Camilla and Livingston; Polk and San Jacinto cos. Put in either side of river below dam, OK beginners, good fishing, particularly in spring, good campsites but on private land, no particular hazards or rapids, can canoe up Long King Creek, take out on right side up steep bank near hwy. brdg.

Trip 12—USGS Livingston and Rayburn; Polk, Liberty, and San Jacinto cos. From Hwy. 59 to Hwy. 105, 22 mi., 1–2 days; 2 access pts. near Taylor Lake and Horseshoe Lakes Development; scenery ranges from farmland and for. at first to beautiful hardwood fors., headwinds common, sandbars, no particular dangers, no rapids. Take out either side.

Trip 13—From Hwy. 105 to Hwy. 162, 19 mi., 1 day; USGS Rayburn; Liberty Co. Vacation Homes along river, campsites at both ends, chain of lakes near with good fishing in the sandbars in river, no particular dangers, no rapids. Take out right side.

Trip 14—From Hwy. 162 to Liberty, 30 mi., USGS Rayburn and Liberty; Liberty Co.; 1½ days, no rapids, no particular dangers, sandbars, private land both sides, scenic, small lakes along side have wildlife and fishing, Tanner Bayou worth exploring.

Trip 15—From Hwy. 90 to I 10, 27 mi. USGS Liberty, Moss Bluff, Shiloh, Anhuac, Cove; Liberty and Chambers cos. Coastal marshes begin 15 mi. below Liberty, much wildlife, threatened by Wallisville Res., sandbars in parts. Take out on left above large shell and sand dumps, is at W. end of Miller St. in Anhuac.

(Credit—Don Purinton, *Texas Rivers and Rapids,* and *Texas Waterways*)

Trinity River—Clear Fork: Parker, Tarrant, Dallas cos. From Aledo to jctn. with Elm Fork, 3–4 days.

Trip 1—Aledo to blacktop rd. crossing on rd. that goes to

Hwy. 377, 6–7 mi., 3 hrs. Access—cross RR tracks in Aledo, turn right 1 mi. on blacktop rd. to Clear Fork, put in N.W. side of brdg. at small sandbar. Obstacles—1 fence ¼ mi. downstream, a few large fallen trees, several steel channel beams 1–2 ft. above water below low-water brdg. (watch out in high water). Best canoeing when water is between first and second yellow stripes on rock at put-in, cold stream, 18–25 ft. wide, depth varies from ins. to 4 ft., steady current, steep banks, sand and gravel bottom, winding channel, very little litter, no pollution, beautiful stream, OK for novice, no good campsites.

Trip 2—from blacktop rd. crossing on rd. that goes to Hwy. 377 to headwaters of Lake Benbrook, 8 mi. Take-out pt. is 200 yds. S. of Hwy. 377 brdg.

Trip 3—Lake Benbrook to Hwy. 360, canoeable, some obstacles that require ptgs., dangerous in high water, not too much pollution, about 40 mi.

Trip 4—Hwy. 360 to Belt Line Rd. in Irving, easy ½ day, OK beginners, some easy rapids, some possible obstacles, pleasant trip until sewage plant for Grand Prairie, many snakes.

Trip 5—Hwy. 360 to jctn. with Elm Fork, 1 day, not recommended, not dangerous but not scenic nor much fun, channel confusing in W. Dallas.

(Credit—Hans Weichsel)

Trinity River—E. Fork: Rockwell, Kaufman, and Dallas cos. From Hwy. I 20 to jctn. at Hwy. 34, 38 mi., can break into two trips: from Hwy. I 20 to Hwy. 175, 15 mi.; from Hwy. 175 to Hwy. 34, 23 mi. Wooded, some logjams and overhang.

Trinity River—Elm Fork: Dallas Co. From Garza Little Dam to jctn. with Clear Fork, 2–3 days.

Trip 1—Garza Little Dam to Sandy Lake Rd., 1 day, 11 mi., put into well below dam outflow. DANGER—near outflow, 1 mi., some small rapids; open, prairielike ctry. at first, nice runs at first, then river changes at RR crossing—1 rapid here, becomes wooded on both sides after RR crossing. DANGER—

dam at Sandy Lake Rd.; dam is under rd., take out well above dam and ptg.

Trip 2—Sandy Lake Rd. to Wildwood Dr. (Tom Braniff Dr.) near Elm Fork Nature Trail and Univ. of Dallas, 1 day, 12 mi., 1 small rapid at RR crossing above Belt Line Rd. DANGER—Dam near California Crossing, don't run— LIVES HAVE BEEN LOST HERE, can take out at brdg., after 1 at California Crossing. Bass, catfish, and bream on Trips 1 and 2, not much pollution.

Trip 3—Wildwood Drive (Tom Braniff Dr.) to jctn. with Clear Fork, 12 mi. DANGER—don't take it—dam about 1 mi. below Loop 12 brdg., LIVES HAVE BEEN LOST HERE, water OK between brdg. at Wildwood Dr. and dam; pretty, fair fishing, below dam the river is lousy, often too low, junk cars in stream, no scenic value, a real loser.

(Credit—*Texas Rivers and Rapids* and personal experience)

White Rock Creek: Dallas Co., below Loop 12 Crossing, 2 mi., round trip, shaded and quiet canoeing with sufficient water, don't run in flood stage. (Credit—Don Purinton)

UTAH

Big Bear River: Northern Ut., no rapids, good scenery, easy going, ends at bird refuge near Brigham City. (Credit—Max Gardner)

Green River: Daggett Co.

Trail 1—Red Canyon Dam to Red Creek, 12 mi., frigid water, levels change rapidly, excel. fishing—rainbow, brown, native cutthroat; gen. safe. DANGER—Red Creek rapid in lower end of canyon. Dam to Little Hole Cmpgrnd., 7 mi. Little Hole to Brown's Park, 9 mi. Brown's Park—long, mt.-rimmed valley, slow, peaceful. Canyon of Din. Natl. Mon. rough, dangerous, guide necessary, poor fishing.

Trail 2—Emery, Wayne cos. maps—USGS "Canyonlands Natl. Park and Vicinity, Ut." From Green River, Ut., to confluence with Col. River. Distance—117½ mi., 9 days. Put-in—St. Park in Green River, Ut. Take-out—there are no rds. to take out, arrange for motorboat pickup for 70 mi. return trip upstream to Moab, can make arrangements with Tex. Tours, Inc., of Moab; approx. cost—$32 per person plus $25 for boat and gear. Calm water entire trip, no major obstacles or ptgs., windy in canyons, don't drink untreated water, many good campsites, spectacular, canyons up to 1,200 ft. deep, Indian Rivers, petroglyphs, old uranium prospects. Fishing—good for catfish, best climate in spring and fall.
(Credit—Stuart Smith)

Gunnison River: Southern Ut., short stretches only, mostly easy, but also many rocky stretches that should be avoided. Good fishing. (Credit—Max Gardner)

Provo River: Starts in High Uintah Mts., ends at Ut. Lake near Provo, several exciting stretches, some easy floating, one of top fishing streams in st., excellent scenery. (Credit—Max Gardner)

Weber River: Near Morgan, lively at spots upstream, rocky and dangerous in canyons above Ogden. (Credit—Max Gardner)

VERMONT

NOTE: It is strongly recommended that you purchase and consult the *AMC New England Canoeing Guide* for further information.

A special word of thanks to Stewart Coffin, who generously shared his notes with me. These were collected over many years by a great canoeist.

Black River: *Section A*—USGS sheets—Irasburg, Memphremagog (northern Vt).

Trip 1—Craftsbury to Irasburg, 15 mi., high water only, narrow, winding brook, slow going.

Trip 2—Irasburg to Rte. 14 brdg., 3½ mi. Put-in—below Irasburg where river goes N. away from hwy., 1 mi. to covered brdg. Ptg.—barbed-wire fence near covered brdg., then easy rapids—Dif. II, too low in summer. Below Rte. 14 brdg., not recommended, mostly smooth water. DANGER—2 falls (first at Stony Brook and second in deep ravine near Coventry Center), 6 mi. of dead water below last brdg. to S. Bay, last 6 mi. OK for canoeing.

(Credit—Stewart Coffin)

Section B—USGS sheets—Ludlow, Claremont (southern Vt.).

Trip 1—Above Whitesville, pleasant, several ptgs. around dams. Put-in—one of Plymouth Lakes, short ptgs. between lakes; from reservoir to Cavendish Gorge, mostly placid, good current, riffles, dam at each town, water polluted. Ptg.—hydroelectric sta. at Cavendish Gorge—left side, river steeper below gorge, low dam at Whitesville.

Trip 2—Whitesville to Downers, 6 mi., steep river below Whitesville, 3 mi. to heavy rapids—Dif. III, worst pt.—1½ mi. below left turn—old brdg. abutment here. Ptg.—this pt. in high water, rapids continue heavy for 2 mi. to Downers, run in late Apr. Take-out—covered brdg. or continue ½ mi. to gravel pit on left.

Trip 3—Downers to Springfield, 10 mi., strong current at first. Ptg.—Perkinsville Dam—right side, ¼ mi. below to chute—can be run. From N. Springfield to Springfield—6 dams.

(Credit—Stewart Coffin)

Clyde River: USGS sheets—Is. Pond, Memphremagog; from Is. Pond to Lake Memphremagog. Put-in—2 mi. below vil. of Is. Pond near jctn. with Osegatchie Brook, 16 mi. to Pensioner Pond. Below Pensioner Pond, ½ mi. slow water, power dam, impossible gorge, and short pond to W. Charleston, then another dam, impassable drops through W. Charleston. Ptg.—1½ mi. by rd. around both dams; below W. Charleston, ½ mi. mod. rapids, then good current ½ mi., then 1 mi. slack water to Salem Pond (Salem Pond 2 mi. long); Salem Pond to Clyde Pond, 3 mi rapids with attractive cedar banks. Ptg.—1 small dam ⅔ mi. below Rte. 105 brdg. in Derby; Clyde Pond to Newport, 2 mi., impassable or unattractive, don't run this part. (Credit—Stewart Coffin)

Connecticut River: See description under New Hampshire.

Deerfield River: USGS sheets—Wilmington, Rowe, Plainfield, Ashfield, Heath, Shelburne Falls, Greenfield. Not canoeable above No. 5 Powerhouse. From No. 5 Powerhouse to Conn. River, 40 mi. Powerhouse is below rd. in W. side of river 2 mi. below Monroe Brdg. From below powerhouse to sharp bend at Hoosac Tunnel Sta.—rapids—Dif. IV, DANGER—LIVES HAVE BEEN LOST HERE. Below sta. river flattens but with strong current. DANGER—steep drop, can be run with care, then minor rapids and good current to Charlemont. Charlemont to Conn. River, 28 mi., 4 power dams through Shelburne Falls, some good canoeing below last dam. (Credit—Stewart Coffin)

Dog River: USGS sheets—Barre. Riverton to Montpelier, 10 mi, white water in spring runoff, mod. rapids, Dif. II, no ptgs., sand and rock bottom.

E. Creek: Listed as a canoe trail by the Vt. Dev. Dept.

Green River: USGS sheets—Brattleboro, Colrain, Greenfield. Green River to Water Supply Dam, 14 mi. Green River to W. Leyden, 7 mi. Put-in—below mill dam, usually can run all rapids in first few mi.; inspect before running, run in high water, small river, steep, many ledges, tough—near E. slope of Pulpet Mt. Ptg. —sawmill dam at Stewartville; W. Leyden to Water Supply Dam, 7 mi., best part from W. Leyden to next brdg., continuous rapids, not tough, deep pools, beautiful. Ptg. left—Greenfield water supply dam; last 6 mi. to Greenfield, few rapids, less interesting, flat farm country. (Credit—Stewart Coffin)

Lamoille River: USGS sheets—Lyndonville, Hardwick, Hyde Park, Mt. Mansfield, Milton; Hardwick to Lake Champlain, 74 mi.

Trip 1—Hardwick to Hyde Park, 19 mi. Put-in—Jackson Brdg. 1 mi. W. of Hardwick—below Hardwick Lake Dam mostly farm ctry., good current, some rapids, spring best time. After 5 mi. ptg.—Pottersville Dam, then 10 mi. to dams and millponds in Morrisville—ptg. by car. Put in again below Cadys Falls.

Trip 2—Hyde Park to Fairfax Falls, 34 mi., popular canoeing sec., mostly smooth, good current, 8 mi. to pair of falls—ptg. or line to left, good scenery, good picnic sites, Ithiel Falls—4 mi. below Johnson (most obstructions removed), then river slows and winds 9 mi. to Jeffersonville. Take-out—at brdg.

Trip 3—Fairfax Falls to Lake Champlain, 21 mi., some rapids first 7 mi. to E. Georgia, then 4 mi. deadwater to 2 dams in Milton. Ptg.—dam 3 mi. below Milton, then smooth water to the lake.

(Credit—Stewart Coffin)

Mad River: USGS sheets—Lincoln Mt., Waterbury, Montpelier. Spring run, white water, clear water, rocky bed, run before mid-May. From Waitsfield to dam, 1 day. Put-in—Waitsfield or several mi. above with sufficient water. Rapids—Dif. III to Moretown. Ptg.—Moretown Falls—take out for ptg. at Rte. 107 brdg. above Moretown—1-mi. ptg. to foot of falls, then 4 mi. white water to dam backwater. Take-out—before dam; remaining 3 mi. to jctn. not recommended. (Credit—Stewart Coffin)

Missisquoi River: Listed as a canoe trail by the Vt. Dev. Dept.

Moose River: USGS sheets—Burke, St. Littleton. Gallop Mills to St. Johnsburg, 29 mi.

Trip 1—Gallop Mills to Victory, 11 mi. Tiny rocky stream at Gallop Mills—run in high-water area to brdg., is steep, several unrunnable spots, then 7 mi. slow, twisty, then rapids Dif. III 1 mi. above Victory at old brdg.

Trip 2—Victory to St. Johnsburg, 18 mi. Medium rapids

through Victory, then tough rapids near brdg. above N. Concord, then swift current and medium rapids, 1 bad drop under RR brdg. in E. St. Johnsburg—don't run, lower part not a good canoe run. Take-out—above bad drops in St. Johnsburg.
(Credit—Stewart Coffin)

Ompompanoosuc River: USGS sheets—Strafford, Mt. Cube; W. Farilee to Union Vil. 13 mi., challenging rapids all the way, can't run in spots. Ptg.—170-ft. dam above Union Vil.; experts only.
(Credit—Stewart Coffin)

Ottauquechee River: USGS sheets—Rutland, Woodstock, Hanover. From dam at W. Bridgewater to Bridgewater, 9 mi., all easy rapids, first 5 mi. prettiest; above W. Bridgewater too steep for canoeing. (Credit—Stewart Coffin)

Otter Creek: USGS sheets—Wallingford, Rutland, Castleton, Brandon, Middlebury, Port Henry. From S. Wallingford to Lake Champlain, 93 mi., 5–6 days, OK for beginner.
Trip 1—From put-in to Proctor, put in at right bank below True Temper Tool Co., dam at S. Wallingford, at first small stream, good current, sharp bends, shallow riffles, polluted at Rutland. Ptg. the dam at Rutland—30 yds. left, trip unattractive from Rutland to Proctor, current sluggish. Ptg. dam at Rutland Center—approach with caution and ptg. right, ptg. to Proctor.
Trip 2—Proctor to Brandon, beautiful ctry., nice mts., no dams or dangers.
Trip 3—Brandon to Middlebury, good current, river wanders, clear water, sandy bottom, ptg. Middlebury dam. Take out ahead of retaining walls, keep right, then left across brdg. and right again on other side down between buildings ¼ mi. to launching pt.
Trip 4—Middlebury to Weybridge, 4 dams with carries at 1 mi. below town, at Beldens, at 1½ mi. below mouth of New Haven River, and last at Weybridge, rapids below lock—can run at one water level, most dangerous rapid below Beldens, a gorge is here; this sec. best part of river.

Trip 5—Weybridge to Lake Champlain, first 2 mi. slow current, ctry. flat. Ptg.—Vergennes Dam—take out left, cross street and down rd. to river, Dead water after Vergennes to Lake Champlain, much shipping.
(Credit—Stewart Coffin)

Paul Stream: Not recommended; too steep to canoe.

Saxtons River: USGS sheets—Saxtons River, Bellows Falls. Nice white-water run, run Apr., fast drop between Grafton and Saxtons River Vil. Valley small and for., scenic. From Grafton to upper dam at Gageville, 11 mi. Put in at forks, many rocks in river, just below brdg., 3 mi. from start is bad part, at Cambridgeport river broadens, not so steep, rapids still good 1 mi. below Cambridgeport to covered brdg., then 1 mi. to unrunnable spot, take out ½ mi. above Saxtons River Vil. 2 dams at Saxtons River Vil., river slows down at Barber Park; 3 dams in Gageville. Pull out at right of brdg., above upper one; river drops 150 ft. in last 1½ mi.
(Credit—Stewart Coffin)

Trout River: USGS sheets—Jay Peak; tributary of Missisquoi River. Run in high water only. From Montgomery Center to E. Berkshire, 12 mi., mostly easy, shallow gravel rapids. Rte. 118 follows on right, mountainous, quick runoff, not very attractive, few trees. (Credit—Stewart Coffin)

Waits River: USGS sheets—E. Barre, Woodsville, Mt. Cube. From Waits River P.O. to Bradford, 14 mi., 1 day, high water, usually until late May, Dif. III, don't run in flood stage, narrow valley, mixture for. and pasture, clear water, rocky. Take-out pt. at Rte. 25 brdg. (Credit—Stewart Coffin)

West River: USGS sheets—Londonderry, Saxtons River, and Brattleboro: Can run from Londonderry but in high water only. CAUTION—heavy pitches. From S. Londonderry to Brattleboro, 36 mi.
Trip 1—S. Londonderry to Jamaica, 9 mi., white water, run in spring, continuous rapids, first mi. easy, then it gets tougher. Ptg.—dam at Ball Mountain. DANGER—1 mi.

above Jamaica, "The Dumplings"—don't run "Dumplings" in high water.

Trip 2—Jamaica to Brattleboro, 27 mi., river widens, less dif., OK into late spring. Ptg.—dam above Townshend. Ptg. dams in Townshend and Dummerston. CAUTION—chute near granite works on Black Mt., near Brattleboro, river is flat.

(Credit—Stewart Coffin)

White River: Listed as a canoe trail by the Vt. Dev. Dept.

Winhall River: USGS sheets—Londonderry. Don't run above Rawsonville; below Rawsonville, steep, rocky; from Rawsonville to W. River, 2½ mi., white water, not for beginners, very dif. (Credit—Stewart Coffin)

Winooski River: USGS sheets—Plainfield, Barre, Montpelier, Camels Hump, Burlington, Milton, and Plattsburg. From last brdg. in Montpelier to Lake Champlain; run in high water only above Plainfield, many small dams, easy ptgs., current good through Plainfield and E. Montpelier, some good rapids, below Montpelier polluted but runnable all summer. Ptg.—dam at Middlesex. Ptg.—Bolton Falls Dam 4 mi. below Waterbury. DANGER—river is in narrow gorge at Bolton Falls, ptg. right. Ptg.—dams at Essex Jctn. and Winooski, then flat water to Lake Champlain. (Credit—Stewart Coffin)

VIRGINIA

Appomattox River: Upriver from Hopewell; good canoeing.

Back Creek: Bath Co.; Rte. 600 brdg., above Mt. Grave to Rte. 603 brdg., 10 mi., 3–4 hrs., great white water until June, beautiful, small river, exciting rapids, may be dammed by Corps of Engineers; 3 ledges, experienced only. Trout, small-mouth bass.

Big Totuskey: Richmond Co. Below Warsaw on N. Neck Hwy., tidal creek. Variety of fish.

Big Walker Creek: USGS—Va., Radford, and Pearisburg; Giles Co. From brdg. 1 mi. N. of Poplao Hill at confluence with Little Walker Creek to New River above Ripple Mead, 19 mi., Dif. I–II, run until June 1. Access pt.—opposite filling sta. near Bane, some·easy rapids, not an exciting river, private land, no camping, panfish. (Credit—*Canoeing White Water River Guide*)

Broad Run River: USGS—Thoroughfare, Gainesville, Nakesville; Prince William Co. From Rte. 29–211, 3 mi. from Gainesville, to Rte. 28 brdg., 4 mi. S. of Manassas, 14 mi., 5 hrs. Dif. I–II. DANGER—barbed-wire fences below, run stream only after rain, 2 broken-down mills in river that make rapids of Dif. II–III, a slow trip, some nice scenery, camping along river. Fish—smallmouth and large-mouth bass, sunfish. Take-out pt. is dif. due to high ledge. (Credit—*Canoeing White Water River Guide*)

Bull Pasture River: USGS—Va., McDowell 15 ft., Monterey, Williamsville; Highland and Bath cos. From McDowell to Cowpasture River at Williamsville, 15 mi. Dif. II–IV. DANGER —an 8-ft. drop (run on right only), some Dif. V rapids, run in spring, small stream, many ledges and bldrs., very fast-moving stream, trip for experts only, most dif. part is Bullpasture Gorge, avg. drop of 45 ft. per mi., use all necessary safety equipment. Fish—small-mouth bass, sunfish, trout, and fallfish. (Credit— *Canoeing White Water River Guide*)

Catoctin Creek: 4 mi. above Taylorstown. Dif. I; 4–5 mi. below, Dif. II.

Cedar Creek: USGS—Middletown, Va.; Shenandoah, Frederick, and Warren cos. From N.W. of Strasburg, Rte. 55 to U.S. Rte. 11, 20.1 mi.
    Trip 1—Rte. 55 to Rte. 628 (Stephen's Fort), 10 mi., early spring or after rain but not in flood, sharp turns, a beginner's

white-water stream, all shallow water, some barbed-wire fences.

Trip 2—Rte. 628 to U.S. Rte. 11, 10.1 mi., early spring or after rain but not in flood, some waves, 10 per cent of river has rapids of 60 yds., submerged obstacles, fences, 1 low-water brdg., blind curves, logjam, low limbs. (Credit—*Blue Ridge Voyages*)

Clinch River: USGS 15 ft.—Pounding Mill, Richlands, 7½ ft.—Elk Garden, Lebanon, Carbe, St. Paul, Toms Creek, Plum Grove, Looneys, Kyles Ford; Tazewell, Russell, Scott, and Wise cos. From Pounding Mill Rtes. 19 and 460 near Tazewell to Kyles Ford, Tenn. Rte. 70 brdg., 136 mi., 45 days. Dif. I–IV. Starts as small river, ends as large one. Good camping.

Trip 1—Pounding Mill Rtes. 19 and 460 to Blackford Brdg. at Rte. 80, 30 mi. Dif. I–III. DANGER—old dam with 5 ft. in Cedar Bluff near hwy. old dam 10 ft. high above Richlands.

Trip 2—Blackford Brdg. to Cleveland, 26 mi. Dif. III–IV, white water. DANGER—3-ft. waterfall about 6 mi. below Blackford, then another 3-ft. fall ½ mi. more, 2-ft. falls, then 4-ft. falls about 1 mi. below jctn. with Big Cedar Creek, wild entry, beautiful.

Trip 3—Cleveland to Dungannon, 33 mi. Dif. II–III; 1½ days. DANGER—ledge with a chute about 1 mi. below St. Paul, scout this one, beautiful sec.

Trip 4—Dungannon to Kyles Ford, Tenn., 47 mi., 1½ days. Dif. I–II. DANGER—old mill dam about 2½ mi. below Clinchfield RR crossing, scout before running, very little white water. Fish—small-mouth bass and sunfish upper sec.; cats, carp, and suckers lower sec.

(Credit—*Canoeing White Water River Guide*)

Cowpasture River: USGS—Williamsville, Millboro Springs, Clifton Forge; Bath, Allegheny, and Highland cos. From Rte. 614 brdg. above jctn. with Bull Pasture to lndg. below jctn. with James River below Rte. 220 brdg., 72 mi., 2–3 days. Upper river is small, increases in size and slows down downstream, run through summer, beautiful until last part.

Trip 1—Rte. 614 brdg. to Fort Lewis Brdg., 12 mi., no particular dangers. Dif. II–III. White water, exciting.

Trip 2—Ft. Lewis Brdg. (Rte. 678) to Millboro Springs, 20 mi., no particular dangers. Dif. I–II. Good for beginners.

Trip 3—Millboro Springs to Rte. 60 brdg., 32 mi. DANGER —5-ft. dam below Millboro Springs, then bad rapid below RR brdg. at Coleman Tunnel.

Trip 4—Rte. 60 brdg. to lndg. below jctn. with James River, 8 mi. DANGER—heavy water and deep hole about 1 mi. below Rte. 60 brdg.; run on right, beautiful scenery but pollution in lower part. Fish—small-mouth bass and sunfish.

(Credit—*Canoeing White Water River Guide*)

Dismal Swamp Traverse: 4 days.

Day 1—Put-in terminus of "Jericho Ditch" at Suffolk, Va., sluggish, some deadfalls, 9 mi. to Lake Drummond, easy day.

Day 2—Cross Lake Drummond. DANGER—in wind, enter Reddick Ditch. Ptg. is ½ mi. long.

Day 3—Enter Feeder Ditch on E. Shore of lake, ptg. over perm. flood-control dam, continue to jctn. of Dismal Swamp canal at Carbuncle Lndg., continue S. on Dismal Swamp canal (part of intercoastal canal), camp at N.C.-Va. line; total, 11 mi.

Day 4—Canoe 9 mi. to South Mills, N.C. NOTE—ditches dug by slaves in early 1800s. DANGER—water moccasins.

(Credit—Eigel Hansen and Jon Smith)

Farnum Creek: Tidal creek. Variety of fish.

Goose Creek: USGS—Leesburg, Sterling, Lincoln. Loudoun Co. From 1 mi. below Rte. 50 on Purceville Rd. Rte. 611 to Rte. 7 brdg., 30 mi., mudbed at first then rocky bed, run until June 1 or after rains, rises and falls fast. Dif. II–III.

Trip 1—From Rte. 611 to Oatlands Rte. 15, 14 mi. Dif. II–III. DANGER—none in particular, a Dif. II–III rapid about 2½ mi. below put-in and another 2½ mi. below Rte. 626 brdg.; logjam and low trees.

Trip 2—Rte. 15 brdg. to Rte. 7 brdg. at clubhouse, 16 mi. Dif. II–III. DANGER—several broken dams, especially one at end near clubhouse; some exciting rapids. (Credit— *Canoeing White Water River Guide*)

Grays Creek: Runs far inland, good canoeing.

Hazel River: USGS—Luray; Rappahannock, Culpeper, Fauquier cos. From Near Boston to Remington at Rte. 15 brdg., 30 mi., Dif. I. No white water. OK beginners.

Trip 1—From Near Boston to Monumental Mills low-water brdg., 15 mi. Dif. I. DANGER—old power dam ½ mi. above jctn. with Thornton—ptg. this dam.

Trip 2—Monumental Mills to Remington at Rte. 15 brdg., 15 mi. Dif. I. Flat water, slow-moving.

(Credit—*Canoeing White Water River Guide*)

Holston River—Mid. Branch: USGS—7½ ft. Damascus, Abington, and Shady Valley; Virginia, Washington, and Wise cos. From De Busk Mill, 2 mi. above Rte. 91 brdg. to Creek Water Intake Tower in S. Lake Holston, 25 mi. Dif. I–III. DANGER—20-ft. dam 7 mi. below put-in; fast, rocky sec. 1 mi. below dam, falls just above jctn. with S. Fork of Holston, fast sec. in narrow gorge below jctn., and then Dif. IV–V rapids below, scout this area. Fishing—panfish, large-mouth bass, trout. (Credit—*Canoeing White Water River Guide*)

Holston River—N. Fork: USGS—Va., Chatham Hill, Saltville, Glade Spring, Hayters Gap, Brumley, Nansonville, Wallace, Mendota, Hilton, Tenn., and Kingsport; Wash., Scott, and Smyth cos. From Chatham Hill to Rte. 23 brdg. at Weber City, 108 mi., 4 days, exciting river in upper part, sluggish in lower part.

Trip 1—From Chatham Hill to Saltville to Holston Rte. 19 brdg., 28 mi.; 4 mi. after put-in is a very fast sec. of Dif. III, very dif. rapid here, Dif. IV, scout first, another bad rapid 9 mi. from Saltville.

Trip 2—Holston Rte. 19 brdg. to Rte. 23 brdg. at Weber City, 54 mi. Dif. I–II. DANGER—7½ mi. after Holston, small dam across is., then 4 more. (Credit—*Canoeing White Water River Guide*)

Holston River—S. Fork: USGS—7½ ft. Damascus, and Abington; Wash. Co. From Laurel Creek at Damascus to S. Holston Lake, 7 mi. Dif. I–III. Run in spring. DANGER—old mill dams, Dif. III rapid below old mill dam near Roe Town, fast water and Dif. IV–V rapids in the Narrows. (Credit—*Canoeing White Water River Guide*)

Hughes River: USGS—Luray; Rappahannock and Culpeper cos. From Peola Mills to Boston (Rte. 522), 8 mi. W. of Culpeper, 12 mi., 4 hrs. Dif. II–III. Start—¼ mi. below Rte. 231 on Rte. 603; trees and brush above this pt. DANGER—old Rte. 603 brdg., fallen trees, small river, fast current, white water, some ledges, exciting parts, fair scenery, small-mouth bass, trout, sunfish. (Credit —*Canoeing White Water River Guide*)

Jackson River: USGS—Williamsville and Warm Springs; Bath Co. From Hwy. 220 brdg. to environs of Covington, 46 mi.
    Trip 1—Hwy. 220 brdg. to Hwy. 39 brdg., 12 mi., 4 hrs. Dif. III. DANGER—waterfall 4 mi. below start, many fences, watergaps, several low-water brdgs., small and fast river, run till June 1, rapids, white water, experts only.
    Trip 2—Hwy. 39 brdg. to brdg. at Nat. Well, Va., 22 mi., 8 hrs., experts only, dangerous rapids, waterfall, being destroyed by dam.
    Trip 3—Nat. Well to environs of Covington, Va., 12 mi., 4 hrs., fairly easy. Trout, small-mouth bass.
    (Credit—*Canoeing White Water River Guide*)

James River: USGS—Bon Air, Richmond, Buena Vista, Scottsville, and Dillwyn; city of Richmond; Amherst, Rockbridge, and Fluvanna cos.
    Trip 1—From Fluvanna Gauging Sta. up from Huguenot Brdg. in Richmond to Robert E. Lee Brdg., 6 mi., 3 hrs.,

some flat stretches, many rapids. Dif. I–VI. Some extremely dangerous rapids. DANGER—Williams Isle and Belle Isle dams, rapids below Belle Isle Dam; experts only run falls below Belle Isle.

Trip 2—From Clifton Forge via Iron Gate to Eagle Rock, Buchanan to Balcony Falls, slow-moving, beautiful, polluted.

Trip 3—Balcony Falls to Snowden, 4 mi., 1 hr.; Dif. III–IV. Beautiful, white water.

Trip 4—Scottsville to Bremo Bluff, 13 mi., 5 hrs. Dif. I–II. DANGER—right side of first isle, many isles on trip, relatively wild, ledges, long rapids, some dif. rapids, OK for beginners in low water. Fish—small-mouth bass, crappie, large-mouth bass, and sunfish.

(Credit—*Canoeing White Water River Guide*)

Little River: USGS—Hanover Academy, and Ashland; Hanover Co. Rte. 685 to Rte. 1, 6 mi., 4 hrs. Dif. IV. DANGER—25-ft. waterfall, white water. Ptg.—falls, riffles below falls; beautiful scenery, trout. (Credit—*Canoeing White Water River Guide*)

Little Totuskey River: Richmond Co. Below Warsaw on N. Neck Hwy. Tidal creek, var. of fish.

Little Walker Creek: Giles Co. 1 mi. above Big Walker Creek, in ample water only, experts only, white water, exciting. (Credit—*Canoeing White Water River Guide*)

Mattaponi River: King William and King and Queen cos. Bowling Green Hwy. to Aylett; 4 access pts., brdgs. at No. 2 Hwy., Stephens Run, Munday, Tappahannock Hwy. Fast, clean, sharp bends, deep pools, sand bottom, some rapids. Fair to excel. fishing —pike, bass, perch.

Maury River: USGS—Lexington; Rockbridge Co. From Goshen to Lexington, Rte. 631, 24 mi., 10 hrs. Dif. II–VI.

Trip 1—From Goshen to Rockbridge Baths, 11 mi., 6 hrs. DANGER—impassable sec.—don't run, mean rapids, experts only on this trip.

Trip 2—From Rockbridge Baths to Lexington (Limekiln Brdg.), Rte. 631, 13 mi., 4 hrs., experts only, white water, sharp bends, exciting. Small-mouth bass, large-mouth bass, sunfish. (Credit—*Canoeing White Water River Guide*)

Moccasin Creek: USGS—Hilton, Gate City. Scott Co. From Snowflake on Rte. 71 to Gate City RR brdg., 12 mi., 4 hrs. Dif. II–IV. DANGER—3 waterfalls 3 mi. below Snowflake. DANGER—Slabtown Mill Dam, fast white water, exciting, wild area, beautiful, run till Apr. 15. Small-mouth bass, rock bass, sunfish. (Credit—*Canoeing White Water River Guide*)

Moormans River: USGS—University, Charlottesville; Albemarle Co. From Rte. 810 to dam above Rte. 29, 18 mi., 7 hrs. Dif. II–III.
Trip 1—From Rte. 810 at Whitehill to Rte. 601, 8 mi., 3½ hrs. Dif. II–III. Sharp bends, rapids, overhanging brush.
Trip 2—From Rte. 601 to dam above Rte. 29 near Charlottesville, 10 mi., 3½ hrs. Dif. II. DANGER—some fences and high dam ½ mi. above Rte. 29 brdg. Small-mouth bass, sunfish, trout. (Credit—*Canoeing White Water River Guide*)

Mt. Landing Creek: Essex Co. N. of Tappahannock; var. of fish, tidal creek.

North Anna River: USGS—Va. 7½ ft. Partlow, Beaver Dam, Hewlett, and Ruther Glen; Caroline Co. From Smith Mill Brdg. to Rte. 1 brdg., 23 mi., 8 hrs. Dif. I–V. DANGER—10-ft. dam with falls 6 mi. below Smith Mill Brdg., North Anna Falls. Dif. V rapids, run till June 1. Ptg.—danger pts., white water, ledges, sunfish, large-mouth bass. (Credit—*Canoeing White Water River Guide*)

Nottoway River: USGS McKenney; Sussex Co. From Rte. 609 to Rte. 619 (off Rte. 301–95, 8 mi. W. of Jarrott). Dif. I–III, 11 mi., 4 hrs., several Dif. I–II rapids, pleasant, some exciting rapids at end. Small-mouth bass, sunfish. (Credit—*Canoeing White Water River Guide*)

Pamunkey River: New Kent, King William, Hanover cos. Not fast, often muddy, widens into bays, poor fishing. Wash. brdg., Hwy. 11 to Lille Pt., 2 days, popular.

Passage Creek: USGS Va.—15 ft., Strasburg; Warren and Shenandoah cos. From brdg. above George Wash. Cmpgrnd. to Rte. 55, 5 mi. W. of Front Royal, 7 mi., 3 hrs., small "rip-snorter." Dif. IV rapids, barbed-wire fences, tight turns, little river, ledges. DANGER—low-water brdg. after RR brdg., and 6-ft. dam below gorge. Rock bass, small-mouth bass, sunfish, trout. (Credit— *Canoeing White Water River Guide*)

Potomac River: See description under Maryland.

Rapidan River: USGS—Gordonsville, Unionville, Culpeper, Germanna, Richardsville, Salem Church, Chancellorsville, Mine Run; Orange, Culpeper, and Spotsylvania cos. From Rte. 29 near Ruckersville to jctn. with Rappahannock, 66 mi.

Trip 1—Rte. 29 near Ruckersville to Old Madison Rte. 15 near Orange, 18 mi., 6 hrs. Dif. I–II. Ptg.—low dam 8 mi. below Rte. 15 brdg.

Trip 2—Madison Mill Rte. 15 to jctn. with Rappahannock 10 mi. above Fredericksburg, 48 mi., 14 hrs. Dif. I–III. A slow-flowing river, high mudbanks, scenery poor, few rapids. Large-mouth and small-mouth bass, sunfish.

(Credit—*Canoeing White Water River Guide*)

Rapidan River—Upper Conway River Sec.: USGS Madison; Madison Co. From Kinderhook 4 mi. above Rte. 231 to Rte. 29 brdg. near Ruckersville, Va. (called Mid. River on St. 231 brdg.), 11 mi., 5 hrs. Dif. V. Very fast, fallen trees, don't run in high water, dif. rapids, 50-ft. waterfall 1 mi. below start, barbed wire, run till mid-Apr., experts only. Small-mouth bass, sunfish. (Credit —*Canoeing White Water River Guide*)

Rappahannock River:
NOTE: Rather than trying to combine descriptions for the

Rappahannock from two books it was decided to give the reader both.

Description 1: USGS—Luray, Warrenton, Germanna Brdg., Storch, Salem Church, Fredericksburg; Rappahannock, Culpeper, Fauquier cos. (See descriptions under Thornton and Hazel rivers.) From 211 brdg. near Waterloo to Fredericksburg, 54 mi., Dif. I–III.

> *Trip 1*—211 brdg. near Waterloo to Remington Rte. 15 brdg., 18 mi. Dif. II. A few rapids, slow river, scenery not particularly good, OK for beginners, mostly farmland, high mudbanks.

> *Trip 2*—Remington to Fredericksburg. Dif. I–III, 36 mi., wide, long flat stretches broken with fast and white water, rock bed, ledges in rapids, excellent rapids, 1 mi. of continuous rapids at Kelly's Ford, experienced canoeists only.

> (Credit—*Canoeing White Water River Guide*)

Description 2:

> *Trip 1*—Upper Rappahannock. From Rte. 647 to Rte. 211, 6 mi. W. of Warrenton, USGS 15 ft. Warrenton, 15 ft. Sperryville, 15 ft. Front Royal, 7½ ft. Orlean. A little stream; put-in is below jctn. with Jordon River, fast water, white water, shallow, good campsites, don't canoe when gauge at brdg. on Rte. 211 is above 3 ft.

> *Trip 2*—Lower Rappahannock. From No. 620 (gravel rd.) via U.S. Rte. 1, 9 mi. W. of Fredericksburg to take-out pt. at picnic area above Rte. 1 brdg., 10 mi., pleasant summer trip, many riffles, a few flat areas, many good swimming spots, can be exciting trip if rocks above Motts Lndg. are barely covered or just out of water. DANGER—Don't canoe rapids below take-out pt., avoid feeder canal at Vepco Dam about 1 mi. above take-out pt., area below dam has strong rapids; not for beginners—ptg. left.

> (Credit—*Blue Ridge Voyages*)

Reed Creek: USGS—Max Meadows 15 ft.; Wythe Co. From Max Meadows to New River, 16 mi., 5 hrs. Dif. I–III. Ptg.—waterfall, few nice rapids, run till May. Small-mouth bass, rock bass, cats, sunfish. (Credit—*Canoeing White Water River Guide*)

Roanoke River: USGS Elliston, Salem, and Roanoke. Montgomery, Roanoke cos. From Elliston to Roanoke Stadium Park Area, 26 mi. Dif. II–III.

Trip 1—Elliston to rd. S. side of river W. of Salem. Dif. II–III, 14 mi., 5 hrs.

Trip 2—W. of Salem near small dam on river side to Roanoke Stadium Park Area, small river, not very fast, many low-water brdgs., 2 low-water dams below Elliston ¾ mi., W. of Salem, and in Roanoke City area. Small-mouth bass, sunfish, trout, rock bass. (Credit—*Canoeing White Water River Guide*)

Russell River: USGS Clintwood 15 ft., Elkhorn City 7½ ft.; Dickenson Co. Through Grand Canyon of E. from Haysi, Va., to Elkhorn City, Ky. Dif. III–VII, 13 mi., 11 hrs. DANGERS— many, incl. 10-ft. waterfall, 6-ft. waterfall, 5-ft. waterfall, long run of continuous waterfalls and ledges, experts only, a terror of a river, beautiful. Small-mouth bass, sunfish, cats. (Credit—*Canoeing White Water River Guide*)

Shenandoah River—N. Fork: USGS—Orkney Springs, Broadway, Mt. Jackson, Edinburg; Rockingham Co. From brdg. between Bergton and Criders via Brooks Gap to the dam just below the hwy. brdg. at Front Royal, 115 mi., 5 days.

Trip 1—From brdg. between Bergton and Criders to ¼ mi. below Cootes Store, Rte. 259, 17 mi., 5 hrs. Dif. III. CAUTION—low-water brdg. above Brooks Gap, don't run in high water, run early spring, beautiful, exciting, narrow.

Trip 2—From Cootes Store to low-water brdg. about 3 mi. below Mt. Jackson via Timberville, 25 mi., 1 day. Dif. II–III. CAUTION—5-ft. dam above Timberville—easy ptg. CAUTION—heavy rapid in high water 3 mi. below Timberville. CAUTION—heavy rapids in high water.

Trip 3—Low-water brdg. 3 mi. below Mt. Jackson to low-water brdg. 5 mi. below Edinburg, 12 mi., 4 hrs. Dif. I–II. DANGER—12-ft. dam 8 mi. below start or ¾ mi. below King Crossing—ptg. right, mostly slow river, run till mid-

May, first 3 mi. drab, then some nice fast water. Fish—trout, bass, bream.

Trip 4—From low-water brdg. on St. Rte. 672 2 mi. below Edinburg to Stonewall Mill Rte. 663 at Pughs Run below Woodstock, 19 mi., 6 hrs. Dif. I–II. DANGER—16-ft. dam, 12-ft. dam, and a 4-ft. dam above Stonewall Mill, very twisty river, run till June 1, not an exciting trip.

Trip 5—From Woodstock to Strasburg to Front Royal, 42 mi., 12 hrs. Dif. I–II. Many low-water brdgs. CAUTION— low dam below Strasburg. DANGER—10-ft. dam at end of trip below hwy. brdg.—stay away from this dam, run river till July 1, good camping. Fish—small-mouth and rock bass, bream.

(Credit—*Canoeing White Water River Guide*)

Shenandoah River and S. Branch: USGS—Va.—Strasburg, Front Royal, Winchester, Berryville; W. Va.—Martinsburg; Md.— Antietam; Warren and Clarke cos., Va.; Jefferson Co., W. Va. From Bentonville low-water brdg. Rte. 613 to Harpers Ferry at Knoxville, 67 mi., 2–3 days. Dif. II–IV.

Trip 1—From Bentonville low-water brdg. Rte. 613 to Morgan Ford low-water-brdg. Rte. 624, 25 mi., 8 hrs. Dif. II. Wide, slow, beautiful, and clear water, don't drink water, run anytime except dry summer. DANGER—4 mi. below Front Royal is high power-plant dam—dif. ptg. to right; 1 Dif. II rapid at Karo Lndg.

Trip 2—From Morgan Ford low-water brdg. Rte. 624 to 1 mi. above power plant above Millville, 33 mi., 10 hrs. Dif. II–III. CAUTION—dif. rapid 1 mi. above power plant, clear, wide, OK for beginners, fair scenery, good camping, best sec. below Rte. 50 to Castelman's Ferry Brdg., 14 mi., very popular run, riffles, good put-in and take-out pts.

Trip 3—From below power plant above Millville to Harpers Ferry at Knoxville, 9 mi., 4 hrs. Dif. IV. DANGER—Bull Falls after the first rapids ending the long flat stretch of about 2 mi. below the power plant—scout. DANGER—White Horse rapids ¼ mi. below Harpers Ferry, not for beginners, wear lifejacket. DANGER—old dam spikes that stick up in riverbed, a wide and powerful river, many old dams, run any-time except in high water, excel. white water, beautiful, flows through deep gorge. Take-out—left bank at is. opposite Knoxville.

(Credit—*Canoeing White Water River Guide* and *Blue Ridge Voyages*)

Shenandoah River—S. Fork: USGS—Harrisonburg, Elkton, Mt. Jackson, Stony Man, and Strasburg; Rockingham, Page, Warren cos. From Port Republic to water brdg. at Bentonville, Rte. 613, 73 mi. Dif. II–III, 3 days.

Trip 1—Port Republic to Shenandoah. Dif. II–III, 24 mi., 8 hrs., nice canoeing river, some rapids, some dif. rapids, some pollution, many long, flat stretches. DANGER—several low dams, particularly the one at old Harrisonburg power plant—this is 7 mi. below Port Republic—ptg., run river all summer unless drought.

Trip 2—Shenandoah to Massanutten Power Plant Dam above Newport off Rte. 340. Dif II, 2 mi., 4 hrs., slow, unexciting, beautiful, run anytime except in drought.

Trip 3—Newport, Foltz Mill to Rte. 211 brdg., 9 mi., 3 hrs., Dif. II–III. Rocky bed, some ledges, best rapid is old dam, run anytime but in dry summer; beautiful. Don't run below old mill dam on Rte. 646; high-power dam below.

Trip 4—Luray low-water brdg. at Bixler's Ferry (Rte. 675) to low-water brdg. at Bentonville, Rte. 613, 28 mi., 10 hrs. Dif. II–III. Wide river, drops over many ledges, rock bed, clean water, beautiful scenery. DANGER—rapid at Comptons opposite high RR brdg. DANGER—rapid on a left-hand bend. DANGER—rapids above Millville power plant—dangerous in high water—water above 2 ft. is high. Good fishing—small-mouth bass, cats, bream, good camping.

(Credit—*Canoeing White Water River Guide*)

Shenandoah River—S. Fork, N. River: USGS Harrisonburg; Rockingham Co. From Bridgewater to Port Republic, 20 mi., 7½ hrs. Dif. I–II. Ptg.—6-ft.-dam, small river, easy canoeing. Small-mouth and large-mouth bass, sunfish. (Credit—*Canoeing White Water River Guide*)

Shenandoah River—S. Fork, S. River: USGS—Waynesboro, Harrisonburg; Augusta and Rockingham cos. From River Rd. opposite Dooms below Waynesboro to Port Republic. Dif. II–IV, 19 mi., 6 hrs., small river, many dif., fallen trees, quick turns, polluted from city of Waynesboro, run early spring, white-water river. DANGER—many old dams; don't take this run in flood stage, not good fishing. (Credit—*Canoeing White Water River Guide*)

Shenandoah River—S. River and Back Creek: USGS—Waynesboro, Lexington; Augusta Co. From Sherando to Waynesboro, 10 mi., 4 hrs. Dif. II–IV. Barbed wire, small river, brush piles, overhanging brush, upper part fast, don't run in high water. Smallmouth bass, trout. (Credit—*Canoeing White Water River Guide*)

Stony Creek: USGS—Edinburg; Shenandoah Co. From Camp Strawderman to Shenandoah through town of Edinburg, 15 mi. Dif. II–III. DANGER—low-water dams and low-water brdgs., fast-flowing river, some long, fast rapids, run in spring, white water, nice scenery, small river. (Credit—*Canoeing White Water River Guide*)

Swift Creek: Canoeable halfway from mouth to jctn. with Appomatox River.

Thornton River (Rappahannock River): USGS—Sperryville; Rappahannock Co. From Sperryville to Monumental Mills low-water brdg., 21 mi., small stream, good white water, run in Feb., too low to canoe much of year, ideal water level is 2 ft. through brdg. at Rock Mills; when above 2½ ft., don't run.

    Trip 1—From Sperryville to Fletcher's Mill, 1 mi., several fences.

    Trip 2—From Fletcher's Mill to Rock Mills, 6½ mi. DANGER—Bldr. Ledge Rapid 1.3 mi. after Fletcher's Mill; scout this before running.

Trip 3—Rock Mills to Monumental Mills low-water brdg., 12½ mi., no particular danger. (Credit—*Blue Ridge Voyages* and *Canoeing White Water River Guide*)

Wards Creek: Floridieu Hundred Creek—canoeable.

Wolf Creek: USGS—Bland, Pocahontas and Narrows; Giles and Bland cos. From S. Gap Brdg. to Narrows Mill Dam, 24 mi. Dif. I–IV. DANGER—low-water brdgs.; scout river before running, wire fences on river, upper part between S. Gap and Rock Gap for experts only. Fish—rock bass, small-mouth bass, sunfish, trout. (Credit—*Canoeing White Water River Guide*)

WASHINGTON

Bogachiel River: Clallam Co. Approx. 10 mi. to jctn. with Sloeduck River. Dif. II.

Cascade River: Skagit Co. Approx. 6–8 mi. to Marblemount. Dif. IV.

Cedar River: USGS—Maple Valley, Hobart. From Seattle Water Supply Intake to Maple Valley, 6.8 mi. Dif. II–III. Run in spring, not for novice in high water. CAUTION—drop under second RR brdg., keep in mid., water level changes rapidly because of dam. (Credit—*Kayak and Canoe Trips in Washington*)

Chehalis River: Lewis, Grays Harbor cos. Rainbow Falls to mouth at Grays Harbor. Dif. II.

Cherwack River: Okanogan Co. Dif. III.

Cle Elum River: Kittitas Co.
Trip 1—From 4 mi. above Cle Elum Lake to dam. Dif. III.

Trip 2—From 6.6 mi. below to mouth. Dif. II at med. water level.
(Credit—Raymond J. Parker)

Columbia River: USGS—Beverly Priest Rapids. From Wanapum Dam to Priest Rapids Dam, 13 mi. Dif. I. Wind can whip up whitecaps, no rapids. (Credit—*Water Trails of Washington*)

Cowlitz River: Lewis, Cowlitz cos. Jctn. Hwys. 123 and 12 to mouth. Dif. II–VI, mostly II–III; 2 dams, Mossy Park and Mayfield. Ptg.—falls below Randle.

Crab Creek—Lower: USGS—Beverly. From brdg. that is 5½ mi. from Beverly to left bank of Columbia River below mouth of creek, 6⅕ mi. Dif. I. Desert ctry., run in spring, runs through Columbia Wildlife Refuge, OK for novice, 1 rapid in tight "S" curve. (Credit—*Kayak and Canoe Trips in Washington*)

Deschotes River: Thurston Co. Approx. 13 mi. Dif. II.

Dungeness River: Clallam Co. Dif. II.

Duwanisn River: King Co. Dif. I.

Entiat River: Chelan Co. Dif. IV.

Grand Coulee Chain of Lakes: USGS—Ephrata, Jameson Lake, Park Lake; old riverhead of Columbia River, easy ptgs. CAUTION—motorboats. Dif. I, 11½ mi. (Credit—*Water Trails of Washington*)

Green River: King Co. Lester to Flaming Geyser. Dif. III–VI. Green River Gorge is dangerous, 2 dams, Hanson and low dam below; below Flaming Geyser Dif. I–II.

Hoh River: USGS—Olympic Natl. Park. From Olympic Natl. Park near Ranger Sta. to Pacific Ocean, 34 mi., may wish to terminate at brdg. 4 mi. above ocean or continue on to access near

Oil City just before ocean. Dif. II–III. Logjams may be present, true channel not easy to find at first, then river flattens and slows down. (Credit—*Water Trails of Washington*)

Humptulips River: USGS Humptulips, Quinalt Lake. From Fish Trap Rd. access to brdg. off 101 near Humptulips, 21 mi. Dif. II. Goes through Olympic For., overhanging trees, fern-covered cliffs, logjams, can paddle on to Grays Harbor but less interesting. (Credit—*Water Trails of Washington*)

Kachees River: Kittitas Co. Not canoeable. (Credit—Raymond J. Parker)

Lewis River: Cowlitz Co. Driel Dam to mouth. Dif. I.

Lost River: Okanogan Co. Mile 70 (7 mi. above Mazama); here is where it joins W. Fork of the Methow to form the main stem of the Methow River. No rd. access to the Lost River above Mazama. On the main stem there are logjams, not good canoeing. (Credit—Raymond J. Parker)

Methow River: Okanogan Co. Mazama to Pateros (jctn. with Columbia River), total 63 mi.
  Trip 1—Mazama to Winthrop, 15 mi. Dif. III.
  Trip 2—Winthrop to Twisp, 10 mi. Dif. II.
  Trip 3—Twisp to Carlton, 12 mi. Dif. II.
  Trip 4—Carlton to Methow, 14 mi. Dif. III.
  Trip 5—Methow to Pateros, 12 mi. Dif. II–IV with Dif. IV in Black Canyon. See also the description of Lost River.
  (Credit—Raymond J. Parker)

Nisqually River: USGS—Yelm and Anderson Is. From McKenna to power plant, 9 mi. Dif. III–IV. Several large rapids, swift water, a demanding trip. Can paddle past power plant to Nisqually Delta (10 mi.), but no way out, so have to paddle back. (Credit—*Water Trails of Washington*)

Nooksack River: Whatcom Co. Forks to mouth. Dif. I–II.

Nooksack River—N. Fork Branch: Below Glacier to forks. Dif. II–III.

Nooksack River—S. Fork Branch: Whatcom Co. Saxen Brdg. to forks. Dif. I.

North River: Grays Harbor; Pacific Co. Dif. II.

Okanogan River: Okanogan Co. Dif. II.

Pilchuck Creek: USGS—Clear Lake, Marysville. From Rte. 9 brdg. N. of Arlington to Hwy. 5 brdg., 5 mi. Dif. II–III, several small rapids, some logjams, steep, mossy banks, gravel bars. Take-out pt. is swampy. Above Rte. 9 brdg. river flows from Lake Cavanaugh over Dif. V–VI waterfall, then through canyon with Dif. III–IV water. (Credit—*Water Trails of Washington*)

Pilchuck River: USGS—Granite Falls, Marysville, Everett. From brdg. near Granite Falls to Pilchuck River Park in city of Snohomish, 18 mi. Dif. II–III. Beautiful, rain-fed, farmland, and wooded banks; fast at first, many logjams, then river becomes larger. (Credit—*Water Trails of Washington*)

Potholes Lakes: USGS—Othello. Chain of 7 small lakes, easy ptgs. except for last, much wildlife, scenic, inside Columbia Natl. Wildlife Refuge. (Credit—*Water Trails of Washington*)

Puyallup River: Pierce Co. Electron to Fisk, Dif. VI. Fisk to Summer, Dif. II.

Queets River: Jefferson Co. Approx. 20 mi. to mouth. Dif. II.

Quinault River: USGS—Olympic Natl. Park; Grays Harbor and Jefferson cos. From S. side of brdg. near jctn. with N. Fork to Mi. 8 above Quinault Lake; alt. take-out is Falls Creek Cmpgrnd., 10½ mi., Dif. II. Logjams, flood channels change yearly; best time of year is June–Aug.; best to take out at Mi. 8 and avoid lake paddling. Sec. upstream from brdg. put-in—not recommended.

Sec. below Lake Quinault to ocean, part of Indian Res., can't run without permission. (Credit—*Kayak and Canoe Trips in Washington*)

Quinault River–N. Fork: Not recommended.

Sammamish River: King Co. Lake to lake. Dif. I.

Satsop River—Mid. Fork: USGS—Wynoochee Valley and Elma. From brdg. 4 mi. N. of Cougar Smith Rd. to brdg. 3½ mi. N. of Brady, 17½ mi. Dif. 4 mi. of Dif. III, lively rapids at first, then deep canyon, usually only upper part is run; normal to float 4 mi. and end at Cougar Smith Rd. brdg. (Credit—*Water Trails of Washington*)

Satsop River—W. Fork: USGS—Wynoochee Valley and Elma. From Cougar Smith Rd. brdg. 3½ mi. N. of Brady, 17 mi. Dif. first 10 mi. Dif. II. Normal to end at Swinging Brdg. Park, easy trip, open farmland. (Credit—*Water Trails of Washington*)

Sauk River (Upper):
 Trip 1—USGS—Bedla and White Chuck. From Camp Bedal to White Chuck Cmpgrnd., 8.3 mi. Dif. III. For. camps at both ends. Trip starts with rapids and logjams, go to left of logjam, headwall at 3-mi. pt.—to right, bldrs. in last part of trip. DANGER—beyond take-out pt. is Dif. IV–V. (Credit —*Water Trails of Washington*)

Skagit River: From New Halem to mouth, approx. 100 mi. Dif. I–III.
 Trip 1—From New Halem powerhouse to Bacon Creek Cmpgrnd., 10 mi. Dif. III. CAUTION—"S" bend on upper portion, scout before running; "S" bend has fast-flowing water, water level varies without warning, depends upon release from dam; lower river peaceful, generally Dif. I. (Credit—*Water Trails of Washington*)

Skokomish River: Mason Co. Forks to mouth. Dif. II.

Skookumchuck River: Thurston, Lewis cos. Dam in Thurston Co. to mouth. Dif. I–II.

Skykomish River: USGS—Skykomish, Grotto, Baring, Monroe, Index. From Skykomish to Monroe.

   Trip 1—Skykomish to Baring. Dif. II–III, 8.7 mi., mt. scenery, harsh rapids; can bypass by going to one side.

   Trip 2—Baring to Eagle Falls, no information.

   Trip 3—Eagle Falls to Gold Bar, Dif. IV. Approx. 11 mi. No other data.

   Trip 4—Gold Bar to Sultan, 9 mi. Dif. II. Helmet and life-jacket required by co. law for first 100 ft. to co. line at RR brdg.; rapid at first, CAUTION—rapid 4.5 mi. after put-in. Beautiful scenery, good camping.

   Trip 5—Sultan to Monroe, 9.3 mi. Dif. I. OK beginners. CAUTION—rapid 1 mi. after put-in and rapid upstream from Ben Howard Public Fishing area. Take-out—public fishing area in Monroe.

   (Credit—*Kayak and Canoe Trips in Washington* and *Water Trails of Washington*)

Skykomish River—S. Fork: USGS—Sultan. From gate near Sunset Falls to pt. above Boulder Drop, 3.3 mi. Dif. III–IV. Not for novice, dif. stretch, many rapids, don't run. Boulder Drop—Dif. IV, scout river before running. (Credit—*Water Trails of Washington*)

Snohomish River: Snohomish, King cos. Forks to mouth, approximately 50 mi. Dif. I.

Snohomish River—N. Fork: King Co. Approx. 12–15 mi. to forks. Dif. II–IV.

Snohomish River—S. Fork: King Co. Edgewick to forks, approx. 8 mi. Dif. II.

Soleduck River: Clallam Co. Fairholm to mouth. Dif. IV–VI.

S. Prairie River: Pierce Co. Dif. II.

Stillaquamish River—S. Fork: U.S. For. Ser. Mount Baker Natl. For. Ser.

> *Trip 1*—From Riverbar to Verlot, 7 mi. Dif. III. Tough to run in high water, may be impassable in low water, several rapids, many campsites.
>
> *Trip 2*—From Granite Falls to Arlington, 15 mi. Dif. I. Some rapids.
>
> (Credit—*Kayak and Canoe Trips in Washington*)

Suiattle River: Skagit Co. Approx. 8 mi. to jctn. with Sauk River. Dif. III.

Tieton River: Yakima Co. Dif. III or above in all secs., including lower stretches. (Credit—Raymond J. Parker)

Tilton River: Lewis Co. Near Mortin to jctn. with Cowlitz River. Dif. II first 10–12 mi., then Dif. VI for approx. 5 mi.

Tolt River: USGS—Carnation and Lake Joy. From rd. access pt. (4 mi. N. of intersec. with Rd. 202 from Carnation) to Snoqualmie River, 5.7 mi. Dif. III. Many rapids, many logjams, many boulders. (Credit—*Water Trails of Washington*)

Wenatchee River: Chelan Co. From brdg. near forks to Columbia River. Dif. II–VI; Dif. VI in Tumwater Canyon, many rapids have been run only in low water, 1 extremely dangerous set of rapids in canyon, low dam below Peshastin.

> *Trip 1*—From brdg. on Hwy. 2 below Lake Wenatchee to Tumwater Cmpgrnd., 19.1 mi. Dif. II. Rapids of Dif. II in "The Rock Gardens" just upstream from brdg. at plain. End at brdg. above Tumwater Canyon; don't run canyon.
>
> (Credit—*Kayak and Canoe Trips in Washington* and Raymond J. Parker)

White River: Chelan Co. Uncanoeable in spring. Dif. I in lowest water season, in general—above Lake Wenatchee, approx. 8 mi. Dif. II–III. (Credit—Raymond J. Parker)

Yakima River: Kittitas, Yakima, Benton cos. Canoeable almost all of its 100 mi. Dif. I–III, 10 mi. of III, 50 mi. of II and rest I. Obstacles—6 dams, highest is 12 ft., in first 22 mi. there are 8 low weirs with logjams. (Credit—Raymond J. Parker)

WEST VIRGINIA

Anthony Creek: Neola to Greenbrier River, 15 mi., beautiful, small trout stream, sharp turns, fallen trees, some dif. rapids below Blue Bend Rec. Area, run in spring. (Credit—*A Canoeist's Guide to the Whitewater Rivers of West Virginia*)

Big Sandy: Preston, Monongalia cos. Pa.-W. Va. st. line to Cheat River, 17 mi. St. line to Bruceton Mills, 5 mi., no danger spots, small rapids at Clifton Mills, flat water below, use care in high water. Good fishing—trout, bass. Bruceton Mills to Rockville, 6¼ mi. Dif. II–IV. Progresses from dif. to very dif. rapids, OK intermed. skill, check carefully—Hazel Run Rapids, 1 waterfall—ptg. left. Rockville to Cheat River, experts only, 5½ mi., remote, beautiful, exciting, hazardous white water. Dif. V. Ptg. left, 2 large waterfalls, many 4–6-ft. falls. (Credit—*A Canoeist's Guide to the Whitewater Rivers of West Virginia* and *Canoeing Guide to Western Pennsylvania and Northern West Virginia*)

Blackwater River: Northern West Virginia. From Blackwater Falls to jctn. with Dry Fork of Cheat at Hendricks, 8½ mi., very dangerous. Dif. V–VI. Upstream falls flat. No other information. (Credit—*Canoeing Guide to Western Pennsylvania and Northern West Virginia*)

Buchannon River: W. Va. Moving water and good white water.

Alton to Tenmile, 5 mi., Class III. Tenmile to Sage, 5 mi., Dif. IV–V.

Cacapon: USGS—W. Va. Wardensville, Middletown, Capon Brdg., Paw Paw. Hampshire Co., from Wardensville to Great Cacapon, 80 mi. Dif. I–III. Small stream, white water, beautiful, flows over ledges and rocks, a good canoe stream.

Trip 1—Wardensville to Capon Brdg., 29 mi., 1 day, no particular dangers.

Trip 2—Capon Brdg., on Rte. 50 to Rte. 45, 12 mi., no particular dangers.

Trip 3—Rte. 45 to Largent, 18 mi., no particular dangers.

Trip 4—Largent to Great Cacapon, 21 mi., 1 day. DANGER —high dam 4 mi. above Great Cacapon. Ptg. left side, dif. ptg.; wildlife along stream, a wild river, several ledges—scout ahead, don't run in flood stage, water rises and falls fast, run in spring or rainy season. Fish—panfish and trout.

(Credit—*Canoeing White Water River Guide* and *Blue Ridge Voyages*)

Cacapon—N. River Tributary: USGS—Capon Brdg. and Hanging Rock; Hampshire Co. From Rte. 50 brdg. to forks of Cacapon, 24 mi., 1 day. Dif. I–II. DANGER—7 fences, very small river, rocky bed, cold, clear, beautiful, run in spring, takeout at last brdg. before the forks. (Credit—*Canoeing White Water River Guide*)

Cheat River: Tucker, Preston cos. Parsons to St. 73 brdg., 71 mi. Parsons to Rowlesburg, 36 mi. or St. George to Rowlesburg, 24 mi., scenic, some riffles, threatened by dam, OK for beginner, excel. bass fishing. Rowlesburg—Manheim to RR brdg., 5.2 mi. Dif. III–IV. Narrow below cement works, huge waves, deep holes. RR brdg. to Albright power dam, 8 mi., rapids, some dif.—some waves, white water, strip-mine pollution. Albright to Jenkintown brdg., 11 mi. Dif. IV–V. Experts only, white water, wilderness, canyon, water vol. makes dif. Jenkins brdg. to St. 73 brdg., 10 mi., Dif. III for 4 mi. with easy white water, some dif. rapids, rest is a lake. (Credit—*A Canoeist's Guide to the Whitewater Rivers* *of West Virginia* and *Canoeing Guide to Western Pennsylvania and Northern West Virginia*)

Cheat River—Black Fork: Tucker Co. Mouth of Blackwater River to Parson Tannery, 4 mi., good white water, not too dif. (Credit—*A Canoeist's Guide to the Whitewater Rivers of West Virginia*)

Cheat River—Dry Fork: Tucker Co. Jenningston to Hendricks, 13½ mi. Dif. III–IV, scenic, bear and wild turkey common, first 9 mi. Dif. II+ or III, last mi. dif., 2 Dif. IV rapids. End—100 yds. from mouth of Blackwater River; can be extended—U.S. Rte. 33 brdg. to along W. Va. Rte. 32. Dif. II. (Credit—*A Canoeist's Guide to the Whitewater Rivers of West Virginia* and *Canoeing Guide to Western Pennsylvania and Northern West Virginia*)

Cheat River—Gladys Fork: Randolph Co. Rte. 33 brdg. to mouth on Dry Fork (Gladwin), 16½ mi., no major dif., continuous rapids, small stream ideal for well-coached beginner. Dif. mostly II, ends in III. Fallen trees, overhanging trees, beautiful, wilderness, run early spring. (Credit—*A Canoeist's Guide to the Whitewater Rivers of West Virginia* and *Canoeing Guide to Western Pennsylvania and Northern West Virginia*)

Cheat River—Shavers Fork: Randolph Co. Bemis to Porterwood, 36 mi. Bemis to Bowden brdg., 9 mi., Dif. IV, experts only, wilderness, very fast, large boulders. DANGER—dam under Bowden brdg. Bowden brdg. to Rte. 33 brdg., 5 mi. Rte. 33 brdg. to Porterwood, 22 mi., great scenery, OK for beginner, numerous nice rapids, Dif. II. (Credit—*A Canoeist's Guide to the Whitewater Rivers of West Virginia*)

Cherry River: Nicholas Co. Richwood to Curtin brdg., 9 mi., white water, med. dif. to very Dif. IV, spring thaws and early April. (Credit—*A Canoeist's Guide to the Whitewater Rivers of West Virginia*)

Cranberry River: Nicholas Co. 1 mi. above Big Rock Camping Area to Rte. 20 brdg. over Gauley River, Dif. III–IV, med. dif. to very dif. rapids, small stream, spring thaws and early April. (Credit—*A Canoeist's Guide to the Whitewater Rivers of West Virginia*)

Decker's Creek: Monongalia Co. Dellslow at St. Rte. 7 brdg. to Monongalia River, 6 mi., polluted with mine acid, limestone washing, foundry effluent, and some raw sewage last 3 mi., some high-standing waves, junk and other hazards, some dif. areas. (Credit—*A Canoeist's Guide to the Whitewater Rivers of West Virginia*)

Elk River: Kanawha, Clay cos. Sutton Dam to Kanawha River, 97 mi., peaceful, meandering, many easy riffles; take care in heavy runoff. (Credit—*A Canoeist's Guide to the Whitewater Rivers of West Virginia*)

Gauley River: Nicholas Co. Rte. 20 brdg. to Donegal Mine No. 10, 6 mi., med. dif. to very dif., not for novice; Donegal Mine No. 10 to Rte. 39 brdg., 10 mi., first 2 mi. vigorous rapids—then reservoir. Below Summersville Dam 24 mi. roadless, Dif. V–VI, a super project for experts only. (Credit—*A Canoeist's Guide to the Whitewater Rivers of West Virginia*)

Greenbrier River: USGS—Durbin, Cass, Mingo, Marlington, Labella, White Sulphur Springs, Ronceverte, Alderson, and Big Bend; Pocahontas, Greenbrier, and Summers cos. From Durbin to Hinton, 150 mi., 5–6 days; river starts as small trout stream in wilderness, gets larger downstream, exciting white water in lower sec. Fishing—panfish and bass in upper part, then walleye, pike, and musky in lower part. Good camping along river.

Trip 1—Rte. 250 brdg. W. of Durbin to Cass, 17 mi., beautiful, small stream, wilderness, no major dif. rapids.

Trip 2—Cass to Marlington, 27 mi., uncomplicated rapids, no obstruction. Dif. II–III on Trips 1 and 2, no particular dangers on Trips 1 and 2.

Trip 3—Marlington to Renick, 35 mi. Dif. II–III, no particular danger, river now wider, gravel bed.

Trip 4—Renick Rte. 219 to Anthony Sta., 12 mi., rapids mixed with long flat pools, 1 dif. rapid.

Trip 5—Anthony Sta. to Ronceverte, 18 mi., occasional rapids, scout rock dam at Ronceverte, scarcely populated, beautiful scenery on Trips 4 and 5. Dif. of Trips 4 and 5 is II–III, some good rapids; rapids, strong current, some waves, some dif. rapids.

Trip 6—Alderson to jctn. with Rtes. 3 and 12 is 24 mi., experienced canoeists only. DANGER—falls and ledges, Dif. IV, run only in decked canoes. Bacon Falls is on this section, keep to left side, there is a sheer rock cliff on right bank before Bacon Falls. Above Hinton, 5 mi., DANGER—3-ft. falls 1 mi. below Rtes. 3 and 12 brdg., many good rapids on this trip. DANGER—keep away from cliffs, particularly those above Bellepoint on left bank.

(Credit—*Canoeing White Water River Guide* and *A Canoeist's Guide to the Whitewater Rivers of West Virginia*)

Lost River: Moving water, S. of Wardensville, 2–3 mi., dif. white water, dangerous; the 5 mi. above Rte. 55 brdg. for experts only.

Meadow River: Fayette, Greenbrier cos. Green Siding to Russelville, 15 mi., quite easy first 8 mi. to RR brdg., then watch out, last part very dif. white water in canyon, some ptgs. or lining. (Credit—*A Canoeist's Guide to the Whitewater Rivers of West Virginia*)

Moorefield River: See S. Fork of S. Branch of Potomac.

New River: Summers, Raleigh, Fayette cos. Bluestone Dam to Fayette Sta., 56 mi. Bluestone Dam to Sandstone, 11 mi. Scout—Brooks Falls. Sandstone Falls are unrunnable, some dif. rapids, flat stretches with riffles; Sandstone to Prince, 16 mi. Prince to Thurmond, 15 mi., some heavy rapids, wide and powerful river, big waves. Thurmond to Fayette Sta., 14 mi., biggest white-water river in W. Va., whirlpools, large standing waves, experts only, some rapids most dif. there are, approach entire river with caution when above 2½ ft. at Hinton. (Credit—*A Canoeist's Guide to the Whitewater Rivers of West Virginia* and *Canoeing Guide to Western Pennsylvania and Northern West Virginia*)

N. River: Hwy. 50 to Rte. 45 forks of Cacapon, 21 mi., terrific, skilled only, fast, clear, cold water, narrow, fences, low trees, beautiful, 1 dam—ptg. left, sharp bends; before May 15 or after rain. (Credit—*A Canoeist's Guide to the Whitewater Rivers of West Virginia*)

Paint Creek: Fayette, Raleigh cos. Mossy to Westerly, 4 mi., some very dif. rapids. DANGER—movable wooden brdg.—no passage in heavy rapids, don't go below RR brdg.—falls below. Below Westerly to Burnwell, 6 mi., bad scenery, junk, garbage, slag piles, access pts. dif. to find; second brdg. below falls, impassable and rock 400 yds. upstream from brdg., Dif. I–III, after first spring thaws. (Credit—*A Canoeist's Guide to the Whitewater Rivers of West Virginia*)

Potomac River—Upper Sec.: From Greenspring to Williamsport. See description under Maryland.

Potomac River—N. Branch: USGS—W. Va. and Md., Oakland, Elk Garden; Grant and Mineral cos. From Gormania, W. Va., to Bloomington, Md., 38 mi. Dif. IV–VI. Top experts only, very dangerous, river flat first 3 mi., then turns wild, run until May 1, use decked canoe and survival gear.

   Trip 1—Gormania to Rte. 50 at Kitzmiller, 16 mi. Dif. V–VI.
   Trip 2—Kitzmiller to Bloomington, Md., 22 mi. Dif. IV–V. Remember: a very dangerous river. (Credit—*Canoeing White Water River Guide*)

Potomac River—N. Fork of S. Branch: USGS—Circleville, Onego, Petersburg; Pendleton and Grant cos. From Circleville to Smokehole Caverns, 30 mi. Dif. III–IV.
   Trip 1—Circleville to Mouth of Seneca, 15 mi. Dif. III. No

particular dangers, beautiful river, small river, white water, good current, mostly continuous action, exciting, one of best white-water runs in the East.

Trip 2—Mouth of Seneca to Dolly Cmpgrnds., 10 mi. Dif. II–III. Pretty much same description as Trip 1, some overhanging branches. Excel. fishing for trout and bass.

Trip 3—Dolly Cmpgrnds. to Smokehole Caverns, 5 mi. Dif. III–IV, can be dangerous in high water, steep rapids, more dif. than upper parts.

(Credit—*Canoeing White Water River Guide* and *A Canoeist's Guide to the Whitewater Rivers of West Virginia*)

Potomac River—S. Branch: USGS—Onego, Circleville, Petersburg, Greenland Gap, Moorefield, Keyser, Hanging Rock, and Oldtown; Pendleton, Hardy, Hampshire, and Grant cos. From Franklin to jctn. of N. Branch of Potomac, Dif. II–VI, 118 mi., 4–5 days, upper part (Smoke Hole Run) for experts only.

Trip 1—Franklin to cmpgrnd. in Smoke Hole Canyon, 22 mi., Dif. III–IV, run spring–early summer, experts only, 1 out of 10 beginners' canoes are destroyed on this run. DANGER—5-ft. dam. DANGER—rock blockage of river— ptg. left side. DANGER—3 mi. of very dangerous water below rockslide. DANGER—low-water brdg.

Trip 2—Smoke Hole cmpgrnd. to Petersburg Brdg., 21 mi., Dif. II–VI. DANGER—waterfall 7 mi. after cmpgrnd. Beautiful river on both secs., white water, experts only, good trout fishing.

Trip 3—Petersburg to Hwy. 220 brdg. below Moorefield, Dif. I–II, 17 mi., no particular dangers.

Trip 4—Hwy. 220 brdg. to Romney, 24 mi., Dif. II, rapids above RR brdg. and below RR brdg.

Trip 5—Romney to jctn. with N. Branch, 34 mi., Dif. I–II, lower part (Trips 3–5) less pretty than upper sec., parts are very scenic. Panfish, cats, and small-mouth bass on lower sec.

(Credit—*Canoeing White Water River Guide* and *Blue Ridge Voyages*)

Potomac River—S. Fork of S. Branch (Moorefield River Gorge):

USGS—Fort Seybert, Petersburg, Orkney Springs, and Moorefield; Haring, Pendleton, and Hardy cos. From Fort Seybert to Moorefield, 35 mi. Dif. I–IV.

Trip 1—Fort Seybert to brdg. below Gorge, 10 mi., experts only. Dif. IV–V. DANGER—Dif. V rapids below New Bethlehem Church. Gorge is uninhabited, very dangerous, long walk to help. Fish—small-mouth bass and panfish.

Trip 2—From hwy. brdg. below The Gap to Moorefield, 25 mi. Dif. I–III. DANGERS—tricky rapid 6 mi. after put-in, low-water brdg., can run this trip until June 1, can extend trip 3 mi. to brdg. on S. Branch. Fish—small-mouth bass and panfish.

(Credit—*Canoeing White Water River Guide*)

Seneca Creek: Pendleton Co. USGS—Seneca cmpgrnd. 7 mi., wild ride, all white water, blind bends, sudden drops, irregular chutes. DANGER—dangling cable below little white church on right. Run after spring thaws. (Credit—*A Canoeist's Guide to the Whitewater Rivers of West Virginia*)

Tygart River: Randolph, Barbour, Taylor cos. Mill Creek to brdg. at W. edge of Elking, 32 mi., easy meandering, scenic, spring only. Belington to mouth of Buchannon River, 11 mi., continuous rapids, spectacular gorge, experts only, very dangerous. Belington to Philippi. Start—Weise Camp below Belington. End—Lilian above Philippi, experts only, decked canoes, more dif. than Cheat Canyon, 11 mi., Dif. IV–V, line rapids, 10-ft. waterfall—can't be run, suicide for open canoes in med. water, beautiful ctry., very dangerous. Arden Run—6 mi., rapids, standing waves, very dangerous sec., exceedingly dif. secs., 15-ft. waterfall. Valley Falls to Hammond, 1 mi., experts only, utmost dif.; drops 60 ft. over 8 major rapids, several Dif. VI. Hammond to Colfax, 5 mi., no danger spots, normally pleasant. Below Grafton Dam, water level constant, run in summer or fall, like the Youghiogheny. (Credit—*A Canoeist's Guide to the Whitewater Rivers of West Virginia* and *Canoeing Guide to Western Pennsylvania and Northern West Virginia*)

WISCONSIN

Bad and Marengo rivers: Ashland Co. Odanah Rd. to Elm Hoist Brdg., 20 mi., pleasant trip, good fishing, some rapids.

Baraboo River: Sauk, Columbia cos. Hwy. G. to Wisconsin River, easy canoeing, no rapids, no dif. ptgs., no long stretches of fast water. Ptg. dams—La Valle, Reedsburg, 3 times at Baraboo.

Bear River: Iron Co. Flambeau Lake to Flambeau River, 1 day, several rd. crossings, wild entry, no rapids, good trip.

Big Elk River: Price Co. 2 days, Musser Dam to S. Fork Flambeau River below Musser Lake Dam to Phillips, 10 mi., several easy rapids, some dif. in low water, good fishing. Phillips to co. trunk W., brdg. on S. Fork Flambeau, 14 mi., 2 good rapids—run Fleming Rapids in center, run Soo Rapids on right. Ptg.—Soo Dam on right.

Black River: Jackson, La Crosse cos. Lake Arbutus to Mississippi River. Start—N. States Power Co. below Hatfield, 1 day to Black River Falls Dam, some rapids, rocky. Black River Falls to mouth, 3 days, no rapids, no dams, good camping.

Bois Brule River: USGS—Brule, Ellison Lake; Douglas Co. From Co. Hwy. S. brdg. to mouth at Lake Superior, 36 mi. Dif. I–III. Good trout fishing.
   Trip 1—From Co. Hwy. S. brdg. to Co. Hwy. B. brdg., 9 mi., normally sufficient water, nice scenery, some civilization, rapids.—Dif. I.
   Trip 2—Co. Hwy. B. brdg. to U.S. Hwy. 2 brdg., 4 mi., rapids. Dif. I–II, can be Dif. III in high water.

(Credit—*Whitewater, Quietwater: The Wild Rivers of Wisconsin, Upper Michigan, and Northeast Minnesota*)

Brule River: *Section A*—Forest, Florence cos. Nelma to Menominee River, 2 days, wild country, shallow rapids in upper stretches. DANGER—Big Bull Rapids below mouth of Michigamme River. Trout fishing.

Section B—Douglas Co. Co. Hwy. P. to Stones Brdg., 9 mi., 10 hrs., clean, clear water, stable flow, slow and winding, beaver dams, submerged logs, overhanging limbs, no rapids, good trout fishing. Stones Brdg. to U.S. Hwy. 2, 12 mi., 7 hrs., one of finest trips in Wis., stable water level, superb rapids, rapids get more dif. downriver, motorboats outlawed, wild entry, popular with avg. canoeist. Excel. trout fishing. U.S. Hwy. 2 brdg. to N. P. Johnson Brdg., 10 mi., 9 hrs., first stretch easy, last 3 mi. continuous white water—for expert canoeist only, some ptgs., excel. fishing; N. P. Johnson Brdg. to Lake Superior, 13 mi., 7 hrs., 1 extreme hazard rapid below Johnson Brdg., run other rapids and riffles, flat water before lake, novice canoeists avoid stretch to St. Hwy. 13, some ptgs., good fishing.

Chippewa River: Ashland, Sawyer, Rusk, Chippewa cos. Glidden to Stockfarm Brdg., 20 mi., 9 hrs., need med. or higher water level, some wading, some spots unnavigable, some obstacles, semi-wilderness. Start—pub. lndg. on Fishback Rd. W. of Hwy. 13, many riffles, good white water. End—Stockfarm Brdg. on F.R. 164. Good fishing—musky, bass, panfish. Stockton Brdg. to Blaisdell Lake, 15 mi., 7 hrs., easy rapids, some wading. End—pub. lndg. on upper Blaisdell Lake. Blaisdell Lake to Winter Dam, 12½ mi., 6 hrs., lake and river canoeing, many rapids, some challenging part in low water, at Snaptail Rapids, in low, high, or very high water use canal and ptg. dam. Ptg.—Winter Dam; Winter Dam to Ojiba, 8 mi., 3 hrs., scenic, med. current, riffles, 1 low hazard rapid, bottom stony. End—pub. lndg. right bank—below Co. Hwy. G. brdg.

Chippewa River—W. Fork: Washburn, Burnett, Sawyer cos. Upper Clam Lake to Belsky Fire Lane Brdg., 6 hrs., 9 mi., mostly slow current, few low rapids, sandy bottom. Start—stream from St. Hwy. 77 brdg., some wading, dif. Fish Trap Rapids in low water. Belsky Fire Lane Brdg. to Co. Hwy. B. brdg., 15 mi., 7 hrs. slow–med. current, many rapids.

Clam River: Burnett Co. N. Fork, Matteson Brdg. to Lynch Brdg., 10 mi., 9 hrs., slow water, wild shorelines, no rapids, short ptgs. around obstacles. S. Fork, Burnikel Rd. to Lynch Brdg., 6 mi., 5 hrs., small stream, slow current, no rapids, logjams, and fallen trees. Upper Clam River: Lynch Brdg. to Meenon Park, 13 mi., 8 hrs., med.–slow current, no rapids. Excel. fishing. Meenon Park to St. Croix River, 20 mi., 2 days, mostly slow current, logjams, fallen trees. Good fishing—small-mouth bass, northern pike.

Courderay River: Sawyer, Washburn cos. Windigo Lake to Billy Bog Dam, 12 mi., 9 hrs., mostly lake canoeing, Windigo, Grindstone, Court Oreilles, and Little Court Oreilles lakes. Start—where W. arm of Lake Windigo meets St. Hwy. 27. Ptg.—½ mile to Grindstone Lake. End—pub. lndg., right bank, Billy Bog Dam; Billy Bog Dam to Radisson, 13 mi., 6 hrs., or to Chippewa River, 16 mi., low rapids, excel. fishing, med.–slow current, OK all canoeists. DANGER—Swift Dam, use left chute, whirlpools below dam. Ojibwa to Co. Hwy. D. brdg. near Exeland, 15 mi., 6 hrs., med. current, several low hazard rapids, 1 short stretch of white water. DANGER—Belisle Falls. Ptg.—Arpin Dam 7 Belisle Falls. Excel. fishing. Co. Hwy. D. brdg. to Imalone, 11 mi., 5 hrs., 25 rapids, 2 with high hazard rating, deep holes. DANGER —Soo Line Rapids. End—Harris-Eddy at iron brdg. Imalone to Bruce, 9 mi., 5 hrs., fast, wild, rapids, separated by long, quiet water. Dinner and Lundgrens holes—excel. fishing, some tricky rapids. Bruce to Chippewa-Flambeau jctn., 18 mi., 9 hrs., mostly quiet water, few easy rapids. Excel. fishing—small-mouth bass, walleye, musky, cats. Chippewa-Flambeau jctn. to N. States Power Co. Dam, 10½ mi., 7 hrs., mostly lake canoeing, winds make trip tough. Fishing excel.—musky, walleye, panfish.

Crystal River: Waupaca Co. Fast-running little stream, some exciting rapids near Parfreville, small-mouth bass, spring runs of white bass and walleyes.

Deer Trail Creek: Rusk Co. St. Hwy. 27 brdg., 5 mi. S. of Ladysmith to Co. Hwy. D. brdg., 3 hrs., 7 mi., riffles, low rapids, quiet pools. Excel. fishing—walleye, musky, small-mouth bass.

Eau Claire River: Douglas Co. Second brdg. to St. Croix River, 13 mi., 8 hrs., wild shoreline, med. current, low rapids, some shallows in low water, good trout fishing in fast water. Ptg.—low dam below put-in. DANGER—6-mile logging dam.

Embarras River: USGS Tigerton; Shawano Co. From St. Hwy. 45 brdg. at Tigerton to Co. M. brdg., 3 mi. Dif. II–III. Don't run in low water, windfalls, barbed wire, quiet with rapids. Dif. I first 2 mi., then logjam, then drop with Dif. II–III, scout first; then quiet water, then strong pitches near Dells—ptg., dangerous hole follows, then continuous rapids, Dif. II–III in Dells, steep canyon, strong waves; take out after canyon (Credit—*Whitewater, Quietwater: The Wild Rivers of Wisconsin, Upper Michigan, and Northeast Minnesota*)

Flambeau Flowage: Iron Co. 17,000 acres, hundreds of mi. of wild shoreline, isles. Excel. fishing—pike, musky, walleye, panfish. Turtle–Flambeau trip, 8½ mi., 6 hrs. Falls at Co. Hwy. F. to Turtle Dam, superb fishing, ptg. right at dam. Manitowish–Flambeau rte., 9 mi., 7 hrs., lake canoeing. Murray Lndg. to Turtle Dam.

Flambeau River: Rusk, Price cos. Upper—Turtle Dam to Park Falls, 18 mi., 6 hrs., fast, exciting, beautiful, good rapids. DANGER—Notch Park Rapids. Ptg.—¼ mi. at Park Falls, left bank, excel. fishing. Park Falls, 2 ptgs.—Pixley Dam, left; Crowley Dam, right; 9 mi., Creek to Babbs Isle, 22 mi., 9 hrs., wild, fast, lower—large, exciting rapids, strong current. Ptg.—Flambeau Falls—nonskilled, no take-out at Forks, go on to Hewas Camp 2 mi. beyond. Forks to Big Falls Dam, 13 mi., 4½ hrs., outstanding white water, several skills required for several rapids.

DANGER—Beaver Dam rapids. Ptg.—Big Falls Dam, over dike —left bank. Big Falls to Ladysmith, 12 mi., 7 hrs., lake canoeing. Start—Lake Superior Dist. Pur. Co. cmpgrnd., stick close to shore, good fishing. Ptg. left—Ladysmith Dam. Ladysmith to Thornapple Dam, 10 mi., 5 hrs., some fast water below dam, mostly med.–slow current. Start—below Hwy. 27 brdg. Ptg.— Thornapple, left. Thornapple Dam to Chippewa–Flambeau jctn., 8½ mi., 3 hrs., med. current, easy rapids. Start—below Thornapple Dam—left bank. End—Flater's Pub. Lndg., right bank above forks.

Flambeau River—S. Fork: Price Co. Round Lake to Cedar Rapids, 12 mi., 7 hrs., relatively wild, beautiful. Ptg.—Round Lake Doering Dam, 3 small dams, can run, some dif. rapids. End —F.R. 149 brdg. Cedar Rapids to Fifield, 19 mi., 9 hrs., high-hazard rapids, ptg. Blockhouse Dam and Divine rapids Rock Dam; Fifield to Co. Hwy. F., 12 mi., 5 hrs., several good rapids. DANGER—Rocky Carry—white water. End—right bank above Co. Hwy. F. brdg. Co. Hwy. F. brdg. to County Hwy. W. brdg., 10 mi., 4 hrs., good white water, in med. or higher water, some dif. rapids End—pub. lndg. below Co. Hwy. W. brdg. Co. Hwy. W. brdg. to Flambeau forks, 13 mi., for experts, white water, many rapids—some high-hazard ptg.—Little Falls.

Fox River: Marquette, Columbia cos. Ptg. to Wolf River minor obstacles—old dams. Some cats, bass, and northern pike.

Horsehead—Lac du Flambeau Trail: Vilas Co. Start—W. of Presque Isle at N. end of Horsehead Lake. End—village of Lac du Flambeau. Trail—Horsehead Lake to Armour Lake to N. Crab Lake to Little Crab Lake to Manitorist and Alder lakes to Wild Rice Lake via Trout River to Ike Walton Lake to Little Sand, White Sand, and Pokegam lakes to Lac du Flambeau. Several ptgs., some river travel.

Jump River—N. Fork: Price Co. U.S. Hwy. 8 to Co. Hwy. I., 8½ mi., 3 hrs., many riffles, sometimes beaver dams, wild, scenic, untraveled, dif. in low water, fishing good in Oxbow. Co. Hwy. I. to forks, 10 mi., 3½ hrs., scenic, primitive, rocky shallows, med.–high water necessary, some wading, no hazardous rapids.

Jump River—S. Fork: Price, Taylor, Chippewa cos. Prentice to St. Hwy. 86, 11 mi., 6 hrs., mostly quiet water, go in high water; minor rapids and riffles. St. Hwy. 86 to Co. Hwy. M., 3 mi., about same as from Prentice, dif. in low water. Co. Hwy M. to forks, 19 mi., 7 hrs., exciting, many rips and small rapids.

Kickapoo River: 125 mi.; flows through Occoch Mountains and Kickapoo Valley, rugged hill country, high bluffs, roads, parallel river most of way, winding river, many brdgs. Trip—Ontario–Wauzeka; 3 ptgs.—right ptg. La Farge Dam, left ptg. Teadstone Dam, left ptg. Gays Mills.

Lemonweir River: Juneau Co. Hwy. H. to Wisconsin River, mod. fast; 3 ptgs.—New Lisbon Dam, Mauston and Lemonweir dams. HAZARD—slough below Hwy. HH. brdg., easy to get lost in.

Little Fox River: Racine, Kenosha cos. Big Bend to Ill. st. line, lazy river, some shallow spots, several dams, easy to canoe, many motorboats.

Little Wolf River: USGS—Tigerton; Waupaca Co. From Mud Lake Rd. brdg. to Co. Hwy. C. brdg. at town of Big Falls, 8 mi. Dif. II. Fair to good scenery, trout fishing. Rapids—Dif. II. CAUTION—culverts under McNinch Rd. brdg.; scout first.

Lower Ox Creek: Douglas Co. 3 hrs., med.–high water levels necessary, several rapids.

Main Creek: Chippewa, Rusk cos. Conrath to Lake Holcombe, 8 mi., very dif., wading, few small rapids, good fishing.

Manitowish River: Vance Lake to Flambeau Flowage, 22 mi., mostly slow water, scenic—wilderness, few easy rapids. Excel. fishing—musky, walleye. End—Murray's Pub. Lndg., E. end of Flowage.

Marengo River: USGS—Mellen; Ashland Co. From brdg. N. of town of Highbridge to Elm Hoist Trail Brdg., 12 mi. Dif. I–II. Run in spring, excellent scenery, trout and walleye fishing, windfalls, rapids with Dif. I–II. (Credit—*Whitewater, Quietwater: The Wild Rivers of Wisconsin, Upper Michigan, and Northeast Minnesota*)

Menominee River: Marinette Co. Brule River to Green Bay, many ptgs.—rough water upstream from mouth of Pine River, Little Portage Falls, below Niagara Sturgeon Dam, Pemene Dam, Pemene Falls. DANGER—Sturgeon Dam. Easy rapids and more ptgs. below Sturgeon Dam.

Montreal River: USGS—Little Girls Point, Ironwood. Iron Co. in Wis. and Gogebic Co. in Mich. From W. Branch of Montreal below Gile Flowage at Hwy. 77 brdg. to Wis. Hwy. 122 brdg., 9 mi. Dif. II–III.
    Trip 1—Hwy. 77 brdg. to Wis. Hwy. 2 brdg., 5 mi., water level depends on dam release, beautiful scenery. DANGER—RR rapids about 1 mi. after put-in; ptg. right—watch for large boulders to mark spot where rapids begin. CAUTION—rapids Dif. III after Chicago and North Western RR brdg., scout first. DANGER—waterfall at steel brdg.
    Trip 2—Below Saxon Falls Dam to Wis. Hwy. 122 brdg., rapids Dif. II, beautiful canyon, not as tough a trip as Trip 1. (Credit—*Whitewater, Quietwater: The Wild Rivers of Wisconsin, Upper Michigan, and Northeast Minnesota*)

Namekagon Lake: Bayfield Co. N. of bay to Namekagon Lake Dam, 4 mi., 2–8 hrs. scenic; vil. of Namekagon to Namekagon Lake Dam, 6 mi., 3–8 hrs., excel. fishing.

Namekagon River: Bayfield, Sawyer cos. Namekagon River to Pacwawong, 16 mi., 6 hrs., semiwilderness, narrow, avg. current, several low-hazard rapids. Pacwawong Dam to Hayward, 15 mi., 6 hrs., stream and lake canoeing, some low-hazard rapids, 1 ptg. —Phipps Dam. Hayward to Groat Lndg., 11 mi., 4 hrs., mod. current, several good rapids, excel. small-mouth bass fishing.

Groat Lndg. to Trego, 17 mi., 7 hrs., good rapids—some tricky, long stretches—slow current. Trego to Byrkit Lndg., 15 mi., 5 hrs., lake and river canoeing ptg.—Trego Dam, fast current, no hazardous rapids. Good fishing—northern pike, walleye, bass, panfish. Byrkit Lndg. to Namekagon Trail Brdg., 16 mi., or to St. Croix River, 21 mi., near wilderness, few easy rapids, good fishing, musky, northern pike, small-mouth bass.

Oconto River, N. Branch: USGS—Thunder Mt.; Langlade, Oconto cos. From F.S. 2104 brdg. to Co. Hwy. W. brdg., 8 mi. Dif. II.

Trip 1—From F.S. 2104 brdg. to Hwys. 32 and 64 brdg., 4 mi. Beautiful, run in spring or after heavy rain, don't run when Cap Buettner's gauge on the Wolf is less than 15 ft., fast current, not for beginners. Several rapids Dif. I–II, windfalls, blind curves.

Trip 2—Hwys. 32 and 64 brdg. to Co. Hwy. W. brdg., 4 mi. Same general description as Trip 1 but more civilization. CAUTION—barbed wire, continuous rapids; good trout fishing above Bagley rapids.

(Credit—*Whitewater, Quietwater: The Wild Rivers of Wisconsin, Upper Michigan, and Northeast Minnesota*)

Pecatonica River: Lafayette Co. 2 forks to Ill. st. line, either fork good, few easy rapids in both, farmland, many brdgs., some fences, some fallen trees.

Pelican River: Oneida Co. Moen's Lake to Hwy. 8, easy, 1-day trip, rapids below N. Pelican Lake Dam, no ptgs., dif. in low water.

Peshtigo River: Marinette Co. Hwy. C. to Green Bay, wild entry, some dams, flowages, white water, N. Woods scenery, water levels vary, several ptgs. Ptg. rough water below Johnson Falls unless expert—one of state's toughest trips.

Pike River: Marinette Co. Very limited canoeing.

Pine River: Marinette Co. Very limited canoeing.

Popple River: USGS—Florence Co. From F.S. 2398 brdg. to jctn. with Pine River, 19 mi. Dif. I–III. Don't run after mid-May; excellent scenery, wild country.

> *Trip 1*—F.S. 2398 brdg. to F.S. 2159 brdg., 9 mi. Dif. I–II. Several rapids.

> *Trip 2*—F.S. 2159 brdg. to jctn. with Pine River, 10 mi., experts only in covered craft, scout rapids first, many areas Dif. III, 1 area Dif. IV at Washburn Falls—ptg. right. Take out on Bass Lake Road.

> (Credit—*Whitewater, Quietwater: The Wild Rivers of Wisconsin, Upper Michigan, and Northeast Minnesota*)

Rock River: Dodge, Jefferson, Rock cos. Hwy. 49 to Ill. st. line. Long, leisurely river, shallow in Horicon Marsh; several ptgs.—dams.

St. Croix River: Burns, Polk, St. Croix cos. Upper St. Croix Lake to Cut-away Dam, 6½ mi., 7 hrs., mostly lake canoeing, slow water, 1 easy rapid, ptg. second bridge in high water. Excel. fishing—bass, northern pike, panfish. Gordon Dam to co. line rd., 12½ mi., 8 hrs., beautiful, quite wild, 35 rapids—mostly low–med. hazard, some wading in low water. Good fishing—small-mouth bass, northern pike. Dry Landing to Riverside, 10 mi., 4–5 hrs., med.–fast current, wild, scenic area, good rapids, 1 high-hazard rapid—Big Fish Trap. Good fishing—northern pike, walleye, small-mouth bass. Riverside to St. Hwy. 77 brdg., 13½ mi., 6 hrs., mod. current, no ptgs. Norway Pt. to Soderbeck Lndg., 10 mi., 5 hrs., varies from slow to turbulent water, some mod.-hazard rapids, great scenery. Soderbeck Lndg. to Old Rush City Ferry, 12½ mi., 6 hrs., slow–mod. current, no rapids, no ptgs., scenic, good fishing. Old Rush City Ferry to Nevers Dam, 16 mi., 6 hrs., mod. current, few easy rapids, wild, scenic, excel. fishing. Nevers Dam to St. Croix-Taylors Falls, 10 mi., 3½ hrs., slow water, no rapids, sandbars, scenic, some motorboats, 3 ptgs. —low dam at outlet from Upper Eau Claire Lake, outlet from Mid. Eau Claire Lake and Monney Dam. Upper Eau Claire Lake to second brdg., 8½ mi., 7 hrs., mostly lake canoeing, many different trips possible, short ptgs. necessary. Excel. fishing—northern pike, walleye, bass, panfish, musky.

Thornapple River: Sawyer, Rusk cos. St. Hwy. 27 8 mi. N. of Ladysmith to U.S. Hwy. 8 brdg. E. of Bruce, 6 hrs., many riffles, several good rapids, wild, secluded. DANGER—in flood, rapids above Soo Line RR brdg.—hazardous, fallen trees.

Three Lakes—Eagle River Trail: Vilas, Oneida cos. Big Lake to Eagle River, calm water, good fishing, fine scenery. Start—outlet of Big Lake. End—Long Lake outlet or on into Wisconsin River. Good campsites, good side trips.

Tomahawk River: Oneida, Lincoln cos. Minocqua Lakes to Wisconsin River, 60 mi., 4 days, lake and river canoeing. Ptg.—Prairie Rapids and Half Breed Rapids. Many access pts., dif. in low water.

Totogatic River: Washburn Co. Duck Dam to Hwy. 53, 24 mi., wilderness stream, in high water only. From Duck Dam to Colton Dam—Apr.—series of rapids, experts only. Ptg.—High Falls, Buck Falls. From Colton Dam to U.S. Hwy. 53 mostly slow, many short ptgs., wild, good fishing. U.S. Hwy. 53 to Lake Nancy Rd., 16 mi., 9 hrs. Shallow, upper part, slow current; below lake, med. current, low-hazard rapids. Lake Nancy Rd. to Namekagon River, 15 mi., 7 hrs., wild and secluded, fluctuating flow, some easy rapids. Excel. fishing—northern pike, walleye, bass.

Trout River: Vilas Co. Trout Lake to Manitowish Lake and river trip.

Turtle River: Iron Co. Shea Dam to the falls at Co. Hwy. FF., 14 mi., 9 hrs., small, scenic lakes, wild shore, some wading—low water, 10 rapids—low–med. hazard, OK avg. canoeist.

Waupaca Chain of Lakes: Waupaca Co. 23 clear, spring-fed lakes with connecting channels, wooded shorelines, sand beaches, good trout streams nearby.

Waupaca River: Waupaca Co. Chain of Lakes to Wolf River, interesting, short trip.

White River: USGS—Grandview, Marengo; Ashland, Bayfield cos. From Town Rd. E. of town of Mason to Hwy. 112 brdg., 14 mi. Dif. I–II. Trout fishing, windfalls, muddy water, can be very dangerous with heavy release from dam, in normal flow the river has continuous rapids Dif. I–II. (Credit—*Whitewater, Quietwater: The Wild Rivers of Wisconsin, Upper Michigan, and Northeast Minnesota*)

Wisconsin River: Many cos. Lac Vieux Desert to Mississippi River; Lac Vieux Desert to Vilas-Oneida co. line, starts at river's source, no danger rapids, no obstructions, water fast at first, becomes slower, 2 short ptgs.; Vilas-Oneida co. line to Merrill, 4 dams, 1 straight sec. easy with 1 ptg. and easy rapids, second sec. from Rhinelander to Tomahawk, some hazardous rapids, ptg.— Whirlpool rapids, Merrill to Nekoosa, several ptgs.—dams; deep and slow water; Nekoosa to Prairie du Sac, flows through Wisconsin Dells from Dekoosa to Prentwell Dam—35 mi., no falls, no rapids, no ptgs. below Prentwell. Ptgs.—dams, river deep and swift from Stand Rock to dam at Wisconsin Dells, DANGER— backwash from motorboats in canyon. Prairie du Sac to Mississippi River is easiest sec. of river, no ptgs., some wading, river rises and falls rapidly, hwy. parallels river. Excel. fishing—bass, walleye, northern pike, catfish, panfish in river and sloughs.

Wolf River: Langlade, Menominee, Shawano, Outagamie, Waupaca cos. Post Lake to Shawano, not for beginners, many falls and rapids, can be dangerous, good trout stream, several access pts. Shawano to Lake Winnebago, no rapids or dams, good for novices, some speedboats. Walleye and white bass.

Yahara River: Dave, Rock cos. Lake Mendota to Rock River, runs through "Four Lakes" of Madison, some connecting portions dif., several dams, many access pts., watch lakes on windy days, generally pleasant.

Yellow River: *Section A*—Taylor, Chippewa cos. For. Ser. Rd. 108 to For. Ser. Rd. 575, 11 mi., 6 hrs., quiet, wild country, some riffles, med.–slow water. For. Ser. Rd. 575 to Miller Dam, 7 mi., 3½ hrs., half stream, half lake; slow–med. current, low rapids and riffles. End—right bank Miller Dam; Miller Dam to Mattes Brdg., 15 mi., last 8 mi dif. and dangerous. Upper part—low rocky rapids and long, slow pools; canoeing not advised from Co. Hwy. B. to Mattes Brdg.

Section B—Burnett Co. The Culverts to Hwy. H., 16 mi., 10 hrs., quiet, secluded, few gentle rapids. Excel. fishing—northern pike, good for trout. Co. Hwy. H. to Keyser Brdg., 20 mi., 16 hrs., no rapids, wild shoreline, slow–mod. current. Keyser Brdg. to St. Croix River, 25 mi., 12 hrs., stream and lake canoeing, slow–mod. current, few easy rapids. DANGER—don't canoe on Yellow Lake in storm or wind.

(Credit for Wisconsin information—*Wisconsin Water Trails, Wisconsin's North Central Canoe Trails,* and *Canoeing the Wild Rivers of Northwestern Wisconsin*)

WYOMING

Buffalo River: Teton Wilderness and Grand Teton Natl. Park. Teton For. Rd. 007 near Trupin Meadow Lodge to Snake River, good 1-day trips, approx. 25–30 mi., fair fishing, much wildlife, no obstacles or ptgs., can start higher but must pack into "wilderness."

Green River: Sublette, Lincoln cos. Bridger Natl. For. Green River Lakes to Fontenelle Res., approx. 108 mi. Lakes to Kendall, ptgs.—between lakes, shallow and rocky in upper stretches, poor fishing above Dollar Lake; Kendall to Old Fort Bonneville, most float trips start at Kendall, short stretches white water, not critical hazards; Old Fort Bonneville to Fontenelle Res., no serious obstacles, not often floated.

Greys River: Lincoln Co. Bridger Natl. For. Corral Creek For. Ser. Sta. to jctn. with Snake River, approx. 50 mi., short stretches white water; high-quality rapids below Poison Hollow.

Gros Ventre River: Teton Wilderness, Grand Teton Natl. Park, canoeable with proper flow, run in midseason; above Slide Lake, narrow, parallels Rd. 114, easy access; below Slide Lake, steep and rocky first few mi., ptg.—first few mi. below lake, then flows leisurely to Snake River, fair fishing.

Hoback River: Teton Wilderness. Teton Natl. For. Canoeable with proper flow, run in midseason. Access—good in lower half— Hwy. 189—187 runs parallel, access dif. for several mi. above and below town of Bondurant, access easy upstream on Teton Natl. For. land. Superb scenery in lower half—Hoback Canyon; many small rapids mixed with quiet stretches on river, fair fishing.

Platte River: Carbon Co. Sanger Ranch (access fee required) to BLM camping area—Bennett Peak, 4 mi., 1½ hrs. BLM area to Saratoga, 21 mi., 8 hrs. Cow Creek to Saratoga, 10 mi., 4 hrs. Saratoga to St. Picnic Area, 6 mi., 2½ hrs. Saratoga to Pick Brdg., 10 mi., 4 hrs. Saratoga to Bolten Ranch, 28 mi., 8 hrs. Saratoga to Ft. Steele, 42 mi., 2 days. River easy to run, watch for trees or bank washouts in high water, some rapids in sharp bends, fishing good, rainbow and brown trout, no ptgs. in high water, some wading in low water.

Shoshone River—N. and S. branches: Park, Big Horn cos. Shoshone Natl. For. Canoeable with right water conditions, dangerous in spring, good fishing; no other information.

Snake River: Teton, Lincoln cos. S. Gate of Yellowstone Park to Palisades Res. Approx. 125 mi., excel. DANGER—white water in small rock-walled canyon between S. Gate and Flagg Ranch, experts only, several large rapids in bottom end of Grand Canyon of the Snake, 90 mi., between those pts.—easy canoeing with minor rapids; below Jackson Lake dam to Moose Lndg., 25 mi. Non fee permit required from Natl. Park Ser., not particularly dangerous, water level OK through summer and fall, no dangerous rapids, some rough water at Deadmans Bar—can be avoided, many channels—some dif. in finding main one, strong current. Wildlife, incl. moose. Water not drinkable; some wading in fall. Dam to Pacific Creek 4½ mi. Pacific Creek to RKO site, 4 mi. RKO to Deadmans Bar, 7 mi. Deadmans Bar to Moose Lndg., 9½ mi. Fair–good fishing in summer, very good in fall.

FURTHER SOURCES
SUGGESTED

ALABAMA

Orr, John V. For. Supervisor, U.S. For. Ser., USDA, P.O. Box 40, Montgomery, Ala. 36101.

Tatum, W. M. and Hackney, P. A. "The Beautiful Cahaba River," *Alabama Conservation,* Vol. XXXLX, No. 4 (Aug. 1969), pp. 4–8. St. of Alabama Conservation Dept., 64 N. Union St., Montgomery, Ala. 36104.

ALASKA

Alaska Canoe Trails, U. S. Dept. of Interior, Bureau of Land Management; Write to: U. S. Dept. of Interior, Fish and Wildlife Sec., Bur. of Sport Fisheries and Wildlife, Kenai National Moose Range, P.O. Box 500, Kenai, Alas. 99611. Free.

ARIZONA

Coleman, Bert R. Chief, Visitor Develop. Sec., Dept. of Economic Planning and Develop., Ariz. Travel Information Sec., Suite 1704, 3303 N. Central Ave., Phoenix, Ariz. 85012.

Gillies, Robert B., Jr. District Ranger, USDA, For. Ser., Coconino Natl. For., Beaver Creek Ranger District, Rimrock, Ariz. 86335.

Holzhauser, Scott. "Arizona Fun," *American Whitewater,* Vol. XVI, No. 4 (Winter 1971), pp. 143–47.

McComb, John. 752 S. Forgeus Ave., Tucson, Ariz. 85716.

ARKANSAS

Bly, Harold D. P.O. Box 343, Pocahontas, Ark. 72455.

Boyles, F. Maps, "White and N. Fork River Trout Fishing" (1966) and "Little Red River" (1968), Ark. Game and Fish Commission.

Ouachita River Float Trip. USDA, For. Ser., Ouachita Natl. For., Hot Springs, Ark. 71901. Free.

Ozark Society Bulletin. (Winter 1969–70, Spring 1970, Summer 1970). The Ozark Society, P.O. Box 38, Fayetteville, Ark. 72701.

Wellborn, Jack, Jr. *A Guide to Canoeing the Cossatot,* 1625 Slattery Bldg., Shreveport, La. 71104.

CALIFORNIA

Dwyer, Ann. *Canoeing Waters of California,* Canoe California, P.O. Box 61, Kentfield, Calif. 94904. $4.00 with shipping.

Gardner, Max. Features Editor, *Scouting* magazine, Boy Scouts of America, North Brunswick, N.J. 08902.

Martin, Charles. *Sierra Whitewater.* Fiddleneck Press, P.O. Box 114, Sunnyvale, Calif. 94088.

Schwind, Dick. *River Touring.* The Touchstone Press, P.O. Box 81, Beaverton, Oreg. 97005. $7.00.

Trost, Carl. 257 Pacheco St., San Francisco, Calif. 94116.

Trowbridge, W. C. Canoe trips and canoe rentals. P.O. Box 942, Healdsburg Beach, Healdsburg, Calif. 95448.

COLORADO

Bovee, B. G. Adm. Asst., Parks and Rec. Planning Dept. of Nat. Res., St. of Colo., 6060 Broadway, Denver, Colo. 80216.

Eberhard, Tom. For. Ranger, U.S. For. Ser, USDA, Conejos Ranger Dist., La Jara, Colo. 81140.

Smith, Ray. Director, Challenge/Discovery, The Prescott Institutions, Prescott, Ariz. 86301.

Winn, Bill. "The Animas of Colorado," *American White Water,* Vol. XIII, No. 4 (Spring 1968), pp. 4–6.

CONNECTICUT

AMC New England Canoeing Guide. Appalachian Mountain Club, 5 Joy St., Boston, Mass. 02108. $5.00.

Canoeing in Connecticut. St. of Conn., Park and Forest Commission, Hartford, Conn. 06101.

Coffin, Stewart T. Old Sudbury Rd., RFD 1, Lincoln, Mass. 01773.

Grinnell, Lawrence I. *Canoeable Waterways of New York State and Vicinity* (1956). Pageant Press, Inc., Brooklyn, N.Y. 11201.

Hawley, Robert A. *A Guide for the Canoeist on the Farmington and Map* (1969). The Farmington River Watershed Assoc., Inc., Avon, Conn. 06001

The Farmington River and Watershed Guide (1970). The Farmington River Watershed Assoc., Inc., Avon, Conn. 06001 $2.50 for booklet, $.50 for map.

FLORIDA

Arthurs, David S. Editor and Publisher, Citrus Co. Publishing Co., Citrus County *Chronicle*-Dunnellon Press—The Poster, Box 65, 103 N. Opoka, Inverness, Fla. 32650.

A Proposed System of Canoe Trails. St. of Fla., Dept. of Nat. Res., Larson Bldg., Tallahassee, Fla. 32304.

Florida Canoe Trail Guide and Supplement. State of Fla., Dept. of Nat. Res., Div. of Rec. and Parks, Larson Bldg., Tallahassee, Fla. 32304. Free.

Map and News Release. U. S. Dept. of Interior, Natl. Park Ser., Everglades Natl. Park and Fort Jefferson Natl. Monument, P.O. Box 279, Homestead, Fla. 33030.

Truesdell, William G. *A Guide to the Wilderness Waterway of the Everglades National Park.* Univ. of Miami Press, Coral Gables, Fla. 33124. $2.50.

GEORGIA

Cannon, Raymond S. *The Satilla River Development Project* (Sept. 1969), pp. 26–32. For Slash Pine Area Planning and Dev. Comm., Adm. by S. Reg. Educ. Brd., 120 6th St., N.W., Atlanta, Ga. 30313.

Canoe Guide to the Alapaha River Trail. Coastal Plains Area Tourism Council, Box 1223, Valdosta, Ga. 31601.

Canoe Guide to the Scenic Satilla River. Slash Pine Area Planning and Development Comm., P.O. Box 1276, Waycross, Ga. 31501.

Canoe Guide to the Withlacoochee River Trail. Coastal Plains Area Tourism Council, Box 1223, Valdosta, Ga., 31601 and St. of Fla., Dept. of Natl. Res., Larson Bldg., Tallahassee, Fla. 32304.

Canoeing Georgia's White Water Rivers. Georgia Mountains Planning and Development Comm., P.O. Box 1294, Gainesville, Ga. 30501.

Carter, Randy. *Canoeing White Water River Guide.* Appalachian Outfitters, Box 11, 2930 Chain Bridge Rd., Oakton, Va. 22124. $4.75.

Georgia Mt. Planning and Development Comm., P.O. Box 1294, Gainesville, Ga. 30501.

Harper, Robert A. Rec. Staff Officer, USDA, U.S. For. Ser., P.O. Box 1437, Gainesville, Ga. 30501.

Mitchell, G. R. Rte. 2, Box 215B, Camilla, Ga. 30317.

Various pamphlets and miscellaneous information from Refuge Mgr., Okefenokee Natl. Wildlife Refuge, P.O. Box 117, Waycross, Ga. 31501. Phone 912-283-2580.

Wilderness Canoeing in Okefenokee. Slash Pine Area Planning and Development Comm., 120 6th St., N.W., Atlanta, Ga. 30313.

HAWAII

Shima, Stanley. Aquatic Biologist, St. of Hawaii, Dept. of Land and Nat. Res., Div. of Fish and Game, 1179 Punchbowl St., Honolulu, Hawaii 96813.

IDAHO

Middle Fork of the Salmon. USDA, For. Ser., Intermountain Region, Ogden, Ut. 84401.

Miller, Jack M. Branch Chief, U.S. For. Ser., USDA, Targhee Natl. For., St. Anthony, Ida. 83445.

The Salmon, River of No Return. For. Ser., USDA, Northern and Intermountain Reg. Federal Bldg., Missoula, Mont. 09801.

ILLINOIS

Illinois Canoeing Guide. St. of Ill., Dept. of Conservation, Boating Sec., 400 S. Spring St., Springfield, Ill. 62704. Free.

IOWA

Iowa Canoe Trips. Iowa Conservation Comm., E. 7th and Court, Des Moines, Ia. 50309.

Knudson, G. E. *A Guide to the Upper Iowa River* (1971). Luther College Press, Luther College, Decorah, Ia. 52101. $1.50.

KANSAS

Bransom, N. W. P.O. Box 248, Coldwater, Kan. 67029.

Helwic, John. 400 Ridgecrest Dr., Richardson, Tex. 75080.

Nighswonger, James L. *A Methodology for Inventorying and Evaluating the Scenic Quality and Related Recreational Value of Kansas Streams.* Kansas Planning for Development, Report No. 32, Kansas Dept. of Economic Dev. Write to James L. Nighswonger, Landscape Architect, Dept. of Horticulture and Forestry, Kansas State University, Manhatten, Kans. 66502.

The Scenic Quality and Related Recreational Value of Selected Kansas Streams. St. of Kans., Dept. of Economic Dev., St. Office Bldg., Topeka, Kans. 66612.

KENTUCKY

Cosgrove, C. E. P.O. Box 44, Oak Ridge, Tenn. 37830.

Daniel Boone Natl. For. Float Trip Summary and Map of Daniel Boone Natl. Forest, U.S. For. Ser., USDA, P.O. Box 727, Winchester, Ky. 40391.

Stokley, Ronald L. 607½ Silverleaf Dr., Lexington, Ky. 40505.

LOUISIANA

Gibson, Lamar, Director-Liaison Officer, and Ryan, Patrick W., Interagency Co-ordinator. Letter of May 26, 1970, State Parks and Rec. Comm., P.O. Box Drawer 1111, Baton Rouge, La. 70821.

Louisiana Wildlife and Fisheries Comm., P.O. Box 44095, Capitol Sta., Baton Rouge, La. 70804.

Major, Lou, Jr.; Busby, Bruce; and Major, Steve. P.O. Box 820, Bogalusa, La. 70427 or the *Daily News* of Bogalusa, La.

Norton, Rick. Rte. 1, Box 375, Bogalusa, La. 70427. Phone 504-732-9635. Rents canoes, will serve as guide.

Williams, Richard and Mrs. *Canoeing in Louisiana.* Lafayette Nat. History Museum and Planetarium, 637 Girard Park Dr., Lafayette, La. 70501. $2.20 ea., incl. postage.

MAINE

Allagash Wilderness Waterway. St. Park and Rec. Comm., Augusta, Me. 04330.

AMC New England Canoeing Guide. Appalachian Mountain Club, 5 Joy St., Boston, Mass. 02108. $5.00.

Canoeing Map for the St. Croix River (Apr. 30, 1969). Me. For. Ser., Augusta, Me. 04330.

Coffin, Stewart T. Old Sudbury Rd., RFD 1, Lincoln, Mass. 01773.

Escape to Me. The Great St. of Maine, Flat Water Canoeing, Vacation Planner 4, Dept. of Econ. Dev., St. House, Augusta, Me. 04330.

Tuthill, Arthur H. "The Not So Dead River," *American White Water* Vol. XVI, No. 1 (Spring 1971), pp. 26–27.

Wild Me.: The Great St. of Maine, White Water Canoeing, Vacation Planner 3, Dept. of Econ. Dev., St. House, Augusta, Me. 04330.

MARYLAND

Corbett, Roger H., Jr., and Matacia, Louis J., Jr. *Blue Ridge Voyages,* Vol. I, 2nd ed. (1968) and *Blue Ridge Voyageurs,* Vol. II (1966). P.O. Box 32, Oakton, Va. 22124. $2.50 each.

Gray, Thomas L. *Canoeing Streams of the Potomac and Rappahannock Basins—Map.* 11121 Dewey Rd., Kensington, Md. 20795. $1.00.

MASSACHUSETTS

AMC New England Canoeing Guide. Appalachian Mountain Club, 5 Joy St., Boston, Mass. 02108. $5.00.

Coffin, Stewart T. Old Sudbury Rd., RFD 1, Lincoln, Mass.
01773.
Waite, Richard A. Executive Director, Westfield River Watershed
Assoc., Inc., P.O. Box 114, Middlefield, Mass. 01243.
Printed map of drainage area.

MICHIGAN

Canoeing in West Michigan. West Michigan Tourist Council, 107
Pearl St., N.W., Grand Rapids, Mich. 49503.
Huron River Canoeing Maps. Huron-Clinton Metropolitan Au-
thority, 600 Woodward Ave., Detroit, Mich. 48226. Free.
Michigan Canoe Trails. Michigan Dept. of Conservation in co-
operation with the Michigan Tourist Council, Stevens T.
Mason Bldg., Lansing, Mich. 48926. Free.
Michigan Guide to Easy Canoeing. Michigan Dept. of Nat. Res.,
Lansing, Mich. 48926. Free.
Palzer, Bob and Jody. *Whitewater, Quietwater: The Wild Rivers
of Wisconsin, Upper Michigan, and Northeastern Minnesota.*
Evergreen Paddleways, Two Rivers, Wis. Order from Out-
door Programs Office, Wis. Union, 800 Langdon St.,
Madison, Wis. 53706. $7.50.

MINNESOTA

Crow Wing Canoe Trail. Box 210, Sebeka, Minn. 56477.
Big Fork Canoe Trail. Box 256, Big Fork, Minn. 56628.
Inguadona Canoe Tour. Chippewa Natl. For., For. Supervisor,
Cass Lake, Minn. 56633. Free.
Kettle River. Pub. 9-41, St. of Minn., Documents Sec., 140 Cen-
tennial Bldg., St. Paul, Minn. 53155. $1.20.
Minnesota Voyageur Trails. Minnesota Dept. of Conservation,
Div. of Parks and Rec., 320 Centennial Bldg., St. Paul, Minn.
55101. $2.00.
Palzer, Bob and Jody. *Whitewater, Quietwater: The Wild Rivers*

of Wisconsin, Upper Michigan, and Northeastern Minnesota. Evergreen Paddleways, Two Rivers, Wis. Order from Outdoor Programs Office, Wis. Union, 800 Langdon St., Madison, Wis. 53706. $7.50.

Rice River Canoe Tour. Chippewa Natl. For., For. Supervisor, Cass Lake, Minn. 56633. Free.

Root River. Canoe Trails Assoc., Rushford, Minn. 55971.

Rum River. Pub. 9-42, St. of Minnesota, Documents Sec., 140 Centennial Bldg., St. Paul, Minn. 53155. $1.49.

St. Croix River. Book 1, Pub. 9-43, $1.49; Book 2, Pub. 9-44, St. of Minn., Documents Sec., 140 Centennial Bldg., St. Paul, Minn. 53155. $1.20.

Snake River. Pub. 9-45, St. of Minn., Documents Sec., 140 Centennial Bldg., St. Paul, Minn. 53155. $1.20.

Turtle River Canoe Tour. Chippewa Natl. For., For. Supervisor, Cass Lake, Minn. 56633. Free.

MISSISSIPPI

Black Creek Float Trip. DeSoto Natl. For., F72-R8 (1967) and map of DeSoto Natl. For., Leaf River Div., U.S. For. Ser., USDA, P.O. Box 1291, Jackson, Miss. 39205. Information in letter from Mr. G. W. Wasson, Rec.-Watershed Staff Officer.

Rickerson, Stephen R. Wildlife Biologist, U.S. For. Ser., Delta Ranger Dis., 717 E. Walnut St., Rolling Fork, Miss. 39159.

MONTANA

Burdge, R. W. and Ross, R. A. *Floating, Fishing, and Historical Guide to Yellowstone State Waterway: Gardiner to the Big Horn River.* 2047 Custer Ave. or 712 Central Ave., Billings, Mont. 59001. $2.00.

Craig, Vern. "Floating Through the Yellowstone Waterway,"

Montana Wildlife (July 1966), pp. 1–11. St. of Montana, Dept. of Fish and Game, Helena, Mont. 59601.

Montana's Popular Float Streams. Montana Fish and Game Dept. Information Bul. reprint from *Montana Outdoors* (Aug. 1969), Helena, Mont. 59601.

"Ride the Wide Missouri Historic Water," *Montana West, Magazine of the Northern Rockies* (Spring 1970). Box 894, Helena, Mont. 59601.

MULTI STATES

Burmeister, Walter Frederick. *Appalachian Waters.* Vols. I and II. Published privately by members of the Canoe Cruisers Assoc., Washington, D.C., in co-ordination with Walter Kirschbaum, Guidebook Chairman of the American Whitewater Affiliation, Copyright 1962 by Walter F. Burmeister. NOTE: This is almost impossible to find anywhere; it is one of the earliest guide books and a classic. It covers streams throughout the East Coast as far west as Kentucky.

Guide to Rivers, U.S.A., Imaginations XX. Champion Papers, Marketing Services, 245 Park Ave., New York, N.Y. 10017. Two beautiful volumes, historical and with fantastic pictures.

NEBRASKA

"Canoe Trails," *Outdoor Nebraskaland* (Mar. 1965).

Canoeing in Nebraska. The Nebraska Game and Parks Comm., 2200 N. 33rd St., Lincoln, Nebr. 68503.

"Feel of a River," *Nebraskaland* (Oct. 1967).

Nebraskaland, Boating Guide. (1970). Nebr. Game and Parks Comm., 1-70 St. Capitol, Lincoln, Nebr. 68509. Free.

"Paddles on the Platte," *Nebraskaland* (Nov. 1965).

Thomas, Fred. Special Projects Editor, Omaha *World-Herald,* Omaha, Nebr. 68102. Phone 402-341-0300.

Wegman, Pete. 1226 N. Irving, Fremont, Nebr. 68025.

NEVADA

Lee, Henry S. Branch Chief, R & L, U.S. For. Ser., USDA, Humboldt For., 976 Mountain City Hwy., Elko, Nev. 89801.

Maw, Edward C. For. Supervisor, U.S. For. Ser., USDA, Toiyabe Natl. For., P.O. Box 1331, Reno, Nev. 89504.

Riffice, Paul E. Box 236, Bonanza, Oreg. 97623.

NEW HAMPSHIRE

AMC New England Canoeing Guide. Appalachian Mountain Club, 5 Joy St., Boston, Mass. 02108. $5.00.

Canoeing on the Connecticut River. (Mar. 1964). Vt. St. Board of Rec. and Water Res. Dept., Montpelier, Vt.

Summer Canoeing and Kayaking in the White Mountains of New Hampshire. White Mountain Region Assoc., Box K, Lancaster, N.H. 03584.

NEW JERSEY

Canoeing in New Jersey. St. of N.J., Dept. of Cons. and Economic Dev., Div. of Parks, For., and Rec., Bur. of Rec., P.O. Box 1889, Trenton, N.J. 08625.

Cawley, James and Margaret. *Exploring the Little Rivers of New Jersey.* New Brunswick, N.J.: Rutgers University Press, 1961. $1.95.

Delaware River Basin Comm., 25 Scotch Rd., P.O. Box 360, Trenton, N.J. 08603. Maps—price $1.00 per set.

Hansen, Eigel and Smith, Jon. 137 E. High St., Glassboro, N.J. 08028.

Murray Hill Canoe Club, c/o W. J. Schreibers, Bell Laboratories, 600 Mountain Ave., Murray Hill, N.J. 07974.

NEW MEXICO

Carnes, C. Rafting. "Kayaking & Canoeing on the Rio Grande and the Chama Rivers in Northern New Mexico, Sheets A & B," *The Rio Grande Gurgle,* 1970. 130 Rover Blvd., White Rock, Los Alamos, N.M. 87544.

McComb, John. 752 S. Forgeus Ave., Tucson, Ariz. 85716.

NEW YORK

Adirondack Canoe Routes. (1970). St. of N.Y., Dept. of Environmental Conservation, Albany, N.Y. 12226.

AMC New England Canoeing Guide. Appalachian Mountain Club, 5 Joy St., Boston, Mass. 02108. $5.00.

Binger, David. "Trip Report, Boreas River," *American Whitewater,* Vol. XVI, No. 4. (Winter 1971), pp. 124–25.

Delaware River Basin Comm., 25 Scotch Rd., P.O. Box 360, Trenton, N.J. 08603. Maps $1.00 per set.

Grinnell, Lawrence I. *Canoeable Waterways of New York State and Vicinity.* New York: Pageant Press, 1956.

Grose, C. H. Journal Newspapers, 72 W. High St., Ballston Springs, N.Y. 12020.

McNett, Victor G. 1356 Westmoreland Ave., Syracuse, N.Y. 13210.

Phinizy, Coles. *Sports Illustrated,* Vol. 35, No. 21 (Nov. 22, 1971), pp. 98–101, 104, 106, 109, 110, 113–15.

NORTH CAROLINA

Carter, Randy. *Canoeing White Water River Guide.* Appalachian Outfitters, P.O. Box 11, 2930 Chain Brdg. Rd., Oakton, Va. 22124. $4.75.

Cosgrove, C. E. P.O. Box 44, Oak Ridge, Tenn. 37830.

Georgia Canoeing Assoc., Race Information, H. P. Holden, Race Chrm., Camp Chattahoochee, P.O. Box 565, Roxwell, Ga. 30075.

Hansen, Eigel and Smith, Jon. 137 E. High St., Glassboro, N.J. 08028.

Mills, Richard A. U.S. For. Ser., USDA, P.O. Box 2750, Asheville, N.C. 28802.

NORTH DAKOTA

Ertresvaag, Rolf W. Deputy Director, N.D. Park Ser., St. Capitol Bldg., Bismarck, N.D. 58501.

Garrison Dam and Master Plan Drawing. U.S. Army Eng. Dis., Corps of Engineers, 7410 USPO and Court House, 215 N. 17th St., Omaha, Nebr. 68102.

Little Missouri River Float Trips. USDA, U.S. For. Ser., Medora Ranger Dist., 1409 W. Villard, Dickinson, N.D. 58601. Free.

Rollings, Robert G. *Why Not Wakopa?* Dist. by N.D. Park Ser., St. Capitol Bldg., Bismarck, N.D. 58501.

OHIO

Mohican Canoe Livery. Loudonville, O., and Loudonville Canoe · Livery, Loudonville, O. 44842. Folders.

Ohio Canoe Adventures. Ohio Dept. of Natl. Res., Div. of Water Craft, 1350 Holly Ave., Columbus, O. 43212.

OKLAHOMA

Floating the Illinois. Dept. of Wildlife Cons., 1801 Lincoln, Okla. City, Okla. 73105.

Jones, Jim. 501 E. Craig, Broken Bow, Okla. 74728. Guide and float ser.

Outdoor Oklahoma. Okla. Dept. of Wildlife Cons. (Feb. 1969, June 1970, Oct. 1970), 1801 Lincoln, Okla. City, Okla. 73105.

Smith, Melvin E. 305 N.E. Morningside, Bartlesville, Okla. 74003.

Weichsel, Hans. 5801 Rock Hill Rd., Ft. Worth, Tex. 76112. Phone 817-GL1-6379 (may call for information).

OREGON

Bonn, Richard I. Biologist, USDA Soil Cons. Ser., 2216 E. 9th St., Albany, Oreg. 97321.

Garren John. *Oregon River Tours,* ed. L. K. Phillips. Thomas Binford, 2536 S.E. Eleventh, Portland, Oreg. 97202. $4.00.

Helfrich, Prince E., and Sons. Licensed guides, White Water River Trips, Vida, Oreg. 97488.

Jackson, Mel. Willamette River Res., Cons., and Dev. Project, Oregon St. Hwy. Depts. Bldg., Salem, Oreg. 97310.

Master Plan for the Rogue River Component of the Natl. Wild and Scenic River System (Oct. 9, 1969), House Doc. No. 91-175. Washington, D.C.: U.S. Govt. Printing Office.

Riffice, Paul E. P.O. Box 236, Bonanza, Oreg. 97623.

PENNSYLVANIA

Canoe Country Pennsylvania Style. Commonwealth of Pa., Dept. of Environmental Resources, P.O. Box 1467, Harrisburg, Pa. 17120. Free.

Canoe Routes. Commonwealth of Pa., Dept. of Fors. and Waters, Harrisburg, Pa. 17120. Mimeo.

Canoeing Guide to Western Pennsylvania and Northern West Virginia, ed. III. Pittsburgh Council, American Youth Hostels, Inc., 6300 Fifth Ave., Pittsburgh, Pa. 15232.

Carter, Randy. *Canoeing White Water River Guide.* Appalachian Outfitters, P.O. Box 11, 2930 Chain Bridge Rd., Oakton, Va. 22124. $4.75.

Chase, P. W. and Hoecker, O. A. *Map of Canoeable Waters of Western Pennsylvania and West Virginia* (May 10, 1970). Dist. by Pittsburgh Council, American Youth Hostels, Inc., 6300 5th Ave., Pittsburgh, Pa. 15232.

Delaware River Basin Comm., 25 Scotch Rd., P.O. Box 360, Trenton, N.J. 08603. Maps $1.00 per set.

Gardner, Max. Features Editor, *Scouting* magazine, Boy Scouts of America, N. Brunswick, N.J. 08902.

Geertz, Lloyd. *Canoeing in the Pittsburgh Area*. Pittsburgh Council, American Youth Hostels, Inc., 6300 5th Ave., Pitts., Pa. 15232.

Gray, Thomas L. *Canoeing Streams of the Potomac and Rappahannock Basins*. 11121 Dewey Rd., Kensington, Md. 20795. Map for $1.00.

Grinnell, Lawrence I. *Canoeable Waterways of New York State and Vicinity,* New York: Pageant Press, 1956.

Olson, Harry A. *Canoeing in Delaware and Susquehanna Watersheds of Pennsylvania*. Pa. Fish Comm., Waterways Div., P.O. Box 1673, Harrisburg, Pa. 17120.

Ruskin, William R. *Canoeing in Kinzua Country*. Kinzua Dam Vacation Bureau, Box 844, Warren, Pa. 16365. $1.00.

Select Rivers of Central Pennsylvania, 4th ed. Pa. St. Outing Club, Pa. State University, Room 4, Intramural Bldg., University Park, Pa. 16802. $.75.

Sloan, David H. 113 Howard Ave., Lancaster, Pa. 17602.

Wilhoyte, Jeff. *Canoeing in the Delaware and Susquehanna River Watersheds of Pennsylvania*. Mimeo.

RHODE ISLAND

AMC New England Canoeing Guide. Appalachian Mountain Club, 5 Joy St., Boston, Mass. 02108. $5.00.

Pawcatuck River and Wood River. St. of R.I., Dept. of Nat. Res., Div. of Cons., 83 Park Street, Providence, R.I. 02903.

SOUTH CAROLINA

Canoeing the Chattooga. Sumter Natl. For., USDA, U.S. For. Ser., P.O. Box 1437, Gainesville, Ga. 30501.

Chattooga River: Wild and Scenic River Study Report. USDA, U.S. For. Ser., Southern Region (May 15, 1970).

Connell, John L. Rec. Asst., U.S. For. Ser., USDA, 1801 Main St., Columbia, S.C. 29201.

Harper, Robert A. Recreation Staff Officer, USDA, U.S. For. Ser., P.O. Box 1437, Gainesville, Ga. 30501.

SOUTH DAKOTA

Norman, Dean. "Canoeing Crazy Horse Canyon," *American White Water,* Vol. XIII, No. 3 (Winter 1967–68), pp. 6–11.

TENNESSEE

Bombay, John. *American White Waters Magazine* (Summer 1962).

Buffalo River Float Map. Tenn. Game and Fish Comm., Ellington Agr. Center, P.O. Box 9400, Nashville, Tenn. 37220.

Canoeing in Tennessee. Tenn. Tourism Dev. Div., Andrew Jackson Bldg., Nashville, Tenn. 37219. Free.

Cosgrove, C. E. P.O. Box 44, Oak Ridge, Tenn. 37830.

Hollenbeck, P. D. *Float Trip Guides for Duck River, Tennessee.* (May 28, 1970). 614-G. Chateau Dr., Huntsville, Ala. 35804. $1.00.

Little Tennessee River Map, Tenn. Game and Fish Comm., Ellington Agr. Center, P.O. Box 9400, Nashville, Tenn. 37220.

Scott Co. Chamber of Commerce. Oneida, Tenn. 37841.

Stokley, Ronald L. 607½ Silverleaf Dr., Lexington, Ky. 40505.

The Oneida Trail. Wild Rivers, Inc., P.O. Box 18, Oneida, Tenn. 37841.

The Tennessee Conservationist. Issues: Oct. 1958, pp. 24–27; Dec. 1961, pp. 3–4; Mar. 1966, pp. 20–21; June 1966, pp. 24 and 27; Feb. 1968, pp. 6–8.

TEXAS

Brazos River Authority. 4400 Cobbs Dr., P.O. Box 7555, Waco, Tex. 76710.

Burleson, Bob. Suggested river trips through the Rio Grande canyons in the Big Bend Region of Tex. as charted by the Tex. Explorers Club. P.O. Box 844, Temple, Tex. 76501.

Cook, Neal. "Discover the Wild Water," *Texas Parks and Wildlife* Vol. XXVIII, No. 2 (Feb. 1970), p. 14.

Douglas, Roy. Asst. Gen. Mgr., Upper Neches River Municipal Water Authority 220, Municipal Bldg., P.O. Drawer Y, Palestine, Tex. 75801.

Evans, Harry R. 7224 Meadowbrook, Ft. Worth, Tex. 76112. Phone: 817-451-5079 (may call for information).

Kelsey, John and Amye. 18 Shady Oaks, La Marque, Tex. 77568.

Nolen, Ben M. and Narramore, Robert E. *Texas Rivers and Rapids,* Vols. I and II. High Trails Co., 12421 N. Central Expressway, Dallas, Tex. 75243. $6.55 for each vol., incl. postage and handling.

Oliver, Biggs, Finney, and Thuma. *Pathways and Paddleways* (Aug. 1971). Tex. Parks and Wildlife Dept., Austin, Tex. 78701 (excellent description of Guadalupe River).

Purinton, Don. 1312 Apache Dr., Dallas, Tex. Phone 214-231-3167 or office phone 214-424-6571.

Sabine River Authority, Fourth Floor, 3 Americas Bldg., 118 Bridgeway, San Antonio, Tex. 78205.

San Marcos River Texas Safari, P.O. Box 721, San Marcos, Tex. 78666.

Speckt, John H. Asst. Gen. Mgr., Guadalupe-Blanco River Authority, P.O. Box 271, 933 E. Court St., Seguin, Tex. 78155.

Stowers, Henry. "It's Fun to Float," *South West Scene,* Dallas *Morning News* (May 24, 1970).

Texas Waterways: A Feasibility Report on a System of Wild, Scenic, and Recreational Waterways in Texas. Texas Parks and Wildlife Dept., John H. Reagan Bldg., Austin, Tex. 78701.

Top Spot for Fun: Highland Lakes in Central Texas. The Highland Lakes Tourist Assoc.

Weichsel, Hans. 5801 Rock Hill Rd., Ft. Worth, Tex. 76112. Phone 817-GL1-6379 (may call for information).

UTAH

Flaming Gorge Natl. Rec. Area. Map. Ashley Natl. For., U.S. For. Ser., USDA, and Bureau of Rec., U.S. Dept. of the Interior, Washington, D.C. 20137.

Gardner, Max. Features Editor, *Scouting* magazine, Boy Scouts of America, N. Brunswick, N.J. 08902.

Mutschler, Felix E. *Guide to the Canyons of the Green and Colorado Rivers,* Vol. II, *Labyrinth, Stillwater, and Cataract Canyons.* Powell Society Ltd., 750 Vine St., Denver, Colo. 80206. $3.00.

Smith, Stuart. 811 N. 17th, Philadelphia, Pa. 19130.

Three Faces of the Green River, Below Flaming Gorge Dam. U.S. Dept. of the Interior and USDA, Washington, D.C. 20137.

VERMONT

AMC New England Canoeing Guide. Appalachian Mountain Club, 5 Joy St., Boston, Mass. 02108. $5.00.

Canoeing on the Connecticut River (Mar. 1964). Vt. St. Board of Rec. and Water Res. Dept., Montpelier, Vt.

Coffin, Stewart T. Old Sudbury Rd., RFD 1, Lincoln, Mass. 01773.

VIRGINIA

Carter, Randy. *Canoeing White Water River Guide.* Appalachian Outfitters, P.O. Box 11, 2930 Chain Bridge Rd., Oakton, Va. 22124. $4.75.

Chase, P. W. and Hoecker, D. A. *Map of Canoeable Waters of*

Western Pennsylvania and West Virginia (May 10, 1970). Dist. by Pittsburgh Council, American Youth Hostels, Inc., 6300 Fifth Ave., Pttsburgh, Pa. 15232.

Corbett, Roger H., Jr., and Matacia, Louis J., Jr. *Blue Ridge Voyages,* Vol. I, 2nd ed. (1968), and *Blue Ridge Voyageurs,* Vol. II (1968). P.O. Box 32, Oakton, Va. 22124. $2.50 each.

Gray, Thomas L. *Canoeing Streams of the Potomac and Rappahannock Basins*—Map. 11121 Dewey Rd., Kensington, Md. 20795. $1.00.

Hansen, Eigel, and Smith, Jon. 137 E. High St., Glassboro, N.J. 08028.

Tyler, Franklin A. "Canoe Trails of Eastern Virginia," *Virginia Wildlife* (Sept. 1949), Va. Comm. of Game of Inland Fisheries, Richmond, Va. 23213.

WASHINGTON

Bauer, Wolf G. Map, 14th printing (1950–1965). Washington Kayak Club, 5622 Seaview Ave., Seattle, Wash. 98107. $1.00.

Furrer, Werner. *Kayak and Canoe Trips in Washington.* Signpost Publications, 16812 36th Ave., W. Lynnwood, Wash. 98036. $2.25.

————. *Water Trails of Washington.* Signpost Publications, 16812 36th Ave., W. Lynnwood, Wash. 98036. $2.50.

Parker, Raymond J. 18028 187th Ave. S.E., Renton, Wash. 98055.

WEST VIRGINIA

Burrell, Bob, and Davidson, Paul. *A Canoeist's Guide to the Whitewater Rivers of West Virginia.* W.Va. Wildwater Assoc., Rte. 1, P.O. Box 95, Ravenswood, W.Va. 26164. $2.50.

Canoeing Guide to Western Pennsylvania and Northern West Virginia, ed. III. Pittsburgh Council, American Youth Hostels, Inc., 6300 Fifth Ave., Pittsburgh, Pa. 15232.

Carter, Randy. *Canoeing White Water River Guide.* Appalachian Outfitters, P.O. Box 11, 2930 Chain Bridge Rd., Oakton, Va. 22124. $4.75.

Chase, P. W., and Hoecker, D. A. *Map of Canoeable Waters of Western Pennsylvania and West Virginia* (May 10, 1970). Dist. by Pittsburgh Council, American Youth Hostels, Inc., 6300 Fifth Ave., Pittsburgh, Pa. 15232.

Corbett, Roger H., Jr., and Matacia, Louis J., Jr. *Blue Ridge Voyages,* Vol. 1, 2nd ed. (1968), and *Blue Ridge Voyageurs,* Vol. II (1968). P.O. Box 32, Oakton, Va. 22124. $2.50 each.

WISCONSIN

"Canoe Trails of Southern Wisconsin," *Wisconsin Trails* magazine, 6210 University Ave., Madison, Wis. 53075. $4.95.

Jipson, William A., and Laury, Gerald R. *Wisconsin's North Central Canoe Trails.* North Central Canoe Trails, Inc., Box 9, Ladysmith, Wis. 54848. $3.00.

Lowry, Gerald R., and Kahl, Norman. *Canoeing the Wild Rivers of Northwestern Wisconsin.* North Western Wisconsin Canoe Trails, Inc., Gordon, Wis. 54838. $3.00.

Occoch Mts. and the Kickapoo Valley Assoc., Mr. Bernard Smith, Rte. 2, P.O. Box 211, La Farge, Wis. 54639.

Palzer, Bob and Jody. *Whitewater, Quietwater: The Wild Rivers of Wisconsin, Upper Michigan, and Northeast Minnesota.* Evergreen Paddleways, Two Rivers, Wis. Order from Outdoor Programs Office, Wis. Union, 800 Langdon St., Madison, Wis. 53706. $7.50.

Wisconsin Water Trails. Pub. 104-70, Wis. Dept. of Nat. Res., Madison, Wis. 53701.

WYOMING

Calkins, Charles S. Dist. Ranger, USDA, U.S. For. Ser., Medicine Bow Natl. For., Brush Creek Dist., Saratoga, Wyo. 82331.

Carringer, W. D. Branch Chief, Rec. and Lands, USDA, U.S. For. Ser., Bridger Natl. For., Kemmerer, Wyo. 83101.

Floating the Snake River in Grand Teton National Park. U.S. Dept. of Interior, Natl. Park Ser., Grand Teton Natl. Park, Moose, Wyo. 83012.

Hirsch, Ernest C. Chief, Branch of Rec. and Lands, USDA, U.S. For. Ser., Teton Natl. For., Jackson, Wyo. 83001.